Śāntideva and the Dynamics of Tradition

Also available from Bloomsbury

Buddhist Ethics and the Bodhisattva Path: Śāntideva on Virtue and Well-Being
by Stephen E. Harris
Ethnic and Religious Diversity in Myanmar: Contested Identities
edited by Perry Schmidt-Leukel, Hans-Peter Grosshans, and Madlen Krueger
Interreligious Comparisons in Religious Studies and Theology: Comparison Revisited
edited by Perry Schmidt-Leukel and Andreas Nehring

Śāntideva and the Dynamics of Tradition

Doctrinal, Social, and Interreligious Contexts

Edited by
Stephen E. Harris and Perry Schmidt-Leukel

BLOOMSBURY ACADEMIC
LONDON • NEW YORK • OXFORD • NEW DELHI • SYDNEY

BLOOMSBURY ACADEMIC
Bloomsbury Publishing Plc, 50 Bedford Square, London, WC1B 3DP, UK
Bloomsbury Publishing Inc, 1359 Broadway, New York, NY 10018, USA
Bloomsbury Publishing Ireland, 29 Earlsfort Terrace, Dublin 2, D02 AY28, Ireland

BLOOMSBURY, BLOOMSBURY ACADEMIC and the Diana logo are trademarks of Bloomsbury Publishing Plc

First published in Great Britain 2026

Cover image: CPA Media Pte Ltd / Alamy Stock Photo

A catalogue record for this book is available from the British Library.

A catalogue record for this book is available from the Library of Congress.

ISBN: HB: 978-1-3505-3233-5
ePDF: 978-1-3505-3234-2
eBook: 978-1-3505-3235-9

Typeset by RefineCatch Limited, Bungay, Suffolk

For product safety related questions contact productsafety@bloomsbury.com.

To find out more about our authors and books visit www.bloomsbury.com and sign up for our newsletters.

Contents

Notes on Contributors

Francis Brassard is Associate Professor at RIT-Croatia. Previously, he taught at Berry College (Rome, GA) and at Miyazaki International College (Japan). He received his PhD from McGill University in Religious Studies in 1997 and studied at the Institut für Kultur und Geschichte Indiens und Tibets of Hamburg University and at Somaiya Bharatiya Sanskriti Peeth in Mumbai. His research interests include Buddhist philosophy and psychology, comparative religions and philosophies, and interreligious dialogue. Among his publications are *The Concept of Bodhicitta in Śāntideva's Bodhicaryāvatāra* (2000) and, more recently, *Meeting the Others in their Differences: Toward a Christian Approach to the Scientific Study of Religions* (2021).

Amber D. Carpenter is currently Senior Research Fellow with the Einstein Forum (Potsdam), and Visiting Professor (King's College London), and will soon be taking up a position at St Anne's College, Oxford. She works in ancient Greek philosophy and Indian Buddhist philosophy, both separately and jointly, focusing topically on questions at the intersection of metaphysics, epistemology, and ethics. She taught for several years at Yale-NUS College (Singapore) and has held research fellowships at Yale, Melbourne, York, and with the Templeton Religion Trust for a project on 'Ethical Ideals and their Formations of Character'. She is the author of several articles on Greek philosophy, as well as of the monograph *Indian Buddhist Philosophy* (2014); co-editor of *Portraits of Integrity* (2020), emerging from The Integrity Project (integrityproject.org); and co-editor, with P.-J. Harter, of *Crossing the Stream, Leaving the Cave: Buddhist-Platonist Philosophical Inquiries* (2024). Her current work develops a distinctive Buddhist-Platonist approach to ethics.

Douglas Duckworth is Professor of Religion and the Director of Graduate Studies in the Religion Department at Temple University in Philadelphia. His research engages the nature of Buddhist philosophy and practice, and their relation. Duckworth is the author of *Mipam on Buddha-Nature: The Ground of the Nyingma Tradition* (2008), *Jamgön Mipam: His Life and Teachings* (2011), and *Tibetan Buddhist Philosophy of Mind and Nature* (2019). He co-edited (with Jonathan Gold) *Readings of Śāntideva's Guide to Bodhisattva Practice* (2019). Duckworth has translated Kunzang Sönam's overview of the ninth chapter of Śāntideva's *Way of the Bodhisattva*, entitled *The Profound Reality of Interdependence* (2019), and most recently, completed a translation of Minyak Kunzang Sönam's extensive commentary on the first eight chapters of this text, *The Great Hūṃ: A Commentary on the Way of the Bodhisattva* (2025).

Jay L. Garfield is Doris Silbert Professor in the Humanities and Professor of Philosophy and Buddhist Studies, emeritus, at Smith College, and Professor of Philosophy at Melbourne University. Garfield's research addresses topics in the philosophy of mind, metaphysics, the history of modern Indian philosophy, epistemology, ethics, and topics in Buddhist philosophy, particularly Indo-Tibetan Madhyamaka and Yogācāra. He is the author or editor of over thirty books and over two hundred articles, chapters, and reviews. Garfield's most recent books are *How to Lose Yourself* (with Maria Heim and Robert Sharf, 2025); *How to be Caring* (Princeton 2025); *Losing Ourselves: How to be a Person Without a Self* (2022); *Knowing Illusion: Bringing a Tibetan Debate into Contemporary Discourse* (with the Yakherds, 2021); *Buddhist Ethics: A Philosophical Exploration* (2021); and *What Can't Be Said: Paradox and Contradiction in East Asian Thought* (with Yasuo Deguchi, Graham Priest, and Robert Sharf, 2021).

Stephen E. Harris is University Lecturer (Universitair Docent) at Leiden University's Institute for Philosophy. He received his PhD from the University of New Mexico's department of philosophy in 2014, where his dissertation focused on the relationship between Śāntideva's *Bodhicaryāvatāra* and issues of moral demandingness in Western ethics. He specializes in cross-cultural and Indian philosophy, with a particular interest in Buddhist accounts of personhood and Mahāyāna ethics. He has published numerous articles in academic journals, including *Journal of Buddhist Ethics*, *Journal of Indian Philosophy*, *Philosophy East and West*, and *Sophia*. His recent research focuses on Śāntideva's views on well-being, virtue, and the relation between metaphysical selflessness and ethical commitment. He is the author of *Buddhist Ethics and the Bodhisattva Path: Śāntideva on Virtue and Well-Being* (2024).

S. Mark Heim is Samuel Abbot Professor of Christian Theology at Andover Newton Seminary at Yale Divinity School. He has written extensively on issues of religious pluralism, comparative theology, Christology, atonement, and Christian ecumenism. His books include *Salvations: Truth and Difference in Theology* (1995); *The Depth of the Riches: A Trinitarian Theology of Religious Ends* (2001); *Saved from Sacrifice: A Theology of the Cross* (2006); *Crucified Wisdom: Christ and the Bodhisattva in Theological Reflection* (2019); and *Monotheism and Forgiveness* (2022). He has received a Henry Luce III Fellowship in Theology and a Pew Evangelical Scholars' Research Fellowship. An ordained American Baptist minister, he has represented his denomination on the Faith and Order Commissions of the National Council and World Council of Churches.

Emily McRae is Associate Professor of Philosophy at the University of New Mexico. She earned her PhD in 2011 at the University of Wisconsin-Madison with a study on ethics, feminism, and Buddhism. She specializes in Tibetan Buddhist philosophy, ethics, moral psychology, and feminism. Much of her work is in the philosophy of emotions and the philosophy of interpersonal relationships. She has published articles on these topics in *American Philosophical Quarterly*, *Philosophy East and West*, *Journal of Religious Ethics*, and *History of Philosophy Quarterly*. She translated Patrul Rinpoche's *Essential Jewel of Holy Practice* (with Jay Garfield, 2017) and co-edited *Buddhism and*

Whiteness. Critical Reflections (with George Yancy, 2019). With the support of the National Endowment for the Humanities Award for Faculty, she is currently writing a book on Indo-Tibetan philosophical approaches to moral ignorance and misunderstanding.

Carola Roloff (Bhikṣuṇī Jampa Tsedroen) is currently Senior Research Fellow in Pluralistic Dialogical Religious Education at the Faculty of Education, University of Hamburg. From 2018 to March 2025, she served as Visiting Professor of Buddhism and Dialogue in Modern Societies at the Academy of World Religions. A trained Tibetologist and ordained Buddhist nun, she specialises in Buddhist ethics, gender justice, and interreligious dialogue. Her publications include *The Buddhist Nuns' Ordination in the Tibetan Canon* (2020), *Buddhismus im Westen* (2011, co-edited with Wolfram Weiße and Michael Zimmermann), and *Buddhistischer Religionsunterricht: Bestandsaufnahme und Perspektiven* (2023, co-edited with Thorsten Knauth).

Perry Schmidt-Leukel is Senior Professor of Religious Studies and Intercultural Theology at the University of Münster. He taught at the universities of Munich, Innsbruck, Salzburg, Glasgow, and Münster. His research focuses on Buddhist studies, interfaith relations, Buddhist–Christian dialogue, and interreligious theology. He has published more than thirty books in different languages, including *Understanding Buddhism* (2006); *Buddha Mind - Christ Mind. A Christian Commentary on the Bodhicaryāvatāra* (2019); *To See a World in a Flower. Buddhism and Christianity - a Fractal Interpretation of Their Relation* (in English and Chinese, 2020); and *The Celestial Web. Buddhism and Christianity - A Different Comparison* (2024). His 2015 Gifford Lectures have been published as *Religious Pluralism and Interreligious Theology* (2017).

Reza Shah-Kazemi is Senior Research Associate at the Institute of Ismaili Studies, London, and Managing Editor of *Encyclopaedia Islamica*. He received his PhD in Comparative Religion from Kent University in 1994. His research focuses on Islamic Studies and Comparative Religion. His publications include *Paths to Transcendence: According to Shankara, Ibn Arabi and Meister Eckhart* (2006); *The Other in the Light of the One: The Universality of the Qur'an and Interfaith Dialogue* (2006); *Justice and Remembrance: Introducing the Spirituality of Imam 'Ali* (2006); *My Mercy Encompasses All—The Koran's Teachings on Compassion, Peace and Love* (2007); and *Common Ground between Islam and Buddhism* (2012).

Andrew Skilton, retired, has taught at a number of universities, including Cardiff, McGill, SOAS, King's College London, Dongguk University Seoul, Mahidol University Bangkok, and is now teaching Buddhist Studies, Pāli language and literature, and Buddhist Sanskrit texts in Oxford. He was editor of *Contemporary Buddhism* for ten years. He has published articles and books, including a translation and study of Śāntideva's *Bodhicaryāvatāra* (with Kate Crosby, 1995); *How the Nagas Were Pleased* (2009); a translation of the Buddhist drama *Nāgananda*; and *A Concise History of Buddhism* (1994). Currently, he is writing an introduction to the study of Pāli language and literature, and researching aspects of the *boran kammathan* meditation tradition in Thailand; the *vīthicitta* or 'consciousness process' in the *Jie tuo dao lun* 解脱道論 (**Vimuttimagga*); and revising the *Dīpavaṃsa* from new manuscript evidence from Myanmar. He has recently been writing about rules on surgery in the *vinaya*, coercive control in the *Jātaka*, early Buddhist relations with the Jains, and monastic waterbottles.

Fabian Völker is Postdoctoral Research Assistant at the Institute of Intercultural Philosophy of Religion at the University of Vienna. He taught at the Vrije Universiteit Amsterdam and the University of Münster. He earned his PhD in 2019 at the University of Münster with a study on David Loy's non-dualism. His research focuses on Buddhism, Hinduism, transcendental philosophy, intercultural philosophy of religion, and mysticism. He has published *Philosophie der Nondualität* (2020) and edited two books: *Transzendentalität und Transkulturalität* (2024) and *Beyond Boundaries: Essays on Theology, Dialogue, and Religion in Honor of Perry Schmidt-Leukel* (2024). His articles include *Methodology and Mysticism: For an Integral Study of Religion* (2022); *The Plurality of Nonduality: Towards a Tripartite Typology* (2023); *Overcoming Nishitani: Nihilism and Nationalism in Keiji Nishitani's Political Philosophy of Religion* (2024); and *Transcendence, Reason, and Self-Annihilation: Interreligious Theology and Transcendental Philosophy of Religion* (2024).

Dorji Wangchuk is Professor of Tibetan Studies at the University of Hamburg. His main teaching and research interests lie in Indo-Tibetan Buddhist texts and ideas, Tibetan Buddhist intellectual history and history of ideas, and Tibetan Buddhist intellectual, literary, and textual cultures, topics on which he published extensively, including *The Resolve to Become a Buddha. A Study of the Bodhicitta Concept in Indo-Tibetan Buddhism* (2007). In addition to teaching at the University of Hamburg, he was Lecturer at the University of Copenhagen (2005–6), Numata Visiting Professor at McGill University (2011), Visiting Scholar at Renmin University of China, Beijing (2013–14), and Visiting Professor at the University of Tsukuba (2014–21). He is the founder and co-director of the Khyentse Center for Tibetan Buddhist Textual Scholarship (KC-TBTS, since 2011). He is also involved in a number of collaborative research projects such as the ERC Synergy project "Intellexus."

Introduction

Stephen E. Harris, Perry Schmidt-Leukel

1. Śāntideva and the *Bodhicaryāvatāra*

As is frequently the case with early Indian thinkers, we know virtually nothing about the life of "Śāntideva," as the author of the *Bodhicaryāvatāra* is most often named by the tradition. He lived in India sometime between the late seventh and the eighth century, was a Mahāyāna Buddhist, and a (presumably monastic) scholar. But we do not know with certainty, for instance, where in India he lived, how many texts he wrote, whether the texts we have inherited under the name "Śāntideva" are by a single author, and so on. There are many legends about his life that emerged over the centuries. All of them take him to have been a resident monk at the academic monastic university of Nālandā in North India. But the legends do so with rather opposing intentions. Some present him as having little or no learning of his own, and his text as being verbally inspired by Manjuśrī, the supra-natural Bodhisattva of wisdom, while other (presumably later) legends claim that he was a great scholar. Unfortunately, there is no way to determine whether his association with Nālandā has preserved some reliable memory (for an account and discussion of the legends, see Schmidt-Leukel 2019: 13–52).

According to tradition, Śāntideva is the author of at least two texts: the *Bodhicaryāvatāra* and *Śikṣāsamuccaya* ("Training Anthology"). The second text is mainly composed of extracts from Mahāyāna *sūtras*, interspaced with brief commentary in Śāntideva's own voice, all structured around twenty-seven verses summarizing the core points of bodhisattva practice. The first text exists under two titles: *Bodhicaryāvatāra* and *Bodhisattvacaryāvatāra*. *Bodhi-carya* can be translated as the "course / practices" (*carya*) leading to "awakening" (*bodhi*) and *Bodhisattva-carya* as the "course / practices of a *bodhisattva*." *Avatāra* may be understood either as "entering" this course / practice or, alternatively and in a more scholastic sense, as an "introduction" or "guide" to such life and practice. The text offers a vivid record of the life of someone who decides to follow the path of a bodhisattva—that is, the path to full Buddhahood—not for the sake of one's own liberation but for the greater benefit of all beings. Hence special attention is given to the virtues or mental characteristics of a bodhisattva and to *bodhicitta*, the "spirit of awakening,"—that is, the aspiration to attain awakening for the sake of all.

The *Bodhicaryāvatāra* exists currently in two different versions. The longer, canonical version consists of 913 verses in ten chapters and is preserved both in

Sanskrit and Tibetan. The second, shorter version, which has 701 verses in nine chapters (Chapters 2 and 3 of the longer version forming here just one chapter), was discovered in Dun-huang and exists only in Tibetan translation. Many of the chapters are largely identical in content in both versions, but there are significant differences in both the contemplation (*dhyāna*) and wisdom (*prajñā*) chapters (Chapters 8 and 9 in the longer version). The two versions of these chapters differ quite radically from each other; each lacks some verses contained in the other version, possesses its own extra verses, and has a different structure with partly different aims.

There is no scholarly consensus for how to understand the relation between these two versions of the *Bodhicaryāvatāra* and the other text ascribed to Śāntideva, the "Training Anthology." One possibility is that one author composed the shorter version of the *Bodhicaryāvatāra*, while another, later author composed the "Training Anthology" and the longer *Bodhicaryāvatāra* (see Saito 1993). An alternate theory suggests that the longer version is a revision of the shorter version by the original author in light of the "Training Anthology," which he had composed in the meantime (see Harrison 2019). But even then, additional editorial work by others may not be excluded. What is beyond doubt is that the longer version of the *Bodhicaryāvatāra* has become the more influential; there is no published critical edition and no contemporary translation of the shorter version, and the vast majority of both traditional commentaries and contemporary academic scholarship focuses on the longer version. It is the primary source consulted by almost all of the authors represented in this collection, although several authors reference the "Training Anthology" as well.

The *Bodhicaryāvatāra* (hereafter BCA) gives its purpose as "cultivating" or "imbuing the mind" (BCA 1:2), and it soon becomes clear that this refers to the development of the various virtuous mental states and character traits of the bodhisattva. The first chapter praises the value of *bodhicitta*, the "spirit of awakening." The second and third chapters perform the bodhisattva liturgy known as the "supreme worship" (*anuttarapūja*), through which the practitioner turns to the Buddhas and supra-natural Bodhisattvas for support. This is a common Mahāyāna ritual, usually presented in seven or eight parts (see Huntington 2019). Śāntideva's version of the ritual is composed of eight parts: (a) praise, (b) offering, (c) refuge, (d) confession of faults, (e) rejoicing in goodness, (f) requesting the teaching, (g) supplication for the buddhas to remain, and (h) dedication of merit. It is in the middle of this ritual, at verses 3:22–3, that the bodhisattva takes or regularly renews their vow:

> Just as the earlier Buddhas have grasped the spirit of awakening (*bodhicitta*) and as they have remained ever steadier in the practices of a bodhisattva, so too would I like to bring forth the spirit of awakening for the benefit of the world, and in just this way I wish to perform these practices one after the other.
>
> trans. Steinkellner

The next six chapters of the *Bodhicaryāvatāra* are devoted primarily to the development of one, or a pair of closely related virtues. Chapter 4 focuses on the virtue of non-negligence (*apramāda*), a watchful state of mind whose primary purpose in this chapter is to protect and preserve *bodhicitta* against its "enemies", the *kleśas*—that is, greed, hate, and delusion. This is followed by a chapter focused on mindfulness and introspection (*smṛti* and *saṃprajanya*, Chapter 5). Chapters 6–9 are dedicated to four of the traditionally six bodhisattva virtues: patience (*kṣānti*, Chapter 6), commitment (*vīrya*, Chapter 7), contemplation (*dhyāna*, Chapter 8), and wisdom (*prajñā*, Chapter 9). The other two traditional virtues of generosity (*dāna*) and ethical discipline (*śīla*) are not given their own chapters. They are briefly mentioned in BCA 5:9–10, but play an important role in the overall treatment of the bodhisattva path (e.g., BCA 3:11), as is also the case with compassion (*karuṇā*), which is given careful treatment in the second half of the eighth chapter, and is a recurring theme throughout the entire text. The *Bodhicaryāvatāra* ends with a chapter dedicating the karmic merit that has been acquired through cultivating virtue for the benefit of all sentient beings.

There are a number of controversies about how to understand the structure of the text. Any reasonable interpretation will emphasize as a central goal of the early chapters the development and nurturing of *bodhicitta*. Scholars differ, however, as to the organizational structure of the chapters that follow. A common reading takes Śāntideva to employ a modified version of the schema of the six traditional bodhisattva virtues called perfections (*pāramitā*s), mentioned in many Mahāyāna texts (see Harris 2021). The structure of the six perfections is, for example, found in Āryaśūra's Compendium of Perfections (*Pāramitāsamāsa*) (see Meadows 1986). Śāntideva can be understood as employing it as well, in somewhat elliptical and idiosyncratic form. One could argue that, although generosity and ethical discipline have no chapters on their own, they are, as said above, by no means missing. In addition, one could also hold that generosity is being developed in Chapter 2 in a sequence of visualized gifts to Buddhas and supra-natural Bodhisattvas (BCA 2:1–21), and in Chapter 10 in which merit is dedicated to all sentient beings. The second perfection of ethical discipline can be understood as being illustrated in the fourth, and especially fifth chapter. This is because Śāntideva frequently psychologizes ethical action, analyzing the psychological conditions necessary for appropriate or inappropriate verbal and physical actions to occur (see BCA 5:9–14). In terms of ethical discipline, therefore, Śāntideva's emphasis will not be on rules of conduct, such as a prohibition against killing, but rather on purifying the mind of aggression which incites violence (see BCA 5:11–12). Chapter 5, focused on mindfulness and introspection, two virtuous qualities of attention, can therefore be understood as giving the psychological conditions of ethical actions in general, that being a mind under the control of mental discipline. The final four perfections are then treated sequentially in order in the chapters which bear their name.

However, it has also been argued that the schema of the six bodhisattva virtues is only used in a way subservient to something else. The central topic would then be *bodhicitta*, which Śāntideva describes as being twofold: the "resolution to strive for awakening and the actual striving" like the resolution to embark on a journey and the actual journeying (BCA 1:15–16). The first chapter emphasizes the crucial role of *bodhicitta* for the pursuit of a bodhisattva. Chapters 2 and 3 deal with its arousal and adoption. Chapters 4–8 show how *bodhicitta* is protected against its mental enemies (*kleśa*s) and developed throughout the journey toward its final perfection in wisdom (Chapter 9) and compassion (Chapter 10) (see Schmidt-Leukel 2019: 53–8).

2. Dynamics of tradition

Howsoever one interprets the title and structure of the *Bodhicaryāvatāra*, it is beyond dispute that Śāntideva deals with the bodhisattva path as the core ideal of Mahāyāna Buddhism—an ideal which may have actually been at the root of this tradition in as much as *mahā-yāna*, the "great" or "superb" (*mahā*) "vehicle" or "pursuit" (*yāna*) was probably originally the designation for the bodhisattva career—that is, for those Buddhists who strove to attain Buddhahood. "For them the Bodhisattvayāna became the Great Vehicle, the Mahāyāna" (Peter Skilling, quoted in Anālayo 2010: 132; see also Nattier 2003; Fronsdal 2014). Thus, Śāntideva's interpretation of this persuasion stands within a tradition that existed for almost a millennium before he composed the *Bodhicaryāvatāra* and it had a lasting and astonishing impact after its composition.

Today, the *Bodhicaryāvatāra* has become, next to the famous *Dhammapada*, the most often and most widely translated (both in Asian and Western languages) Buddhist text (Schmidt-Leukel 2019: 75–82). Since the eighth century it gradually assumed prominence throughout the Buddhist world from Central Asia and Mongolia down to Sri Lanka, where one of its verses (BCA 10:39) has even become part of the present Constitution (Schmidt-Leukel 2019: 505–6). It enjoyed a particularly high esteem in Tibet, where over the centuries many of the leading intellectuals from multiple philosophical lineages composed commentaries on it, even if they differed in their interpretations of Mahāyāna fundamental tenets. The *Bodhicaryāvatāra*'s spiritual-ethical contemplations were agreeable to Buddhists across different doctrinal positions (Douglas 2025). Thus, it became a foundational source for the Tibetan practice of mind-transformation (*Lojong*) in which the practitioner overcomes disturbing emotions by mentally taking on the suffering of all beings (Jinpa 2019). The text continues to be used in Tibetan monastic education, and is incorporated into rituals such as the taking of the bodhisattva's vow. It is a favored text of many influential Tibetan Buddhist teachers including the 14th Dalai Lama (Harris 2021).

In the last thirty years, the availability of dependable affordable translations of the *Bodhicaryāvatāra* has contributed greatly to its contemporary influence; it is now easily accessible for study by the spiritually minded broader public. It has also become a central primary source for the study of Mahāyāna Buddhist ethics. Being taught frequently in dharma centers around the world it also remains of vital importance for contemporary Buddhist practitioners far beyond the boundaries of Tibetan Buddhism. It is part of the dynamics of tradition that the text takes on new and partly controversial meanings within such processes of religious globalization. For instance, Amod Lele has argued that Śāntideva himself shows little interest, at least within the *Bodhicaryāvatāra*, for addressing immediate social needs such as poverty and injustice (Lele 2019). Other contemporary treatments of the *Bodhicaryāvatāra*, in contrast, are likely to turn to the text for inspiration for direct engagement in these kinds of social issues. The popular commentary by Pema Chödrön, for instance, portrays the bodhisattva as being inspired by compassion and *bodhicitta* to take as a goal the transformation of contemporary society (Chödrön 2005; see also Clayton 2019). Moreover, the *Bodhicaryāvatāra* is now increasingly attracting attention beyond the boundaries of Buddhism itself, whether from other religious traditions or the modern secular quest to determine whether there is still some value in the religious heritage of the world. In other words, Śāntideva's writings are influenced by a long tradition proceeding them and have themselves influenced an even longer tradition succeeding them. Looking at Śāntideva as part and parcel of a dynamic tradition is the overall aim of the chapters in this volume.

Adopting this viewpoint is not self-evident. In 1963, Wilfred Cantwell Smith published his study *The Meaning and End of Religion*, where he proposed to replace, in academic use, the concept of "religion" or "religions," by the binary of "faith" and "cumulative tradition." This, he argued, would allow distinguishing more clearly between individual religiosity or spirituality—i.e., "faith," ultimately observable only to the person of faith him- or herself—and that multifaceted side of religion that is open to public scrutiny and scholarly observation—i.e., "cumulative tradition." The latter comprises such various phenomena as beliefs, doctrines, narratives, poetry, scriptures, rituals, rules, contemplations and customs, buildings and institutions, songs and dances, music and artwork, and so on—just everything that, in contrast to faith, can be studied from the outside but is somehow connected to faith.

One reason why Smith coined the term "cumulative tradition" was to underline the tremendous internal diversity of so-called "religions" and especially "world-religions" and the undisputable fact of their persistent transformations. While the concepts "religion" and "religions" can misleadingly insinuate an immutable essence of each religion, historical investigation shows that such essentialization exists only in the minds of believers and/or their critics and is itself subject to diversity and change. For example, many concepts of what the true dharma really is existed side by side and changed over the course of time. "Cumulative tradition" would capture such diversity and dynamic much better than the concept of "religion." And this, of course, does not merely apply to Buddhists and their traditions but to all humanity.

Smith understood the relation between personal faith and cumulative tradition in terms of reciprocal influence. Cumulative tradition, or certain facets of it, can be expressive of faith and is nourished and shaped by the faith of those persons who live in and with the tradition. Conversely, cumulative tradition nourishes and shapes faith but should never be identified with faith, which is always personal and always new. Hence Smith distinguished strictly between "faith" as "an orientation of the personality" and "belief" as "the holding of certain ideas" which are part of the tradition (Smith 1979: 12).

In conceptualizing the relation between faith and tradition as interactive, Smith recognized not only interdependency but also some independency—that is, a certain irreducible autonomy of each of the two factors. This implies that a person's faith is by no means only the product of a tradition nor is it the only driving force within the dynamics of cumulative tradition. Cumulative traditions develop a life of their own in which many factors appear to play a more or less decisive role. Here the whole complexity of a web in which culture and religious tradition are interwoven comes into sight, without making both interchangeable. Still, one specific tradition can be found in different cultures as much as one culture can encompass different religious traditions. It seems that religious views and practices, as part of dynamic traditions, cannot be reduced to social and psychological realities, but shape and express a person's faith in a way going beyond both dimensions. Exploring in more detail the interplay of the different factors within the dynamics of religious traditions will be an ongoing task in academia.

3. The chapters

The dynamics of cumulative traditions can be studied backward or forward. Both directions are important. Studying history backwards—that is, perceiving anything "in terms of its antecedents"—forgets "that in fact time's arrow points the other way. History is not the past; history is process" (Smith 1989: 155). Hence, any look at antecedents may and should be complemented and perhaps even corrected by looking at things "in terms of its subsequent ramifications, its effects" (156). The chapters in this volume adopt both perspectives in examining the work of Śāntideva. Naturally, they can do this only by way of case studies. In sum, they take into account three different and significant fields of the dynamics of tradition: *first*, the realm of inner-Buddhist doctrinal dynamics; *second*, social dynamics—both as feasible within the text itself and in its further influence and reception history; and *third*, dynamics emerging when the text is considered through eyes shaped by non-Buddhist religious traditions.

The *first part* of the volume focuses on the embeddedness of Śāntideva's ideas in a Buddhist intellectual culture as well as their contribution to the ongoing development of Buddhist thought by identifying some of the driving doctrinal issues at work in this development.

A crucial point in understanding Śāntideva is his conception of wisdom in relation to the bodhisattva's action in the saṃsāric world. Amber Carpenter addresses this issue by contrasting Śāntideva's account of wisdom with that developed by the earlier Mādhyamika commentator, Candrakīrti. She takes Śāntideva's account to differ from Candrakīrti's in several important respects. According to Carpenter, Candrakīrti develops a "content-based" account of wisdom, where it is defined as correct understanding of ultimate reality. Moreover, for Candrakīrti wisdom takes as its content ultimate truth; conventional truth is not part of its proper domain. Finally, for Candrakīrti, the bodhisattva's compassion for others is not intimately related to wisdom itself, but is a distinct commitment taken on at earlier stages of the path. Carpenter argues that for Śāntideva, none of these claims hold true. The domain of wisdom is both conventional and ultimate truth, rather than ultimate truth alone. Likewise, wisdom is not (at least most centrally) the correct understanding of conventional and ultimate truth, but is rather the practical skill of determining which level of truth to engage with at any given time, in order to eliminate suffering, thereby facilitating shifting between them as needed. This is necessary, since the perspectives represented by the truths are incompatible, and cannot be kept in view simultaneously. Moreover, the bodhisattva's commitment to liberating all sentient beings requires engaging with conventional truth, the domain in which sentient beings, as well as the elements of the liberative path, exist. Unlike Candrakīrti, therefore, Śāntideva's account of wisdom is centrally related to compassion, given its role in enabling the bodhisattva to keep suffering sentient beings in view.

In the next chapter, Stephen Harris deals with Śāntideva's conceptualization of suffering, and the role it plays in his presentation of the bodhisattva path. According to

Harris, Śāntideva integrates appeals to suffering in two ways into his trainings in the *Bodhicaryāvatāra*. First, in line with the approach found in the early Buddhist tradition, suffering inspires *saṃvega*, a spiritually potent fear which destabilizes saṃsāric value and motivates commitment to Buddhist practice. Second, contemplating the wish to be free of suffering that is shared by all living beings motivates compassion and thereby dedication to the bodhisattva path. Initially these motivations appear to be in tension, in inspiring a wish to leave *saṃsāra*, paired by a commitment to remain within it. Harris suggests we can resolve this tension by attention to the way Śāntideva presents wisdom as enabling engagement with conventional reality in a purified mode of perception. As a result, the bodhisattva continues to engage with conventional reality free from the pathological emotions (*kleśa*s) which constitute saṃsāric experience.

The section continues with Jay Garfield and Emily McRae's analysis of the quality of *vīrya*, which they translate as "commitment," and the role it plays in the seventh chapter of the *Bodhicaryāvatāra. Virya* is usually translated as "effort," or "zeal," in order to highlight its role in motivating progress on the bodhisattva path. Garfield and McRae, however, warn against a purely adjectival reading of *vīrya*, insisting rather that it must be understood as non-egocentric motivation for moral action, which enables a fundamental reassessment of human values. Understood in this way, *vīrya* takes its proper place as a constituent of the bodhisattva path, which facilitates the shift from intellectual knowledge of what is right, to the bodhisattva's active caring engagement with the world. It also explains the placement of the *vīrya* chapter in Śāntideva's text, as mediating between the preparatory virtues which come before (such as generosity, patience, and introspective vigilance), and Śāntideva's focus on the deeply transformative virtues of meditative concentration and wisdom which follows.

The section concludes with Douglas Duckworth's analysis of the relationship between metaphysics and ethics in the context of the bodhisattva path. In accepting the core Mādhyamika tenet of the emptiness of all phenomena, Śāntideva, as Candrakīrti before him, is open to the charge of ethical relativism and a nihilism about values which reduces all evaluative distinctions to mere ungrounded opinion. In view of the later interpretations of Śāntideva, Duckworth points out two different responses to this charge. On the one hand, Śāntideva's emphasis on the commonality of human experience, in relation to suffering and the shared wish for happiness, provides a way of supporting universal commitment to the well-being of all without appealing to transcendent metaphysical foundations. On the other hand, Śāntideva can be and actually has been read by the Tibetan Nyingma Great Perfection (*rdzogs chen*) tradition in a way that grounds ethics on the non-dual realization of transcendent ultimate truth. Although in apparent tension, Duckworth argues that the two readings are in fact compatible, with each successfully illustrating a central facet of Śāntideva's thought.

Chapters in the *second part* move the focus to issues of social dynamics which are at several points closely entangled with doctrinal questions. At the beginning of his chapter on wisdom, Śāntideva correlates the traditional Madhyamaka distinction between two truths/realities with a distinction between two types of "worlds" or "people"—that is, the world of ordinary, non-yogic people and the world of yogic people (BCA 9:3–4). Dorji Wangchuk investigates possible antecedents of this distinction and its later impact on especially Tibetan Buddhism under six different perspectives: the possible exchange or "dialogue" between those two types of people (1); the significance of this distinction for Madhyamaka methodology (2); ontology (3); epistemology (4); and axiology (5); and finally its implications regarding various aspects of the relationship (6) between the ordinary and yogic people, including both doctrinal and social issues.

In the next chapter, Perry Schmidt-Leukel investigates the function of mockery, sarcasm, and irony as they appear frequently in the *Bodhicaryāvatāra*. Numerous scholars have emphasized the confessional and existential character of Śāntideva's writing. Schmidt-Leukel shows that such features are accompanied, and in part even carried out by a subtle mocking sarcasm. Śāntideva uses humor not only to express his cynicism about ordinary conceptions of value but also about his own spiritual state, identifying the typical features of worldly ways of thinking in himself. Via his sarcasm a pessimism about the human ability to comply by one's own efforts with the extremely high demands of the bodhisattva ideal becomes seizable. This is closely connected to the persistent exhortation to rely on the protection and support of the supra-natural Bodhisattvas and Buddhas—a feature of the text that is often neglected or downplayed by contemporary interpreters, but is much in line with the growing importance of faith or trust in the context of Mahāyāna Buddhism. For, if the bodhisattva ideal exists in striving for awakening for the benefit of all others, it becomes possible for those others to rely on the compassion of those Bodhisattvas who are close to their aim or have already achieved it and become Buddhas.

Carola Roloff explores the *Bodhicaryāvatāra* through a feminist lens, revealing its contemporary relevance and challenging traditional interpretations. She begins with a critical examination of how translations influence the text's reception, particularly regarding gender inclusivity. She questions the presence and representation of female figures within the text, examining both explicit and implicit references. She also scrutinizes Śāntideva's perspectives on women and gender roles, juxtaposing these with modern feminist thought. Her analysis extends to the concept of precious human birth, probing into the implications of gender in the path to enlightenment. Furthermore, she delves into the depiction of women in various roles and the ascetics' interactions with them, offering a unique perspective on Buddhist teachings and societal norms of the time. Her chapter aims to provide a nuanced understanding of the *Bodhicaryāvatāra*, suggesting that Śāntideva's work, when viewed through a feminist perspective, can offer valuable insights for contemporary discussions on gender equality in Buddhism. This reinterpretation not only sheds light on historical gender dynamics but also paves the way for a more inclusive and empathetic approach to Buddhist teachings.

Andrew Skilton, finally, focuses not on Śāntideva's writings but on the way Śāntideva is seen as a role model in the context of the relation between organizational hierarchy and a practitioner's actual level of spiritual insight. Skilton analyzes multiple axes of hierarchical influence that can be achieved in monastic settings. These include seniority acquired by the date of one's ordination, or one's gender; organizational roles taken on such as temple abbot, individual preceptor or spiritual instructor; and influenced gained through being perceived as spiritually advanced, or through display of supernatural powers. Through a careful reading of traditional hagiographic accounts of Śāntideva's life, with additional references to the stories of the lives of the Chan monk Huineng, and Indian Mahāyāna monastic, Nāropa, Skilton argues that these narratives illustrate that these many forms of institutional authority do not necessarily or even reliably track actual spiritual progress. This tension between organizational authority and spiritual advancement is exemplified clearly in some versions of the Śāntideva legend, in which he is shown as abandoning his monastic institution of Nālandā upon being recognized as a spiritual authority by the community.

The *third part* turns to the perception of Śāntideva beyond the confinements of the Buddhist tradition. It begins with Francis Brassard's interpretation of Śāntideva's idea of *bodhicitta* from the perspective of comparative spirituality. According to Brassard, the twofold *bodhicitta* (as the resolution to strive for awakening and the actual striving, BCA 1:15–16) corresponds to two different dynamics of spiritual transformation, two stages, each having its own aspiration and benefits in the process of one's emancipation. Starting from here, he suggests a hermeneutic based on the idea that religious discourses are to be distinguished in terms of their respective mode of resolving a problem, be it practical, existential, or social. These modes differ from each other, among other things, in terms of the relation between knowledge and action. By analyzing the structure of the twofold *bodhicitta* through these modes of resolution, he highlights the universal nature of the path of the *bodhisattva* as well as its specificity with regard to other philosophical, religious, or spiritual traditions.

After a preliminary exposition of the central points of contention that structure the general debate between Mahāyāna Buddhists and Advaita Vedāntins, Fabian Völker examines the apparent similarities and basic differences between the doctrines of Buddha-nature (*tathāgatagarbha*) and Self (*ātman*). By a list of ten criteria that would identify a Buddhist as Advaitin, he discusses the wisdom chapter of the *Bodhicaryāvatāra* focusing on Śāntideva's views on consciousness and ultimate reality in respect to whether they align with Śaṇkara's perspective. Despite Śaṇkara's and Śāntideva's irreconcilable approaches to consciousness, which seem to reflect deep insuperable differences regarding their metaphysical visions of ultimate reality, there is still an option to interpret Śāntideva as presupposing a transconceptual ultimate reality. However, even this assumption could close the philosophical gap between Śaṇkara and Śāntideva only partially, because the abiding and irreconcilable point of contention resides in the crucial question of whether the absolute appearance of the ultimate may be consistently conceived in terms of pure consciousness or not.

Mark Heim employs the methodology of comparative theology to argue for the relevance of Śāntideva's conception of the emptiness of the person, in deepening Christian understandings of what it means to be a "creature"—that is, a being created by and radically dependent on their creator. Learning to be empty, for Śāntideva, is in many ways akin to learning to be a creature, for the Christian. For both, it requires insight into the lack of self-existence, and therefore acceptance of the radical dependence of persons. Likewise, it diagnoses the root sources of spiritually harmful actions and negative emotions to the false belief in the independence of the self. Moreover, embracing one's emptiness or creatureliness entails positive psychological and spiritual transformation, manifesting in impartial benevolent commitment toward all beings (for Śāntideva), and a recognition of the commonality of all beings as created and dependent on God (for the Christian). Heim's paper concludes with a suggested connection between Śāntideva's emphasis on the non-dual realization of emptiness, and the idea that a kind of "creaturely emptiness" can be realized by the Christian in apophatic experience of divine immanence.

Reza Shah Kazemi investigates the relation between the Buddhist bodhisattva ideal and Muslim concepts of spirituality, which, so far, has not been much researched, despite the fact that religious practice is of crucial significance for Buddhist–Muslim dialogue. His chapter offers a comparative analysis of Śāntideva's *Bodhicaryāvatāra* and the treatise on spiritual ethics, *Makārim al-akhlāq* ("Noble Character Traits") by ʿAlī b. Husayn Zayn al-ʿĀbidīn (d. 713), fourth Shia Imam, great-grandson of the Prophet. The main theme of the comparison is the way in which ethico-spiritual dynamics operate within the respective texts, principally the interplay between ethical imperatives and contemplative praxis. According to Shah Kazemi, a functional parallel and perhaps even metaphysical convergence can be discerned between the flow of compassion from the contemplation of emptiness and the dynamics of merciful grace, despite the differences between the non-theistic approach of Buddhism and the theistic approach in Islam.

4. A diversity of views

The contributors to this volume do not only discuss Śāntideva in relation to different aspects of the dynamics of tradition. They also differ in certain aspects of their interpretation of Śāntideva and hence are themselves part of the diversity of the ongoing reception history of Śāntideva's work.

As mentioned above, there are widespread differences in understanding the title and structure of the *Bodhicaryāvatāra*. In addition, differences in translation can be indicative of sometimes severe differences in interpretation. For example, translating the "enemies" of *bodhicitta*, the *kleśa*s, as "pathological emotions" or as "mental defilements" can be expressive of a different understanding of how Śāntideva conceives the nature of human persons. A related difference is the question of the role of support from supra-natural Bodhisattvas and fully enlightened Buddhas, and correspondingly the role of faith in them on the part of the developing bodhisattva. Some interpreters emphasize that Buddhas and highly advanced Bodhisattvas are referenced repeatedly in the text: the developing bodhisattva invokes their aid (BCA 3:3), asks for their protection against the consequences of his/her own bad karma (e.g., BCA 2:22, 33, 51), and praises them as those who evoke the crucial spirit of *bodhicitta* (BCA 3:3; 10:13). Other contemporary interpreters deemphasize these themes of faith and divine support, focusing instead on Śāntideva's therapeutic method of prescribing trainings to develop the aspirant's mind. These authors are more likely to describe Śāntideva's project as developing a moral psychology of virtuous mental states, or a virtue theory training positive habitual dispositions, where this includes virtuous mental habits of response (see Harris 2024). A related approach is to describe Śāntideva's method as one of moral phenomenology, in which the mind is purified of egocentricity and the negative emotions which constitute self-centered attitudes (see Garfield 2021). These approaches have in common a more naturalistic approach to the *Bodhicaryāvatāra*, in which specifically religious presuppositions (such as the existence of celestial

Bodhisattvas who are at work within *saṃsāra*) are deemphasized. Such approaches will emphasize instead Śāntideva's arguments and meditative exercises given throughout the text to enhance moral development.

Our guiding method as editors is to embrace diversity in approaches and one will find variations of different approaches represented in the subsequent chapters. At the outset, however, it is worth emphasizing that there is also a great deal of overlap between the two interpretive trends referenced above. This is in part because Śāntideva references specific virtuous mental states which constitute the novice bodhisattva's reverential attitude to Buddhas and supra-natural Bodhisattvas. These include faith (*śraddhā*) and serene joy (*prāmodya*), both attitudes of confidence toward and respect for the efficacy of the Buddhist path, and those who complete it. Moreover, these mental states themselves play a central role in calming the bodhisattva's mind, enlivening it for bodhisattva practice, and diminishing the pull of negative emotions. Offerings to Buddhas and Bodhisattvas, and invocations for their aid at the beginning of the bodhisattva path and throughout (BCA 5:98), stimulate the bodhisattva's mind for developing and increasing the strength of *bodhicitta* and compassion. The invocations of divine aid, therefore, are deeply entwined with Śāntideva's moral psychology, and the relevant qualities of faith and confidence are themselves a constituent part of the bodhisattva's moral and spiritual development.

A final—and somewhat crucial—area of divergence in interpretation of the *Bodhicaryāvatāra* that should be mentioned in this Introduction is the question of Śāntideva's account of wisdom, in particular his understandings of conventional and ultimate truth/reality (note that *satya* may be translated both ways), as well as the relation between them. There is, among many commentators, general agreement that Śāntideva means by conventional truth/reality the deceptive world of commonsense partite objects and entities comprising everyday experience, such as chariots, tables, cats, desks, persons, etc., although there are differences in interpretation as to how radical his understanding of its illusion-like or illusory nature is. This is related to an issue where interpretations sharply diverge: the question of ultimate truth/reality, and what Śāntideva takes to be its relation to conventional truth/reality. In one reading, ultimate truth/reality refers to the true reality beyond concepts and language, experience of which is the chief component of liberation. Conventional truth/reality, in contrast, is the realm of illusion, a fabricated web of concepts habitually superimposed on the true nature of reality. Scholars taking this interpretation can draw upon verses like BCA 9:2 to support their interpretation, which can be read to suggest that ultimate truth/reality refers to the inconceivable nature of true reality underlying conventional entities:

> The conventional (*saṃvṛti*) and the ultimate (*paramārtha*), these two realities (*satya*) we accept. Ultimate reality is not a domain of cognition. Cognition is called the conventional reality.
>
> trans. Steinkellner

On this reading, the liberative practices of the bodhisattva are consciously enacted within the illusory realm (BCA 9:53, 76–7; according to a different numbering 9:75–6) while ultimately all beings are already saved (BCA 9:151).

A competing interpretation rejects the idea of any true reality beyond language undergirding conventional reality. In this interpretation, all that exists are conventionally existing phenomena, which by their nature are radically dependent, on external causal conditions, their own parts, and conceptual imputation by a perceiving consciousness. Conventional phenomena are like illusions (see BCA 9:5), in that they appear one way, as possessing independent existence, while their real mode of existence is of radical dependence. This is not to be taken literally as claiming that they are non-existent, however; rather such phenomena function dependably when not analyzed, and interact in reliable causal relations (see BCA 9:9–14). Correspondingly, there is no independent realm of reality undergirding conceptually structured conventional truth/reality; rather ultimate truth becomes the mode in which conventional phenomena exist, as empty of intrinsic nature. Conventional phenomena, in this reading, take on a more robust ontological role, as the only kind of thing that can exist. All the components of the bodhisattva path, the bodhisattvas themselves, the virtues they develop, the beings they save, and so on, are all conventional phenomena, with sufficiently robust existence to make intelligible the practices of liberation Śāntideva gives in the *Bodhicaryāvatāra*.

Both readings of the text sketched above can be traced to divergences of interpretation in how to understand the thought of the Madhyamaka school's founder, Nāgārjuna, as well as his Indian commentator, Candrakīrti. As with the other interpretive disagreements surveyed above, however, we can acknowledge some common points of agreement among both interpretive trends. For both readings of Madhyamaka, conventional reality will be conceived of as deeply misleading, at least to non-liberated persons. Likewise, most commentators will agree that central to Śāntideva's goals in the *Bodhicaryāvatāra*, and especially the wisdom chapter, is arguing for the positive therapeutic and soteriological consequences of realizing this deceptive nature of conventional reality: this eliminates negative emotions, develops virtuous mental states, and represents a central point of progress toward liberation.

Most of the chapters in this volume are revised and expanded versions of papers that were presented during an expert symposium that took place in May 2023 at the University of Münster (Germany) that was jointly organized by Stephen E. Harris and Perry Schmidt-Leukel. We are grateful to the Cluster of Excellence "Religion and Politics" which sponsored the symposium and also contributed to some of the costs involved in the publication. We would also like to extend our gratitude to the anonymous reviewers who recommended the publication of the papers and to Aimee Brown and the team of Bloomsbury who were so helpful and indeed indispensable in the process that finally brought the book about.

References

Anālayo, Bhikkhu (2010), *The Genesis of the Bodhisattva Ideal*, Hamburg: Hamburg University Press.

Chödrön, P. (2005), *No Time to Lose: A Timely Guide to the Way of the Bodhisattva*, Boulder, CO: Shambala.

Clayton, B. (2018), "The Changing Way of the Bodhisattva," in D. Cozort and J. M. Shields (eds.), *The Oxford Handbook of Buddhist Ethics*, New York: Oxford University Press.
Duckworth, D. S. (2025), "Translator"s Introduction," in Minyak Kunzang Sönam, *The Great HŪṂ. A Commentary on Śāntideva's* Way of the Bodhisattva, 1–18, New York: Wisdom Publications.
Fronsdal, Gil (2014), *Dawn of the Bodhisattva Path. The Early Perfection of Wisdom*, Berkeley: Institute of Buddhist Studies and BDK America.
Garfield, J. (2021), *Buddhist Ethics: A Philosophical Exploration*, New York: Oxford University Press.
Harris, S. E. (2021), "Śāntideva's Introduction to the Practices of Awakening (Bodhicaryāvatāra)," in *Oxford Research Encyclopedia of Religion* online.
Harris, S. E. (2024), *Buddhist Ethics and the Bodhisattva Path: Śāntideva on Virtue and Well-Being*, London: Bloomsbury.
Harrison, P. (2019), "Śāntideva: The Author and His Project," in J. Gold and D. Duckworth (eds.), *Readings of Śāntideva's Guide to Bodhisattva Practice*, 27–44, New York: Columbia University Press.
Huntington, E. (2019), "Ritual Structure and Material Culture in the *Guide to Bodhisattva Practice*," in J. Gold and D. Duckworth (eds.), *Readings of Śāntideva's Guide to Bodhisattva Practice*, 132–45, New York: Columbia University Press.
Jinpa, T. (2019), "Bodhicaryāvatāra and Tibetan Mind Training (Lojong)," in J. Gold and D. Duckworth (eds.), *Readings of Śāntideva's Guide to Bodhisattva Practice*, 146–61, New York: Columbia University Press.
Lele, A. (2019), "Disengaged Buddhism," *Journal of Buddhist Ethics* 26: 237–89.
Meadows, C. (1986), *Ārya-Śūra's Compendium of the Perfections: Text, translation and analysis of the Pāramitāsamāsa*, Bonn: Indica et Tibetica Verlag.
Nattier, J. (2003), *A Few Good Men. The Bodhisattva Path according to The Inquiry of Ugra (Ugraparipṛcchā)*, Honolulu: University of Hawai'i Press.
Saito, A. (1993), *A Study of Aksayamati (=Śāntideva)'s Bodhisattvacaryāvatāra as Found in the Tibetan Manuscripts From Tun-Huang*. Project number 02801005, Faculty of Humanities, Miye University.
Schmidt-Leukel, P. (2019), *Buddha Mind – Christ Mind. A Christian Commentary on the Bodhicaryāvatāra*. With a new translation by E. Steinkellner and C. Peck-Kubaczek, Leuven: Peeters.
Smith, W. C. (1963), *The Meaning and End of Religion. A New Approach to the Religious Traditions of Mankind*, New York: Macmillan.
Smith, W. C. (1979), *Faith and Belief*, Princeton: Princeton University Press.
Smith, W. C. (1989), *Towards a World Theology. Faith and the Comparative History of Religion*, Maryknoll, NY: Orbis Books.
Williams, P. (1998), *Altruism and Reality: Studies in the Philosophy of the Bodhicaryāvatāra*, Richmond: Curzon.

I

Doctrinal Dynamics

1

Candrakīrti's *prajñā*, Śāntideva's *phronēsis*

Alternative Models of Mādhyamika Wisdom

Amber D. Carpenter

1. Introduction

The ninth chapter of the *Bodhicaryāvatāra* seems to inspire in scholars a cautious and respectful distance: it is clearly vital, and yet it is difficult philologically as well as philosophically. In order to bring into sharper relief one exciting strand of that chapter, this study considers the treatment of *prajñā* in two Mādhyamika Buddhist *avatāras*: Candrakīrti's *Madhyamakāvatāra* and Śāntideva's *Bodhicaryāvatāra*. For *prajñā* I shall largely use the English "wisdom," for the concept of wisdom occupies that crucial space of overlap between the cognitive and the moral, and it operates as a perfection—coming in degrees and difficult to attain. Wisdom is good in itself while making other things good, and at the same time the concept is agnostic about exactly what sort of cognition is involved (is it a kind of understanding? a kind of insight? a kind of mental grasp? intuition?). Since this is an examination of texts, not of what might be the authors' wider views, phrases such as "according to Candrakīrti" or "Śāntideva's view" should be taken as conventional shorthand for the views that can be found articulated in Chapter 6 of the *Madhyamakāvatāra* or Chapter 9 of the *Bodhicaryāvatāra*.[1]

In what follows, I shall argue that Candrakīrti has a more familiar and conservative conception of wisdom as content-based: *prajñā* just is the apprehension of certain content, even if that content is of a rather peculiar unspecifiable sort.[2] While one uses

1 The authorship of the *Bodhicaryāvatāra* is particularly complicated, there being an earlier text, call it (with Saito) BCA-I, which later editorial hands changed and supplemented, particularly in the wisdom chapter (see §5, below), resulting in the received text (or BCA-II) which is conventionally known as Śāntideva's. Akira Saito's invaluable, but not always readily available, work on the earlier version of the text includes Saito 1993, Saito 1994, Saito 2006. For *Bodhicaryāvatāra* 9, I will follow the verse numbering of Crosby and Skilton 1995. Regarding Candrakīrti, this is specifically *not* a study of what the tradition has made of his thought more widely, which may for good reason differ from what the text of the *Madhyamakāvatāra* itself, and Chapter 6 in particular, says.

2 Sweet 1979 explores in some detail the subsequent debates over whether it is appropriate to describe ultimate reality as an *object* of cognition at all. This is an interesting and important matter in the philosophy of mind, but not one that will concern us here. I want to speak of "contents" of cognition in the widest possible sense, which may include non-dual apprehension (hence, *realization*) of reality.

the conventional as a means to attain this end, the attainment of this end consists in the cognitive stillness hailed by Nāgārjuna in the homage to the Buddha in the *Mūlamadhyamakakārikā* (dedicatory verse) as "the auspicious cessation of *prapañca* [conceptual proliferation]".[3]

Śāntideva, by contrast, takes the mode of *prajñā* to be itself a caring attitude; it is not just motivated by care. The content of wisdom, moreover, is the *two* truths (not just the one): ultimate emptiness and the illusions of conventional conceptually rich reality, recognized as such.[4] Wisdom itself, however, is not defined as simply the caring apprehension of this content, but consists rather in the skill of moving between the two. *Prajñā* according to Śāntideva is the dynamic ability to discern well which aspect of wisdom's incompatible content is to be entertained at a given moment so as to best eliminate suffering. In its conception of *prajñā* as a sensitivity to what is required now, Śāntideva's wisdom might be considered something like Aristotelian *phronēsis*—with the rather substantial caveat that what the bodhisattva discerns is *not* "what action to take," but rather which perspective to take or "how to see," at a given moment.

This dynamic conception of *prajñā* is better able than more conservative content-focused conceptions to do justice to Nāgārjuna's challenging assertion in the *Root Verses* that "there is no distinction whatsoever between *saṃsāra* and *nirvāṇa*" (MMK 25:19). It offers a more satisfying explanation of Nāgārjuna's insistence that both conventional and ultimate reality are necessary for enlightenment. And it is better placed to address the difficulty inherent in the bodhisattva ideal of how full appreciation of the insubstantiality of reality, including of selves *and* of suffering, can be compatible with caring responsiveness.

2. Comparative *avatāra*s

Both texts under consideration are *avatāra*s—introductions or inductions (Einleitungen)—written by Buddhist Madhyamaka thinkers working perhaps a century apart, and both introductions are structured around the *pāramitā*s or "perfections." Candrakīrti's *avatāra*, however, is an introduction to Madhyamaka, to Nāgārjuna's distinctive interpretation of Mahāyāna Buddhism as Candrakīrti understands that; and it is structured as an exposition of ten perfections, with *prajñā* coming sixth (followed by *upāya* [skillful means], *praṇidhāna* [resolution, aspiration],

[3] Translations from the *Mūlamadhyamakakārikā* are by Siderits and Katsura 2013, with modifications: in particular, using "(dependent) arising" for their "(dependent) origination," and generally omitting material they supply in square brackets. Here I also leave "*prapañca*" in place, offering "conceptual proliferation" as a gloss rather than their translation as "hypostatization."

[4] In what follows, I use the alliterative and conventional "two truths," with all the appropriate caveats about "truth" and "reality." I use "conventional" for *saṃvṛti* (also "the world" and "worldly" for *loka**-words, e.g., *lokam, laukikī*, MA 1:16, 2:9, 3:4, 3:10, 4:22–35, 6:98–113; *lokacaritaiḥ*, worldly ways, worldly affairs, BCA 8:185; *lokena, lokayoḥ*, BCA 9:5; associated with *saṃvṛti* at MA 6:28–30, 6:159; BCA 9:8) and "ultimate" for *paramārtha*. It is proverbial in Madhyamaka discourse to say that one must know the two truths; but while *Bodhicaryāvatāra* 9 is quite explicit in this regard, *Madhyamakāvatāra* 6 is not, and in fact rather indicates that *prajñā* is of ultimate reality.

bala [power], and *jñāna* [knowledge]). Śāntideva's *Bodhicarāvatāra*, by contrast, offers an induction into bodhisattva conduct, structured around *six* perfections, culminating with *prajñā*.[5] The aim of the text is to make its audience into a bodhisattva advancing along the path, and accordingly the aim of its wisdom chapter is to make one wise.[6]

The *avatāra* to being a bodhisattva is relatively evenly balanced across the six *pāramitā*s, even if it is not entirely clear where we should locate the text's treatment of *dāna*. Wisdom and mental cultivation are treated at greatest length, but there are substantial expositions of restraint (Ch. 5), *kṣānti* (Ch. 6), and *vīrya* (Ch. 7) as well. The *Bodhicaryāvatāra* may culminate in wisdom, but each step in that direction warrants sustained attention in its own right, essential to the wholesale transformation that becoming a bodhisattva entails. In the *Madhyamakāvatāra*, by contrast, while Candrakīrti's selection of ten *pāramitā*s may situate Nāgārjuna's thought as an exposition of the ten stages of the bodhisattva's progress, the aim of the text is not to transform but to introduce the Madhyamaka understanding of the Mahāyāna. It is indicative, then, of what Candrakīrti thinks Madhyamaka is that he takes *prajñā* to be of overwhelming centrality: more than 70 percent of the *Madhyamakāvatāra* consists in the sixth chapter's discussion of wisdom, which at 226 verses is nearly six times longer than the treatment of the other nine perfections *combined*; four perfections have just a single verse devoted to them (Chs. 5, 7, 9, and 10). Evidently Candrakīrti at least does not think there is anything specifically Madhyamaka in the other nine perfections. Madhyamaka is distinguished by its understanding of wisdom.[7]

3. Candrakīrti's content-based conception of wisdom

This understanding of wisdom is, however, remarkably conservative, all the distinctiveness due to the distinctiveness of what it is *of*. It is no part of my plan to give

5 The structure of the *Bodhicarāvatāra* is not quite so neat, since there are competing structuring elements, with the liturgy of the Supreme Worship structuring Chapters 2 and 3 on developing *bodhicitta*, which were originally a single chapter (see Crosby and Skilton 1995: 9; Saito 1993: 14). These might serve as Śāntideva's treatment of *dāna*, typically the first of the six perfections, for it is not treated elsewhere (the fourth chapter concerns "vigilance concerning the awakening mind"); the remaining five *pāramitā*s are then taken in the ordinary sequence in Chapters 5–9. Schmidt-Leukel 2019: 53–8 offers a slightly different interpretation of the *Bodhicaryāvatāra*'s "creative variation" (54) on the six *pāramitā* schema, on which "the *pāramitā*s are understood as perfections of different aspects of *bodhicitta*" (57).

6 Note the first- and second-person address of the *Bodhicarāvatāra*, for instance, and frequent appeals to the psychology of the bodhisattva in training. On the *protreptic* nature of the *Bodhicarāvatāra*, see Carpenter 2019 and Harris 2024: 43–7. Schmidt-Leukel 2019: 59–60 observes that these directly personal forms of address are diminished in most of the wisdom chapter. This is perhaps fitting, if the chapter is meant to address primarily someone who is already largely free from the sorts of personal thinking the previous chapters treat. Its style is nevertheless notably attentive to the phenomenological and experiential content of the bodhisattva (Harris 2024: 163), and very dialectically engaged and thus marked by a distinct situational responsiveness relevant to wisdom. (The more sectarian, set-piece debates are usually latter additions; see note 1.)

7 This distinctive wisdom may yield modified versions of the other perfections (e.g., "To give without a giver, gift, recipient, Now this is a perfection which transcends the world," MA 1:6, may be a particularly Mādhyamika understanding of generosity); but these modifications evidently do not warrant or require exposition beyond what is found in the description of wisdom itself.

a definitive account of the distinctively Mādhyamika "object" or contents of wisdom. Rather, I want to show something much more contained, namely that Candrakīrti *does* conceive of *prajñā* as a cognitive condition defined by its content.

Consider first, then, the verse with which Candrakīrti opens MA 6:

> On Presence, with their minds now placed in equipoise,
> They're in the presence of the traits of buddhahood.
> *Dependent rising is the fact they now perceive* —
> And reach cessation, resting in intelligence [*prajñā*].
>
> trans. Liland, emphasis mine[8]

This seems to set out a fairly straightforward content-focused characterization of wisdom. Naturally, it will have to be conceived a bit differently from any usual conception of "contents," for they cannot be properly thought of as discrete individuate-able objects at all.[9] But so far as conventional language can at all get a grip on the situation, we can ask: "What does *prajña* know (perceive, understand, grasp, apprehend)?" and expect the correct answer to be: "Dependent-arising."

Or perhaps the correct answer is "emptiness," for in verse 6:4 Candrakīrti introduces emptiness—"Some common people, when they hear of emptiness, Will find that great delight comes surging from within"—with the implicit suggestion that this is what the wise person knows. And this initial positioning of emptiness as "what wisdom is of" is reiterated at the end of the chapter, which sets out the sixteen forms of emptiness made canonical by Asaṅga.[10] This exposition of emptiness takes up over forty-three verses (vv. 180–223) or nearly a fifth of the whole chapter, reinforcing the impression that the important thing about understanding *prajñā* correctly lies in getting the content right. Emptiness here, however, should not be taken as an alternative to dependent arising, but rather as a specification of it. In keeping with Nāgārjuna's *Mūlamdahyamakakārikā,* Candrakīrti intends us to recall Nāgārjuna's 'dependent arising we declare to be emptiness' (MMK 24:19), repeated in his commentary on verse 70 of the *Vigrahavyāvartanī.*[11] Thus the correct understanding of dependent arising, of that which wisdom apprehends, is as emptiness, and the chapter from beginning to end is committed to spelling this out.

Thus the greater proportion of *Madhyamakāvatāra* 6 is concerned with some version or another of what it is wisdom apprehends—whether conceived as dependent

[8] Further quotations of the *Madhyamakāvatāra* and the *Madhyamakāvatāra-Bhāṣya* are from Liland 2020, unless otherwise noted. The Sanskrit of *Madhyamakāvatāra* 6, without Candrakīrti's auto-commentary, can be found in Li 2015. While the Austrian Academy of Sciences have published critical and diplomatic editions of the Sanskrit text with auto-commentary of the first five chapters (Lasic, Li, and MacDonald 2022), the remainder—and Chapter 6 in particular—has yet to appear.

[9] See Carpenter 2022 for this way of taking *pratītyadamutpāda* in Nāgārjuna as concerned primarily with individuation.

[10] In the *Madhyānta-Vibhāga.* According to Tucci 1947: 54, the fact that Dignāga's *Prajñāpāramitā-piṇḍārta* also treats emptiness under sixteen heads (rather than eighteen, as the *Mahāvyutpatti*, or twenty, as Haribhadra's *Abhisamayālaṅkārāloka*) sufficiently indicates that Dignāga took the *Madhyānta-Vibhāga* as his source text.

[11] In which context, Westerhoff 2010: 130 observes that "emptiness is to be understood in terms of dependent origination has been stressed frequently by Nāgārjuna."

arising or as emptiness or as no-self. Over a third of the text (ninety-five verses, from v. 8 to v. 103) is hung on *Mūlamadhyamakakārikā* 1 in particular, the examination of causes, which Nāgārjuna presents as clearing the way for the correct understanding of dependent arising.[12] And since the crux of dependent arising and emptiness is the lack of substantial, well-individuated entities, another central way of specifying the content of *prajñā* is as "no self." Thus Candrakīrti devotes a further sixth of the chapter (nearly fifty verses, vv. 122–70) to no-self. In total, over 80 percent of Candrakīrti's discussion of the perfection of wisdom concerns specifying its content, what it is that wisdom knows or apprehends. The remaining forty-ish verses act as sinews connecting the different parts of the discussion, sometimes articulating things like the relation of *prajñā* to the other *pāramitās* (MA 6:2), or the purpose of a teaching (MA 6:179); but they offer nothing significant theoretically to shift the basic conception of wisdom.[13] Even in Chapter 11, Candrakīrti persists in presenting wisdom in terms of the apprehension of reality: "To know the true reality, which is unchanging, has no types, Will be the only way that one can rid oneself of every stain. The wisdom that discerns it can't be classified in any way" (11:45).

This content-focused conception of *prajñā* is reinforced by the polemical argumentative style in which this material is presented, which lays implicit emphasis on getting some content *right* (and especially on not getting it wrong). Instead of setting out and defending his particular understanding of Madhyamaka, Candrakīrti takes the argument to the opponent—going on the offense to prove alternative views wrong.[14] Thus vv. 8–13 demonstrate that production from self is incoherent (6:12), while vv. 14–97 argue against production-from-another. (The final two horns of the tetralemma do not merit much discussion, just vv. 6:98–100.) In the chapter's second act—which begins by observing that misapprehension of the conclusion of the tetralemma is responsible for confusion[15]—Candrakīrti spends the bulk of the section demonstrating that other theories will not survive analysis (6:115), or in Liland's vivid rendering:

> And as all things arise interdependently
> These theories will not withstand analysis.

[12] The correct interpretation, that is, of such canonical texts as SN 12:17, in which the Buddha advises, "[if one thinks,] 'The one who acts is the same as the one who experiences [the result]' . . . this amounts to eternalism. But, Kassapa, [if one thinks,] 'The one who acts is one, the one who experiences [the result] is another' . . . this amounts to annihilationism. Without veering towards either of these extremes, the Tathagata teaches the Dhamma by the middle: 'With ignorance as condition, volitional formations [come to be]; with volitional formations as condition, consciousness . . .'" (trans. Bodhi).

[13] Take away ten verses which act as bookends at either end, and this leaves thirty-six verses in the chapter that might *not* be content-focused. This suggests that not only is wisdom about getting the content right; for Candrakīrti, that's *all* it is.

[14] The passage in *Bodhicaryāvatāra* 9 which most resembles *Madhyamakāvatāra* 6 in argumentative style is the extended interpolated passage at BCA 9:118–37, where Nyāya and Saṃkhya views are engaged with.

[15] "Because things don't arise from self, other or both, Nor causelessly, they're nothing in and of themselves. The clouds of dense confusion lie across the world, And therefore objects are perceived mistakenly" (6:104, trans. Liland).

Submitted to interdependence's arguments
All complex nets of faulty views are ripped to shreds.

One might see this aggressive mode of argument as an implication of Candrakīrti's *prasaṅgika* commitments: if all rivals are refuted, what is left standing is confirmed as correct, without one having had to defend or even define it. But it is strikingly different from the style of Chapter 9 of the *Bodhicaryāvatāra,* which is much more often responding to concerns that anyone might have when told, for instance, "Ordinary people see existent things and also imagine them to be real, that is to say not an illusion. It is in this regard that there is disagreement between the ordinary person and the spiritually developed" (BCA 9:5).[16] As we will see below, the fundamentally responsive mode of engagement which characterizes Śāntideva's exposition of wisdom will turn out to be highly revealing of and fitting to the *Bodhicaryāvatāra*'s distinctive conception of *prajñā*. But for now we may simply take this as evidence that there are other ways than Candrakīrti's to engage as a Prāsaṅgika (or else Śāntideva is a bad Prāsaṅgika, or no Prāsaṅgika at all).[17]

Even if Candrakīrti's aggressive style is all in the methodological service of refraining from asserting a substantial claim, it nevertheless underscores the basic, conservative object-oriented conception of *prajñā* that Candrakīrti presumes. What is of essential, overriding importance to attaining awakening is to grasp the truth of dependent arising/emptiness correctly—for instance, by not mistaking it for the assertion of non-being (e.g., MA 6:34); by working through, over forty-four verses, the received concise and elaborate expositions of emptiness until "Thus brightened by the rays of clear intelligence They see the triple world as unborn from the start As clear as a myrobalan plum in their palm" (MA 6:224); and generally through recognizing that "no other source presents This dharma in this accurate way" (MA 11:53).

4. What does Candrakīrti care?

At the end of this extensive investigation of what *prajñā* sees, Candrakīrti suddenly turns to care or compassion (*karuṇā*), asserting: "Although remaining in cessation all the time, Compassion for defenseless ones will still occur" (MA 6:225). This is sudden because until now, *karuṇā* has appeared in Chapter 6 only as a characteristic of one suited to be taught Madhyamaka emptiness (MA 6:6), and as a defining mark of the Buddha (6:212). The exposition of what wisdom consists in operates completely independently of, and without reference to, *karuṇā*. It is simply an assertion because once wisdom is defined in a content-based way, and defined without any reference to care built into that content, it is not at all obvious what the place of *care* would be in wisdom or its related cessation.

[16] This and all following quotations of the *Bodhicaryāvatāra* are as translated by Crosby and Skilton 1995, unless otherwise noted.

[17] See Saito 1996 for careful and informed consideration of Śāntideva's place within Madhyamaka as presenting views distinguishable from those of Candrakīrti.

This does not mean of course that for Candrakīrti care is *not* proper to a Buddha or that concerned engagement is irrelevant to the bodhisattva path—it is most emphatically relevant. The *Madhyamkāvatāra* opens with praise to *karuṇā* (MA 1:1–2); and the final chapter concludes with emphasizing the compassion of the Buddha (MAB 11:49–51). But here, care is '*the seed of* all qualities of Buddhahood' (MAB 1:2, emphasis mine); it is not internal to *prajñā* itself, as that is described in Chapter 6.[18] The auto-commentary tells us that the subsequent four perfections "are in fact particular aspects of *prajñā* itself" (MAB 7:1), supplementing the wisdom "of analytical investigation" set out so comprehensively in Chapter 6. But the six verses describing those four perfections do not build care into wisdom either. The auto-commentary on Chapter 8 does exhort the audience, in the words of the *Daśabhūmikasūtra*,

> O son of good family, although you are now resting within the liberation of peace, you must consider the ordinary immature beings who are not at peace, who being ravaged by many afflictions and beleaguered by swarms of conceptual thoughts, are not at all at peace. O son of good family, remember the aspirations you made in the past! . . .

But what we are given here, if anything, is once again simply the assertion that *karuṇā* is still operative at the eighth bodhisattva level—that is, even after *prajñā* is perfected. We are given no indication of how that is, nor of how it relates to *prajñā*. This is particularly puzzling because apprehending dependent arising/emptiness should consist in cessation—the cessation of *prapañca*, of conceptualizing, of purposiveness, and so on. Yet aspiring to assist beings requires seeing them *as* beings and *as* in need of help, which implies individuating and purposive thought.[19] How can one "resting within the liberation of peace" *at the same time* "consider the ordinary immature beings . . . ravaged by many afflictions and beleaguered by swarms of conceptual thoughts"?

5. Śāntideva: Care and wisdom

The ninth chapter of the received text of the *Bodhicaryāvatāra* is particularly affected by the work of later editorial hand(s).[20] In particular, while BCA-II (the received text)

[18] The auto-commentary on MA 1:4 suggests the relation may in fact be reversed, and wisdom is not just caused by compassion, as at MAB 1:2 (discussion below), but is an *expression of* perfected *karuṇā*: "The various levels encompassed by the bodhisattvas' *compassion of undefiled wisdom* receive the name *grounds* (*bhūmi*)." A fuller study of the best considered view of the *Madhyamakāvatāra* on the question is beyond the purpose of this current study, which aims to use the description of perfect *prajñā* in Chapter 6 as a counterpoint to illuminate Śāntideva's own perfection of wisdom chapter.

[19] Finnigan and Tanaka 2011 attempt to address the difficulty by insisting that both of the two truths remain in view; but the very question—to which we will return below—is *how* that can be.

[20] According to Kapstein, "the ninth chapter as we now know it was the result of an expansion of the entire *Guide* dating to some centuries after the work's original eight-century composition. The ninth chapter, in particular, was almost doubled in size to include substantial new material, particularly in its arguments criticizing non-Buddhist schools" (2019: 95 n.7).

has 168 (or 167) verses devoted to wisdom, BCA-I has only 90.5, of which about twenty-two verses do not appear in the BCA-II.[21] Overall the two versions of the wisdom chapter share only about thirty-six verses,[22] and much of the explicitly argumentative material, engaging opposing views, was added later. Nevertheless, I think it is possible to discern in the text a rather different approach to *prajñā*, and one which may have more resources for addressing the perennial puzzle of the bodhisattva's simultaneous realization of emptiness and care for beings.

Śāntideva opens his discussion of *prajñā* by framing it as something purposive:

> It is for the sake of wisdom that the Sage taught this entire collection of preparations. Therefore, in the desire to put an end to suffering, one should develop wisdom [*prajñā*].[23]
>
> BCA 9:1

Wisdom is that-for-the-sake-of-which—not just the goal but that which gives meaning to what has come before. Contrast this teleological and relational framing with Candrakīrti's static description of *prajñā* in MA 6:1, quoted above:

> On Presence, with their minds now placed in equipoise,
> They're in the presence of the traits of buddhahood.
> Dependent rising is the fact they now perceive —
> And reach cessation, resting in intelligence.

Notice also that Śāntideva does not simply offer wisdom as cessation, as Candrakīrti does, where this means primarily the cessation of all conceptualization, or quiescence. Śāntideva specifies that the cessation of *suffering* is what is at issue. In addition, he calls it *putting an end* to suffering, not merely cessation arising. And finally, where Candrakīrti speaks to one who has accomplished something, Śāntideva is addressing one *desiring*, one with an aim or goal: namely, to bring about the cessation of suffering.

In all of these respects we see what we noted earlier about Śāntideva's practical bent in this text: it is addressed directly to an audience that should be changed by it. But there is something more. For Śāntideva, care is no mere afterthought to wisdom. It is built in to the conception of wisdom right at the start, in the desire to bring about the end of suffering. Care is the motivation to wisdom; but this motivation is so internal to the wisdom acquired that it becomes more like the mode of wise apprehension.[24]

The presence of care in wisdom is reinforced periodically throughout the chapter—for instance, in the way that the analysis of *vedanā* at vv. 88–99 takes place primarily

[21] See Saito 1993: 25.

[22] Crosby and Skilton 1995: 110–11 have a concise overview of concordance between the wisdom chapters of BCA-I and BCA-II. Saito 1993: 25 lists only thirty-two common verses.

[23] I leave *prajñā* untranslated where Crosby and Skilton have "understanding," since "understanding" suggests a determinate specification of the sort of thing *prajñā* is that "wisdom" leaves open.

[24] Wisdom is conceived in the desire to end suffering in the way that, in Plato's *Symposium*, wisdom is conceived in beauty. What is thus attained is characterized by the medium in which it arose; if one must describe care as a "means" then it is an internal means (as described in MacIntyre 1981: Ch. 14, esp. p. 184).

with reference to felt suffering. It is particularly significant that the chapter closes by returning to suffering which, after having been declared unreal (BCA 9:151–3), is vividly depicted as all too real (BCA 9:154–66). This sets up an explicitly dual aspiration in the final verse: "When shall I teach emptiness *and* the accumulation of merit . . .?" (BCA 9:167). The accomplished bodhisattva does not just understand, grasp, or have insight into ultimate reality; that insight, arising in concern for suffering, is experienced as a desire to teach.

This integration of the attitude or orientation of care into wisdom itself can also be seen in Śāntideva's different use of *svabhāva*, which is comparatively infrequent and typically not used as a term of art.[25] A partial exception to this, and one which underscores the point, may be found at *Bodhicaryāvatāra* 9:151–2:

> When all things are empty in this way, what can be received, what taken away? Who can be honoured or humiliated by whom?
>
> From what can there be happiness or misery, what can be liked and what loathed? What craving can there be? For what is that craving, when examined as to its *svabhāva*?

These verses, common to the earlier and the canonical version of the text, are striking for the way they immediately relate the abstract and technical notion of *svabhāva* to the afflictive emotions.[26]

It is common in the Mahāyāna to say that both wisdom and *karuṇā* are required for awakening, as if these were two independent legs on which one walks, or indeed, as Candrakīrti says of ultimate and conventional reality (MA 6:226), two wings on which the king of the swans soars ahead to the farther shore.[27] But in the *Bodhicaryāvatāra*, it looks as if Śāntideva is setting out a more intimate connection between the two. It is care that gives rise to wisdom, to be sure; but also the wisdom thus arisen is itself a caring attitude toward reality, or is perhaps even just what wisdom feels like—as suggested perhaps by the *Śikṣa-samuccaya*'s observation that "in a *bodhisattva* who sees things as they are, great compassion unfolds for sentient beings."[28]

[25] Śāntideva's favored way of articulating Madhyamaka is overwhelmingly in the language of being/non-being, or existence/non-existence. *Svabhāva* is not generally used in that special technical sense of as that the lack of which is equivalent to emptiness: BCA 9:148 argues that existence/non-existence would have the undesirable result (*prasaṅga*) of something having two natures (*dvisvabhāva*), while BCA 9:152 asks rhetorically "what is that craving, when examined as to its *svabhāva*?" The remainder of the few occurrences of *svabhāva* in Chapter 9 arise in engagement with non-Buddhist views which were probably introduced later: BCA 9:64–5 engages the Saṃkhya *triguṇa* view, in a passage not in the BCA-I; BCA 9:121 engages the Nyāya view of God, and BCA 9:128 Saṃkhya *triguṇa* again, in the most extended passage added to the BCA-II by a later hand.

[26] *Svabhāva*, for its part, is simply a concise way of alluding to the foregoing discussion of the non-existence of things (BCA 9:142–50), which is to say their lack of "real" existence (BCA 9:144), which is to say their dreamlike nature (BCA 9:150).

[27] "They soar ahead of beings, like the king of swans, On white and outstretched wings of truth, the relative And ultimate, and speed ahead on virtue's wind Across the ocean of the Victor's qualities" (MA 6:226).

[28] SS 119 *ad* 9a–b, trans. Goodman. I thus agree with, for instance, Warren Lee Todd, who says that in Śāntideva's path "compassion runs right the way through" (2013: 136), though our reasons for and understandings of this may differ.

6. Wisdom's alternative content in the *Bodhicaryāvatāra*

This integration of care into wisdom is reflected in the distinctive content of *prajñā* that the *Bodhicaryāvatāra* puts forward. For to the question "What does wisdom apprehend?", Śāntideva offers a rather different answer from the *Madhyamakāvatāra*.

After the opening declaration that everything else is for the sake of wisdom, Chapter 9 immediately continues with "It is agreed that there are these two truths: the conventional and the ultimate" (BCA 9:2ab). Strictly, all this says is that in order to inculcate wisdom, recall that there are two truths. But placed where it is, it strongly suggests that if we were to ask Śāntideva "what is wisdom *of*?" he would say, "The two truths." For this statement about the two truths dominates (if it does not quite structure) the discussion that follows, occasioning the introduction of "illusion" (BCA 9:5) as a central metaphor for conventional reality, which move prompts in turn the greater part of the discussion that follows.[29] This has the effect of keeping conventional truth front and center throughout the chapter, not as an alternative to ultimate truth but alongside it, as something which itself is a proper object of wisdom.[30]

That is to say, understanding the two together is what *prajñā*, for Śāntideva, requires. Indeed, the closing verse of *Bodhicaryāvatāra* 9 mirrors the duality set up in the second verse, with the aspiration to share one's wisdom by teaching emptiness *and* the accumulation of merit, or conventional reality rightly (which is to say, caringly) engaged with. The two verses together thus bookend the exposition of wisdom with an assertion of its dual content.

This is not in any way to claim that *saṃvṛtisat* is irrelevant to Candrakīrti. It quite patently is not—see the oft-quoted verse about the two wings of a swan, above.[31] But conventional reality is not for him the object of *prajñā*, and in fact is explicitly *external* to *prajñā*. "Conventional truth works as a means to reach an end," Candrakīrti says (MA 6:80). "The ultimate is like the end one tries to reach." One *uses* the conventional as a means to the ultimate—but it is apprehension of the ultimate (emptiness) that wisdom consists in. One could say that Śāntideva himself does this in practice, when in the foregoing chapters he draws on the misconceived psychology of the ordinary person to achieve his aim of transforming them. But this is not what happens in Chapter 9, where the bodhisattva audience addressed can be presumed already to have been significantly transformed by the foregoing chapters. Here, in the inculcating-examination of wisdom, whatever the relation Śāntideva envisages between conventional and ultimate reality, it is certainly *not* one of means to end. We do not merely need conventional reality, and the correct grasp of it, in order to get to some other thing: apprehension of ultimate reality, a.k.a. wisdom. There is no wisdom—not merely no attaining wisdom—there is no wisdom at all without correct grasp of

[29] Śāntideva, we might say, uses this conventional–ultimate distinction to set out his account of wisdom in much the way Candrakīrti uses the central tetralemma of *Root Verses* I to set out his account of wisdom.

[30] One might argue that, in this respect, Śāntideva is an astute interpreter of the *Mūlamadhyamakākārikā*, in particular Chapter 24.

[31] On the two truths in Nāgārjuna, see MMK 24:8, 9; Candrakīrti engages with this at MA 6:23 et seq. In some respects, Candrakīrti makes more of the two truths than Nāgārjuna did, in ways that have proved both compelling and deeply problematic.

both conventional *and* ultimate. Both truths together are the proper contents of wisdom, and as such are partially constitutive of it.

But even considering just wisdom's apprehension of ultimate reality, Śāntideva seems to differ from Candrakīrti. He may not explicitly challenge Candrakīrti's use of emptiness, yet neither does he reproduce it in his own exposition of *prajñā*. When Śāntideva introduces emptiness rather later in *Bodhicaryāvatāra* 9, he does not offer it as that which *prajñā* is *of*; in fact, Śāntideva rather tends—as at 9:52–105—to turn talk of emptiness to talk of selflessness.[32] When Śāntideva does appeal to "the influence of emptiness," it is as a tool to counteract desires raised by illusions recognized as illusions (BCA 9:31–2a), thus reversing Candrakīrti's means–end relationship. Śāntideva then advises the eradication of emptiness, too:

> The influence of phenomena is removed by employing the influence of emptiness, and even that is later eradicated by inculcating the realization, "nothing really exists."
>
> BCA 9:32

In keeping with this, in the lengthy discussion of "why emptiness?" which follows (BCA 9:40–53), the non-scriptural part of Śāntideva's answer[33] focuses not on the sixteen forms of emptiness but on the positive *benefits* of emptiness:

> Without emptiness a mind is fettered and arises again
>
> (9:48a)

and

> Remaining in *saṃsāra* for the benefit of those suffering through delusion is achieved through freedom from the two extremes, attachment and fear. This is the fruit of emptiness.
>
> 9:52

While Śāntideva recognizes the quiescence of realizing emptiness that is so important to Candrakīrti (BCA 9:34), he places this rather early in the chapter and does not offer it as a definition of what perfect wisdom and therefore liberation consist in.[34] As the subsequent discussion indicates, Śāntideva more emphatically values its distinct effects or fruit—namely, the ability to engage with *saṃsāra* and its suffering.

Insofar as the content of wisdom is "ultimate reality," no-self more decisively animates Śāntideva's account of what that content is. Even this central passage on

[32] This feature is even more obvious in the earlier edition, for a greater part of the verses present in the BCA-I but absent from the BCA-II (the received edition) concerns the examination of selflessness. There is also an important thematic shift between how the two chapters engage with no-self: BCA-I, according to Saito, "focuses on the criticism of 'I,'" while BCA-II critiques "the Self as defined by some philosophical schools such as Sāṃkhya and Vaiśeṣika" (2006: 36–7).

[33] Verses 9:40–5 and 9:49–51 answer by appeal to scripture, and these verses do not appear in the BCA-I.

[34] Under the "influence of emptiness" (9:32), "neither entity nor non-entity remains before the mind, [and] . . . it becomes tranquil" (9:34).

emptiness moves seamlessly to discussion of no-self. Śāntideva's wisdom chapter, unlike *Madhyamakāvatāra* 6, does not culminate in an exposition of the forms of emptiness, as if this were the culmination of wisdom. On the contrary, in *Bodhicaryāvatāra* 9, emptiness is situated in the middle of the chapter, as a means whose fruit is more valuable than the realization of emptiness itself. Moreover, that fruit is not mere quiescence but engagement. For Śāntideva, wisdom renders one a bodhisattva—not just a being with insight into ultimate reality, but above all a being whose insight manifests as the ability to help those who still suffer. This is not an afterthought or an adjunct to wisdom, but is simply what wisdom is, given that its proper contents or objects are the *two* truths, and not just the one. Thus if we consider, finally, how Śāntideva *does* end his wisdom chapter, it is with a detailed iteration of the ordinary world of suffering (BCA 9:151–67), as seen from the perspective of recognizing that "there is in substance no difference between those who have obtained liberation and those who have not" (BCA 9:150). These verses articulate not just what the wise person sees, but *how* they see it: full of opportunities (9:162a) and pitfalls (9:157a) and with a questioning attitude of how it might be made otherwise (9:160). Wisdom culminates, for Śāntideva, in the simultaneous recognition of ultimate and conventional, which recognition occurs in the mode of care.

7. Not just apprehension of the right object in the right way

For Śāntideva, then, wisdom is an orientation of care toward the *two* truths apprehended, where apprehending the one (emptiness-selflessness) does not preclude the other.

But it is not at all clear that this is a possible mental state. One can easily *say* "both truths together are the proper contents of wisdom" and that wisdom is "the simultaneous recognition of ultimate and conventional" or that a buddha can "have direct and simultaneous knowledge of the two realities,"[35] but is it coherent to suppose there could be any such cognitive state?

Consider the person well advanced in realizing *prajñā*: on both Śāntideva's and on Candrakīrti's accounts, this person sees everyday reality differently from the rest of us—they see it, namely, *as* empty, essence-less, dependent-arising, as an illusion (BCA 9:5). But recognizing dynamically changing forms as without self cannot be identical to the great quiescence that, for Candrakīrti at least, either *is* or is consequent upon realization of emptiness, for this insight is quiescent inasmuch as it is non-conceptual—and in order to see forms or entities *as* empty (or *as* anything at all) one must *in some sense* see entities. But this means that *any* engagement with conventional reality, howsoever enlightened, is by definition not quiescent—at any rate, not that quiescence in which awakening consists.[36] A thoroughly non-conceptual apprehension/realization

[35] Thakchöe 2011: 49 is describing Tsongkhapa's interpretation of Candrakīrti here.

[36] As Nāgārjuna says, "these are the characteristics of [true] reality (*tattva*): not dependent upon another, quiescent, unelaborated by conceptual proliferation, without determinations, undifferentiated" (*aparapratyayaṃ śāntaṃ prapañcair aprapañcitam nirvikalpam anānārtham etat tattvasya lakṣaṇam*, MMK 18:9, trans. mine), and likewise characterize the apprehension of reality as it is.

of reality might well transform one's (subsequent) experience of conceptual/ conventional reality, enabling one to see this too *as* ultimately empty, essence-less, dependently-arising. But this latter must be "seeing emptiness" in a second and distinct sense—a mere byproduct of the first, or perhaps a stepping stone to it. And whether as byproduct or as stepping stone, conceptually structured apprehension necessarily displaces thoroughly non-conceptual cognition.

This leads to a motivational problem: once one can directly experience ultimate reality non-conceptually, what motivation could there be for ever doing otherwise? Presumably such motivation may come from care (*karuṇā*); but as we have seen, care is for Candrakīrti an adjunct to and not inherent in wisdom. It is one of the three causes that give rise to bodhisattvas (MAB 1:1) and it motivates one to acquire *prajñā* (MAB 1:2), but it does not characterize wisdom itself. Wisdom cognizes emptiness in a way that it *realizes* it—makes the non-structured objectlessness of reality pure, devoid of confused demarcations, conventional boundaries, and provisional individuations. But since care requires objects of care in view, once objectless non-conceptual cognition is attained, it is hard to see how care for suffering could nevertheless be present.[37]

One way to avoid the difficulty is to sweep the whole matter behind the capacious screen of the "mysteries of the Buddha mind." This may in fact be Candrakīrti's solution,[38] perhaps with the magic being worked in whatever supplementation *prajñā* acquires on the way to the tenth perfection, the perfection of *jñāna* characteristic of the fully realized bodhisattva. The associated motivational problem is then just solved by *fiat*, declaring (as Candrakīrti does) that care is also characteristic of the Buddha. But such a proposed solution is not a very satisfying one, inasmuch as it amounts to the assertion of a mystery and the demand that it be accepted.

At any rate, this is not a solution that Śāntideva could avail himself of in the same way, since he presents a six-perfection path culminating in *prajñā*—there is no space between the perfection of *prajñā* and the fully realized bodhisattva for any supplementation by care. And the wisdom chapter shows no indication of claiming there might be a contradictory cognition at once conceptual and non-conceptual. On the contrary, the structure and dialectic of *Bodhicaryāvatāra* 9 suggest a quite different approach to the problem.

37 Of course, Candrakīrti claims that great compassion *does* characterize the fully realized bodhisattva. It is simply difficult to see *how* a bodhisattva could enjoy both wisdom and care simultaneously.

38 The auto-commentary says, for instance, that generosity "when free from the reference points of something given, a recipient and a giver, is a perfection transcending the world . . . *This is not something those who have not reached the stage of a bodhisattva are able to comprehend*" (MAB 1:16ab, emphasis mine); the comment on MA 11:16 makes reference to previous merit stored up by buddhas to explain how it is that "Although there are no concepts involved, they work for the benefit of the limitless realms of beings in ways that suit those to be trained" and advises one to pray that "Just as the illustrious buddhas, without conceptual ideas, assiduously work in the most beneficial way for the betterment of beings—like wish-fulfilling jewels or trees of plenty—and whilst not departing from the *dharmadhātu* even for an instant, never miss an opportunity to train beings, I shall do the same." The objection "If true reality is peace, the mind cannot engage with it" is raised at MA 11:12; but instead of engaging with the difficulty of simultaneous conceptual and non-conceptual cognition, Candrakīrti turns it into a problem about subject-object relations and addresses this question instead (MAB 11:12–13).

First, if I am right that for Śāntideva the proper contents of wisdom are the *two* truths, and not just the one, then so far from sweeping the problem under the carpet, Śāntideva puts it front and center, positively calling our attention to it. Both truths together are the proper contents of wisdom; yet one cannot at once see *things*—even things recognized as illusory—and not see *things*. Granted, there is an enlightened experience *of the world* and it is normative and distinct from ordinary experience (BCA 9:3–5): the enlightened mind sees that the apparent things of the world lack thingy-ness. Still this apprehension of objects-as-illusory is not identical to the enlightened experience of no-world, of ubiquitous selflessness, the quiescent, unelaborated, undifferentiated ultimate reality described in *Mūlamadhyamakakārikā* 18:9.

This is reflected in the structure of Chapter 9, which rather than moving relentlessly toward the focal point of non-conceptual realization of ultimate reality instead moves continually back and forth between ultimate reality as such (empty, without self, insubstantial) and the spiritually advanced recognition of illusions *as* illusions.[39] For instance: first, while "there is no fault in the use of conventional truth by the spiritually developed" (BCA 9:8), it is "when neither entity nor non-entity remains before the mind" that the mind "becomes tranquil" (BCA 9:34); but after this, we find a conceptually rich analytical investigation deconstructing the "I" (BCA 9:57–69),[40] continued in verses 78 to 105. Or, a second instance: emptiness "should be meditated on without reservation" (BCA 9:53b) in order to remove attachment and fear (9:52); but subsequently *karma*-thinking is redeemed with the argument that an "I " is not necessary for *karma* (BCA 9:70–2), because "it is taught that there is an agent and an experiencer of the consequence in terms of a unity of the continuum of consciousnesses" (BCA 9:73). And third, following a lengthy interpolated passage arguing against non-Buddhist views (BCA 9:106–40), the chapter engages in the sort of tetralemmic analysis of causation from Nāgārjuna that Candrakīrti focuses on in his wisdom chapter (BCA 9:141–50); this is followed, however, not with increasing push toward non-conceptual realization, but on the contrary with deliberate use of emptiness to dissolve the fear and attachment induced by value-laden terms such as "gain" and "loss," "honor" and "humiliation," "happiness" and "misery," "death," "birth" and "friend" (BCA 9:151–3). Fourth and finally, as previously noted, the chapter on *prajñā* ends not in emptiness but in a vivid recollection of the suffering of the world.[41] Thus the need to cognize both truths, and yet the impossibility of manifesting conceptual and non-conceptual cognition simultaneously, shows up in the text's refusal to settle on one or the other, nor to move from one to the other, but to continually move back and forth between the two.

Not only does Śāntideva posit two (incompatible) truths to be apprehended by *prajñā*, he demonstrates in the dialectical presentation of the two *how* it is *prajñā* may

[39] Todd 2013 emphasizes this dynamic character of wisdom for Śāntideva, which he calls "flickering."

[40] A passage Crosby and Skilton 1995 identify as following the four foundations of mindfulness exercise.

[41] This movement back and forth between seeing conventionally (wisely) and seeing ultimately seems to be characteristic of the chapter even without the abrupt changes caused by later interpolations, though this is difficult to determine with certainty.

be of both, even while cognizing the two simultaneously remains impossible. Wisdom, that is to say, consists not just in grasping each truth severally, but in moving between the two aptly. This dynamic response to the need for wisdom to have incompatible contents is directly thematized in the middle of the chapter:

> If you argue: for whom is there compassion if no being exists?, [our response is] For anyone projected through the delusion which is embraced for the sake of what has to be done.
>
> 9:75

> [Objection] Whose is the task to be done, if there is no being? [Mādhyamika] True. Moreover, the effort is made in delusion, but, in order to bring about an end of suffering, the delusion of what has to be done is not prevented.
>
> 9:76

> However, egotism, which is the cause of suffering, increases from the delusion that there is a Self, and, if this is the unavoidable result of that, it is better to meditate on no-Self.
>
> 9:77

Śāntideva implicitly acknowledges, in voicing the objection, that care requires the discernment of beings,[42] both as object of care (9:75) and as an agent doing the caring (9:76). He does not address the objection by disputing the fact. Instead, he has the Mādhyamika bite the bullet without hesitation: true, there is no being and therefore no one whose task is to care, and no being to care for. But the person wise enough to recognize no-self will actively refrain from preventing the delusion of agency, so as to ameliorate suffering. Here Śāntideva recognizes that there is something other than seeing reality as it is that the wise bodhisattva does—namely, they project a delusion, the illusion of there being suffering beings, and of themselves as one with a task to discharge. It belongs to the bodhisattva's wisdom to project this delusion;[43] and yet this projecting of delusion cannot be what wisdom as such consists in, for then perfected wisdom would perpetually project delusion, thus *maintaining* the suffering it desires to end.[44]

Moreover, as Śāntideva acknowledges in verse 77, there are psychological and not just logical difficulties in taking wisdom as such to consist in knowingly entertaining

[42] The Sanskrit of 75a is *yadi sattvo na vidyate*, which could also be rendered "if no being is discerned." Presumably because the foregoing debate took a metaphysical line, Crosby and Skilton (and also Gomez) translate *vidyate* existentially. However, the epistemic aspect is just as relevant and articulates aptly the deeper concern that *cognizing* no being is what makes care impossible.

[43] And since wisdom is grasping the two truths in the mode of care, equally the aim to end suffering belongs to wisdom and is not external to it.

[44] Wisdom cannot consist entirely in seeing conventional reality *as* dependently arising, no-self, empty—and not also in seeing dependent arising *simpliciter* (what Harris 2024: 167 describes as "non-conceptual, direct perception of emptiness")—for if conventional objects must be in view in all wise apprehending, then persisting in practicing wisdom will be a perpetuation of conventional reality and therefore of suffering. (It will not help to add "as illusory" to the suffering seen, for it is as illusory that the suffering seen by the bodhisattva is "to be removed.")

delusion. For even wisely entertaining the delusion of agency and being is apt to lead to harmful self-thinking: "egotism . . . increases from the delusion that there is a Self," even if that delusion is projected (or not prevented) by one knowing it as a delusion—for it is such a person who is under discussion here.[45] This being so, one should at some point cease to entertain the delusion and meditate on no-self—and the text goes on to do just that, engaging in a lengthy (twenty-seven verses) dissolution of self by analysis of its constituents.

Thus while in verses 75 and 76 the wise person knowingly permits the self-delusion, in verse 77 (and following) they cease to entertain the delusion and cultivate no-self. Wisdom as such cannot consist in either one of these cognitive states alone, nor is there a possible cognitive state which comprises them both. Instead what we are shown here, and in the dynamic structuring of the chapter, is *good judgement*, or apt responsiveness, about when to entertain which of the two truths: when possible to do so without harm, entertain the delusion of self and beings (recognized as an illusion); when entertaining the delusion starts to induce egoism, recognize the ultimate essencelessness of reality, free of heuristic illusions. Wisdom for Śāntideva requires recognition of the two truths, and it involves moving between the two; but it consists, more specifically, in fitting responsiveness to prevailing conditions to determine which of these ways of cognizing reality is to be realized at a given moment. This is exhibited in the very texture of Chapter 9, in which Śāntideva casts himself in the traditional "defensive" role of entertaining and dispelling objections, so that the text itself manifests a constant responsiveness to whatever is needed, here and now, in order best to serve the end of cessation and awakening. The mode of presentation thus exhibits precisely the apt responsiveness in which wisdom itself consists.

Wisdom, then, is engagement in perfectly appropriate perspective shifting: entertaining the self-delusion when that is necessary to eliminate suffering, and eliminating that same delusion when that is what is needed to eliminate suffering.[46]

[45] Could someone of perfected wisdom entertain the delusion without pernicious self-thinking ever arising, so they would have no need to revert to no-self (ultimate reality as it is)? Todd 2013 seems at times to think this, although sometimes he allows that the "flickering," as he calls it, between seeing conventional reality and seeing essencelessness is endemic, characteristic therefore of the most perfect of wisdom. Harris 2024: 166–7 takes BCA 9:77 as "advice to developing bodhisattvas who are still susceptible to tendencies to reify conventionally existing persons" and adds that "when wisdom is perfected . . . [such alternating] will no longer be necessary." However, I see no suggestion in the text, neither here in response to the explicit objection nor elsewhere in the chapter, of some supremely realized state in which seeing oneself as an agent, even while recognizing it is delusive, will *not* have the corrosive effect of causing one to relate to the world in terms of self. If there is such a condition, it seems it is not, according to Śāntideva, that of a bodhisattva.

[46] This may be original to Nāgārjuna: in their introduction to the *Ratnāvalī*, Dunne and McClintock observe: "The work thus invites us to experience oscillating perspectives as Nāgārjuna moves back and forth among them" (14). As Schmidt-Leukel 2019 puts it, "understanding emptiness . . . provides the ultimate foundation upon which the flexible and creative handling of illusions can be based" (66). The flexibility interests me here; I have not tried to show that or how apprehension of ultimate reality makes this possible. Harris 2011: 119–22 highlights this "switching between viewpoints" as a meditational practice in Chapter 8's apparent argument from no-self to altruism (BCA 8:101–3), and calls in these verses from the wisdom chapter to support and illustrate "switching viewpoints" as a strategy. Harris points to the use of the strategy at earlier stages of bodhisattva development (e.g., BCA 6:32); I am arguing that mastery of this skill in perceptual responsiveness characterizes perfect wisdom itself.

This picks up the care that is built into wisdom as a constitutive attitude, and the teleological, purposive character of the perfection of wisdom. Wisdom so conceived is a *skill:* a skill in recognizing appropriateness for the sake of the correct goal—and in these ways it is *phronēsis*-like.[47] But it is nothing like "practical judgement" as the neo-Aristotelians describe it, for what is discerned is not what action is required, but which aspect of wisdom's content is to be realized here and now.

8. Conclusion

Candrakīrti's conception of *prajñā* is classical and conservative—conventional, if you like—specifically in the fact that it is defined with reference to the "right content," rightly grasped. But this conservative view of *prajñā* can seem to leave the essentially ethically good aspect of wisdom to be a kind of dispensable adjunct.

If wisdom grasps non-conceptual ultimate reality as it is, this very apprehension seems to undermine the motivation for seeing things in a way that makes care possible. It is no help to collapse, as some modern Mādhyamikas would like, cognition of emptiness and cognition of conventional reality *as* empty. For if to see conventional reality *as* conventional—empty, dependently arising, etc.—is what perfect insight amounts to here, then there is and can be no basis for challenging or changing accepted conventions—"The Buddha does not quarrel with the world" (MA 6:166). This is the rigid conservatism inherent in skepticism: all appearances are equally appearances and so all that is left is to follow the appearances there are (without endorsing them). "The truth of everyday conventions should not be subjected to analysis" (MA 6:35); and "we speak in harmony with worldly folk And grant that things exist, though they do not" (MA 6:81). In this way, insight into ultimate reality as directed toward conventional reality may indeed lead to quiescence of a sort—but it seems a distinctly morally problematic sort of quietism that cannot dispute, say, the basic conceptual apparatus of slave and master.[48] Sometimes a bodhisattva must quarrel with the world.

Śāntideva's skill-conception of *prajñā* offers distinctive means for escaping the pernicious quietism of the skeptic that lurks in the content-based conception of wisdom. For Śāntideva clearly distinguishes enlightened experience of conventional reality from ordinary experience, and insists on the normativity of the former with respect to the latter, so there is a basis of critique of ordinary practice. At the same time, this enlightened experience of conventional reality is not *all there is* to wisdom: the experience of selfless reality as such enables the bodhisattva to have the enlightened experience of ordinary reality she does have. Her wisdom consists not in either one of these apprehensions of reality, but in a responsiveness guided by care for ending

[47] Particularly if one's account of *phronēsis* is quasi-perceptual, as McDowell 1979 or Nussbaum 1992: Ch. 2.

[48] This worry is not original. Tillemans 2011 raises the concern about "dismal relativism," and several chapters in The Cowherds 2011 attempt to bring out Mādhyamika resources for addressing it.

suffering in determining which part of wisdom's content to engage at any given moment.[49]

References

Bodhi, Bhikkhu (2000), *Connected Discourses of the Buddha*. Boston: Wisdom Publications.

Carpenter, A. D. (2019), "Reason and Knowledge on the Path: A Protreptic Approach to the *Bodhicaryāvatāra*," in J. C. Gold and D. S. Duckworth (eds.), *Readings of Śāntideva's Guide to Bodhisattva Practice*, 45–59, New York: Columbia University Press.

Carpenter, A. D. (2022), "Nāgārjuna: Dependent Arising Without Any Thing Arising," in W. Edelglass, S. McClintock, and P.-J. Harter (eds.), *The Routledge Handbook of Indian Buddhist Philosophy*, 211–35, London & New York: Routledge.

The Cowherds (2011), *Moonshadows: Conventional Truth in Buddhist Philosophy*, Oxford: Oxford University Press.

Crosby, K. and A. Skilton, trans. (1995), *Śāntideva: The Bodhicaryāvatāra*, Oxford: Oxford University Press.

Dunne, J. and S. McClintock, trans. (2024) *Nāgārjuna's Precious Garland: Ratnāvalī*, New York: Wisdom Publications.

Finnigan, B. and K. Tanaka (2011), "Ethics for Mādhyamikas," in The Cowherds, *Moonshadows: Conventional Truth in Buddhist Philosophy*, 221–31, Oxford: Oxford University Press.

Goodman, C., trans. (2016), *The Training Anthology of Śāntideva: A translation of the Śikṣa-samuccaya*, Oxford: Oxford University Press.

Harris, S. E. (2011), "Does Anātman Rationally Entail Altruism? On Bodhicaryāvatāra 8:101-103," *Journal of Buddhist Ethics* 18: 92–123.

Harris, S. E. (2024), *Buddhist Ethics and the Bodhisattva Path: Śāntideva on Virtue and Well-Being*, London: Bloomsbury.

Kapstein, M. (2019), "An Intoxication of Mouse Venom," in J. C. Gold and D. S. Duckworth (eds.), *Readings of Śāntideva's Guide to Bodhisattva Practice*, 84–98, New York: Columbia University Press.

Lasic, H., Xuezhu, L. and A. MacDonald, eds. (2022), *Candrakīrti's Madhyamakāvatārabhā #dusya, Chapters 1 to 5: Critically and diplomatically edited on the basis of preparatory work by Helmut Krasser*. Vienna: China Tibetology Research Center. Austrian Academy of Sciences Press.

Liland, F. (2020), *Madhyamakāvatāra-Bhāṣya: Candrakīrti's Auto-Commentary to Entering the Middle Way*. Bibliotheca Polyglotta. Revised edition. Online: https://www2.hf.uio.no/polyglotta/public/media/libraries/file/2/Liland%202019,%20Chandrakirti's%20Auto-Commentary%20to%20Entering%20the%20Middle%20Way.pdf

[49] I owe thanks to David Eckels, whose invitation to speak at Boston University first prompted me to formulate these ideas; and to Perry Schmidt-Leukel and Stephen Harris, whose invitation to participate in the Śāntideva conference in Münster enabled me to pursue them further. I also thank participants on both occasions for their insightful suggestions and criticisms, as well as participants at the Ancient Wisdom conference at the Humboldt University (2024) for probing discussion of the issues involved. I am very grateful again to Perry Schmidt-Leukel and Stephen Harris, who as volume editors offered astute and constructive comments which have improved the final version.

MacIntyre, A. (1981), *After Virtue*, Notre Dame: University of Notre Dame Press.
McDowell, J. (1979), "Virtue and Reason," *The Monist* 62: 331–50 (repr. in *Mind, Value and Reason*, Cambridge, MA: Harvard University Press 1998, 50–73).
Nussbaum, M. (1992), "The Discernment of Perception: An Aristotelian Conception of Private and Public Rationality," in *Love's Knowledge*, 54–105, Oxford: Oxford University Press.
Saito, A. (1993) *A Study of Akṣayamati (=Śāntideva)'s Bodhisattvacaryāvatāra as found in the Tibetan Manuscripts from Tun-huang*, Project Number 02801005, Miye University.
Saito, A. (1994), "On the Difference Between the Earlier and the Current Versions of Śāntideva's *Bodhi(sattva)caryāvatāra*, with special reference to Chapter 9 (/8) entitled 'Perfection of Wisdom (*prajñāpāramitā*),'" Research paper presented at the IXth World Sanskrit Conference, 9–15 January 1994, Melbourne, Australia.
Saito, A. (1996), "Śāntideva and the History of Mādhyamika Philosophy," in K. Sankaranarayanan, M. Yoritomi, and S. A. Joshi, eds., *Buddhism in India and Abroad: An Integrating Influence In Vedic and Post-Vedic Perspective*, 257–63, Mumbai & New Delhi: Somaiya Publications.
Saito, A. (2006), "Śāntideva's Critique of 'I' or Self in the Earlier and Later Recensions of the *Bodhi(sattva)caryāvatāra*," *Studies in Indian Philosophy and Buddhism* 13: 35–43.
Schmidt-Leukel, P. (2019), *Buddha Mind - Christ Mind. A Christian Commentary on the Bodhicaryāvatāra*. With a new translation by E. Steinkellner and C. Peck-Kubaczek, Leuven: Peeters.
Siderits, M. and S. Katsura, trans. (2013), *Nāgārjuna's Middle Way: Mūlamadhyamakakārikā*, Somerville: Wisdom Publications.
Sweet, M. J. (1979), "*Bodhicaryāvatāra* 9:2 As A Focus For Tibetan Interpretations of the Two Truths In the Prāsangikā Mādhyamika," *Journal of the International Association of Buddhist Studies* 2 (2): 79–89.
Thakchöe, S. (2011), "Prāsaṅgika Epistemology in Context," in The Cowherds, *Moonshadows: Conventional Truth in Buddhist Philosophy*, 39–55, Oxford: Oxford University Press.
Tillemans, T. (2011), "How Far Can a Mādhyamika Reform Conventional Truth? Dismal Relativism, Fictionalism, Easy-EasyTruth, and the Alternatives," in The Cowherds, *Moonshadows: Conventional Truth in Buddhist Philosophy*, 151–66, Oxford: Oxford University Press.
Todd, W. L. (2013), *The Ethics of Śaṅkara and Śāntideva: A Selfless Response to an Illusory World*, Farnham: Ashgate.
Tucci, G. (1947), "Minor Sanskrit Texts on the *Prajñā-pāramitā*: 1. The *Prajñā-pāramitā-piṇḍārtha* of Diṅnāga," *Journal of the Royal Asiatic Society of Great Britain and Ireland* 79 (1): 53–75.
Westerhoff, J. (2010), *Nāgārjuna's Vigrahavyāvartanī: the Dispeller of Disputes*, Oxford: Oxford University Press.
Xuezhu, L. (2015), "*Madhyamakāvatāra-kārikā* Chapter 6," *Journal of Indian Philosophy* 43: 1–30.

2

Suffering and Liberation on Śāntideva's Bodhisattva Path

Stephen E. Harris

A frequent complaint raised against the Madhyamaka tradition, to which Śāntideva belongs, is that accepting all phenomena as empty (*śūnya*) of intrinsic existence (*svabhāva*) entails nihilism about ordinary existence and the bodhisattva path. Śāntideva's response to this concern, given in the ninth chapter of his *Guide to the Practices of Awakening* (*Bodhicaryāvatāra*: hereafter, BCA or *Guide*), parallels that given by the founder of the Madhyamaka tradition, Nāgārjuna, in the *Root Verses on the Middle Way (Mūlamadhyamakakārikā)*.[1] To say a thing is empty is not to claim that it does not exist, but rather that it exists in dependence on causes and conditions, its constituents, and conceptual imputation by the mind. An ethical analogue of this metaphysical objection is also responded to by Nāgārjuna, this time in his *Dispeller of Disputes* (*Vigrahavyāvartanī*). One who accepts emptiness, the objection goes, undercuts the liberative Buddhist path, not because the factors of awakening do not exist, but because they are empty of intrinsic value. Nāgārjuna's response is to once more reference relationality as the meaning of emptiness. To say a mental state is virtuous (*kuśala*) or pathological (*kleśa*) is not to reference its essential nature, but rather the role it plays in a network of causes and effects. In particular, the pathological mental states are the causes of an increase in suffering, while the virtuous mental factors diminish it.[2]

In a certain sense, this set of responses leaves everything about the Buddhist path to liberation as it was: virtuous mental states remain efficacious in eliminating pathological mental states which cause or constitute suffering, and so on. Suffering and virtue remain foundational units in Śāntideva's ethics, although their role is not constituted by their metaphysical essence, but rather the centrality of their function in inhibiting or accomplishing the goal of liberation. Significantly, however, both virtue and suffering, in a Madhyamaka psychological framework, are not self-standing mental

1 Nāgārjuna raises and responds to the objection in *Root Verses* Chapter 24. See translations and commentary by Garfield 1995 as well as Siderits and Katsura in Nāgārjuna 2013.

2 See commentary to the *Dispeller of Disputes (Vigrahavyāvartanī)* to verses 7–8 and 52–6. See translation and analysis by Westerhoff 2010: 94–104.

events, but depend on conceptual imputation for both their identity and their existence. This suggests as well that there will be a perspectival aspect to these mental states; as we will see below, both virtuous and pathological mental states are, for Śāntideva, most basically ways of viewing a world shared by ordinary and liberated persons. Scholars of Buddhist ethics have begun to take note of this aspect of Śāntideva's moral thought. Nicolas Bommarito (2014), for instance, argues that patience (*kṣānti*) for Mahāyāna authors like Śāntideva, is best understood as a more realistic perspective on the world, in which one's own desires are not given exaggerated importance, in relation to the needs of others. Jay Garfield (2021), similarly, argues that Śāntideva's thought should be understood as a transformative phenomenology in which one's perception of the world is purified of egocentric bias.

This chapter will focus on the Buddhist first noble truth of suffering (*duḥkha*), as understood by Śāntideva in the *Guide*, with attention given to both the foundational role it plays in his ethical thought, and how suffering must ultimately be understood as an impoverished way of viewing the world. The first section of the chapter explores what suffering is, for Śāntideva; we will see that he takes suffering fundamentally to be constituted by the pathological mental states, which are themselves impoverished ways of viewing the world. The next two sections examine how Śāntideva incorporates a deepening understanding of suffering into his project of moral development. For Śāntideva, recognizing vulnerability to suffering wakens *saṃvega*, the affective fear of *saṃsāra* which motivates taking up the Buddhist path. He utilizes this motivation both to stimulate commitment to bodhisattva training, and to develop specific virtues which constitute progress on the path. These techniques are interwoven throughout the *Guide* with the parallel strategy of recognizing that others suffer from these same afflictions and thereby developing compassion (*karuṇā*) toward them. The final section of the chapter turns to the question of perspective in relation to virtue and suffering. I show how for Śāntideva wisdom functions to enact an altered perspective on the ordinary conventional world.

1. What is suffering?

Śāntideva explores suffering throughout the *Guide*, but most explicitly analyzes its nature in the fourth chapter, dedicated to developing the mental state of non-negligence (*apramāda*). At this point in the text, the bodhisattva has taken her vow (at verses 3:22–3), and now focuses on protecting her commitment to attain full liberation for the sake of all beings. Key to maintaining this commitment is protecting her resolve against the pathological mental states (the *kleśas*), which threaten to undermine it. As an aid to recognizing the dangers of these psychopathologies, Śāntideva meditates upon their harmfulness, identifying them as the underlying cause of all forms of suffering:

> Enemies such as craving and hatred are without arms, legs, and so on. They are neither courageous nor wise. How is it that they have enslaved me?
>
> 4:28

Stationed in my mind, they ruin me, while remaining well-established themselves; and yet I do not get angry at my forbearance with this shameful and improper situation.

4:29

How can I take delight in the cycle of existence when constant, long-lasting enemies, who are the sole cause of the currents and floods of adversities, fearlessly dwell in my heart?

4:34

How can I be happy if the guardians of the prison of the cycle of existence, these murderers and slaughterers in hells and the like, remain in the cage of greed within the dwelling of my heart?

4:35

Therefore, as long as these enemies are not destroyed before my eyes, I shall not forsake my task.

4:36ab[3]

The central pathological mental states for Śāntideva, like most Mahāyāna authors, are anger (*krodha*), craving (*rāga*), and delusion (*moha/avidya*). The verses above use martial imagery to characterize these psychopathologies as the deepest causes of suffering (4:33–4). The pathological mental states are both the sources of the bodhisattva's own suffering, and the factors which inhibit her progress on the bodhisattva path. The virtues of the bodhisattva path function to weaken and finally eliminate the pathological mental states, thereby protecting the bodhisattva's own well-being and enabling her to care more deeply for others.[4]

The forms of suffering caused or constituted by the pathological mental states are multifold. First, and perhaps most basically, they destabilize the mind, disrupting its focus by stimulating harmful trains of thought, which then cause negative actions (see BCA 4:26–7). Second, they are psychologically painful in both subtle and explicit ways. A craving-filled mind, for instance, suffers from longing when lacking its object, but becomes obsessed with jealous clinging when its object is obtained (BCA 8:5–7). Craving also gives rise to arrogant pride and envy, which disrupts social relationships (BCA 8:12–13). At the cosmological level, these mental states result in future negative rebirths, such as in a hell realm (see, for instance, BCA 4:21 and 4:25).

Śāntideva's description of the harms of anger provides another illustration of the grades and modalities of suffering caused or constituted by the pathological mental states. The following verses are found at the beginning of the *Guide*'s Chapter 6, where the focus is on developing patience (*kṣānti*), the antidote to anger:

[3] Translations of Śāntideva's *Guide* are by Wallace and Wallace, from Śāntideva 1997.
[4] See Harris 2024a: Ch. 1 for a more detailed explanation of the relation between the perfections and similar Buddhist virtues, and the pathological mental states.

> Anger destroys all the good conduct, such as generosity and worshiping the Sugatas, that has been acquired over thousands of eons.
>
> 6:1
>
> There is no vice like hatred, and there is no austerity like patience. Therefore, one should earnestly cultivate patience in various ways.
>
> 6:2
>
> The mind does not find peace, nor does it enjoy pleasure and joy, nor does it find sleep or fortitude when the thorn of hatred dwells in the heart.
>
> 6:3
>
> Even dependents whom one rewards with wealth and honors wish to harm the master who is repugnant due to his anger.
>
> 6:4
>
> Even friends fear him. He gives, but is not served. In brief, there is nothing that can make an angry person happy.
>
> 6:5
>
> One who recognizes hatred as the enemy, knowing that it creates sufferings such as these, and persistently overcomes it, becomes happy in this world and in the other.
>
> 6:6

The harms ascribed to anger in these verses span physical, psychological, social, and cosmological dimensions. The comparison of anger to a thorn in the mind (6:3) serves both to indicate its psychological painfulness, and the difficulty of eliminating it. The reference to anger's ability to impede sleep (6:3) shows that it also harms the body. Anger also contaminates ordinary enjoyments (6:3), infecting pleasurable moments by stimulating fantasies about the supposed moment of offense from which anger originated. Social ill effects of anger are then detailed in 6:4–5. Elsewhere in his writing, Śāntideva explores the power of the pathological mental states to instigate arguments and warfare (see Goodman 2016: 22). Here in the patience chapter, however, his approach is more subtle. The disposition for anger to erupt at any moment ensures that even the positive actions of an angry person, such as providing material support and gifts for employees and family members, causes fear rather than gratitude. Anger, therefore, not only actively harms its possessor, but also drains the value out of the good actions the angry person performs.

Śāntideva concludes his detail of the harms of anger in 6:6, by turning to its cosmological implications. This is done through the reference to anger causing suffering "in this world and the other" (*iha paratra ca*, 6:6d). The reference to "this world" indicates the current life, and the various kinds of suffering just listed that anger causes within it. The reference to "the other (world)" refers to future states of rebirth. Śāntideva's implication, which is made explicit later in the chapter, is that anger causes negative effects in future lives, either through rebirth in impoverished human environments, or in negative realms such as in animal form, or in one of the hells (see, for instance, 6:72–4, 6:99, 6:130–1).

Suffering, therefore, for Śāntideva, is most centrally the experiencing of the world under the distorting influence of the pathological mental states.[5] It manifests in physical, psychological, social, and cosmological dimensions. Similar characterizations of the pathological mental states, which we have surveyed above in relation to craving and anger, reoccur throughout the text. We can distinguish within these descriptions two grades in the severity of suffering. Most centrally negative are the pathological mental states themselves, as well as the fear (*bhaya/trāsa*) and mental pain (*daumanasya*) which cause, accompany, and result from them. These negative mental states also cause additional unwanted experiences, such as poor physical health, sensory pain, social isolation, and negative rebirths. This second list of items are described as forms of suffering by Śāntideva because ordinary people are overwhelmed by the pathological mental states when experiencing them. Elsewhere in the text, however, he gives examples of highly developed bodhisattvas experiencing each of these items without psychological distress. The bodhisattva can experience any grade of sensory pain with equilibrium or even joy (see BCA 6:7–20 and Harris 2024a: Ch. 3.3); she delights in solitude in times when this is appropriate (see BCA 8:26–9, and 8:85–8); and she even erupts into joy when visiting hell realms and liberating sentient beings there (see BCA 8:107–8 and Goodman 2016: 179–80). This suggests that, for Śāntideva, it is the pathological mental states themselves which constitute suffering, as well as perhaps the fear and mental pain which accompany them. The rest of the items are neutral in terms of their contributions to human happiness: when they are accompanied by pathological emotions, as is usually the case for ordinary persons, then they are harmful. When experienced by the virtuous bodhisattva, however, they become ways to facilitate her bodhisattva trainings, or instances in which she can contribute to caring for sentient beings, and are thereby no longer damaging to her happiness.[6]

2. Contemplating suffering to develop *saṃvega* and *bodhicitta*

Śāntideva's analysis of these various aspects of suffering, which I reviewed in the last section, plays more than a merely theoretical role in the text. He incorporates these reflections into spiritual trainings to develop virtue. Reflection upon the impoverished state of ordinary experience results in *saṃvega*, the affective fear of saṃsāric existence, which in early Buddhist texts provides the initial motivation for the Buddha and his disciples to take up Buddhist practice.[7] Śāntideva utilizes *saṃvega* in two ways in the *Guide*. First, it serves to deepen motivation to commit to the bodhisattva path. Second, Śāntideva incorporates *saṃvega* into trainings to develop specific virtues; for instance,

5 See Harris 2024a: 77–83 for an argument that, according to Śāntideva, even severe physical pain does not diminish happiness if it is endured by a mind uncontaminated by pathological emotions.

6 See Harris 2024a: Ch. 1, esp. 1.3.3, for a more detailed development of this point.

7 See Brons 2016 and Harris 2024b for studies of *saṃvega* which draw upon Śāntideva's *Guide* in their analysis.

as we see below, it stimulates the virtue of energetic effort (*vīrya*). In line with his Mahāyāna commitments, Śāntideva intertwines meditations to develop *saṃvega* with contemplations to develop compassion and strengthen *bodhicitta*, by reflecting on the suffering of others. These two forces of *saṃvega* and compassion provide mutually supporting motivations for the bodhisattva's moral and spiritual development.

An early sequence of meditations, occurring in the second chapter just prior to the taking of the bodhisattva's vow, stimulates *saṃvega* by contemplating impermanence and death. This sequence is incorporated into a longer series of verses which forms Śāntideva's version of a Mahāyāna ritual called the "ritual of unexcelled worship" (*anuttarapūja*). Śāntideva's version of the ritual is composed out of the following eight parts: praise, worship, going for refuge, confession of misdeeds, rejoicing in merits, request for the buddhas to teach, supplication for them to remain, and dedication of merit (Huntington 2019: 135).[8] Early in the ritual, as part of the worship section, visualized offerings are made to buddhas and bodhisattva as a way of developing joy and reverence. As the text transitions to the confession section of the ritual, however, it takes a dramatically sharp psychological turn. The bodhisattva confesses all pervious harmful actions and develops *saṃvega* by meditating on the negative consequences which will follow from these deeds:

> Whatever offense I have committed, out of disrespect, with my body, speech, and mind against the Three Jewels, against mothers and fathers, and against spiritual mentors and others.
>
> 2:30
>
> And whatever terrible vices I, a sinner, defiled with many faults, have done, O Guides, I confess them all.
>
> 2:31
>
> How shall I escape it? Rescue me quickly! May death not soon creep up on me before my vices have vanished.
>
> 2:32
>
> Death does not differentiate between tasks done and undone. This traitor is not to be trusted by the healthy or the ill, for it is like an unexpected, great thunderbolt.
>
> 2: 33

These verses are an extended meditation on karma, the efficacy of past actions and mental responses to cause positive and negative effects in the future. The karmic effects of a mind dominated by the pathological mental states will be mental confusion, fear, psychological pain, and the strengthening of dispositions for pathological mental states to reoccur. In the confession sequence of the ritual, harmful actions and mental responses which cause these kinds of suffering are recalled and confessed in the

[8] For explanation of the ritual of unexcelled worship in the *Guide*, see Huntington 2019.

visualized presence of past and present buddhas and bodhisattvas. This practice acts as a means of purification of accumulated negative karma and symbolizes the aspirant's commitment to neutralize and finally eliminate the pathological mental states and their negative effects through the trainings of the bodhisattva path. The verses also act as an extended meditation on delusion, with the emphasis here being ignorance of the transient nature of human existence. Repeated attention to the impoverished human situation, in which all desired things will be lost at the time of death, is meant to stun the practitioner out of their complacent attitude.

These verses, whose central purpose is to develop *saṃvega*, follow a set of verses in which refuge is taken in buddhas and bodhisattvas (2:26–7), and are then followed by a series of verses expressing great joy at the recognition of the value of *bodhicitta*, and the bodhisattva path. The effect is to simultaneously turn the aspiring bodhisattva away from pursuit of saṃsāric pleasures, and toward the bodhisattva path. The verses below, praising compassion and *bodhicitta*, occur shortly before the bodhisattva vow is taken at 3:22 and 23:

> May I be the medicine and the physician for the sick. May I be their nurse until their illness never recurs.
>
> 3:7

> With showers of food and drink may I overcome the afflictions of hunger and thirst. May I become food and drink during times of famine.
>
> 3:8

> May I be an inexhaustible treasury for the destitute. With various forms of assistance may I remain in their presence.
>
> 3:9

> For the sake of accomplishing the welfare of all sentient beings, I freely give up my body, enjoyments, and all my virtues of the three times.
>
> 3:10

Central to Śāntideva's method to develop *bodhicitta* in his version of the ritual of unexcelled worship, is his integration of these two apparently contrasting motivations. *Saṃvega*, as theorized in early Buddhist texts, represents a turning away from the world, while compassion, centrally emphasized in the Mahāyāna tradition, returns the bodhisattva to that same world to care for suffering sentient beings. How then can the bodhisattva turn away from and return to the world simultaneously? The solution is that turning away from *saṃsāra* does not mean abandoning conventional reality, but purifying one's mode of perception, so that all factors of experience are perceived as empty of intrinsic existence. This results in the elimination of the bodhisattva's own pathological emotions, but is also, Śāntideva argues, compatible with compassion, the wish to free (empty) sentient beings from suffering. Śāntideva's bodhisattva path, therefore, fully integrates these early Buddhist insights about *saṃvega* and suffering into the Mahāyāna commitment to remaining in the world to work for the benefit of all beings. Śāntideva's development of these themes is most explicit in the *Guide*'s wisdom chapter, to which I will turn shortly. First, however, we will examine a complementary use of *saṃvega* in the *Guide*, in which spiritually efficacious fear is incorporated into trainings to develop specific bodhisattva virtues.

3. Contemplating suffering to develop specific virtues

We have seen thus far that, for Śāntideva, suffering is largely constituted by the mind's domination by the pathological mental states, and the resulting mental instability and psychological pain, which causes social dysfunction, bodily pain, and negative cosmological rebirths. I have suggested as well that the pathological mental states, as well as the mental pain and fear which accompany them, are largely constitutive of suffering for Śāntideva. The other items, such as loss of material possessions, physical pain, and negative cosmological rebirth, are sources of suffering for ordinary persons, but can be endured by the virtuous bodhisattva with ease, once the pathological mental states are eliminated. Thus far we have focused on Śāntideva's method of contemplating these aspects of suffering in order to develop *saṃvega* and compassion as motivations to embrace the bodhisattva path.

This section turns to Śāntideva's utilization of the bodhisattva's growing awareness of their impoverished saṃsāric situation in the development of specific bodhisattva virtues. Once again, we will find him intertwining the two motivations of *saṃvega* and compassion. The general strategy Śāntideva uses is the same that we saw above. Recognizing one's impoverished situation stimulates *saṃvega*, and a turning away from saṃsāric modes of experience. A greater awareness of one's own suffering, however, entails as well greater awareness of the suffering of others, who experience the same kinds of adversities. Developing *saṃvega*, therefore, is also a resource for developing universal compassion. At various places in the text, one or another of these root motivations may be more explicitly emphasized. For instance, in his discussions of the virtuous factors of awareness, mindfulness (*smṛti*) and introspection (*saṃprajanya*), Śāntideva repeatedly references the loss of mindfulness and introspection as leading to a loss of ethical discipline, and corresponding performance of negative actions and thereby negative karmic results for oneself (see 5:2, 5:7, 5:20, 5:29). Likewise, he discusses a mind in which meditative concentration is lacking as caught between fangs of the pathological mental states (8:1). These descriptions are more explicitly directed toward self-benefit and self-protection. Nevertheless, the negative ethical actions in question, which virtuous forms of awareness prevent, are precisely those which harm others, and so in protecting oneself, one protects others as well. Likewise, we have seen already in Śāntideva's treatment of patience that protecting one's mind from pathological mental states harmonizes social relationships, resulting in benefits for oneself and others.

Śāntideva also deploys a careful analysis of pain and suffering in developing a psychological technique to nurture patience and eliminate anger. In the section quoted below, he identifies the psychological causal conditions of anger and develops a strategy to eliminate them:

> Finding its fuel in mental pain (*daumanasya*) originating from an undesired event and from an impediment to desired events, anger becomes inflamed and destroys me.
>
> 6:7, translation slightly altered, my parenthesis

> Therefore, I shall remove the fuel of that enemy, for that foe has no function other than to harm me.
>
> 6:8

> Even if I fall into extreme adversity, I should not disrupt my happiness. When there is frustration, nothing is agreeable, and virtue is forsaken.
>
> 6:9

> If there is a remedy, then what is the use of frustration? If there is no remedy, then what is the use of frustration?
>
> 6:10

These verses articulate a technique whereby anger is eliminated by eliminating its immediate psychological cause, which Śāntideva identifies as mental pain (*daumanasya*) (6:7). This strategy is an application of the shared Buddhist understanding of causality represented in the twelve links of dependent origination (*pratītyasamutpāda*), in which feeling (*vedanā*) is identified as the salient cause of craving (*tṛṣṇā*), which itself acts as causal condition for clinging appropriation (*upādāna*), and eventually all forms of future suffering. In the twelve links, craving is best understood as standing in for all the pathological mental states, including anger, which can be understood as the desire to be free of what one does not want. Implicit in Śāntideva's application of the twelve links is a distinction between physical pain, which arises in dependence on a sense organ, and mental pain, which arises in response to physical pain, or unpleasant ideas.[9] It is mental pain which is the immediate causal condition of anger, and moreover, unlike physical pain, mental pain is an active response to the world which is at least in theory in the control of its experiencer. With appropriate training, Śāntideva believes that the propensity to feel mental pain can be diminished and eventually eliminated, which will result in the elimination of its causal effect, anger (6:8–9). Throughout the *Guide*, Śāntideva offers numerous meditations to build up our capacity to endure difficult situations without mental suffering. A simple but powerful technique is given in 6:10, quoted above. In the verse, Śāntideva points out that mental pain is always an unneeded suffering, given that if the situation which stimulates it can be altered, it is more effective to simply do so. When this is not the case, there is no use in feeling mental pain, which will simply be an additional form of suffering.[10]

[9] See Sumanacara 2019 for a good explication of this distinction in early Buddhist sources.

[10] For a more detailed exploration of Śāntideva's strategy in this section of the *Guide*, see Harris 2024a: Ch. 3.3 and Nelson 2021: Ch. 5, esp. 202–3 and 210–12.

Anger, therefore, is identified as a cause of much of the suffering the bodhisattva experiences. The way to protect the bodhisattva's own well-being, therefore, is to eliminate it, and this is done by keeping the mind joyful (BCA 6:9), since a happy mind will not experience anger's causal condition, mental pain. This illustrates once again the tight connection Śāntideva fashions between self and other benefit, given that experiencing virtuous joy is itself the antidote which eliminates the wish to harm sentient beings. Moreover, as spelled out in the earlier verses in BCA chapter six analyzed in the last section, this itself facilitates beneficial social relationships with those that the bodhisattva has vowed to serve. Once again, a careful analysis of pain and suffering, and in particular the recognition of mental pain as the causal condition of anger, serves as the tool to lessen pathological response and therefore suffering.

Another example of Śāntideva's use of the awareness of suffering to stimulate virtue comes in the *Guide*'s seventh chapter, dedicated to developing energetic effort (*vīrya*).[11] This section uses the contemplation of suffering, which wakens *saṃvega*, as the motivational basis for energetic effort, whose development eliminates laziness (*alasya*):

> Scented out by the hunters, the mental afflictions, you have entered the snare of rebirth. Why do you not recognize even now that you are in the mouth of death?
>
> 7:4
>
> You do not see that those of your own kind are gradually being killed. You even fall asleep like a buffalo among butchers.
>
> 7:5
>
> When Yama watches you and your path is blocked on all sides, how can you enjoy eating, and how can you sleep and have sexual intercourse?
>
> 7:6
>
> Since death will come swiftly, with its implements prepared, what will you do then even if you have abandoned spiritual sloth at this wrong time?
>
> 7:7
>
> Thinking: "I have not achieved this. I have just started this, but it remains half-done. Death has suddenly arrived. Oh, I am wretched!"
>
> 7:8, translation slightly altered

These meditations on the suffering caused by impermanence and death are also an analysis of delusion, with the focus being on how it manifests in relation to the pleasures of ordinary life. Delusion is not merely the ignorance that we will die—in fact, it is not that at all in this case, given that we all have knowledge of our own mortality. Rather, delusion in relation to impermanence and mortality clouds over intellectual

[11] For good treatments of *vīrya*, see Garfield and McRae 2026 and Gold 2018.

understanding, enabling a bad faith in which we live as if we will not die even while knowing that this is not the case. This feature of delusion is captured in verse 7:5 with the image of the cow, who is oblivious to his impending execution, even while the other members of the herd are culled one by one for their meat. The purpose of these verses is once more to develop *saṃvega*, which functions here to create disinterest in the saṃsāric pursuits detailed in verse 7:6. Instead, the Buddhist path is recognized as the only way to free oneself of the pain of a death under the power of the pathological mental states.

The tenor of these verses, in their stimulation of *saṃvega* as a spiritually potent fear, is similar and indeed almost interchangeable with the reflections during the confession section of the ritual of unexcelled worship treated above. Nevertheless, their application differs, in that now Śāntideva's goal is not to nurture commitment to the bodhisattva path as a whole (although these verses can still serve that function), but more specifically to act as an antidote to laziness, which is one of the opposing factors preventing the development of energetic effort. Once again, the self and other benefiting structure of Śāntideva's account of virtue is revealed, given that effort itself is defined as enthusiasm for virtue (BCA 7:2), where the virtues in question are those of the bodhisattva path, dedicated to the liberation of all from suffering.

4. Suffering and liberation as perspectives on the world

We have seen in the last section that careful attention to the forms suffering takes plays multiple roles in Śāntideva's liberative psychology.[12] In its manifestations as *saṃvega*, fear of our saṃsāric condition motivates the bodhisattva to deeply engage in the bodhisattva path, stimulates commitment to maintaining careful awareness and concentration, and provides motivational energy for effort (*vīrya*) in acting as the antidote to laziness. Further, the identification of mental pain as a necessary causal condition of anger facilitates the therapeutic technique of preventing anger through developing virtuous joy as its antidote. Finally, Śāntideva offers numerous contemplative techniques directing attention toward the suffering of others, as a way of developing compassion and strengthening *bodhicitta* (see 8:90–103 and 8:140–86).

All these strategies are based in the moral psychology of the early Buddhist tradition, that was further refined by the Abhidharma schools. Each is moreover an application of the root Buddhist tenet of dependent origination. For much of the Abhidharma tradition, a presupposition for the success of these strategies is the ontological grounding of the relevant psychological terms: because of its intrinsically pleasurable

[12] Śāntideva's goal in the *Guide* is to develop the virtuous qualities of the bodhisattva path, such as the mental states of generosity (*dāna*), patience (*kṣānti*), wisdom (*prajñā*), and so on. We can understand his goal as providing a "liberative psychology," in that these mental states eliminate suffering and free the practitioner from saṃsāric modes of experience. Likewise, it can be called a "moral psychology," in that these same mental states are virtuous, in constituting perfected experience, and in enabling beneficial actions in service of others. His development of the bodhisattva path, therefore, can be described as both "moral philosophy" and "religious soteriology."

or unpleasurable feel, the mental factor of feeling (*vedanā*) gives rise to craving, given the presence of adequate supporting conditions, and so on. Likewise, virtuous mental factors like patience and generosity, because of their intrinsic efficacy, function to eliminate the pathological mental states. The path to liberation can be articulated, joint by ontologically grounded joint, through specifying the intrinsic natures of liberative and afflictive mental states and marking out their causal relations.

For Śāntideva, as a Madhyamaka, in contrast, these basic psychological terms are empty of intrinsic nature, and this raises the question of how they can play the same foundational role in his ethics and moral psychology. Śāntideva's response to this concern is the same as the one given by Nāgārjuna in his own reply to the charge of ontological nihilism in the *Root Verses on the Middle Way*: to say something is empty is not to say that it doesn't exist, but to understand it as dependently arisen (See BCA 9:9–14 and Garfield 1995: 304–8). All soteriologically relevant factors, such as the pathological mental states, the perfections of virtue, compassion, the five aggregates, and so on, conventionally function to bring about suffering and the liberation from suffering. To say a mental state exists without intrinsic existence, and therefore only conventionally means that it depends for its identity and existence on causes and conditions, its parts, and conceptualization from a given perspective. All phenomena are like illusions, in appearing in a way they do not exist—that is, as possessing intrinsic existence when they are in fact empty. Nevertheless, they function reliably.[13] One can therefore eliminate the (conventionally existing) causes for (conventionally existing) suffering, through developing the (conventional) virtues, and so on.[14]

None of this is new ground within the Madhyamaka tradition. It does, however, account for a repeating feature in Śāntideva's characterization of virtue. Basing one's liberative psychology on an ontology of emptiness and the corresponding rejection of objective essences entails that there will be a perspectival aspect to every element of reality, including virtue and vice. The perfections, the pathological mental states, and so on, therefore, will be affective accompaniments to certain ways of viewing the world, rather than merely psychological responses to it.[15] Moreover, these perceptual frameworks themselves will obtain their moral valence depending on how they are contextualized within Śāntideva's overall soteriological framework.[16] This does not

[13] See BCA 9:5, where Śāntideva claims that things are "*māyāvad*"—that is, they are similar to illusions. Śāntideva's meaning is they exist only conventionally, and are deceptive in appearing as if they possess intrinsic existence. He is not, however, claiming that they are literally illusions, in being unreal.

[14] See Harris 2024a: Ch. 6 for a longer exploration of Śāntideva's response to concerns about the entailment between emptiness and nihilism

[15] This aspect of Śāntideva's moral thought is emphasized in Garfield's phenomenological reading of the *Guide*. See Garfield 2021: esp. Ch. 3.

[16] For a complimentary approach to Śāntideva's utilization of negative mental states for soteriological gain, see Harris 2017. In this prior article, I emphasize Śāntideva's use of afflictive energy, particularly that of fear, as being channeled into liberative purposes. The present work further clarifies his strategy by emphasizing that the fear in question is *saṃvega*, the affective terror at our saṃsāric condition which stimulates commitment to the Buddhist path.

mean that the virtuous and pathological mental states will lose their positive or negative valence, but it does suggest that the pathological mental states themselves may be able to perform provisionally positive roles in liberative practice. In this essay, we have already seen Śāntideva employ fear, in its liberative form as *saṃvega*, in exactly this way. Fear, which is usually a form of suffering, can be a cause of liberation when employed as a motivational resource to dedicate oneself to spiritual practice. An even clearer example of this technique is found in the patience chapter, in which Śāntideva emphasizes the soteriological efficacy of suffering itself:

> Suffering has another quality since arrogance diminishes because of despair, and one feels compassion for beings in the cycle of existence, fear of sin, and a yearning for the Buddha.
>
> 6:21, translation slightly modified

The word translated as "suffering" in the verse is *duḥkha*, and Śāntideva does not here clarify its meaning, in relation to the broad semantic range of the Sanskrit term. In its context within the chapter, it is not unnatural to take it as having the narrower referent of physical pain, given that the verse follows a section of the sixth chapter in which Śāntideva encourages the bodhisattva to develop the ability to tolerate physical pain without mental distress. One can also take *duḥkha* here as having a broader meaning, encompassing any kind of negative experience, and most centrally indicating a mind dominated by the pathological mental states. In either reading, the verse should be understood as offering techniques to alter our attitude toward pain and suffering, which can be recognized as valuable, to the extent that they act as a resource for spiritual progress. As the verse argues, experiencing suffering can be helpful as a stimulus for deepening *saṃvega*, which strengthens motivation to deeply engage in Buddhist practices. Likewise, experiencing suffering exposes one's own human vulnerability, and thereby diminishes the disposition for arrogant pride. Finally, careful reflection on one's own suffering stimulates compassion for others who suffer in similar ways, thereby acting as a resource for the development of *bodhicitta*.

This is not to say that Śāntideva's approach to virtue, vice, suffering, and liberation is wholly non-dual; the overarching emphasis throughout the text is to equate pathological mental states with suffering and to conceive of virtuous mental states as their antidotes. Yet passages like 6:21 draw attention to the relation between Śāntideva's moral psychology and his Madhyamaka metaphysical commitments. Virtue and vice are, in the final analysis, ways of viewing the world, and there is nothing within experience that cannot be conceived of through an afflicted, or a liberative perspective. This strategy is used piecemeal throughout the text, including in the verse quoted above. It is not explicitly theorized, however, until the text's penultimate chapter, focused on wisdom (*prajñā*), in which the core Madhyamaka tenet of the emptiness of all phenomena of intrinsic existence is explicated and defended. In one part of the chapter, Śāntideva turns his deconstructive gaze to pain and its causal conditions, arguing that they are empty of intrinsic existence, and exploring the psychological consequences of this fact. The verses below are part of a sequence in which Śāntideva provides arguments for the emptiness of all physical and mental phenomena:

> If there is no one to experience feeling and if feeling does not exist, then after understanding this situation, why, O craving, are you not shattered?
>
> 9:98

> The mind that has a dreamlike and illusion-like nature sees and touches.
>
> 9:99ab

The key to understanding Śāntideva's strategy in this passage is, once again, the twelve links of dependent origination. In prior verses, Śāntideva has given arguments for the emptiness of feeling (*vedanā*), which itself is the causal condition for craving (*tṛṣṇā*). In verse 9:97, he claims that craving will be destroyed through this recognition of the emptiness of its causal condition. The argument depends on an implicit distinction between ordinary psychological factors, such as feeling, and the pathological mental states, such as craving. The former can continue to function when perceived accurately, as being empty of intrinsic existence (9:99). The latter, in contrast, can only be experienced by a deluded mind falsely perceiving intrinsic existence. Recognizing the empty nature of craving, as a result of realizing the emptiness of its causal factors, therefore, destroys it.

This distinction is formalized and explicitly applied to all aspects of experience in the beginning of the chapter, in a pivotal verse in which Śāntideva articulates the central difference between ordinary persons and highly developed bodhisattvas:

> Ordinary people see and imagine things as real and not as similar to illusions. It is in this respect that there is disagreement between the contemplatives and the ordinary people.
>
> 9:5, translation slightly altered

The difference between ordinary people and the bodhisattva developed in virtue, Śāntideva claims in the verse, is most basically a difference in perspective. Ordinary persons conceive of all entities as real—that is, as possessing intrinsic existence—while, by contrast, the bodhisattva views them as like illusions, in that they are empty of intrinsic existence. As a result, the highly developed bodhisattva feels no craving or aversion toward them, but can continue to interact with them, as well as the beings she has vowed to save, in a liberated mode of perception. Nevertheless, such entities continue to be experienced as conventionally real, and therefore as able to function. Likewise, conceiving of beings in this way remains compatible with her basic bodhisattva commitment to liberate them. Śāntideva makes this later point explicitly in response to a raised objection:

> [Qualm:] If no sentient being exists, for whom is there compassion?
> [Madhyamika:] For one who is imagined through delusion, which is accepted for the sake of the task.
>
> 9:75

> [Qualm:] If there is no sentient being, whose is the task?
> [Madhyamika:] True. The effort, too, is due to delusion. Nevertheless, in order to alleviate suffering, delusion with regard to one's task is not averted.
>
> 9:76

Śāntideva's opponent, in these verses, objects that the bodhisattva who conceives of all beings as empty of self loses the object of compassion. Śāntideva's response is to apply the insight from 9:5 to this concern. The high-level bodhisattva does not cease experiencing conventional reality, but rather perceives it in a purified mode of perception, as illusion-like, in being empty of intrinsic existence. This is how he conceives of himself, the beings he has vowed to save, and the compassion he feels for suffering sentience beings. Delusion (*moha*), alluded to in the verses as accepted for its pragmatic purposes, represents the bodhisattva's employment of conceptuality as a condition for continuing to engage with conventional reality.

These sets of verses, therefore, suggest that all pathological mental states are, most basically, delusive ways of perceiving, and relating to reality. Given that the pathological mental states are what Śāntideva means by suffering, this entails as well that suffering itself is a delusive way of experiencing the world. It is natural, therefore, that many of Śāntideva's techniques, like those surveyed above, are ways of altering our perspectives. Liberative opportunities exist in any situation, no matter how apparently impoverished. Śāntideva makes this point most explicitly by alluding to the possibilities of bodhisattvas wholly eliminating their own propensities to suffer, even in the hell realms (see BCA 8:107–8 and Goodman 2016: 179–80). These allusions culminate in the final chapter of the text, in which Śāntideva describes buddhas and bodhisattvas as transforming the hell realms themselves:

> May the regions of hell become vast ponds of delight, fragrant with lotuses, beautiful and pleasing with the cries of white geese, wild ducks, ruddy geese, and swans.
>
> 10:7

> May the heap of burning coal become a mound of jewels. May the burning ground become a crystal marble floor; and may the mountains of "the crushing hell" become temples of worship filled with Sugatas.
>
> 10:8

These verses highlight the liberative power of buddhas and bodhisattvas to aid suffering sentient beings. They can also be read as a continuation of Śāntideva's emphasis on the development of character and transformation of perception. For the first nine chapters in the *Guide*, Śāntideva's emphasis is on the transformation of the experience of the developing bodhisattva. This culminates in his claim that virtuous bodhisattvas can flourish even in the hell realms, where they manifest to liberate sentient beings. In the tenth chapter, the text reaches its conclusion as the experience of sentient beings is also transformed, so that the hell realms themselves become places of delight. These verses then provide the social analogue of the psychology of the *Guide*, in which the transformation brought about by the bodhisattva is no longer limited to her own individual perspective, but encompasses the entire environment and, by implication, the perspectives of all other beings within it.

5. Conclusion

In this chapter, I have offered an analysis of Śāntideva's account of suffering, and its role in the soteriology of the *Guide*. Suffering, for Śāntideva, is most basically the domination of the mind by the pathological emotions, and the accompanying and resulting fear and mental pain. Awareness of suffering is incorporated into his liberative psychology in two forms: as *saṃvega*, the affective fear of *saṃsāra* which inspires Buddhist practice, and as compassion, the wish to eliminate the suffering of sentient beings which inspires commitment to the bodhisattva path. Moreover, I have framed this study around a basic question facing an author like Śāntideva who combines a moral psychology grounded in early Buddhist and Abhidharma insights, with a Madhyamaka ontology of emptiness. The concern is that without an Abhidharma commitment to intrinsic nature, it becomes inexplicable how liberative mental factors can possess the power to eliminate pathological mental states. The solution, for Śāntideva, is given explicitly in the ninth chapter of his text; wisdom functions to enact a fundamental transformation of perspective in which all phenomena are conceived of accurately, as empty of intrinsic existence. This itself eliminates all pathological mental states, which are themselves most basically inaccurate and impoverished ways of viewing the world. We can see hints of this solution throughout the text, such as in Śāntideva's utilization of fear, in the form of *saṃvega*, as a motivational resource for liberation, and his suggestion that the experience of suffering itself can be understood as an element of liberative practice. It is developed most explicitly, however, in the ninth chapter, in which the bodhisattva's wisdom is presented as the means to engage with the conventional world in a transformed mode of perception, wholly free from the distorting influence of the pathological mental states.

References

Bommarito, N. (2014), "Patience and Perspective," *Philosophy East and West* 64 (2): 269–86.

Brons, L. (2016), "Facing death from a safe distance: *Saṃvega* and moral psychology," *Journal of Buddhist Ethics* 23: 83–128.

Gold, J. (2018), "Freedom through Cumulative Moral Cultivation: Heroic Willpower (*Vīrya*)," *Journal of Buddhist Ethics* 25: 742–66.

Garfield, J. (1995), *Fundamental Wisdom of the Middle Way: Nāgārjuna's Mūlamadhyamakakārikā*, New York: Oxford University Press.

Garfield, J. (2021), *Buddhist Ethics: A Philosophical Exploration*, New York: Oxford University Press.

Garfield, J. and McRae, E. (2026), "The Wind in the Sails: *Vīrya* in the *Bodhicaryāvatāra*," in S. Harris and P. Schmidt-Leukel (eds.), *Śāntideva and the Dynamics of Tradition: Doctrinal, Social, and Interreligious Contexts*, 55–69. London: Bloomsbury.

Goodman, C., trans. (2016), *The Training Anthology of Śāntideva: A Translation of the Śikṣā-samuccaya*, New York: Oxford University Press.
Harris, S. (2017), "The Skillful Handling of Poison: *Bodhicitta* and the *Kleśas* in Śāntideva's *Bodhicaryāvatāra*," *Journal of Indian Philosophy* 45 (2): 331–48.
Harris, S. (2024a), *Buddhist Ethics and the Bodhisattva Path: Śāntideva on Virtue and Well-Being*, London: Bloomsbury.
Harris, S. (2024b), "Buddhism and Existentialism: *Saṃvega* as Existential Dread of the Human Condition," in K. Aho, M. Altman, and M. Pedersen (eds.), *Routledge Handbook of Contemporary Existentialism*, 376–86, New York: Routledge.
Huntington, E. (2019), "Ritual Structure and Material Culture in the *Guide to Bodhisattva Practice*," in J. Gold and D. Duckworth (eds.), *Readings of Śāntideva's Guide to Bodhisattva Practice*, 132–45, New York: Columbia University Press.
Nelson, B. (2021), "Ksānti in the bodhisattva path of Śāntideva." PhD diss., University of Sydney. Revised edition.
Śāntideva (1997), *A Guide to the Bodhisattva Way of Life* (Bodhicaryāvatāra), trans. V. Wallace and A. Wallace, Ithaca, NY: Snow Lion.
Siderits, M. and Katsura, S., trans. (2013), *Nāgārjuna's Middle Way: Mūlamadhyamakakārikā*. Boston: Wisdom Publications.
Sumanacara, A. (2019), "The Experience of Dukkha and Domanassa among Puthujjanas," *Journal of Buddhist Ethics* 26: 107–38.
Westerhoff, J., trans. (2010), *The Dispeller of Disputes: Nagarjuna's Vigrahavyāvartanī*, New York: Oxford University Press.

3

The Wind in the Sails

Vīrya in the *Bodhicaryāvatāra*

Jay L. Garfield and Emily McRae

So, a patient person should cultivate commitment (*vīrya*).
This is because awakening requires commitment.
Just as motion is impossible without wind,
Virtue cannot arise without commitment.

Bodhicaryāvatāra 7:1

1. Introduction

The bodhisattva path as articulated in path literature beginning with the *Discourse on the Ten Bodhisattva Levels* (*Daśabhūmika-sūtra*) and Asaṅga's *Bodhisattva Stages* (*Bodhisattvabhūmi*) poses a complex puzzle. That puzzle becomes acute when we examine the most precise articulation of the moral dimensions of that path in Śāntideva's *How to Lead an Awakened Life* (*Bodhicaryāvatāra*, hereafter BCA).[1] We can summarize this puzzle in three related questions: (1) Why is the quality of *vīrya* (commitment) a distinct quality to be cultivated, as opposed to an adverbial qualification of all of the other qualities enumerated on the bodhisattva path? (2) Why is the stage at which one cultivates commitment placed after those in which one cultivates generosity, proper conduct, introspective vigilance, conscientiousness, and patience, on the one hand, and before those in which one cultivates meditative absorption and wisdom, on the other? (3) What exactly is commitment anyway?[2]

These are each interesting questions, and we will address each of them in what follows. First, though, let's bring them each into focus. Not much is written about commitment, either in commentary literature or in the contemporary literature on the bodhisattva path.[3] Candrakīrti, for instance, devotes only one verse to this ground and

[1] For an excellent set of essays on *How to Lead an Awakened Life*, see Gold and Duckworth 2019.
[2] For now, we defer our discussion of our choice to translate *vīrya* as "commitment." We justify this in section 4.
[3] The notable exception is Gold 2018 who insightfully locates *vīrya* in relation to the eightfold path and to Buddhist action theory. He shows how the cultivation of *vīrya* enhances spontaneity and moral strength in ethical engagement in the absence of a doctrine of free will. We will be examining a different aspect of this important perfection.

quality in *Introduction to the Middle Way* (*Madhyamakāvatāra*). Even in one of the most extensive commentaries on *How to Lead an Awakened Life*, Kunzang Sonam (1823–1905) in his *Excellent Vase* (*Gyal sras yon tan bum bzang*, Duckworth 2025) devotes no philosophical attention to the importance of *vīrya* except to note that it is an antidote to laziness. Contemporary literature largely ignores this chapter when discussing *How to Lead an Awakened Life*, and when discussing the structure of Buddhist ethics.[4]

We begin by taking stock of where we are on the bodhisattva path at the end of Chapter 6 on patience (*kṣānti*, *bzod pa*) and the beginning of Chapter 7 where commitment is addressed. We will then ask what the conceptual gap is between Chapter 6 and Chapter 8 on meditative absorption (*dhyana*, *bsam gtan*). This investigation will show how Chapter 7 is intended to span that gap. This will also explain why a bodhisattva waits until the *fourth* bodhisattva ground, until *after* the cultivation of generosity, proper conduct, conscientiousness, and patience, to cultivate commitment. This order is not original with Śāntideva: it is the order introduced in the Prajñāpāramitā literature and discussed at length in the *Discourse on the Ten Bodhisattva Levels* and adopted by all subsequent Mahāyāna theorists. Śāntideva's particular articulation of the moral content of each these grounds and his discussion of *vīrya* in Chapter 7 sheds light on the place of *vīrya* in the bodhisattva path simply because his presentation is the most extensive and sophisticated. So, examination of *vīrya* in this context will give us the most insight into its role in Buddhist moral psychology and path literature more generally.

In section 5, we dive deeper into the structure of *vīrya*. One of Śāntideva's greatest contributions to moral psychology is the distinction he draws between egocentric and non-egocentric conative attitudes.[5] In Chapter 7, he demonstrates that non-egocentric states—such as *aspiration*, as opposed to *desire*, and *confidence*, as opposed to *pride*—can motivate moral action. They provide the bridge between moral knowledge and action.[6]

2. Mind the gap: Where does Chapter 6 leave us and where does Chapter 8 pick up?

The chapter on commitment falls between two particularly famous chapters: Chapter 6 on patience and Chapter 8 on meditative absorption. In Chapter 6, Śāntideva defines patience and its domain, and gives instructions for the cultivation of patience through cognitive reframing.[7] Patience is understood as the ability to endure suffering and hardships that would normally give rise to anger calmly, by depersonalizing the agency

[4] A notable exception to this trend is Schmidt-Leukel 2019: 305–29.

[5] For more on this distinction and Śāntideva's approach to it, see Garfield 2022: Chs. 4 and 9.

[6] The Ven. Chökyi Nyima Rinpoche likes to say that the difference between pride and confidence is that one is at the other's expense. Pride is egocentric; confidence is not. To cultivate either is to cultivate an antidote to the other.

[7] There is no single human author of this work. Nor do we have any biographical information regarding the figure to whom we think we refer when we use the name *Śāntideva*. There may or may not have been a monk at Nālandā of that name who composed a draft of this text. We use that name

of those who inflict suffering on us.[8] In this way, patience is not only an antidote to anger and hatred, but also to the dejection that can overwhelm us when we encounter obstacles, and patience also allows us to endure abuse and physical pain (see especially 6:12–21). Patience, like commitment, is cultivatable. It is a premise of Śāntideva's system that we can train ourselves to be less reactive and that, by doing so, we can become more morally responsive. Patience isn't just the only good option in a bad situation; it is the only option that makes any sense. When we cultivate it, it becomes a liberative comportment to conflict and adversity. This is an achievement, and part of Śāntideva's strategy in Chapter 6 is to frame patience as good for us, as opposed to, say, the recourse of the weak. He ends the chapter on this point (6:133–134ab):

> Set aside attaining awakening: can't you see that benefiting sentient beings brings you success, happiness, and reputation in this life?
>
> Even in samsara, through practicing patience, you will become attractive, safe, and well-regarded; you will enjoy a long, happy life and so you will be as blissful as an emperor.[9]

By the end of Chapter 6, we understand what patience is and why it is rational to cultivate it: it is good for everyone—both ourselves and others. It brings us the goods anger can never secure, including happiness, contentment, joy, and freedom.

We also leave Chapter 6 with a well-developed sense of how to cultivate patience, especially in the difficult contexts of high-stakes interpersonal conflict. Śāntideva's strategy here is to lead the reader through a cognitive reframing that destabilizes our understanding of others as independent actors with evil intentions, thereby demonstrating the inappropriateness and irrationality of anger. He replaces an understanding of the interpersonal as fundamentally atomistic and agonistic with a relational understanding of human conflict and the path to its resolution that is thoroughly informed by dependent co-arising, urging us to see that every event—including each of our actions and the actions of others—is the consequence of countless causes and conditions. There are no autonomous centers of agency. For this reason, most of our most natural reactive attitudes are deeply misguided. Moreover, even our

now to refer to the complex collective responsible for the book we read now, with no commitment regarding who the members of that collective were. So, any attributions of intent or motivation are purely hermeneutical, not biographical. Our interest in this chapter is in moral psychology and how that moral psychology is developed in this chapter of this version of the text, not in the fascinating history of the text. We do know that there are many recensions of *Bodhicāryāvatāra*/*Bodhisattvācāryāvatāra*, and the text(s) we have now are the result of a good deal of editing, expanding, and moving around of text. Chapter 7—the focus of this study—was particularly subject to this process, and contains a good deal of material that originally appeared in other chapters, suggesting that the sequence of authors of this text were especially concerned with this topic (see Saito 1993, 2006; Schmidt-Leukel 2019: 305–7).

8 While Śāntideva, like all Mādhyamikas, agrees that the person, like all sentient beings, exists conventionally and is the object of moral attitudes such as care and friendliness, this does not undermine his insistence in Chapter 6 and later in Chapter 8 (see esp. 8:90–103) that agency is not to be understood as originating in persons; instead, he is unambiguous in his assertion that agency is always causally conditioned, and that to understand a person's actions we need to attend to a myriad of antecedent and external causes and conditions.

9 All translations are our own from the Tibetan.

appraisal of events and actions is conditioned by our own perspective, which usually turns out to be pathologically egocentric, and so which must be transcended if we are to see things correctly. This analysis destabilizes the idea that an essentially egocentric conative attitude like desire can ever be a sound moral motivation. It therefore suggests the need for an alternative conative attitude to motivate a bodhisattva.

To use a particularly stark example: "He has the knife, I have the body. They each cause suffering. Since both are wounding me, at which should I be angry?" (6:43). This is but one of many efforts in Chapter 6 to reframe our understanding of hardship, conflict, and wrongdoing as something that is conditioned all the way down. We could read this verse as problematic victim-blaming. But, in the context of Chapter 6, it is part of a larger project of shifting our perspective.[10] We are urged not to see others as independent, atomistic actors but rather as interdependent, conditioned agents.

Our attention is drawn to the fact that our actions and those of others are not initiated spontaneously through an Augustinian free will.[11] Instead, they, like all other events in the universe, depend on countless causes and conditions, including not only our perceptions and intentions, but our conditioning and experience, our biological nature, and many other factors. Realizing this enables us to abandon the egocentricity that leads to anger, and therefore enables us to cultivate the patience that leads to effective agency. When Chapter 6 ends, we know both *why* and *how* to be patient. But we do not yet have an account of how that knowledge can *motivate* us to be patient, and that is task of Chapter 7.

Like Chapter 6, the eighth chapter of BCA on meditative absorption has received much attention in historical and contemporary scholarship, and for good reason. This chapter is the source of the highly influential ethical practice of "exchanging self and other"—the imaginative practices of taking on another's suffering while offering one's own happiness and good qualities to the other (8:120). In Chapter 8, Śāntideva presents his famous argument against egoism, claiming that the notion that I should only care about my own suffering, because it is mine, cannot be justified (8:90–103).[12]

In Chapter 8, meditative absorption is defined as an antidote to distraction. According to Śāntideva, distraction is a major moral problem: "to be distracted is to be gripped by the fangs of psychopathologies" (8:1cd).[13] Śāntideva emphasizes here that the achievement of virtue requires constant attention. Distraction, he argues, inevitably leads us to an egocentric orientation to the world and hence to psychopathology (*kleśa*) and vice. That psychopathology need not be severe; it need not rise to the level of a

[10] See Bommarito 2014; McRae 2012.

[11] For an extended explanation of why Augustinian free will does not figure in Buddhist action theory or ethics including in Śāntideva's account of moral cultivation, see Garfield 2017 and Garfield 2022: Chs. 2 and 4.

[12] Chapter 8 is another chapter that was heavily redacted as the text developed, with a great deal of material, including this passage, moved from earlier chapters to this context. For more extensive discussion, see The Cowherds 2015: Chs. 2 and 6.

[13] We translate *kleśa* as *psychopathology*. This is not to say that to suffer from *kleśas* is *abnormal*. It is to say that they are that from which we *suffer*, that they are *maladaptive*, and that they are maladaptive *psychological* sources of suffering. The Greek root *pathos* has exactly the same semantic range as *kleśa*. This is also completely consistent with the medical metaphors we find in Buddhist philosophy, comparing the Buddha to a physician, the Sangha to a nurse, and the Dharma to a medicine that together cure us of the *kleśas*.

psychiatric diagnosis or profound disability. Nonetheless, it constitutes a kind of suffering and cognitive-affective dysfunction that renders us less than we might otherwise be—less happy, less effective as agents, less skillful as human beings, in short, less *humane.* Because this consequence represents a disorder and increases our suffering and that of others, it is appropriate to regard even a normal level of *kleśa* as a kind of psychopathology—akin to what Freud called "the psychopathology of everyday life."

In the first half of Chapter 8, Śāntideva encourages us to create the conditions that minimize distractions, thereby diminishing the power of the psychopathologies, such as hatred, obsession, delusion, arrogance, and envy. Several verses are devoted to the value of secluded practice, and many more admonish us to give up sexual desire (8:43–69). If achieved, such freedom from the obsessions of attachment—not to mention the quotidian details of everyday life—has its rewards: "Stay as long as you like in an empty hut, at the foot of a tree, or in a cave. Let go of all concern about your things, and lead a carefree life. Independent, unattached, and bound to no one, enjoy the happiness that is difficult even for the powerful to find" (8:87–8). While pleasure may be found in food, drink, and conviviality, happiness is found when we no longer have the need to satiate desires; pleasure is fleeting, while happiness is lasting.

For a lay audience—or, indeed for anyone uncomfortable with the advice to imagine women's bodies as sacks of filth (8:53)—Śāntideva's recommendation to view them that way may seem repellent, as admonitions to have contempt for other human beings. But it is important to remember the motivation for such dramatic practices. They are intended to transform one's life by counteracting habitual attitudes that generate pathological attraction. They thereby reduce the distractions caused by self-concern, the praise or contempt of others, the desire for popularity, and the obsession with material pleasure. Minimizing these distractions, in turn, enables us to focus on uprooting the egocentric biases implicit in the beliefs, judgments, and emotions that mediate our engagement with the world.

Śāntideva immediately follows these prescriptions with "a meditation on the equality of oneself and others" (8:90cd). He reminds us that in order to develop a decentered view of the moral universe we must constantly direct our attention to the fact that there is nothing morally special about our own position. These reflections, although borne in conditions of relative isolation, yield a radically pro-social result. Happiness results not from the satisfaction of desires, or the pursuit of personal pleasure, but from benefiting others, and from developing the capacity to rejoice in others' welfare. This reflects our status as essentially social beings: "I am bound to others!" (8:137). "In this world, all happiness comes from the desire for others' happiness, and all suffering comes from the desire for one's own happiness. Why say more?" (8:129/130a). But, of course, Śāntideva does say more.

3. Bridging the gap

Chapters 6 demands a lot of us, in particular that we foreswear anger and reorient our reactive attitudes; Chapter 8 demands that we change our lives even more radically: we are urged to transform our relation to the world, to devote ourselves to the care of all beings. This radical transformation requires more than just an explanation of how and why to practice these moral skills and virtues (Chapters 1–6): we need the motivation that enables us to spring into action. Otherwise, this knowledge would be inert. This is the point that Hume was after when he argued that reason is the slave of the passions, and that simply knowing that something is right or wrong cannot by itself impel us to do or not to do it.

Consider an apposite analogy to self-improvement through spiritual exercise, our attempts to improve ourselves through *physical* exercise: we can understand *why* we ought to exercise and *how* to exercise, but that doesn't mean that we *will* exercise. We have to *care* about exercise in the right ways, and we have to prioritize it in our lives. This will require us to abandon many practices to which we are attached and seem to make us happy. We can no longer sleep late; we have to change our diet; and we may have to give up social activities, such as late nights at the bar with our friends. To introduce a set of values into our lives—even values that we endorse—requires us to make room for them, and that in turn requires us to reassess our previous values. This kind of transformation is difficult precisely because our lives are never open spaces; they are always already filled with preexisting habits, practices, commitments—habits, practices, and commitments that form a complex that needs to be replaced *in toto*. This is not a "one-and-done" kind of project; it is a long-term, intentional transformation of our fundamental motivations. Such a project takes *commitment*, and that is why Chapter 7 is necessary.

One way to see the significance of commitment in Śāntideva's system and in Mahāyāna moral psychology more generally is to imagine the BCA without it—to suppose Chapter 8 followed directly from Chapter 6—and to ask, what would we miss?[14] The answer is that we lack a conative attitude that could get us from knowledge to action in a non-egocentric way. While most of us do not enter this transformative moral path as philosophically committed egoists, none of us are free from the habits and attitudes that encode egoism. We often (re)act from habit instead of responding by making choices; our understanding of our own moral psychology is typically shallow; and when asked to explain our behaviour we typically fabricate rather than engage in honest introspection.[15] The first step, then, in the bodhisattva path is to develop the awareness of one's habits, the critical distance that allows us to ask whether they really make sense, and the equanimity to admit that they usually don't. Only once we have cultivated this awareness can we begin to cultivate the skills requisite to moral success. This is the work of Chapter 5, which addresses attention and introspective vigilance.

But cultivating this insight and developing these skills are not sufficient to propel us along the bodhisattva path. We also need a conative attitude that takes us from reason

[14] Once again, we are asking about the current extended version of the BCA, which is the basis of the major commentaries; this is the text that provides the most sophisticated understanding of Buddhist moral psychology; the earlier versions can, in our view, best be seen as rough drafts. In the Dunhuang version of the text, parts of Chapter 8 are included in what is now Chapter 7 (see Schmidt-Leukel 2019: 305–7), but this is beside the present point.

[15] "We're sculpted from youth/ the chipping away makes me weary/ And asked for the truth/it seems like we just pick a theory. And it is the one that justifies/ our daily lives/ and backs us with quivers and arrows" (Indigo Girls, "Deconstruction of Love").

to action, and that attitude cannot be egocentrically grounded. To be sure, we are familiar with conative attitudes that can take us from reason to action. Desire and aversion are the most obvious. But from a Buddhist perspective these are pathological, and indeed are the roots of suffering. Take anger, for example. Śāntideva could have encouraged us to become enraged with samsara and to use that rage to work for the welfare of others. But he explicitly declines to do so.[16] Or he could have proposed desire for the good, or to be a good person, as a motivation. But desire—even desire for the good, however better it might be than desire for that which is bad—is problematic: desire, like anger, always involves some degree of ego-clinging, however subtle. This is exactly what Śāntideva sees as the root of suffering and so cannot be the way to achieve liberation, however useful it might be in taking a beginner forward, replacing explicitly self-interested desire with a more salutary desire (a route, as Nāgārjuna puts it in *Precious Garland*, to a better state, if not to definitive goodness).

Even when we are motivated to become better, if that motivation is a *desire* to be a good person, the fact that the satisfaction of our desire is what is motivational for us that that attitude, however laudable it may appear, is in the end egoistic. What looks like moral progress is simply the satisfaction of one more desire; what appears to be virtuous and healthy is instead vicious and pathological. These are what Buddhaghosa would call "near enemies of virtue." The crucial distinction here, as in Buddhaghosa's account of the near enemies of the *brahmavihāras*, is between egoistic desire to be better and disinterested aspiration for the good, a distinction to which we will return in detail below (see Garfield 2022: 135–44). We will see that Śāntideva's analysis of (*vīrya*) provides us with an analysis of the kind of conation that enables ethical development.

4. Chapter 7 and commitment

What is "commitment" in the sense relevant here? The term *vīrya* is variously translated into English as "effort," "diligence," "zeal," "enthusiasm," or "heroism" (even "manliness"—it is cognate both with the English terms "virile" and "virtue"). Śāntideva glosses it at the beginning of his chapter as "taking joy in virtue" (*brtson gang dge la spro ba'o*), and as an antidote to laziness, to attachment to vice, and to self-contempt (*le lo ngan la zhen pa dang/ skyid lug bdag nyid brnyas pa'o*). We choose to translate it as "commitment."[17]

At a most basic level, commitment involves taking moral cultivation seriously as a central life project. When we are *committed* to a project, that project is not one more

[16] Śāntideva does note that *if* we must be angry at something, then it is best to be angry with one's own pathological states (4:43, 6:41). But this is a conditional: if anger is unavoidable, then direct it toward hatred or other pathological states. It is not a general recommendation, but a statement of the extreme irrationality of anger at what we take to be a self. Selves are unreal, while pathologies are at least conventionally real. It is clear from Chapter 6 that Śāntideva thinks that the best option is to prevent or defuse anger whenever possible.

[17] We note that some—but not all—of our interlocutors find "commitment" not sufficiently emphatic a word to translate *vīrya*. That may be one way of hearing "commitment." But we'd like to hear it in an emphatic way as a *serious commitment*, like, say, marriage or ordination. That gives it the power we need for the translation.

item on the to do list, like cleaning out the fridge or trimming the hedges. Instead, it becomes an organizing principle of our lives, one that is not only the *highest priority* on any to-do list, but more importantly one that stands at the highest *node* of the decision tree regarding what do with our time, our lives, and our other projects—the purpose that provides the context and the rationale for all of the others.

For instance, if I am *committed* to the prevention of extinctions—as opposed to merely disapproving of and saddened by extinctions—I organize my life as a vehicle for action directed at preventing them. This may involve rethinking my career, my diet, my mode of transportation, political party, etc. That is, this commitment organizes my life; it defines not only what I *do*, but who I *am*. I am not a teacher who happens to work against extinction; I am an anti-extinction activist, who also teaches. Preferences determine our actions; commitments determine our identities.

So, to be committed to the bodhisattva path is not to be a baker or candlestick-maker who devotes a lot of time to generous acts, who behaves in an ethically salutary way, who is conscientious, patient, and so forth. Instead, to be committed to the bodhisattva path is to be a bodhisattva who *therefore* cultivates these perfections and who might—like Vimalakīrti—bake or make candlesticks. But one who engages in these mundane activities does so always and only in service of *bodhicitta*, the aspiration to awaken in order to benefit sentient beings. The bodhisattva vow organizes one's life; commitment enables it to do so. To be committed to the bodhisattva project is hence to take oneself seriously as a moral agent, first and foremost, and to subordinate the rest of one's life to that identity.

Vīrya is therefore obviously connected to *bodhicitta* (the aspiration for awakening) itself as well as to the *brahmavihāras*, the four divine states of *karuṇā* (care), *maitrī* (friendliness), *upekṣā* (impartiality/equanimity), and *muditā* (sympathetic joy)—especially to *care*. Each serves a motivational function. But it is distinct from them. *Bodhicittā* specifies a path and consists in an aspiration to follow it. But that path is vast and complex: commitment is a component of that path, and hence a *constituent*, but not the whole of *bodhicitta*.[18] *Care* is more specific: it is a response to suffering and a commitment to relieve it. It is one of the *brahmavihāras*, and so is part of a reorientation of moral vision toward a less egocentric comportment to the world. *Commitment* hence differs from *bodhicitta* in that it is a component of it, and from *care* in that it is broader in scope and must infuse *care* itself as well as other virtuous attitudes.

This should help us to see why commitment is not simply adverbial in nature, or in other words, why—like generosity, patience, and conscientiousness—it has a domain of conduct of its own. It involves a distinctive orientation that is not simply a matter of doing other things really well. Generosity, on Śāntideva's view, has as its domain our attitude toward our possessions, bodies, and time. Instead of clinging to them, and seeing them as *ours*, and available for our own benefit, we see them as affordances to

[18] We must bear in mind here Śāntideva's distinction in Chapter 1 between aspirational and engaged *bodhicitta*. *Commitment* is a constituent of *engaged bodhicitta*—and indeed, as we argue, the principal conative constituent of that aspiration.

benefit others—as they are to be given, not to be held. The domain of patience is the attribution of blame and the control of anger; instead of seeing others as autonomous agents of harm, we see them as driven by conditions over which they have no control. We thus come to respond not with anger, but with care. The domain of conscientiousness is our vows and commitments; instead of forgetting about them in the confusion of daily life, we recollect them, call them to mind, attend to them, and ensure that they determine our behavior.

Commitment has an analogous domain: our basic moral identity, the priorities that drive our life. Without commitment, our basic identity—and with it, the structure and hierarchy of goals and values that drive our conduct and that shape our lives—might derive from our social status, our family context, our professional life, our nationality, or from any of a hundred other sources. Each of these distractions encodes attachment to specific beings or entities in samsara, aversion to others, and confusion about what is really a source of suffering or a source of genuine happiness. In short, these distractors each bind us in samsara; commitment, while it might sound like another bond, is liberatory.

Even if we are genuinely devoted to one of these distractors, if that devotion is egocentric, it would not count as the *virtue* of commitment: that, Śāntideva reminds us in the first verses of the chapter, involves joy *in virtue*. For instance, a person might be regarded as a "devoted family man," or a "devoted doctor," but that devotion might be bound up with their own self-image or the pleasure and satisfaction they themselves derive from their work or relationships.[19] This *looks* and *feels* like virtue. But the egocentricity that underlies it gives it a different conative structure and so a different role in our moral psychology. Devotion to these potential distractors is therefore a near enemy—a vice masquerading as a virtue. That, as Buddhaghosa reminds us, is why these distractors are so dangerous.[20] Just as Aristotle argues that strength is only a moral good when attached to virtue, devotion is only a good in the Mahāyāna framework when it is commitment to the other perfections. Commitment is about our orientation to moral life and our sense of our moral agency.[21] Without the other virtues, it would be pointless.

Śāntideva emphasizes both the relation of commitment to the other virtues and its specific role in moral cultivation in 7:3. He writes that lack of commitment, or sloth, arises from preferring pleasure and relaxation, and from failing to reject the suffering of samsara. It is only when motivation is directed to a worthy end that it really qualifies as commitment. While the aspiration to awaken for the benefit of all sentient beings may constitute the broad orientation of bodhisattva's life, and while care may be one of

[19] The issue here is not the fact that one takes pleasure in one's work or relationships, as this kind of pleasure is a natural outcome of virtuous actions on a Buddhist view. The problem occurs when one is motivated to work or relate to others only in order to secure pleasure for oneself.

[20] Buddhaghosa 1999: 311–12.

[21] We hence see why commitment comes after the virtues. In this way, the discussion is analogous to Aristotle's introduction of moral strength following his discussion of virtue in book VII of the *Nicomachean Ethics*. There is, however, an important disanalogy. While Aristotle argues that moral strength is not a virtue on the grounds that it does not have a specific domain, Śāntideva directs our attention to the fact that commitment does have a domain, even if that is a higher-order domain.

the specific attitudes necessary in order to realize that goal, commitment organizes our specific projects in relation to that broad orientation and to that virtue. Commitment, Śāntideva tells us in the subsequent verses, arises from contemplating both the miseries of samsara and the inevitability and unpredictability of death, which together make practice and cultivation urgent.

The life dedicated to pleasure, by contrast, while it might appear to be a pursuit of happiness, in fact traps us in the very sources of suffering—attachment and aversion. In this context Śāntideva contrasts the genuine, unsurpassable joy of Dharma with the evanescent pleasures of frivolous activity and humor (7:15). Commitment, as we are reminded in the opening verse of the chapter, is the wind in the sails that propels us across the ocean of samsara. And, as Śāntideva reminds us in 7:14, that boat is hard to catch.

Throughout the second half of this chapter, in verses such as 7:31–2, 39, and 46, the terms *mos pa* (often used to translate the Sanskrit *adhimokśa*) and *bsam pa* (Sanskrit *chanda*) and their cognates denote the conative state in which commitment issues. These terms are best translated as "aspiration," as opposed to "desire" (*'dod pa*/*kāma*). And the difference is important.[22] The frequent practice of translating *mos pa*, *bsam pa*, and *'dod pa* all as "desire" obscures this important distinction in English translations (see Wallace and Wallace 1997, Crosby and Skilton 2008). The wind in our sails—the motivational force that commitment generates—is *aspirational*, not *desirous*. Desire is always egocentric, as it can always be expressed with an *I want* . . . locution. We desire things that we think will make us happy, or that will give us pleasure. Desire in this sense is always a source of suffering, a species of attraction. Aspiration, though, is *impersonal*, and is better expressed with a *May it be that* . . . locution. It is a recognition of the difference between suffering and the good, between samsara and liberation. While it is conative, it is not egocentric. I am not thematized as the beneficiary, even indirectly.

The point of the moral psychology implicit in this contrast is that conative attitudes can be motivating even when they are not desires, even when my own welfare or personal preference is not at issue. Lack of commitment, or sloth, on this account is just as conative as is commitment. The big difference is that sloth *in this sense* gives rise to desire for the pleasures of an existence unconcerned with others' welfare, and so fails to recognize the reality of suffering, or the nature of true happiness. So, Śāntideva argues that we need a specifically conative state in addition to virtues such as generosity, conscientiousness, patience, and the rest to motivate action. But the state he recommends is not *desire*, but *aspiration*, a state that arises not from *attachment*, but from *commitment*. That is the wind in our sails. Desire would be nothing but an anchor; the boat of our human life might appear to be making progress, but is just circling at the end of the chain that binds us to suffering.

[22] Harris prefers for a tantric reading of Śāntideva's use of desire (2017: 344–5), arguing that Śāntideva advocates using pathological states against pathological states. Despite the virtues of this reading, we do not see a strong tantric orientation to Śāntideva's discussion here because of his clear preference for *aspiration* (*chanda*, *mos pa*) over *desire*.

5. How the gap is bridged

The structure of commitment is tripartite: cognitive reappraisal of the meaning or purpose of one's life, the cultivation of aspiration, and the cultivation of confidence. Cognitive reappraisal is a technique Śāntideva uses throughout the text. In Chapter 6, he argues against anger and defeatism by asking us to rethink agency, replacing a sense of autonomy with an appreciation of radical interdependence. In Chapter 7, Śāntideva asks us to reappraise the fundamental purpose of our life and the identities we habitually inhabit.

By invoking the specter of death and rebirth, he forces the reader to take stock of the meaning of one's life (7:4–14). What is this all *for*? What am I really doing here? "When death is stalking you and when every escape is blocked, how can you enjoy a meal? How can you sleep? How can you make love?" (7:6). Śāntideva is not only trying to whip us into shape with threats of the torturous suffering of the hell realm or the indignities of dying (although he certainly uses this strategy at times, see 7:10–11, 21, 45). He is also introducing a perspective for evaluating our lives here and now. When death comes, we want to have taken our lives seriously. Śāntideva reminds us that that is to take ourselves seriously as moral agents. We do not want to be Ivan Ilyich, wondering on our deathbed whether our life is the real thing.

This cognitive framing trick—evaluating one's life through the lens of one's death—gives us a perspective on what matters. But reframing is not effective by itself. Epiphanies come and go. An effective cognitive reframing requires the skillful targeting of potential obstacles to integrating that new perspective. In everyday life, we constantly confuse trivial goals with important ones (7:15–20). Even if we explicitly reframe our lives as dedicated to the care for others, in the hurly-burly of daily life, we may fail to prioritize what really matters. Like children, we find ourselves confusing what really matters with the satisfaction of momentary desires.

We may ignore reckoning with climate crisis, for example, due to small fears. What if I have to give up my jet-setting lifestyle? What if I have to stop irrigating my yard? What if I have to admit the other side was right? As Śāntideva argues, "although I'm afraid that I might have to give up my hands or feet, because of primal confusion I'm not afraid of failing to distinguish the important from the trivial" (7:20). Commitment requires prioritizing what matters, and this skill is foundational both to understanding what commitment is and to our cultivation of it.

But commitment isn't only about having the right conceptual framework or decision tree; it is entirely possible to fail to be motivated by that conceptual framework. Commitment comprises two conative-affective states: aspiration and confidence (7:31, 39–40):

> One benefits sentient beings through ability, aspiration, persistence, joy, and renunciation. Cultivate aspiration by thinking about how wonderful it is and how terrible suffering is.
>
> Because in the past I lacked aspiration to the Dharma, I'm in terrible trouble now. So how could anyone forsake aspiration to the Dharma?
>
> The Buddha says that aspiration is the root of all virtue, and the root of aspiration is the contemplation of the effects of one's actions.

The only time the Tibetan edition uses *'dod pa* (*ipsu*(*vat*)/desire) in the context of cultivating commitment is by way of analogy (7:62):

> Just like someone drunk with passion, one should be totally immersed in one's actions with an insatiable drive.

Desire and addiction are used here as a provocative and relatable analogy for the depth and *focus* of the commitment one cultivates to the bodhisattva path. But it is only an analogy. The point of the analogy is that the addict is not only *compelled* to take the drugs, but also *confuses* the momentary relief from craving the drug offers for happiness. By doing so, the cycle of suffering that addiction entails is perpetuated. Just as intoxication completely transforms the way we see the world in a *pathological* way, commitment transforms the way we see the world in a *salutary* way. Lest we be misled by the use of this analogy into thinking that desire itself can be virtuous, Śāntideva emphasizes its pathological nature in the following verse (7:64ab):

> Just like honey on a razor's edge, satisfying one's desires brings no satisfaction.

Despite being impersonal, aspiration is not apathetic. On the contrary, it can arise only from caring for others, since it is only that care that releases us from the distortions of self-obsessed deliberation. If I witness a terrible accident, for example, it is important to me that 911 is called. This conviction is not well expressed by "I want to call 911," unless we interpret that as simply a way of saying, "It is important that 911 is called," or "I judge it urgently necessary to call 911." I am not relating to the need to call 911 through an egocentric lens of personal desire. For many of us, deeply conditioned by self-obsessed habits, such clear cases of aspiration may only be obvious in urgent situations like this one. But it is possible, through practice, to expand the scope of our relations to others through aspiration, and to diminish the role of desire in our interpersonal lives.

Because aspiration is non-egocentric, it is not—like desire and anger—pathological. Yet, it still motivates. I am no less motivated to call 911 because I'm not deliberating through the lens of egocentrism; in fact, I may be more motivated to act once I am free from this self-consciousness. This helps us make sense of why Śāntideva says in 7:31 that one only should "cultivate aspiration" as a way to "benefit sentient beings." It also makes sense of his claim that "*aspiration* is the root of all virtue" (7:40).

In addition to aspiration, Śāntideva introduces another non-pathological component of commitment: confidence, which is the remedy for self-defeatism. This section of Chapter 7 (46–61) is tricky, since—unlike his implied distinction between aspiration (*mos pa*) and desire (*'dod pa*)—Śāntideva uses the same word (*māna*/*nga rgyal*) to refer to both pathological *pride* as well as to non-pathological *confidence* (7:53–6, 58–9):

> When you give up because you are discouraged, you'll meet with many obstacles. But if one is buoyed by confidence one can overcome even the greatest ones and become formidable.
>
> Therefore, with resolution, I will triumph over adversity. If I were to let adversity defeat me, my desire to conquer the triple world would be ridiculous.

> I will triumph over everything. Nothing will triumph over me. Since I am the leonine son of the Victors, I will live with confidence.
>
> Anyone who is destroyed by pride really suffers from a pathological lack of confidence. They are controlled by the enemy, pride. No enemy can control a confident person.
>
> [. . .]
>
> The proud are despised everywhere. Inflated by pride, their lives are awful. So, it would be wrong to include them among the confident. What are they really like?
>
> By conquering that enemy, pride, one maintains one's confidence. Such a confident person is an exemplary hero. And one who also absolutely destroys the development of pride has conquered desire for the sake of the world.

In this rhetorically powerful set of verses, Śāntideva is deploying pride in two senses. Indeed, he endorses pride in one of these senses because it releases us from pride in the other. For clarity in English, we will translate pride in its non-pathological sense as "confidence," and use "pride" to translate the pathological variety. Here we follow Gyaltshab (1364–1432) who distinguishes pathological pride (*snyon mongs pa'I nga rgyal*) from virtuous pride (*nga rgyal gyi mchog*) (Gyaltshab 1999: 274). Taking Gyaltshab's distinction seriously, we now turn to an explication of what he calls "virtuous pride" and we call "confidence."

Confidence is the ability to sustain moral effort without over-inflating or under-inflating one's conception of one's own efficacy, and without an egocentric obsession with one's own role. Confidence is to pride as aspiration is to desire: it is distinguished from its pathological cousin in virtue of its being free from egocentric orientation, and in virtue of its being rational as opposed atavistic. Those with confidence do not indulge in self-obsessed evaluations of their own capacities; they do constantly compare themselves to others. They are hence liberated from arrogance, insecurity, and envy.

These three components—cognitive reframing of our priorities, aspiration, and confidence—constitute the structure of commitment. This tripartite structure also shows us how to cultivate commitment, and to troubleshoot failures of commitment. Seeing commitment this way directs us first to reflect on the structure of our priorities, then to develop a non-egoistic determination to achieve our goals, and finally to inhabit the confidence that enables us to do so. This work is necessary for the reflections Śāntideva introduces in Chapter 8 to be successful. Without the foundation provided in Chapter 7, those reflections would be nothing but abstract arguments against egoism. They would not motivate the radical transformation that is Śāntideva's goal, expressed in the eloquent statement, "I am bound to others!" (8:137). Without commitment, even that insight could be but a fleeting thought.

6. Aspiration, desire, and motivation

Michael Smith (1994: 12) identifies what he calls "the moral problem," as a problem about how to account for the motivation to be good. That problem, he suggests, arises out of three apparently mutually inconsistent, but nonetheless all true, theses: (1) moral judgments are claims about matters of fact, viz. that some actions or states of affairs are good, or bad; (2) if someone judges that some action is right or that some state of affairs is good, that is, *ipso facto*, a motivation for performing that action, or for bringing about that state of affairs; and (3) to be motivated to perform an action or to bring about a state of affairs, one must have some instrumental desire that would be satisfied by so doing. The relevant point (Copp 1997: 36–8) is that one might know what a rational person would want to do, but either recognize oneself not to be rational or simply not desire to do what a rational person would do. In either case, that recognition could fail to motivate. One needs another desire, viz. the desire to do what a rational person would do, which is not entailed by any non-conative beliefs.

We think that Śāntideva is alive to this problem, and that this lies behind the need to locate the wind in our moral sails in aspiration grounded in commitment rather than in egocentric desire grounded in preference, and to distinguish desire from aspiration. Śāntideva sees that desire is but one species of conation, and that it is an egocentric species at that. For that reason, acting on desire—even if that is a desire for the good, for liberation, or for the welfare of all sentient beings—binds one to samsara. Even really good honey is always spread on hidden razor blades! Śāntideva's insight is that aspiration can also motivate and, unlike desire, can liberate.

If this is right, the solution to the moral problem lies not in the location of a *desire* to do what is rational or right, but in the rejection of desire in favor of *aspiration*. By articulating both the structure and the role of commitment in Chapter 7, Śāntideva not only illuminates the bodhisattva path but also sheds light on the structure of conation, revealing the possibility of genuinely committed, disinterested moral consciousness. Commitment is the wind in our sails.*

References

Bommarito, N. (2014), "Patience and Perspective," *Philosophy East and West: A Quarterly of Comparative Philosophy* 64 (2): 269–86.

Buddhaghosa (1999), *The Path of Purification* (trans. Bhikkhu Ñāṇamoli), Kandy: Buddhist Publication Society.

Copp, D. (1997), "Belief, Reason, and Motivation: Michael Smith's 'The Moral Problem,'" *Ethics* 108 (1): 33–54.

Crosby, K. and A. Skilton, trans. (2008), *Śāntideva's Bodhicāryāvatāra*, Oxford: Oxford University Press.

Duckworth, D., trans. (2025), *Minyak Kunzang Sönam, The Great Hūṃ: A Commentary on the Way of the Bodhisattva*, Somerville: Wisdom Publications.

Garfield, J. (2017), "Just Another Word for Nothing Left to Lose: Freedom, Agency and Ethics for Mādhyamikas," in R. Repetti (ed.), *Buddhist Perspectives on Free Will and Agency*, 45–58, London: Routledge (repr. from M. Dasti and E. Bryant, eds., *Freedom of the Will in a Cross-Cultural Perspective*, 164–85, New York: Oxford University Press, 2014).

* We thank Amber Carpenter, Stephen Harris, Pierre-Julien Harter, Maria Heim, and Stephen Jenkins for valuable comments on an earlier draft of this chapter.

Garfield, J. (2022), *Buddhist Ethics: A Philosophical Exploration*, New York: Oxford University Press.

Gold, J. (2018). "Heroic Willpower: *Vīrya*," *Journal of Buddhist Ethics* 25: 741–65.

Gold, J. and D. Duckworth, eds. (2019), *Readings of Śāntideva's Guide to Bodhisattva Practice*, New York: Columbia University Press.

Harris, S. (2017), "The Skillful Handling of Poison: Bodhicitta and the Kleśas in Śāntideva's Bodhicaryāvatāra," *Journal of Indian Philosophy* 45 (2): 331–48.

McRae, E. (2012), "Emotions, Ethics, and Choice: Lessons from Tsongkhapa," *Journal of Buddhist Ethics* 19: 344–69.

Saito, A. (1993), *A Study of Akṣayamati (=Śāntideva)'s Bodhisattvacaryāvatāra as Found in the Tibetan Manuscripts from Tun-huang*, Grant-in-Aid for Scientific Research (C), Miye University 1993.

Saito, A. (2006), "Śāntideva's Critique of 'I' or Self in the Early and Later Recensions of the *Bodhi(sattva)caryāvatāra*," *Studies in Indian Philosophy and Buddhism* 13: 35–43.

Śāntideva and rGyal tshab dar ma rin chen (1999), *Byang chub sems pa'i spyod pa la 'jug pa'i rnam bshad rgyal sras 'jug ngogs*, Sarnath: Gelukpa Student Welfare Society.

Schmidt-Leukel, P. (2019), *Buddha Mind – Christ Mind: A Christian Commentary on the Bodhicaryāvatāra*. With a new translation by E. Steinkellner and C. Peck-Kubaczek, Leuven: Peeters.

Smith, M. (1994), *The Moral Problem*, Oxford: Blackwell.

The Cowherds (2015), *Moonpaths: Emptiness and Ethics*, New York: Oxford University Press.

Wallace, V. A. and B. A. Wallace, trans. (1997), *A Guide to the Bodhisattva Way of Life (Bodhicaryāvatāra) by Śāntideva*, Ithaca, NY: Snow Lion.

4

Immanence and Transcendence

Ethical Grounds in Prāsaṅgika and the Great Perfection

Douglas Duckworth

1. Introduction

Buddhist doctrine is distinctive in its denial of a self, and Buddhists typically argue against the identity of an enduring substance, self, or soul. Along with the notion of self, the idea of a creator God is not exempt from critique; it too is frequently denied or incorporated into a system of dependent relations as no more than another node in a network. Buddhists reject God and self as singular, independent agents; as indubitable foundations, the self and God function in parallel, and Buddhist orthodoxies reject typical caricatures of both. In fact, Mādhyamika Buddhists categorically reject the reality of any singular entity. A personal self is said to be simply a designation imputed based upon a collection of aggregates (material form, feeling, consciousness, etc.); there is no special status given to any organism or entity above and beyond its parts. Singular entities thus function as abstractions, for purposes of convenience and/or pragmatic aims, and are held to carry no more than nominal existence (and no less). The lack of reality of any entity (the ultimate truth), paired with nominal existence (the relative truth), is a hallmark of the Madhyamaka or "middle way" Buddhist philosophy and is articulated in the doctrine of emptiness or interrelation, in which all things without exception lack intrinsic nature (*svabhāva*).

Prāsaṅgika-Madhyamaka is commonly held to be the highest interpretation of Madhyamaka by many Buddhist traditions in Tibet. Prāsaṅgika is a philosophy that draws upon Candrakīrti's seventh-century interpretation of Nāgārjuna and gets its name from a distinctive *reductio*-style of argument (*prasaṅga*) when articulating the nature of emptiness. Resembling the way that Pyrrhonean skepticism is opposed to Academic skepticism, Prāsaṅgika contrasts with Svātantrika-Madhyamaka, a system of thought that makes arguments to prove emptiness and defends probative arguments about the nature of this truth (The Cowherds 2011: 121–9). Prāsaṅgika is different and exemplifies the radical nature of emptiness. It does so in a performative way that collapses the presuppositions of fixed claims tied to a rigid duality of two separate truths. The eighth-century Indian monk, Śāntideva, comes to be associated with a Prāsaṅgika-Madhyamaka interpretation in Tibet, where the ethical foundation he articulates in the *Bodhicaryāvatāra* is seen to align with Candrakīrti's philosophy of emptiness in the *Madhyamakāvatāra*.

Tsongkhapa (1357–1419) described Śāntideva and Candrakīrti together as proponents of a distinctive Prāsaṅgika view (Tsongkhapa 1998: 476–7), where the truth of emptiness is characterized by a denial of any transcendent foundations to ground even conventional truth-claims: there is no appeal to irreducible elements (*dharmas*) of dependent arising, ineffable particulars (*svalakṣaṇas*), or an underlying mind (*ālayavijñāna*) as the real substance of the conventional world. This unique characteristic of Prāsaṅgika—not appealing to a transcendent principle—without careful framing can tend toward moral nihilism. This is where Śāntideva's *Bodhicaryāvatāra*, read alongside Candrakīriti's *Madhyamakāvatāra*, can serve as a corrective to nihilistic interpretations of Madhyamaka. This chapter will show how Śāntideva can be read fruitfully with Candrakīrti to offer a robust account of Buddhist ethics without appealing to any transcendent principle.

The appeal to immanence as a foundation for ethics, rather than transcendence, also speaks to modern, naturalistic sensibilities. Yet Candrakīrti and Śāntideva, as Buddhists, also appeal to transcendence. I wish to explore this role of transcendence by drawing upon a Nyingma tantric tradition to show how Prāsaṅgika-Madhyamaka is positioned in relation to the hallmark of this tradition, the Great Perfection (*rdzogs chen*). I will conclude by presenting a way to understand Prāsaṅgika and the Great Perfection as not only compatible, but as mutually illuminating.

2. Groundlessness: The ultimate truth of Candrakīrti

As is well known, in Madhyamaka in general there are two truths: the ultimate truth of emptiness and the conventional truth. There are many different interpretations of Madhyamaka, but the ultimate truth is always understood as emptiness, so it may seem that it doesn't matter much how the conventional truth is understood. That is, sometimes the ultimate truth of emptiness is contrasted with a conventional truth that is understood as atomistic, in accord with the Vaibhāṣikas, such that the world of appearance is held to be best captured in a description of fundamental particles and moments of consciousness, the building blocks of experience. Other interpretations of Madhyamaka might follow a Sautrāntika epistemology when describing the conventional world of appearances and give a pragmatic criterion for truth. In such cases, in contrast to the ultimate truth of emptiness, what counts as conventional reality is efficacious, which is understood to be ineffable particulars rather than extended objects that are distributed in time and space.

Another way that the appearing world of conventional truth might be described in Madhyamaka is as "mind only" since the world is shaped by the mind and its habitual tendencies. While the nature of mind is held to be ultimately empty, the appearing world might be said to be reducible to mind according to this kind of interpretation.

In contrast, in what is a uniquely Prāsaṅgika-Madhyamaka interpretation, nothing is offered to ground phenomena, *even conventionally.* Neither particles nor particulars nor the mind grounds the world; nothing does. In fact, to presume that there is a ground is to fail to understand the ultimate truth of emptiness. This is because, according to Tsongkhapa's influential interpretation of Prāsaṅgika, without realizing that there is nothing to ground phenomena conventionally, one has failed to realize the ultimate truth of emptiness as well. This is because how the conventional is understood is as important as how the ultimate truth is understood; in Tsongkhapa's interpretation of Madhyamaka, the two truths amount to the same thing (Tsongkhapa 1998: 554). This is why, even while the ultimate truth may be explicitly agreed upon as emptiness, it matters how the conventional truth is understood.

While one may *explicitly* claim that the ultimate truth is emptiness, and that the conventional world is reducible to mind only, to atomism, or to anything else, in fact, in doing this reduction one is *implicitly* committed to the metaphysical presuppositions of those grounds, as well as the idea that the appearing world needs a ground or substance, without which it could not function. This, however, is none other than a remnant of realism, and thus is part of the problem of ignorance and reification that holds *saṃsāra* and suffering in place.

The reason why one cannot maintain that ultimately things are empty while conventionally they are grounded in some other, more fundamental substance, like particles or mind, is because the two truths are not really different. The lack of any ground, substance, or essence in anything is the emptiness of that thing; there is no need for a separate substance that serves as a ground that is more real than anything else. Without a hierarchy of one thing being more real than any other, even conventionally, there is only empty appearances, or appearing emptiness, without the slightest separation. When this is not fully understood, emptiness has not been fully understood. It is for this reason that in a Madhyamaka interpretation following Tsongkhapa, there is no liberation outside of a Prāsaṅgika understanding of emptiness: because liberation takes place only through a correct view of reality. This is not necessarily limited to solely a Gelukpa interpretation, for in the Nyingma tradition as well, Mipam claimed that one must perfect the view of Prāsaṅgika to conclusively settle upon primordial purity (Mipam 1997: 19; Duckworth 2008: 74), which is an important feature of this tradition's Great Perfection view.

While a quasi-metaphysical ground of conventional truth may be the extreme of realism, a subtle object of negation that is uniquely overcome in Prāsaṅgika, the other extreme is that of nihilism. A nihilistic view can take shape when the conventional truth is disparaged or otherwise simply rendered in terms of consensus or "what is renowned in the world," without a means to make meaningful distinctions. Denying an independent ground for truth, even conventionally, may be thought to entail just this kind of pernicious relativism with no criterion whatsoever for determining what is right and wrong, or what is true or false. Without any bedrock foundation to ground the conventional truth other than conventions themselves, it might be tempting to lean on simply consensus to describe the world, but consensus on its own simply supports the status quo; such an unreflective, conservative stance cannot be the final arbiter of Buddhist truth. For instance, things like the permanence of the self and the purity of impure things are worldly consensus, yet are rejected by Buddhists like Śāntideva (BCA 9:6). Thus, in order to avoid what Tom Tillemans dubbed the "dismal slough" of conservative consensus and pernicious relativism (The Cowherds 2011), there must be a means to make distinctions within conventional truth and thereby reform it, without which it would be impossible to get any change off the ground, whether it is a scientific revolution, a social revolution, or a revolution on the scale of a liberating personal transformation. This is where Śāntideva steps in, to provide Prāsaṅgika with a means to posit an ethical framework based solely in convention, without a transcendent metaphysical foundation (even while Śāntideva's message is not limited to an immanent-centered interpretation that excludes what is transcendent).

3. Compassion: The conventional truth of Śāntideva

In Tibet, Śāntideva is paired with Candrakīrti as a Prāsaṅgika-Madhyamaka. In a significant way, this pairing provides a means to build an ethics into Candrakīrti's radical philosophy without metaphysical foundations, even conventionally. While Candrakīrti opens his magnum opus, the *Madhyamakāvatāra*, with a praise to compassion (MA 1:2), the bulk of this text elaborates the nature of wisdom rather than compassion. Śāntideva fills out this picture by connecting the dots between conventional ethics and ultimate wisdom.

In the *Bodhicaryāvatāra*, Śāntideva lays the foundation for the ability to ground ethics in a naturalistic world without appealing to what is transcendent. He does so by building a Mahāyāna ethics out from the fact that no one wants to suffer and everyone wants to be happy. Of course, we all may have different ideas of what constitutes "happiness" and ways we think we can achieve it, but sometimes—or rather most of the time—those means and goals are misguided: a child may think happiness lies in cotton candy, a teenager may think happiness equals popularity, an older person may seek happiness in wealth, a partner, and so on—but each of these things is insufficient for a Buddhist; they are impermanent and tied into structures that perpetuate suffering. The only true happiness for a Buddhist is liberation, and for the Mahāyāna Buddhist, true happiness is not just liberation that is individualized and personal, but one that is universal in scope and inclusive of all beings.

The wish to achieve this kind of complete liberation for all beings is *bodhicitta*, the "spirit of awakening," and Śāntideva develops an ethic of *bodhicitta* grounded on equalizing and then exchanging oneself and others. By drawing upon the fact that just as I want to be happy and to avoid suffering, so does everyone else, he builds an altruistic ethics. He deconstructs the assumption of an independent, bounded self to show the irrationality of a self-centered perspective, exposing the fact that there is no reasonable justification for self-centeredness (BCA 8:91–103). By appealing to the universality of the pursuit of happiness, Śāntideva shifts the burden to the one who justifies egocentric behavior. He does not just offer a probative argument or an abstract logical proof to make his case for altruism, but grounds his logic in human experience to reveal that there is no logic that supports the egoist's independent pursuit (Garfield, Jenkins, and Priest 2015).

Challenging the unquestioned assumption of self-preservation at all costs, Śāntideva asks: if things that are different do not need to show concern for that which is other, why does the hand move to dispel the pain in the foot (BCA 8:91)? He extends this argument to show that the boundaries between self and other are arbitrary, and that suffering should be dispelled because it is suffering, no matter where it occurs (BCA 8:94–102). Simply because you do not feel the suffering of another now does not mean that it is unrelated to you: after all, you do not feel the suffering of a future toothache, so why do you brush your teeth now (BCA 8:97; Siderits 2007: 81)? In this way, Śāntideva makes a case for equality:

> I should eliminate the suffering of others
> Because it is suffering, like my own suffering.
> I should benefit others
> Because they are sentient beings, like myself.
> When both myself and others
> Equally want happiness,
> What is exceptional about me,
> Such that I strive for my happiness alone?
> When both myself and others
> Equally do not want to suffer,
> What is exceptional about me,
> Such that I protect myself but not others?
>
> BCA 8:94–6

Śāntideva's ethics extend the range of concern beyond the individual to everyone based on the natural fact that no one wants to suffer and that everybody wants to be happy. Given this immanent truth, it is arbitrary to privilege any one particular individual's interest. The arguments he puts forward, which often take the form of *reductio*s, deconstruct the logic of egoism that presume the reality of a discrete individual or an enduring "self" that could serve to justify egocentrism. Śāntideva's approach is rooted in the logic of interconnectivity at the heart of existence, and he draws upon this logic to undermine the presumption of a singular, independent, and permanent self.

4. Timeless gnosis: The ground of the Great Perfection

Śāntideva's process of equalizing self and other comes to be described as a means to cultivate relative *bodhicitta* in contrast to ultimate *bodhicitta*. Ultimate *bodhicitta* is knowing the nature of things (Minyak Kunzang Sönam 2025: 33–5), while relative *bodhicitta* can be understood as the means by which this comes to be known. This twofold distinction relates to two approaches to Buddhist truth, and another iteration of the "middle way": from the "top-down" (starting from the ultimate, as we see in the Great Perfection) and from the "bottom-up" (as articulated in the first eight chapters of Śāntideva's *Bodhicaryāvatāra*), even while both approaches can be inextricably intertwined.

Ultimate *bodhicitta* is the realization of the unconditioned nature of reality. Meditative practices that disclose a pure nature at the ground of being, unveiled after the obscurations that cloud it are removed, can be said to directly engage a top-down approach based on the view that the qualities of awakening are already here, yet lie beyond an ordinary being's benighted comprehension. A bottom-up approach, in contrast, involves directed training and discipline, like we see in Śāntideva's arguments and contemplative practices of mind-training. Unlike a top-down approach, this is not about "going with the flow" or simply letting the innate qualities of mind express themselves. Rather, the bottom-up approach is better described as "breaking the cycle" of suffering. This technique involves restraint and discipline to train the mind by turning it away from habitual, destructive patterns to shape it into skillful responses and expressions.

In contrast to contemplative exercises that train and condition the mind to be altruistic and ethical, contemplative exercises in the Great Perfection involve a process of *deconditioning*, as ultimate *bodhicitta* is cultivated by an appeal to the natural state, the nature of mind that is nothing other than the natural buddha. Allowing this nature to express itself—unfiltered and uninflected by bad habits of self-centeredness, and the desires and aggressions that this selfishness spawns—is a way to allow the natural qualities of compassion and wisdom to shine forth. These innate qualities of mind shine when we "get out of the way," so to speak, and remove the defilements and hindrances that obscure the light of wisdom and love, in the way that the sun comes out when the clouds disperse (Duckworth 2008: 18–19, 102–4).

With this kind of appeal to a natural buddha there is a shift—a tantric distinction—that undermines not only a temporal path to achieve a future goal but also the place and justification of ethics. While Śāntideva articulates the *conventional* dimension of *bodhicitta* as a dependently arisen development—a conditioned product of rewiring the mind to be more compassionate, from the bottom-up—the *ultimate* compassionate resonance of emptiness and luminosity in the Great Perfection is unconditioned, the feature of a top-down model that turns the process of transformation on its head, such that there is nothing to add or remove with the natural buddha. The primordiality or timelessness of the buddha's unconditioned gnosis, or ultimate *bodhicitta*, reconfigures the role of temporality in a Buddhist interpretation. Since awakening is the nature of being, suffering and even the path to end it are fundamentally illusions. So, rather than grounding ethics solely in a contingent, immanent world, tantric traditions like the Great Perfection derive ethics from a transcendent source, or otherwise can be said to be trans-ethical, which puts them in tension with a naturalistic framework of emptiness and interdependence that is the metaphysical basis of ethics in a uniquely Prāsaṅgika-Madhyamaka framework.

5. Transcendence and Immanence

After he begins his famous ninth chapter of the *Bodhicaryāvatāra* with the claim that the purpose of all the preceding aspects was for wisdom, Śāntideva defines the ultimate as what is beyond the range of mind (BCA 9:2), a description that has sparked a lot of discussion and debate. With this characterization, he leaves open the door to an interpretation of a transcendent ultimate, a realm of gnosis beyond the domain of mind. A debate in Tibet ensues around the import of this verse, and how the nature of wisdom and the ultimate truth is to be understood (Mipham 2017). This debate can be broadly construed to follow two lines of interpretation: those who maintain wisdom's immanence and the knowability of the ultimate truth (Tsongkhapa's interpretation)[1] and those who appeal to wisdom's transcendence and to an ultimate truth that is inconceivable. While the former interpretation lends itself to a naturalistic explanation, the latter interpretation allows space for transcendence.

Another pivotal verse in Chapter 9 marks the place where Śāntideva, according to the legend of his original delivery of this text, ascended into the sky and disappeared when he recited it (BCA 9:34). The text continues after this verse to claim that a buddha's activity functions automatically, through the power of a buddha's previous aspirations (BCA 9:35–7). This kind of activity in the world, that of a buddha that acts in the world with purpose yet without deliberate intention, is *sui generis*, as intentional actions are bound up within karma, ignorance, and suffering.

A parallel passage in Candrakīrti's *Madhyamakāvatāra* explains the buddha's activity to take place effortlessly due to the power of previous aspirations made when a bodhisattva. He says that a buddha's activity continues, like a wheel set in motion by a "strong potter," without effort once set in motion (MA 11:15–16). While it might be unfair to claim that Candrakīrti's example of the potter effectively plays the role of an "unmoved mover," his example exposes the fact that, despite modern interpretations of Buddhism that support a naturalistic (Garfield 2022) or distinctively secular ethics (Dalai Lama 1999), Śāntideva and Candrakīrti make explicit appeals to a transcendent reality in the past and future. While this is not surprising given that they are traditional Buddhist authors, it does invite theological questions like: Does a buddha have a beginning, but no end? Or, like *saṃsāra*, does a buddha have an end, but no beginning?

In the next verse of his *Madhyamakāvatāra*, Candrakīrti says that in the wake of a buddha's awakening "the mind ceases" (MA 11:17), as the mind is tied to intention, karma, and suffering. There are different interpretations of what the cessation of mind really means: is it just the conceptual mind (as opposed to non-conceptual gnosis) that ceases, or is it any and every cognition? A beginning may entail an end, but if there is no beginning, does that also entail that there is no end? The answers to eschatological questions about ends, like those about beginnings, are based in a transcendent domain, and not only bookend a tradition's ethos (with a narrative opening and closure), but also shape the way that the story of the immanent world unfolds.

The tradition of the Great Perfection is unique in the Buddhist world with its narrative of an origin of *saṃsāra*. The origin narrative, contrasting the primordial Buddha Samantabhadra's self-recognition with sentient beings' primordial confusion, is integrally bound to the end of the story—that of the buddha—that is, what the world is like when delusion comes to end. To make sense of the buddha in this tradition, the story of the beginning is as important as the story of the end, and self-existing gnosis (*ye shes*) plays the lead role in this narrative as the agent of creation. Yet the agent here, "the all-creating king" (*kun byed rgyal po*) is certainly not that of a creator God, at least

[1] See, for instance, Tsongkhapa's student Gyeltsapjé's commentary on this verse (Gyeltsapjé 2001: 348–51).

in the sense of a disembodied agent detached from the created world. That is, there is no ontological rift in gnosis between "the three spheres" (*trimaṇḍala*) of creator, creation, and creativity.

In the narrative framework of the Great Perfection, we find not only a beginning, but also an end, in the last of four climactic visions (*snang ba bzhi*), "the cessation of basic nature" (*chos nyid zad pa*) (Longchenpa 1975, vol. 2: 1484).[2] This may be where the curtains close to life with an end to the cosmos, despite most Buddhist traditions describing the universe (of *saṃsāra*) as without beginning—infinite—and thus without end. Yet at least to the extent that there is an origin, there will be a cessation (as the Buddhist "four noble truths" reiterate). The end to life (to a life of suffering at least) is nirvana. Yet for Buddhists, a notion of life is not contrasted with death. Rather, it is *birth* that is the counterpart of death. As long as there is birth, there is death, so in the Great Perfection the notion of *life* may correspond best to the timeless display of gnosis or "buddha" that constitutes not only a potential reality but also the source and substance of the cosmos.

The assertion of the reality of a primordial buddha is not only an article of faith in the Great Perfection, but is a first philosophy in both the ontological and epistemological senses because the buddha's gnosis is both the starting point and the means by which this starting point is understood. Gnosis plays the role of a transcendent foundation, and we can see a parallel here to the appeal to God in theological traditions. We can also extend this parallel to a "scientific" appeal to a primal state of unordered matter and the hypothesis that life emerges from lifeless material. For Buddhists in general, the metaphysical presupposition is not an appeal to the transcendent reality of a creator God or to matter, but rather to karma, which is beginningless. In the Great Perfection, however, the driving force of creation in the cosmos is gnosis, which is the transcendent condition rather than simply karma.

If it is the case that some sort of presupposition or appeal (implicitly or explicitly) to a transcendent ground is unavoidable, even in a naturalistic explanation of the origin of life, we may wonder if a Prāsaṅgika account that aims to avoid any appeal to a transcendent ground could ever succeed on its own, particularly to avoid the "dismal slough" of pernicious relativism. Indeed, there is a debate about whether Tsongkhapa is successful in coherently maintaining Prāsaṅgika as a totalizing system (without appealing to non-Prāsaṅgika systems to account for conventional truth), or whether he must lean on a realist ontological framework to get a coherent epistemology off the ground.[3] In any case, the Prāsaṅgika commitment to deny any transcendent ground is in tension with the Buddhist commitment to the reality of the buddha.

The literature of the Great Perfection, on the other hand, makes explicit claims to a transcendent ground. Yet these claims are also in tension with mainstream Buddhist commitments, in addition to being in tension with the anti-metaphysical character of Prāsaṅgika-Madhyamaka. That is, Buddhist texts frequently reject transcendent

[2] Longchenpa correlates the four visions with the fourfold formation, abiding, destruction, and emptiness of an eon. He also associates the four visions with four life-stages: birth, aging, sickness, and death.

[3] This issue animates the debate studied in *Knowing Illusion* (The Yakherds 2021).

entities as well as origin narratives, which are often dismissed as impotent, metaphysical speculations that distract and deter from pragmatic action (e.g., "the parable of the arrow" in the *Cūḷamālunkya Sutta*, where the Buddha makes the analogy of someone who insists on such speculation to someone who has been shot by an arrow and refuses to take the arrow out until a complete causal story is in place to account for the origin of each of the feathers of the arrow, the wood of the bow, the caste of the shooter, etc.). Further, all things are said to be "nonarising" in Mahāyāna Buddhism; to the extent that there is a Buddhist discussion of origin, it tends to be denied. Nevertheless, we can recognize a Buddhist's foundational presupposition not simply in reference to a *telos* culminating in the buddha's final awakening, but also in the appeal to a "beginningless beginning" as well. Indeed, the idea of a beginningless succession of buddhas is found across historical Buddhist traditions: it is present in Theravāda Buddhism, explicated in Mahāyāna, and developed in tantric forms of Buddhism with the notion of the "original buddha" (*ādibuddha*). Śāntideva as well attributes the rare occurrence of a meritorious mind, which he compares to a flash of lightning in the darkness of night, to the power of the buddha (BCA 1:5). Does the claim to an *original* buddha mark that much of a difference in the transcendent appeal?

In any case, the assertion of the primordiality or timelessness of the buddha's gnosis demonstrates a different relation to *temporality*. In an important way, affirming the illusory status of time is an extension of the logic of Mahāyāna: for if differences between beings in space is an illusion, as Śāntideva suggests, is this not also the case with beings in time? Is it not the case that temporality, too, along with the path, is an illusion? After all, according to Śāntideva, the world is grounded in illusion, and even buddhas are like illusions (BCA 9:9–10). The implications of the illusory nature of time are made explicit with the status of the buddha in Nyingma tantra and the Great Perfection in particular.

Notably, we can see how appeals to transcendence to ground ethical norms in the Great Perfection contrast with Śāntideva's naturalistic rationale for altruism that comes to characterize a unique feature of Prāsaṅgika-Madhyamaka. The justification of ethics in the Great Perfection stems not only from within the illusory nature of empty appearances in an immanent world, but also from the divine nature of transcendent wisdom. This appeal to transcendence ties ethics into a positive foundation that not only supplants a naturalistic ethic, but transcends it. This reflects a shift in the causal story of the origin of the world: from an impure to a pure source. That is, the source of the world, along with the justification for compassionate action, shifts from one that arises from a matrix of mundane pain and delusion to one based on transcendent wisdom and love—in the tripartite ground of the Great Perfection: the empty essence (*ngo bo stong pa*), luminous nature (*rang bzhin gsal ba*), and all-encompassing compassionate resonance (*thugs rjes kun khyab*), which is the ground that enables a buddha's compassionate activity.[4]

[4] The movement from immanence to transcendence parallels the process of development of a key feature in the story of the life of Śāntideva himself. The earliest extant source, which is a Tibetan translation of Vibhūticandra's account, simply states that Śāntideva was one who *meditates while he eats and sleeps*, as a practitioner grounded in the immanent world. Later Tibetan elaborations of his life, however, came to associate him with transcendence as a *bhusuku* who, while seemingly only "eating, sleeping, and shitting," was in reality doing something else, otherworldly (Liland 2009: 15–16).

The feature of transcendence in the Great Perfection contrasts starkly with Prāsaṅgika-Madhyamaka, at least an interpretation of Prāsaṅgika-Madhyamaka that, like one inspired by Tsongkhapa, is framed as a unique and complete metaphysical system (that is not reliant on non-Prāsaṅgika descriptions of conventional truth). The reason for this is that emptiness and interdependence alone serve as the basis for this kind of uniquely Prāsaṅgika ethics *precisely because there is no transcendent principle or ground*, even while the unconditioned reality of a buddha tends to be sidelined to provide a naturalistic account of conventional truth in a benighted world. Ethics in tantric traditions like the Great Perfection, in contrast, are characterized by explicit appeals to a transcendent source "beyond good and evil," yet along with this appeal, ethics tends to be instrumentalized in service of this transcendence since ethics itself (at least ethics tied to duality) is ultimately to be transcended. We will consider the synthesis of these two systems in the conclusion.

6. Conclusion

It is in the immanence of conventional truth, in the collapse of ultimate foundations, where Śāntideva recovers ethics in Candrakīrti's radical emptiness. Building upon the innate wish to be happy, he demonstrates a way to justify an altruistic ethics without appealing to transcendence. In this framework, virtue is not tethered to a transcendent world but is anchored to dependent arising and delusion: the matrix of suffering and the fundamental wish to be free of it. With the Great Perfection, in contrast, a transcendent source is explicitly evoked that grounds ethics.

In contrast to an ethics built solely upon the empty foundation of interdependence—as the conventional reality of suffering and the pursuit of happiness shared by all beings—the Great Perfection grounds the world in the nature of the buddha, in a positive ground of being. Can this kind of appeal be compatible with Prāsaṅgika-Madhyamaka's radical denials? This is a question that faces the Nyingma tradition, where we see traditions emerge that either maintained a clear boundary between the exoteric system of Madhyamaka and the esoteric system of tantra, or they brought them together in a creative synthesis.[5]

The contrast between (1) the bottom-up methods of mind-training and conventional logic drawn from Śāntideva, and (2) the top-down logic of the non-conceptual, "unbounded wholeness" of the Great Perfection, comes into clear focus in the nineteenth century in eastern Tibet with the rise of monastic education in the Nyingma tradition, which was historically a yogic and tantric tradition. The different ways these traditions negotiated the boundaries of this contrast shaped the configurations of their institutions, as we see in alternative Nyingma interpretations of Madhyamaka and responses to issues such as: whether or not Prāsaṅgika has a place at all in the Nyingma tradition (that was traditionally defined by tantra), whether or not Prāsaṅgika is to be

[5] Mipam represents the creative synthesis, and even said that the Great Perfection and Madhyamaka were synonymous: "The great middle way free from constructs and the luminous Great Perfection are synonyms with the same meaning; there is no view higher than this" (Mipam 1997: 50).

relegated to exclusively an exoteric (non-tantric) domain for the Nyingma, and whether or not Prāsaṅgika indeed is an essential component of a tantric view.

The contrast between these two approaches, which mirrors the bottom-up versus top-down versions of the path, is not missed by traditions that draw a clear line between Madhyamaka as an exoteric philosophy and tantra as an esoteric practice. In fact, several Nyingma monastic traditions, including scholars at Katok Monastery, for instance, depict the Great Perfection as aligned with a transcendent "other-emptiness" (*gzhan stong*) interpretation of Madhayamaka, in step with the Jonang, and thus beyond the purview of Prāsaṅgika (Duckworth 2008: 50, 224–5 n.87). Other Nyingma institutions, in contrast, situated an interpretation of Prāsaṅgika following Tsongkhapa within the context of exoteric sutra study, while maintaining a distinctively Nyingma tantric curriculum (Duckworth 2008: xxii). The Nyingma monastic traditions associated with Dzokchen Monastery, however, rendered a creative synthesis of the Great Perfection with Prāsaṅgika-Madhyamaka by representing Prāsaṅgika not as a complete ethical and metaphysical system, but *as an essential yet necessarily incomplete aspect of truth*.

While Tsongkhapa used Prāsaṅgika-Madhyamaka as a meta-framework to support an integrated metaphysics and ethics, in the Nyingma tradition at Dzokchen Monastery, it is the Great Perfection that provides this meta-framework, within which Prāsaṅgika plays an essential part but not the lead role. In notable contrast to a depiction of Prāsaṅgika as a complete system, its features of performativity and incompleteness in this Nyingma synthesis allow for Prāsaṅgika to hold a central place in Buddhist theory while also enabling its constitutive dependence on *non-Prāsaṅgika* claims to render fundamental elements of a Buddhist worldview, including metaphysics and ethics. In contrast to the move to naturalize ethics by grounding ethics in the conventional world in an exclusively Prāsaṅgika system, this synthesis makes room for transcendence while also accommodating the preeminence of a Prāsaṅgika view.

That is, Prāsaṅgika in the Dzokchen synthesis is situated within the unity of the Great Perfection view to convey solely the *empty aspect of primordial purity* (*ka dag*), which is supplemented by the *appearing aspect of spontaneous presence* (*lhun grub*), from which it is inseparable. This view, in consideration of the role Prāsaṅgika plays in tantra, is not necessarily different for Tsongkhapa, for whom the appearing aspect (the subjective dimension of wisdom), not the empty aspect (the objective dimension), marks the difference in how the nature of reality is understand in tantra (Jinpa 2019: 269–71). The interpretation here preserves the indispensable place of a Prāsaṅgika view yet weds it with tantra as it is subsumed within the theory and practice of the Great Perfection. At the same time, this interpretation moves the metaphysical basis of ethics away from the immanent world to a transcendent truth, and thereby shifts the justification for ethics—from the natural expression of no-self (in a uniquely Prāsaṅgika interpretation) to the divine expression of a unified ground of being.

Both Śāntideva's *Bodhicaryāvatāra* and the Great Perfection played an important part in the curriculum of the monastic college at Dzokchen Monastery. With the integration of the bottom-up *logos* of Madhyamaka into the top-down *ethos* of the Great Perfection, the synthesis that Tsongkhapa initiated with his wedding of Candrakīrti and Śāntideva is extended to include a tantric tradition, as the metaphysical basis of ethics (in emptiness) is wed to the ground of the Great Perfection, which is the timeless and transcendent gnosis of the buddha. Here we see that the *Bodhicaryāvatāra* is interpreted not only as a supplement to Candrakīrti—by explicating an immanent ethical framework for Prāsaṅgika-Madhyamaka—but also comes to support a transcendent ground of Buddhist ethics. The interplay and synthesis of these two dimensions—immanence and transcendence—reiterates the view of the middle way.

The middle way is subtle, and when you fall to one extreme, you fall to both. That is to say, the potential shortcomings of Prāsaṅgika, in the "dismal slough," is the tendency toward both realism (in stabilizing the status quo of the conventional truth of the ordinary) and toward nihilism (in denying all foundations). This can be complemented by the Great Perfection's rejection of the default mode of being as being an ordinary, impure world and by its full-throated embrace of reality as the buddha. On the other hand, the Great Perfection carries the potential shortcoming of being misconceived as yet another "pie in the sky," tending toward the instrumentalization of ethics (nihilism) in service of transcendence (essentialism), which embeds a false temporal hierarchy. This can be complemented by Prāsaṅgika's centering of the immanent, human world in its refusal to appeal to some other transcendent reality, one that is inevitably deferred to another place or another time—always and forever in a remote place and distant future.

Both Prāsaṅgika and the Great Perfection are about immediacy, the here and now, when and where the two truths are never really separate. As an integrated vision where there is not only no separation of two truths, but no separation of two times (that of being a sentient being and being a buddha), the two truths are united in a complementary way in the unity of Prāsaṅgika and the Great Perfection. That is to say, both can be seen to share a common ground; as in both traditions, and in their union, there is no real division of two truths nor is there a real temporal structure. Further, these two traditions can also be seen to share the feature of both beginning and ending with ethics in different yet complementary ways: Prāsaṅgika represents a path from the bottom-up, from a foundation in ethics in discipline, to meditation, to wisdom—the three trainings—where wisdom expresses itself in ethical action rather than in a vision that leaves ethics behind. While the Great Perfection draws upon what we may call a path that is top-down, starting from the view of the primordial buddha, in another triad—that of view, meditation, and action that enacts this reality—and like Prāsaṅgika, the source and expression of ethics in the Great Perfection can be seen in the reciprocity of the two truths, and in the unity of the ground and fruition. Thus, Śāntideva's *Bodhicaryāvatāra*, in Tibet and beyond, continues to inspire competing and complementary interpretations of the middle way that express both of these dimensions, the immanent and the transcendent—and their unity—from the bottom-up as well as from the top-down.

References

Cūḷamālunkya Sutta (1995), translated by Bhikkhu Ñāṇamoli and Bhikkhu Bodhi in *The Middle Length Discourses of the Buddha*, 533–6, Boston: Wisdom Publications.

Candrakīrti (1977), *Introduction to the Middle Way* (*Madhyamakāvatāra, dbu ma la 'jug pa*), no. 3861, in *sde dge mtshal par bka' 'gyur: a facsimile edition of the 18th century redaction of Situ chos kyi 'byung gnas prepared under the direction of H.H. the 16th rgyal dbang karma pa*, Delhi: Delhi Karmapae Chodhey Gyalwae Sungrab Partun Khang.
The Cowherds (2011), *Moonshadows: Conventional Truth in Buddhist Philosophy*, New York: Oxford University Press.
The Dalai Lama (1999), *Ethics for a New Millennium*, New York: Riverhead Books.
Duckworth, D. (2008), *Mipam on Buddha-Nature: The Ground of the Nyingma Tradition*, Albany: SUNY Press.
Garfield, J. (2022), *Buddhist Ethics*, New York: Oxford University Press.
Garfield, J., S. Jenkins, and G. Priest (2015), "The Śāntideva Passage: *Bodhicaryāvatāra* VIII.90–103," in The Cowherds, *Moonpaths: Ethics and Emptiness*, 68–74, New York: Oxford University Press.
Gyeltsapjé (*rgyal tshab rje, dar ma rin chen*, 1364–1432) (2001), *Gateway to the Bodhisattvas* (*byang chub sems dpa'i spyod pa la 'jug pa'i rnam bshad rgyal sras 'jug ngogs*), in *spyod 'jug rtsa 'grel*, 100–454, Xining: Qinghai Nationalities Press.
Jinpa, T. (2019), *Tsongkhapa: A Buddha in the Land of Snows*, Boulder, CO: Shambhala Publications.
Liland, F. (2009), *The Transmission of the Bodhicaryāvatāra: The History, Diffusion, and Influence of a Mahāyāna Buddhist Text*, MA Thesis, University of Oslo.
Longchenpa (*klong chen rab 'byams*, 1308–64) (1975), *Treasury of the Supreme Vehicle* (*theg pa'i mchog rin po che'i mdzod*), vols. 1–2, reproduced from *a 'dzom* xylographic edition, Paro: Ngodup.
Minyak Kunzang Sönam (*thub bstan chos kyi grags pa*, 1823–1905) (2025), *The Great Hūṃ: A Commentary on the Way of the Bodhisattva*, translated by Douglas Duckworth, Boston: Wisdom Publications.
Mipam (*'ju mi pham rgya mtsho*, 1846–1912) (1997), *Beacon of Certainty (nges shes sgron me)*, published in *nges shes sgron me rtsa 'grel*, 1–54, Sichuan: Nationalities Press.
Mipham, J. (2017), *The Wisdom Chapter: Jamgön Mipam's Commentary on the Ninth Chapter of the Way of the Bodhisattva*, Boulder, CO: Shambala Publications.
Śāntideva (1977), *Way of the Bodhisattva* (*Bodhicaryāvatāra, byang chub sems dpa'i spyod pa la 'jug pa*), no. 3871, in *sde dge mtshal par bka' 'gyur: a facsimile edition of the 18th century redaction of Situ chos kyi 'byung gnas prepared under the direction of H.H. the 16th rgyal dbang karma pa*, Delhi: Delhi Karmapae Chodhey Gyalwae Sungrab Partun Khang.
Siderits, M. (2007), *Buddhism as Philosophy*, Indianapolis: Hackett Publishing.
Tsongkhapa (*tsong kha pa blo bzang grags pa*, 1357–1419) (1998), *Illuminating the Viewpoint* (*dgongs pa rab gsal*). *Tsongkhapa's Collected Works*, vol. 16, 443–751, Xining, China.
The Yakherds (2021), *Knowing Illusion*, vols. 1–2, New York: Oxford University Press.

II

Social Dynamics

5

Śāntideva's Idea of the Yogic and Non-Yogic Worlds

Its Implications and Possible Antecedents

Dorji Wangchuk

For fear of distortion and misrepresentation of the state of affairs, I dare not say much concerning the status and role of Śāntideva's *Bodhicaryāvatāra* in the past and the present. I do, however, wish to state at least one thing in this regard. rDza-dpal-sprul O-rgyan-'jigs-med-chos-kyi-dbang-po (1808–87), a nineteenth-century East Tibetan Buddhist scholar and *yogin*, who himself has been eulogized by some, so to speak, as the Śāntideva of Tibet,[1] wrote that there is no treatise like the *Bodhicaryāvatāra*, neither in India nor in Tibet, and that it is indispensable for someone who wishes to attain Buddhahood.[2] Indeed, over the centuries and until the present day, the *Bodhicaryāvatāra* has not ceased to serve as one of the most important sources of inspiration and Bodhisattva aspiration. Philosophically, its ninth chapter on the "Perfection of Insight" (*prajñāpāramitā: shes rab kyi pha rol tu phyin pa*) is considered the most important part of the work. This chapter alludes to the idea of the two types of world/people (*loka: 'jig rten*) (*Bodhicaryāvatāra* 9:3–4ab), namely, ordinary (i.e., non-yogic) world/people

[1] The pertinent verse runs as follows: "Supplication to 'Jigs-med-chos-kyi-dbang-po, who is outwardly the (great) Bodhisattva Śāntideva; inwardly Śavarīpā, the king of [all] accomplished ones; and secretly the Supreme Noble One, sDug-bsngal-rang-grol ('one who [causes sentient beings to be] naturally free of pains/sufferings') [a form of Avalokiteśvara in the Klong-chen-snying-thig cycle of teachings] in person!" The verse can be popularly found in liturgical texts of the rNying-ma school of Tibetan Buddhism and has been attributed to 'Jam-dbyangs-mkhyen-brtse'i-dbang-po (1820–92). See, for example, sMyo-shul-mkhan-po, *rDzogs chen chos 'byung* (vol. 1 (E), p. 472.4–6).

[2] rDza-dpal-sprul, *rDo rje'i thal glu* (p. 303.2–3): "The principal [factors] for increasing [*bodhicitta*, the resolve to attain awakening] are the practice of the six perfections. A treatise like the [*Bodhi*]*caryāvatāra*, which is easy to understand, and [whose] teachings strike the core of the quintessential instructions, exists neither in India nor in Tibet. How can there be Buddha[hood for someone] who does not rely on it?"

(*prākṛtako lokaḥ / prākṛtaloka:*[3] *'jig rten phal pa*) and yogic world/people (*yogiloka: rnal 'byor 'jig rten*). In what follows, I wish to focus on this single idea of Śāntideva and discuss the history of its reception including its implications on Tibetan Buddhist thought, as well as its antecedents.

For heuristic reasons, I wish to examine this *prākṛtaloka–yogiloka* dichotomy in terms of (1) communication, (2) Madhyamaka methodology, (3) ontology, (4) epistemology, (5) axiology, and finally (6) in view of their complex relation, all of which are somehow associated with soteriological concerns. Whenever possible, an attempt will be made to show its possible antecedents.

1. No 'quarreling with the world'

One reason why it seems to make sense to examine Śāntideva's *prākṛtaloka–yogiloka* dichotomy is that dialogue in Buddhism seems to be fundamentally presupposed between yogic and ordinary non-yogic worlds. To be sure, terminologically as well as semantically, it is difficult to keep the conceptions of debate and dialogue apart in Indian and Tibetan Buddhist sources, and the borderline between them is either blurred or fluid. Nonetheless, it seems necessary to distinguish one from the other. There is a series of Sanskrit words such as *vāda*, *vivāda*, *saṃvāda*, and *vigraha*, which have often been translated into Tibetan as *rtsod pa* ("dispute" or "debate"). These Sanskrit and Tibetan terms seem to render a wide range of meanings including discourse, discussion, dispute, debate, dialectic, polemic, and dialogue. My impression is that in the Buddhist context, debate and dialogue represent two extreme points on the same scale of conversation between at least two parties, in which certain elements of dissensus and consensus on a given issue have been taken for granted. There may be several ways of defining debate and dialogue but I propose to define debate as an "argumentative conversation or discourse between at least two persons or parties, in which each side as a proponent seeks to prove its own position and/or disprove the position of its opponent," whereas, I would like to define "dialogue," as understood in the Buddhist tradition, as an "exploratory-elucidatory conversation or discourse between at least two persons or parties, in which one is the inquisitive seeker of insight on any given area or theme and the other a benevolent and competent imparter of that insight." The conception of dialogue in this sense, and perhaps in this sense alone, can be said to be extant in Buddhism, whereas the conception of debate in this sense has

3 Śāntideva, *Bodhicaryāvatāra* 9:3–4ab (de La Vallée Poussin 1901–14: 368–70; Bhattacharya 1960: 185): *tatra loko dvidhā dṛṣṭo yogī prākṛtakas tathā |tatra prākṛtako loko yogilokena bādhyate || bādhyante dhīviśeṣeṇa yogino 'py uttarottaraiḥ* |. Note that here only the expression *prākṛtako lokaḥ* occurs but not the compound *prākṛtaloka*. See, however, Āryadeva (ascribed), *Cittaviśuddhiprakaraṇa* 83 (Patel 1949: 6): *yathā prākṛtalokena yogiloko na bādhyate | bādhyante dhīviśeṣeṇa yogino 'py uttarottaraiḥ* ||. In Patel's edition, the compound *prākṛtaloka* does occur (i.e., *si vera lectio*). It does not, however, occur in the Sanskrit text of *Cittaviśuddhiprakaraṇa* 83 cited in de La Vallée Poussin 1931: 414, which reads: *yathā prākṛtako loko yogilokena bādhyate | bādhyante dhīviśeṣeṇa yogino 'py uttarottaraiḥ* ||. The attestation of the compound *prākṛtaloka* is thus not entirely secured. For the English translation of *Bodhicaryāvatāra* 9:3–4 by Ernst Steinkellner and Cynthia Peck-Kubaczek, see Schmidt-Leukel 2019: 416.

been popular, particularly within the Buddhist school of logic and epistemology. The Buddhist conception of debate seems to be more systematic and sophisticated than its traditional understanding of dialogue.

Now for Śāntideva, whose main concern is Bodhisattvayāna soteriology, representatives of *prākṛtaloka* inquisitive about Bodhisattvayāna soteriology and desirous of seeking and obtaining insight regarding it will enter into dialogue with *yogiloka* persons who are willing to impart the soteriologically relevant insights. The elements of consensus and dissensus between the two and the desire to seek and gain insight on the part of the *prākṛtaloka* and the willingness to engage in teaching on the part of the *yogiloka* offer an ideal occasion for a dialogue. If there were only consensus about an issue, there would be no need for a dialogue. If there were only dissensus about it, dialogue would not be possible. If the *prākṛtaloka* does not seek dialogue or if the *yogiloka* does not engage in a dialogue, a dialogue would not take place.

Following Śāntideva, the post-Śāntideva Indian and Tibetan sources have the *prākṛtaloka–yogiloka* dichotomy taken for granted. The question is whether the classification of *loka* into *prākṛtaloka* and *yogiloka* is Śāntideva's own innovation or whether he is simply taking over ideas found in his tradition. For now, it appears that we cannot trace the occurrence of *prākṛtaloka* and *yogiloka* as a pair in pre-Śāntideva sources.[4] What is, however, noteworthy is that also Candrakīrti, a presumably close contemporary of Śāntideva, does seem to admit what I call a *pṛthagjana–āryajana* dichotomy.[5] Throughout his *Madhyamakāvatāra* and its auto-commentary, "ordinary people" (*pṛthagjana: so so'i skye bo*) seems to be juxtaposed to "noble people" (*āryajana: 'phags pa'i skye bo*), for which he also employs the term *yogin* (*rnal 'byor pa*)[6] and "noble one" (*ārya: 'phags pa*). To be sure, the words *ārya* and *āryajana* in the Buddhist context are to be understood only in a spiritual sense of someone who has made the soterial breakthrough, regardless of one's caste or race. The perspectives of the two worlds, too, have been juxtaposed with each other by using a pair of indeclinables, namely, "in reality" (*tattvatas: de nyid du*) and "according to the world" or "by worldly norm" (*lokatas: 'jig rten du*).[7]

[4] I do not have access to the printed edition of the *Guṇakāraṇḍavyūhasūtra* but at least according to the electronic texts available online, the expression *yogiloka* occurs. But unlike our *yogiloka*, which clearly means "world/people consisting of *yogins*" or "world of *yogins*," there it seems to be used in the sense of "*yogins* and [ordinary] world/people."

[5] To be sure, Candrakīrti does employ the terms *pṛthagjana* and *āryajana* together, for example, in *Madhyamakāvatāra* 3.9 (Lasic, Li, and MacDonald 2022: 46): *roṣakṣamādoṣaguṇān avetya pṛthagjanenātha jinātmajena | hitvākṣamām āśu niṣevaṇīyā kṣāntiḥ sadaivāryajanapraśastā* ||; Tibetan in Uryuzu and Nakazawa 2012: 9, 43. For Candrakīrti, *jinātmaja* would be a *bodhisattva* on one of the ten *bodhisattvabhūmis* and hence not be co-extensive with *āryajana*, which should also include *arhacchrāvakas* and *pratyekabuddhas*.

[6] Candrakīrti, *Madhyamakāvatāra* 6.117 (Li 2015: 18): *yā kalpanānāṃ vinivṛttir etat phalaṃ vicārasya budhā vadanti | pṛthagjanāḥ kalpanayaiva baddhā akalpayan muktim upaiti yogī* ||; Tibetan in Uryuzu and Nakazawa 2012: 16, 91.

[7] Candrakīrti, *Madhyamakāvatāra* 6.158 (Li 2015: 23): *na tattvato naiva ca lokataś ca sa saptadhā yady api yāti siddhim | svāṅgāny upādāya vinā vicāraṃ prajñapyate lokata eva caiṣaḥ* ||; Tibetan in Uryuzu and Nakazawa 2012: 19, 104): *de ni de nyid du 'am 'jig rten du || rnam pa bdun gyis 'grub 'gyur min mod kyi || rnam dpyod med par 'jig rten nyid las 'dir || rang gi yan lag brten nas 'dogs pa yin* ||. See also *Madhyamakāvatāra* 6.12 (Li 2015: 5); Tibetan in Uryuzu and Nakazawa 2012: 10.

Such a view of the *prākṛtaloka-yogiloka*, or *pṛthagjana-āryajana*, dichotomy can be said to be extant *ad sensum* even long before Śāntideva and Candrakīrti. Let us for a moment consider the famous statement ascribed to the historical Buddha, "I do not quarrel with the world. The world quarrels with me." Such a statement in varying detail and formulation and in various contexts can be found in several Mahāyāna scriptures such as the *Trisaṃvaranirdeśaparivarta(sūtra)*,[8] which has often been referred to in secondary sources,[9] *Ratnakraraṇḍasūtra*,[10] *Buddhapiṭakaduḥśīlanigrahasūtra*,[11] *Kuśalamūlasaṃparigrahasūtra*,[12] *Garbhāvakrāntisūtra*,[13] *Bodhisattvapiṭaka(sutra)*,[14] *Brahmaviśeṣacintiparipṛcchā(sūtra)*,[15] and *Lokadharaparipṛcchāsūtra*.[16] It can also be found in Mahāyāna scriptures translated into Tibetan from the Chinese such as the **Buddhakośasūtra*[17] and *Mahāparinirvāṇasūtra*.[18] Ultimately, such an idea can also be traced in non-/pre-Mahāyāna sources such as the *Vinayakṣudrakavastu*[19] of Northern Buddhism and the *Pupphasutta* (*Saṃyuttanikāya*)[20] of Southern Buddhism. The idea that the Buddha does not quarrel with the world but the world quarrels with him is also found in commentarial literature such as Candrakīrti's *Prasannapadā*,[21] *Madhyamakāvatāra*,[22] *Madhyamakāvatārabhāṣya*[23] (explained also in Jayānanda's *Madhyamakāvatāraṭīkā*)[24] and Śīlapālita's **Vinayakṣudrakavyākhyāna*.[25] Also, the idea that one who has become salvifically emancipated does not quarrel can be found in the *Suttanipāta* (of the *Khuddakanikāya*)[26] and the occasion of dissent (between the yogic and non-yogic world/people) has already been spelled out in the

[8] *Trisaṃvaranirdeśaparivarta(sūtra)* (T, fol. 14a2–4; P, fol. 10b4–6).

[9] See, for example, Ruegg 2010: 224 n.13; Tillemans 2019: 636–8; Li 2019: 59 n.46. As it would become evident in this present contribution, the *Trisaṃvaranirdeśaparivarta(sūtra)* is not the only Mahāyānasūtric scripture that alludes to the idea in question.

[10] *Ratnakraraṇḍasūtra* (T, fol. 242b5–6; P, fol. 308a3–4).

[11] *Buddhapiṭakaduḥśīlanigrahasūtra* (T, fol. 349a4; P, fol. 21b2).

[12] *Kuśalamūlasaṃparigrahasūtra* (T, fol. 174a4–5; P, fol. 128a3–4).

[13] *Garbhāvakrāntisūtra* (Kritzer 2014: 365).

[14] *Bodhisattvapiṭaka(sutra)* (T, dKon-brtsegs, vol. Ga, fol. 119b3; P, dKon-brtsegs, vol. Wi, fol. 47a3).

[15] *Brahmaviśeṣacintiparipṛcchā(sūtra)* (T, fol. 175b2–4; P. fol. 38a8–b1).

[16] *Lokadharaparipṛcchāsūtra* (T, fol. 44a5–6; P, fol. 36b2–3, and T, fol. 44b4–5; P, fol. 36b7–8).

[17] **Buddhakośasūtra* (T, fol. 80b3; P, fol. 74b2–3).

[18] In the *Mahāparinirvāṇasūtra* translated from the Chinese, the statement that a *bodhisattva* "would not quarrel with the world and would not be tainted by worldly qualities/concerns" (*'jig rten dang mi rtsod cing 'jig rten gyi chos kyis mi gos par 'gyur*) occurs several times. See also the pertinent statement in T, Myang-'das, vol. Ga, fol. 198b6–7; P, Myang-'das, vol. Nyu, fol. 257a4–5.

[19] *Vinayakṣudrakavastu* (T, fol. 227a7; P, fol. 142b7–8).

[20] *Pupphasutta* in *Saṃyuttanikāya* 3.138 (as cited in Seyfort Ruegg 2010: 224 n.13; Tillemans 2019: 637). Bhikkhu Bodhi 2000: 949 translates: "Bhikkhus, I do not dispute with the world; rather, it is the world that disputes with me" (see Analāyo 2009: 720, where *Saṃyuttanikāya* 3.138 has been referred to).

[21] Candrakīrti, *Prasannapadā ad Mūlamadhyamakakārikā* 18.8 (as cited in Seyfort Ruegg 2010: 224 n.13). Also partly cited in Uryuzu and Nakazawa 2012: 107 n.926 and Tillemans 2019: 636.

[22] Candrakīrti, *Madhyamakāvatāra* 6.166d (Li 2015: 24); Tibetan in Uryuzu and Nakazawa 2012: 107.

[23] Candrakīrti, *Madhyamakāvatārabhāṣya* (Uryuzu and Nakazawa 2012: 107; cf. Seyfort Ruegg 2010: 224 n.13; Tillemans 2019: 636, and Uryuzu and Nakazawa 2012: 79). The extant Sanskrit text of the pertinent lines is not accessible to me.

[24] Jayānanda, *Madhyamakāvatāraṭīkā* (D, fol. 274a6; P, fol. 242a4–5).

[25] Śīlapālita, **Vinayakṣudrakavyākhyāna* (P, fol. 64b3–6; D, fol. 56a2–4).

[26] *Suttanipāta* 895 (cited in Analāyo 2009: 720): *vimutto na vivadam eti.*

Ratnaguṇasaṃcayagāthā,[27] one of the earliest Prajñāpāramitā scriptures. To me, it seems quite logical and natural to interpret "the world" here as *prākṛtaloka/pṛthagjana* and the Buddha himself (or a *bodhisattva*) representing the *yogiloka/āryajana*. Also, the juxtaposition of the *bāla*s and *tathāgata*s in the *Udānavarga*[28] can be interpreted as being parallel to our *prākṛtaloka–yogiloka* juxtaposition. One might thus maintain that it was perhaps Śāntideva who made the classification of *loka* into *prākṛtaloka* and *yogiloka* that was implicit in earlier sources explicit. In other words, one might say that he merely expressed *ad verbum* what already existed *ad sensum*.

Tibetan Buddhists may see Śāntideva's *Bodhicaryāvatāra* as a work that deals with "mind training" (*blo sbyong*). While I would readily agree with such a characterization, I am more inclined to see it as a dialogical work, but one that does not deal with a dialogue with an external party. It is an internal dialogue; a dialogue that is taking place in Śāntideva's heart and mind.

2. Implications for Madhyamaka methodology

The next question that concerns us is what is meant by the word "world/people" (*loka: 'jig rten*) in general and what may be the line of demarcation between the non-yogic "ordinary world" (*prākṛtaloka: 'jig rten phal pa*) and "yogic world" (*yogiloka: rnal 'byor gyi 'jig rten*). Any attempt to answer this question can perhaps be only made by examining the methods, approaches, or transactional procedures of what came to be known in Tibet as the *Prāsaṅgika-Mādhyamika (dBu-ma-thal-'gyur-pa). I am not sure who regarded Śāntideva as a *Prāsaṅgika-Mādhyamika for the first time. bCom-ldan Rig(s)-pa'i-ral-gri (1227–1305), a thirteen-century Tibetan scholar, like many later Tibetan scholars, does place Śāntideva together with Candrakīrti clearly, at least in the context of the Buddhological positions, but without explicitly regarding them as *Prāsaṅgika-Mādhyamikas.[29] It is only in much later sources such as the *Shes bya mdzod* by Kong-sprul Yon-tan-rgya-mtsho (1813–99), a nineteenth-century Tibetan scholar, that Śāntideva has been explicitly regarded as a *Prāsaṅgika-Mādhyamika.[30] Now *Prāsaṅgika-Mādhyamikas have also been called 'Jig-rten-grags-sde-spyod-pa'i-dbu-ma-pas, which means something like "those proponents of the Middle Way, who, for their convention, rely on what is known in the world." Such a designation is obviously a Tibetan invention/innovation and it is not clear to me who employed the term for the first time. At any rate, some of the earliest Tibetan sources that I could trace are the writings of the thirteenth-century Tibetan scholar bCom-ldan Rig(s)-pa'i-ral-gri.[31] And it has often been Sanskritized in secondary sources as

27 *Ratnaguṇasaṃcayagāthā* 15.8 (Yuyama 1976: 60; cf. Obermiller 1937: 59). We shall return to this verse below.

28 *Udānavarga* 29.38cd (Bernhard 1965: 382): *prapañcābhiratā bālā niṣprapañcās tathāgatāḥ* ||; Tib. *Udāna* 29.42cd (Zongtse 1990: 318).

29 Rig(s)-ral, *Grub mtha' rgyan gyi me tog* (pp. 378.4–379.6).

30 Kong-sprul, *Shes bya mdzod* (p. 230.10–15).

31 Rig(s)-ral, *bSlab gsum rgyan gyi me tog* (p. 390.5). For some later Tibetan sources, see Seyfort Ruegg 1981: 80 n.259.

"Lokaprasiddha-Mādhyamika."[32] Though Śāntideva and Candrakīrti might not have called themselves "Lokaprasiddha-Mādhyamikas," a closer examination of their works should reveal why they came to be regarded as thus.

Of the names of the two Madhyamaka schools, namely, *Prāsaṅgika-Madhyamaka and *Svātantrika-Madhyamaka, we have been told that the former has neither been attested in Sanskrit sources nor in Sanskrit sources in Tibetan translation, whereas the Tibetan equivalent for the latter, dBu-ma-rang-rgyud-pa, is found in the Tibetan translation of Jayānanda's *Madhyamakāvatāraṭīkā*.[33] We have thus far not been able to disprove the fourteenth-century Tibetan scholar, Bu-ston Rin-chen-grub (1290–1364), who already pointed out that he could not find any Indian treatises that clearly explain these designations (*ming 'dogs*) and terminologies (*tha snyad*).[34]

The expression **prāsaṅgika-madhyamaka*, however, can be said to be *de facto* and *ad sensum* extant already in India although admittedly these *ad verbum* designations were most probably Tibetan innovations. While there is a *dissensus* among Tibetan Madhyamaka interpreters regarding the issue of whether these two Madhyamaka schools independently and successfully establish the same account of true ultimate reality and hence share the same ultimate view, there is apparently a *consensus* regarding their understanding of the methodology followed in establishing true reality. A significant methodological difference between *Svātantrika-Mādhyamika and *Prāsaṅgika-Mādhyamika is that the former resorts to a formal independent syllogism (*svatantraprayogavākya: rang gi rgyud kyi sbyor ba'i ngag*) whereas the latter to an *argumentum ad absurdum* (*prasaṅgavākya: thal bar 'gyur ba'i tshig*). That is, while the former seeks to prove one's own thesis and disprove (or refute) an opponent's antithesis by means of formal independent syllogism, the latter seeks to destroy an opponent's propositions by means of an *argumentum ad absurdum*, without taking any stance of one's own but demonstrating the illogicality in the position of an opponent by virtue of the opponent's own reason(ing)s. A contentious issue among Tibetan scholars has been who exactly is (or should be) a *Prāsaṅgika-Mādhyamika's opponent? Is the opponent "someone whose mind/thought has not been changed by a religio-philological tenet" (*grub mthas blo ma bsgyur ba*), that is, a complete laity, or is he "someone whose mind/thought has been changed by a religio-philosophical tenet" (*grub mthas blo bsgyur ba*)?

[32] Ichigo 1985: lxxxv; Higgins and Draszczyk 2016: 37–8; Almogi 2009. Cf. Loka-prasiddhi-cāri-varga-mādhyamika (Obermiller 1932: 135).

[33] Jayānanda, *Madhyamakāvatāraṭīkā* (P, fol. 336b6–7; D, fol. 281a6). See also Yotsuya 1999: xi n.7, where also references to the occurrence of expressions *rang rgyud pa* and *rang rgyud du smra ba rnams* have been provided.

[34] Bu-ston, *gSung tho bu* (p. 218.6–7): "Regarding this [subclassification Madhyamaka into] *Prāsaṅgika and *Svātantrika Madhyamaka known in Tibet, [such] designations and terminologies have not been seen explained in Indian treatises. Three kinds of Madhyamaka have been explained in decent works, Yogācāra-Madhyamaka, Sautrāntika-Madhyamaka, and *Lokaprasiddha-Madhyamaka. Of these, it appears that the former two are called Svātantrika and the latter Prāsaṅgika." This source has also been identified and cited in Sad-mi-mi-bzhi 2018: 30–1 and Nor-bu et al. 2022: 7 n.1. Note the choice of Bu-ston's words "India treatises" (*rgya gar ba'i bstan bcos*) and "decent works" (*gzhung lugs rnam dag*). He does not seem to imply that subclassification of Madhyamaka into *Yogācāra-Madhyamaka, *Sautrāntika-Madhyamaka, and *Lokaprasiddha-Madhyamaka can be found in Indian sources, and by "decent works" he probably had in mind the writings of, for example, bCom-ldan Rig(s)-pa'i-ral-gri.

In other words, the issue is really whether a Prāsaṅgika-Mādhyamika goes into a dialogue/debate with the *prākṛtaloka*, or rather with *yogiloka*. Obviously, it is not possible to do full justice to the various nuanced Tibetan Buddhist positions on the matter especially because the issue of what precisely is *loka* in the term *lokaprasiddha* is connected with a host of other contentious issues such as *Prāsaṅgika-Mādhyamika's understanding of the two truths or modes of reality, its methodology in establishing the true reality, whether or not there is or should be a "commonly appearing subject [of debate/dialogue]" (*chos can (m)thun snang*), what is actually being negated by Madhyamic reasonings (i.e., *negandum*), whether or not Mādhyamikas have a thesis/proposition of their own and what it really means, and its theories and practices pertinent to its soteriology (i.e., *sa dang lam gyi rnam gzhag* "establishment/scheme of soterial stages and paths").

At any rate, Tibetan interpreters of *Prāsaṅgika-Madhyamaka doctrine seem to form two camps, namely, one for whom *loka* in this context should be understood exclusively as ordinary people, whose minds have not been shaped or influenced by any dogmas, and the other for whom *loka* would include all those who debate with or go into a dialogue with a *Prāsaṅgika-Mādhyamika, be they *prākṛtaloka* or *yogiloka*. rNam-rgyal-rgya-mtsho (1846–1912), a nineteenth-century polymath from East Tibet, for example, clearly presupposes these two positions, while he himself endorses the second position by referring to the idea of the two kinds of people/worlds found in *Bodhicaryāvatāra* 9:3–4ab.[35]

3. Different views of reality

As I suggested above, one of the points of contention between *prākṛtaloka* and *yogiloka* is their conception of reality, let us say, their ontology. What Śāntideva states, in essence, is that the ordinary world sees phenomena to be "existent" (*bhāva: dngos* [*po*]) in reality (*tattvatas: yang dag nyid du*) and the yogic world sees phenomena to be illusion-like (*māyāvat: sgyu ma lta bu*). In other words, the former proposes/presupposes a substantialist view whereas the latter an illusionist view. At least in spirit, such diametrically opposed worldviews have already been expressed by the *Ratnaguṇasaṃcayagāthā*, that I mentioned above, but the crucial difference between the *prākṛtaloka* and *yogiloka* here, in my view, seems to be that the former seeks an ontological substrate (*ālaya: gnas*) in the phenomena whereas the latter knows that the phenomena to be substrate-less (*anālaya/nirālaya: gnas med*).[36] Although the exact correlation between *Prāsaṅgika-Mādhyamikas and those who are called Sarvadharmāpratiṣṭhānavādins (i.e., "those who maintain that all phenomena are

[35] Mi-pham, *dBu ma rgyan 'grel* (fol. 21a5–b3).

[36] *Ratnaguṇasaṃcayagāthā* 15.8 (Yuyama 1976: 60; cf. Obermiller 1937: 59); Tibetan in Yuyama 1976: 173 (cf. Obermiller 1937: 59). Conze 1975: 37 translates: "For beings delight in a place to settle in, they are eager for sense-objects, Bent on grasping, unintelligent, and quite blinded. The Dharma should be attained as nothing to settle in and as nothing to grasp. Its conflict with the world is manifest."

without any metaphysical substrate")[37] is bound to be disputable, both seem to take for granted that both saṃsāric and nirvāṇic phenomena are groundless and rootless. The special Sarvadharmāpratiṣṭhānavāda ontology, which I claim has also been proposed/presupposed by both Candrakīrti and Śāntideva, can be approached from various angles. But here, we may merely allude to the idea of ontological groundlessness and rootlessness conveyed, for example, by the Sanskrit expression *anālaya*/*nirālaya*. Both Candrakīrti and Śāntideva cite several verses from the *Lalitavistarasūtra*, including one that professes the idea that all phenomena are (ontologically) groundless (*anālaya*/*nirālaya: gnas med* [*pa*]).[38] Śāntideva can also be said to propose ontological groundlessness by resorting to the idea of *nirāśraya*/*anāśraya*.[39] Candrakīrti, too, can be said to be a proponent of ontological groundlessness inasmuch as he endorses the idea of *apratiṣṭha* and *nirmūla*/*amūla*),[40] which has been, to be sure, already proposed by Nāgārjuna.[41] Ultimately, the idea of ontological groundlessness can be said to be found, albeit in an incipient form, in conservative sources such as the *Udānavarga* conveyed through expressions such has *ālayo nāsti* ("There is no (ontological) ground").[42]

4. From illusion to insight: An epistemic spectrum

There is a host of epistemology-/gnoseology-related differences between the *prākṛtaloka* and *yogiloka*. If the two kinds of worlds are so far apart, is there at least some shared/common premise to act as a point of departure for a dialogue? Or is there nothing whatsoever in common between them? If there is a common premise, what is it? Obviously, the people of these two worlds differ deeply in their perceptions and conceptions of reality. But is there anything that they perceive and conceive commonly? If so, what is it? If they perceive and conceive the world differently, can one speak of the veridicality of one or another of the two perspectives? That is, can we say that some perceptions are correct and others wrong? If so, what is the criterion for epistemic

[37] See section, "Māyopamavāda-Apratiṣṭhānavāda versus Prāsaṅgika-Svātantrika," in Almogi 2010: 170–81. See also Almogi 2009: 39–43, 226–31.

[38] *Lalitavistarasūtra* 13.117 (Hokazono 1994: 646): *skandhāyatanāni dhātavaḥ śūnya adhyātmika śūnya bāhyakāḥ | sattvātmavivikta 'nālayā dharma ākāśasvabhāvalakṣaṇāḥ ||*. The editor reports variant readings of *sattvātmavivikta*. All his manuscripts omit *ātma* but parallel sources add it. He also notes that, metrically, it should be added. For Candrakīrti's citation of the verse, see his *Madhyamakāvatārabhāṣya* (Uryuzu and Nakazawa 2012: 63), where the Sanskrit text has also been provided (n.559). For Śāntideva's citation of the same verse, see his *Śikṣāsamuccaya* (Bendall 1897–1902: 241).

[39] Śāntideva, *Bodhicaryāvatāra* 9:34 (Bhattacharya 1960: 193–4). See also *Bodhicaryāvatāra* 9:111 (Bhattacharya 1960: 214).

[40] Candrakīrti, *Yuktiṣaṣṭikāvṛtti ad Yuktiṣaṣṭikā* 26 (Li and Ye 2014: 130–3; Scherrer-Schaub 1991: 65–7).

[41] Nāgārjuna, *Yuktiṣaṣṭikā* 26 (Li and Ye 2014: 56): *apratiṣṭham anālambaṃ nirmūlam anavasthitam | avidyābījasambhūtam ādimadhyāntavarjitam ||*; Tibetan in Li and Ye 2014: 56, 130; Scherrer-Schaub 1991: 12, 90. See also Candrakīrti, *Yuktiṣaṣṭikāvṛtti ad Yuktiṣaṣṭikā* 26 (Li and Ye 2014: 130–3; Scherrer-Schaub 1991: 65–7).

[42] *Udānavarga* 33.54 (Bernhard 1965: 488); Tibetan: *Udānavarga* 33.66 (Zongtse 1990: 434).

veridicality and ontic verity? On an earlier occasion, I attempted to discuss these issues.[43] A couple of things seems clear for Śāntideva. Following *Bodhicaryāvatāra* 9:26,[44] we may say that Śāntideva does not deny what is commonly held to be obvious. Let us call this the world of "mere appearances" (*snang ba tsam*). That is, for Śāntideva, *prākṛtaloka* and *yogiloka* are not two parallel worlds and hence mutual communication and interaction are possible between them. Importantly, for all Mādhyamikas, the world of mere appearances should not be proposed as something dogma-specific, for example, as a God-created world of mere appearances. Mere appearances are never the *negandum* of Madhyamic reasonings.[45] What Mādhyamikas seem to be attempting to do is to rip the clothes of manifoldness (*prapañca: spros pa*) off the one and only true reality (*ekaṃ satyam: bden pa gcig*) to reveal it in all its nakedness, thereby enabling aspirants a direct sight of it. Their proposition is that a soterial breakthrough is only possible by gaining direct gnostic access to the true reality.[46]

Śāntideva and Candrakīrti, like many other Buddhist scholars, do not only admit epistemic differences between *prākṛtaloka* and *yogiloka* perceptions in general but also a wide perceptual spectrum of these worlds. The epistemic discrepancy seems to be explained by a difference in the karmic forces and differences in the level of soteric progress of various sentient beings. As opposed/juxtaposed to what one might call a "positive epistemology" of Dignāga and Dharmakīrti, Śāntideva and Candrakīrti seem to propose largely a "negative epistemology." That is, for them, true reality is like empty space where mirage-water appears to originate, continue, and cease even though there never has been mirage-water at all. The oneness of the presence (i.e., arising) of virtual water and the absence (i.e., non-arising) of actual water in the mirage has often been described as the indivisibility of the two modes of reality (*bden pa gnyis dbyer med pa*), for example, by Rong-zom-pa, and an idea that can be *ad sensum* traced back to Mahāyāna scriptures that served as sources for several Madhyamaka authors.[47] I have once claimed that for Rong-zom-pa, ultimately all perceptible/perceived appearances are illusions and all appearances-perceiving perceptions are delusions.[48] I suspect that this is true also for Śāntideva and Candrakīrti, and this seems to become conspicuous especially in their positions on ontology and Buddhology. But although all appearances are illusions and all perceptions are delusions for them, there seems to be a criterion for explaining the varying degrees of ontic verity and epistemic veridicality. The "negative epistemology" of Śāntideva and Candrakīrti may be, thus, formulated as follows: "In so

43 Wangchuk 2009: 227–34.

44 *Bodhicaryāvatāra* 9:26 (Bhattacharya 1960: 191). See also *Catuḥśataka* 6.23 (Lang 1986: 150): "If everything exists by its own-nature, what would be the benefit of perceiving the emptiness [of things]? When one perceives [things] through conceptual constructions, there is bondage. That [bondage] must be stopped here [in our system]." And: Śāntarakṣita, *Madhyamakālaṃkāra* 78 (Ichigo1985: 254).

45 I am thinking, for example, of the statement in Mi-pham's *dBu ma rgyan 'grel* (fol. 14a2–4).

46 For a discussion of this soteriological presupposition, see Wangchuk 2009: 230–1.

47 The idea that everything arising (*jāyati*) dependently on causes and conditions is actually non-arisen (*ajāta*) can be found in the *Anavataptahradāpasaṃkramaṇasūtra* aka *Anavataptanāgarājaparipṛcchā*(*sūtra*) (Li 2012: 61 n.60; Uryuzu and Nakazawa 2012: [Addendum] 8). This *locus classicus* for the idea has been cited by several Indian and Tibetan authors.

48 Wangchuk 2009: 234.

far as all appearances are illusions and all perceptions delusions, the less illusions one perceives, the less is one's level of delusion, and when all illusions and delusions come to cease, one can be said to have seen all phenomena." There appear to be several explicit and implicit sources for this special "negative epistemology,"[49] but *Ratnaguṇasaṃcayagāthā* 12:8–9 can be said to be one of the earliest and most significant sources.[50]

In addition, the idea that the perceptions of more advanced *yogins* can always invalidate those of the less advanced ones but never vice versa has been proposed by both Śāntideva and Candrakīrti.[51] The most difficult and crucial question seems to be this: What makes, in general, the perception of the *yogiloka* more veridical and of the *prākṛtaloka* less veridical? The answer seems to be directly related to Buddhist soteriology. That is, ultimately, that gnostic *Einsicht* ("insight," "perception") that brings about nirvāṇic freedom has been considered valid and that dogmatic or agnostic *Ansicht* ("view," "conceptualization") that brings about saṃsāric thralldom has been considered invalid. How can one then verify or nullify the claim of nirvāṇic freedom and saṃsāric thralldom? The true reality, the direct gnostic access of which is said to bring about the soteriological breakthrough has often been characterized, for example, as *pratyātmadharmatā* ("true reality [to be cognized by] each one for oneself"), *pratyātmagatigocara* ("domain/sphere, the cognitive access to which is to be gained by each one for oneself"), *pratyātmādhigamya* ("to be cognized/attained by each one for oneself"), *pratyātmavedanīya* ("to be experienced by each one for oneself"), *pratyātmavedya* ("to be known by each one for oneself," or "to be known directly and immediately"), and so on. Similarly, the gnostic cognition that brings about the nirvāṇic freedom from saṃsāric thralldom has been often been characterized as *svapratyātmāryajñāna* ("gnosis of the noble one, [which is to be attained by] each one for oneself"), *pratyātmajñāna* / *pratyātmikaṃ jñānam* ("gnosis [to be gained] by each one for oneself"), and the like. All these illustrate that the soterial episode is personal and experiential. Tibetan Buddhist scholars compare such a personal experience to the "a mute's taste of molasses" (*lkugs pas bu ram myong ba*).[52]

49 For a discussion of the idea of "not seeing" (*adarśana: mi mthong ba*) is the "correct seeing" (*samyagdarśana: yang dag par mthong ba*) found mainly in the *Dharmasaṃgītisūtra* cited by several Indic works, associated with the elements of secrecy in the context of Mahāyāna epistemology and "Mahāyāna paradoxology," specifically one pertinent to the "profundity with regard to knowing" (*jñānagāmbhīrya: shes pa la zab pa*), see Wangchuk 2020: 65–9.

50 For a somewhat detailed discussion, see Wangchuk 2020: 66–9.

51 As discussed in Wangchuk 2020: 232–3, Candrakīrti argued that a non-*yogin* who has no gnosis and is not released is not an authority, and that if this were not the case, it would imply that such a person has perceived true reality and eliminated ignorance, and this in turn would imply the redundancy of the spiritual paths of the noble ones (*Madhyamakāvatāra* 6.30, Li 2015: 8). An undefiled cognition of a *yogin*, according to him, can invalidate the defiled cognition of a non-*yogin* but not vice versa (*Madhyamakāvatāra* 6.27, Li 2015: 7). Candrakīrti also proposes that only the gnosis of a *buddha*, and not any other type of gnosis, given their limitation (*ekadeśatva: nyi tshe ba nyid*), can be direct valid cognition (see *Madhyamakāvatāra* 6.214, Li 2015: 29). Following this logic, *buddhajñāna*, or the *yogipratyakṣa* of a *buddha*, will certainly be assumed to be the supreme cognition that can invalidate the perceptions of all *yogins* who have not yet attained Buddhahood.

52 Mi-pham, *Nges shes sgron me* (fol. 9a6).

5. From temporal goods to the highest good: A spectrum of values

One might contend that the two worlds, *prākṛtaloka* and *yogiloka*, are defined and separated by their notions of values, that is, their axiological presuppositions. First, the allegory of the Bodhisattva's final battle with Māraḥ Pāpīyān may be seen not so much as an allegory of war between good and evil, but rather a conflict of values and aspirations. It is a battle between those who hold temporal good (*abhyudaya: mngon par mtho ba*) dear and those who cherish the *summum bonum*, the highest good (*niḥśreyasa: nges par legs pa*), namely, the salvatory release (*mokṣa/nirvāṇa: thar pa / mya ngan las 'das pa*). It may be seen as a war between those who aspire for mundane (*laukika: 'jig rten pa*) goals and those who aspire for supra-mundane (*lokottara: 'jig rten las 'das pa*) ones. Second, there appear to be several ideas in Buddhist sources that reveal a diametrically opposed difference in conceptions of values and value-judgments of the *prākṛtaloka* and *yogiloka*, which we cannot discuss here in detail. I may only briefly allude here to Candrakīrti's intriguing discussion of the issue of sanity and insanity in his narration of a story about a king,[53] whose subjects became insane. The subjects, however, regarded their king to be insane, and he, out of desperation, also became insane. The story illustrates not only a difference in *prākṛtaloka*'s and *yogiloka*'s conception of epistemic values but a host of other issues concerning mundane sanitary and supra-mundane salvatory values. Third, one may go so far as to claim that what Śāntideva attempts to do in the *Bodhicaryāvatāra* is to deconstruct the axiological presuppositions of the *prākṛtaloka* and to offer an alternative axiological orientation.

6. A complex set of relations

One of the most intriguing questions is what exactly is or should be the relation between *prākṛtaloka* and *yogiloka* from a Buddhist perspective. We may consider here five points.

First, historically, in an Indian social/cultural context, the community of ascetics or mendicants (*śramaṇa: dge sbyong*) represented the *yogiloka*, and the community or

[53] Candrakīrti's story narrated in his *Catuḥśatakaṭīkā* has been retold and reused by A-mdo dGe-'dun-chos-'phel (1903–51) in his *Klu sgrub dgongs rgyan* (p. 175.5–19). As pointed out in Lopez 2006: 49 n.2, dGe-'dun-chos-'phel had believed that Candrakīrti narrated the story while commenting on the two verse lines from the *Catuḥśataka*, namely, *de nyid phyir na 'jig rten kun || smyon pa yin zhes cis mi 'thad ||*. Lopez also notes that these verse lines cannot be found in Āryadeva's *Catuḥśataka* itself. It is, however, evident that dGe-'dun-chos-'phel was thinking of *Catuḥśataka* 7.9 (Lang 1986: 72), which states: *rnam shes gnas pa med pa las || gal te smyon par gyur na ni || srid gnas smyon pa ma yin zhes || mkhas pa su zhig smra bar 'gyur ||*. The corresponding Sanskrit text is not available. For an English translation, see Lang 1986: 73. And indeed, like dGe-'dun-chos-'phel, one would expect Candrakīrti to narrate the story in this context, but he does not. Instead, he does so in the context of *Catuḥśataka* 3.22 (Lang 1986: 44). The corresponding Sanskrit text of this verse, too, is not available. For an English translation, see Lang 1986: 45. One can actually understand dGe-'dun-chos-'phel's confusion of the two contexts (i.e., of *Catuḥśataka* 7.9 and 3.22). In each of the two cases, Candrakīrti narrates a story of a king. The story found in *Catuḥśatakaṭīkā ad Catuḥśataka* 7.9 (P, fols. 138a4–139a6; D, fols. 124a4–125a2) is about a king's homosexual inclination and passion toward his own son. For the details of our story of the king who, in the end, voluntarily decides to become insane, see *Catuḥśatakaṭīkā ad Catuḥśataka* 3.22 (P, fols. 79a4–79b8; D, fols. 73b1–74a3).

society of laity represented the *prākṛtaloka*. Let us assume that there was an unwritten social contract between the two, without which it would not have not been possible for the *yogiloka* to sustain itself within the general *prākṛtaloka*. There was a kind of division of labor. The *prākṛtaloka* provided the *yogiloka* with a bare minimum of material support such as daily alms. In return, the *yogiloka* gave the *prākṛtaloka* spiritual guidance, and functioned as a kind of spiritual mentor or idol. In Buddhist terms, it was a bartering of the "gift of the *dharma*" (*dharmadāna*) and the "gift of material goods" (*āmiṣadāna*). In short, the relation between the two is supposed to be a symbiotic and not a parasitic one. It was a kind of give-and-take relation. The basic concept of what came to be known as the preceptor–patron (*yon mchod*; *mchod yon*) relation in Buddhist societies seems to be rooted in such a *prākṛtaloka–yogiloka* symbiotic relation.

Second, perhaps like any other relation, the *prākṛtaloka–yogiloka* relation can be a difficult one. What happens if a household or a community slander and abuses the ordained community of monks and nuns? The Buddhist monastic rule (*Vinaya*) prescribes a kind of protest against a laity called "overturning the alms bowl" (*pātranikubjana: lhung bzed kha(s) dbub/sbub(s)/phub pa*).[54] Similarly, what would be

[54] It is beyond the present scope to discuss in detail the Vinaya act of *pātranikubjana* (Pāli: *pattanikkujjana*) but for the present purpose, six points may be mentioned. First, the act of "turning over the begging/alms bowl" (i.e., a kind of "boycott," "excommunication," "sanction" imposed by the ordained community on a laity) has been ingrained in the Vinaya codex. See, for example, Guṇaprabha, *Vinayasūtra* (cited in Negi et al. 1993–2005, s.v. *lhung bzed khas dbub par bya*): [*pātraṃ*] *krośakaṃ paribhāṣakaṃ ca nikubjayeran* |; Tib. *skur pa dang gshe ba dang spyo ba la lhung bzed khas dbub par bya'o* ||; Dharmamitra, *Vinayasūtraṭīkā* (P, vol. Lu, fol. 303b2; D, vol. Yu, fol. 257b7): *khyim bdag dge slong la yang dag pa ma yin pas skur ba 'debs pa la gsol ba 'ba' zhig gi las kyis lhung bzed kha dbub par bya ba'o* ||. Note that in the *Vinayasūtra* statement, the Tibetan translation has, in addition, *skur pa*, which might have stood for *apavādaka* ("deniers"). Second, without going into the details of the proceeding, according to, for example, the *Vinayasūtraṭīkā* just cited, the legal proposition/declaration or stating of the matter (*karmavācanā: las brjod pa*) can be made before the congregation of monks or nuns through a single/simple/isolated motion (*muktikā jñāptiḥ: gsol ba 'ba' zhig pa* = *gsol ba gcig pa* = *gsol ba nyi tshe ba*), which assumes the form of a demand to be consented by silence and not requiring further questions, objections, or approval. See also Roloff 2020: 210 n.154. Third, the person on whom such a "sanction" is supposed to be imposed is obviously a lay Buddhist, an *upāsaka*/*upāsikā*. Fourth, the list of reasons for the act of *pātranikubjana* seems to vary. The *Vinayottaragrantha*, for example, list two separate lists of five reasons (see *Vinayottaragrantha*, T, 'Dul-ba, vol. Na, fol. 44b1–6; P, 'Dul-ba, vol. Be, fols. 30b6–31a1). For the Theravāda tradition, eight reasons of *pātranikubjana* have been listed (see Rahula 1956: 106 n.7). Fifth, it is perhaps important to note that *pātranikubjana* has hardly been seen as a permanent or long-term measure. The lifting of the "sanction" has been referred to in Tibetan sources as *lhung bzed kha bsrang ba* "setting [again] the begging/alms bowl upright," although more commonly simply *kha bsrang ba*. See, for example, the *mTsho ṭīk* (pp. 1005.9–1007.8). Sixth, a summary of the background stories of the act of *pātranikubjana* might help us understand it in its proper context. The Vinaya scriptures in Tibetan translation tell us about how two monks named *Mitra (mDza'-bo) and *Bhūmajaka (Sa-las-skyes)—counted among the "gang of six" (*ṣaḍvārgika: drug sde*) in Southern Buddhism but not in Northern Buddhism—succeeded in convincing Mahālicchavi (Litstsha-bī-chen-po), an upright man from Vaiśalī who was on his way to pay a visit to the Buddha to bring some "gift of news" (*gtam gyi skyes*). The "news" was that the monk Dravyo Mallaputraḥ slept with his wife. After finding out that it was not true, the *pātranikubjana* sanction was imposed on Mahālicchavi, which was of course duly revoked. For details, see the *Vinayakṣudrakavastu* (T, 'Dul-ba, vol. Ta, fols. 54b6–57b4; P, 'Dul-ba, vol. De, fols. 34b2–36a8). The sources tell us that the two brothers had what one might call "karmic animosity" (*tshe rabs tshe rabs nas rjes su 'brel ba'i (')khon*) with Dravyo Mallaputraḥ and there were often unfortunate circumstances that resulted in some troubles. Once during one "country

the consequence of a member of the *prākṛtaloka*'s negative attitude toward and actions against, let us say, a *bodhisattva* from the *yogiloka*? The consequence is said to be one's destiny in hell.[55]

Third, in my view, Śāntideva's *Bodhicaryāvatāra* reveals the Mahāyāna's reevaluation of the *yogiloka*'s relationship with the *prākṛtaloka*. According to the non-/pre-Mahāyāna tradition, although *yogiloka* maybe for the most part materially dependent on the *prākṛtaloka*, its soteriological success is not dependent on the *prākṛtaloka*. In the Mahāyāna tradition, the *yogiloka*'s relation with the *prākṛtaloka* becomes much more complicated. On the one hand, the *yogiloka* views the *prākṛtaloka* as difficult to please, and no one among the *prākṛtaloka* is said to be friend of the *yogiloka* (*Bodhicaryāvatāra* 8:22–4);[56] the world of *yogiloka* should keep a distance from the world of *prākṛtaloka*, and not familiarize with it too much.[57] On the other hand, now, the soterial value of the *prākṛtaloka* (i.e., *sattvakṣetra*) has been placed on par with the Buddha himself (i.e., *jinakṣetra*).[58] That is, now, we can say that the *prākṛtaloka* plays an indispensable role for the soteriological aspirations of the *yogiloka*. That is why, when a *yogin* encounters an ordinary sentient being, he is supposed to look at them full of gratitude and affection.[59]

Fourth, one of the most intriguing issues in Buddhism seems to be under what circumstances the *yogiloka* should conform with the *prākṛtaloka* and when it should not. In the accounts of the Buddha's life and works, we can find several instances where the Buddha does make concessions and adapts to the world, or yields to worldly demands. For example, it is said that he introduced the practice of staying in one place during the rainy seasons in view of the criticism raised by non-Buddhist teachers (*tīrthika: mu stegs can*).[60] In other instances, he does not seem to make compromises at

tour" (*janapadacārikā: ljongs rgyu*) after the rainy season, Dravyo Mallaputraḥ was appointed to be in charge of distributing food. *Mitra and *Bhūmajaka felt that Dravyo Mallaputraḥ deliberately gave them bad food (*kha zas ngan pa*) three times. As an act of revenge, they instigated their younger sister *Maitrā (mDza'-mo), a fully ordained nun, to falsely report to the Buddha that Dravyo Mallaputraḥ slept with her. This story, however, is not related with the act of *pātranikubjana*.

55 Śāntideva, *Bodhicaryāvatāra* 1:34–5 (de La Vallée Poussin 1901–14: 38, 40; Bhattacharya 1960: 10–11). For an English translation of these verses, see Steinkellner and Peck-Kubaczek in Schmidt-Leukel 2019: 128.

56 Śāntideva, *Bodhicaryāvatāra* 8:22–4 (Bhattacharya 1960: 141; cf. de La Vallée Poussin 1901–14: 294). For an English translation of these verses, see Steinkellner and Peck-Kubaczek in Schmidt-Leukel 2019: 350.

57 Śāntideva, *Bodhicaryāvatāra* 8:15–16 (de La Vallée Poussin 1901–14: 293–4; Bhattacharya 1960: 139). For an English translation of these verses, see Steinkellner and Peck-Kubaczek in Schmidt-Leukel 2019: 350.

58 Śāntideva, *Bodhicaryāvatāra* 6:112–16 (de La Vallée Poussin 1901–14: 231–3; Bhattacharya 1960: 108–9). For an English translation of these verses, see Steinkellner and Peck-Kubaczek in Schmidt-Leukel 2019: 295–6.

59 Śāntideva, *Bodhicaryāvatāra* 5:80 (de La Vallée Poussin 1901–14: 135; Bhattacharya 1960: 72). For an English translation, see Steinkellner and Peck-Kubaczek in Schmidt-Leukel 2019: 236.

60 *Vinayavastu* (T, 'Dul-ba, vol. Ka, fol. 339a4–b5; P, 'Dul-ba, vol. Khe, fol. 223b2–8). This passage contains hefty criticism against the Buddha's disciples, accusing them of trampling and killing small living beings by roaming around during the rainy season. According to them, even *cātaka* (*khug rta*) birds, who are said to subsist on raindrops, are more restrained than these mendicants of Śākyaputra with shaven heads (*muṇḍaka: mgo reg*).

all. For example, no amount of criticism would have caused the Buddha to abandon his soteriology. The *yogiloka*, out of consideration for and as a means of interaction and transaction with the world, does its best to conform to the *prākṛtaloka* and tries its best to refrain from behaviors and conducts that cause the disillusionment of the *prākṛtaloka*, which Śāntideva makes clear in the *Bodhicaryāvatāra* as well as his *Śikṣāsamuccaya*, and which is rooted in Vinaya sources.[61] For the *yogiloka* to communicate with the *prākṛtaloka*, it must resort to the language of the *prākṛtaloka*, an idea made clear, for example, by Āryadeva.[62] This also reminds one of the aspiration of a *bodhisattva* to give teachings in the voices (i.e., languages) of the various sentient beings of the world.[63]

Fifth and finally, the issue of how it is still possible for an awakened being representing the yogic world, who has severed saṃsāric bondage or burnt the saṃsāric seed, to remain in, or return to the non-yogic world, interact with it, and benefit it seems to have culminated in a kind of "Buddhist docetism," often conveyed by expressions such as "conformity to the world" (*lokānuvartanā: 'jig rten dang mthun par mdzad pa / 'jig rten dang mthun par bya ba*), which I cannot discuss here, and Tibetan expressions such as "mere manifestation of the apparitional mode" (*tshul ston pa tsam*).[64] Of the several Sūtric, Tantric, and Śāstric literature that do, in one way or another, convey the idea of docetism, I may merely mention here some early sources such as the *Mahāvastu*,[65] *Lokānuvartanasūtra*,[66] *and*

61 Śāntideva, *Bodhicaryāvatāra* 5:93cd (de La Vallée Poussin 1901–14: 149; Bhattacharya 1960: 75; Negi et al. 1993–2005: s.v. *spang bar bya*). See also the *Śikṣāsamuccaya* (Bendall 1897–1902: 125; noted also in de La Vallée Poussin 1901–14: 149 n.5). For an English translation, see Bendall and Rouse 1922: 125. The *Śikṣāsamuccaya* also cites a Vinaya source which makes the same point (Bendall 1897–1902: 125). For an English translation, see Bendall and Rouse 1922: 125. In the Tibetan Vinaya tradition, there is a proverb similar to the proverb, "When in Rome, do as the Romans do," of which we find three versions: (a) "The Vinaya should conform to the norm of the place" (*'dul ba yul lugs dang bstun*); (b) "The Vinaya should conform to the rule/law of the place" (*'dul ba yul chos dang bstun*); and (c) "The Vinaya should conform to the place and time" (*'dul ba yul dus dang bstun*).

62 Āryadeva, *Catuḥśataka* 8.19 (Lang 1986: 84). For an English translation, see Lang 1986: 85. See also Wangchuk 2020: 99 n.212, where I also allude to Candrakīrti's citation of *Catuḥśataka* 8.19 (i.e., in his *Madhyamakāvatārabhāṣya* and *Prasannapadā*). I take this occasion to correct the wrong page number provided there, that is, "Lang 1986: 82" to "Lang 1986: 84."

63 *Bhadracarī* 18 (Watanabe 1912: 31; cf. *Bhadracarī* 19 in Devi 1958: 16). For a German translation, see Watanabe 1912: 43.

64 That "Buddhist docetism" is indeed a kind of docetism (from Greek *dokein*, "to seem") can be supported by the idea conveyed by the Tibetan expression *tshul ston pa tsam*, often to be found in syntactical constructions such as "mere manifestation of (or manifesting) the apparitional mode of birth and death" (*skye 'chi'i tshul ston pa tsam*), "Śākyamuni has been merely manifesting the apparitional mode of becoming awakened in the realm of (sexual) desire" (*shā kya thub pa 'dod khams su 'tshang rgya ba'i tshul ston pa tsam yin*), "mere manifestation of the apparitional mode of a worldly body" (*'jig rten pa'i skur tshul ston pa tsam*), "merely manifesting the apparitional mode of coming and going" (*gshegs pa dang bzhud pa'i tshul ston pa tsam*), and the like.

65 See, for example, *Mahāvastu* (as cited and discussed in Kuan 2013: 619 n.54): *lokānuvartanāṃ buddhā anuvartanti laukikīṃ | prajñaptim anuvartanti yathā lokottarām api || ... auṣadhaṃ pratisevanti vyādhi caiṣāṃ na vidyate ... eṣā lokānuvartanā || jarāṃ ca upadeśenti na caiṣāṃ vidyate jarā ... eṣā lokānuvartanā ||*.

66 Candrakīrti cites in his *Madhyamakāvatārabhāṣya* seven stanzas (from the *Lokānuvartanasūtra*) and attributes them to Pūrvaśaila offshoot of the Mahāsāṃghika school (Uryuzu and Nakazawa 2012: 66). sKa-ba dPal-brtsegs in his *gSung rab rin po che'i gtam* also cites the *Lokānuvartana(sūtra)* on two occasions (P, fol. 189b3–5; D, fol. 281a2–4, and P, fols. 197b8–198a1; D, fol. 289a1–2). The only

Ratnaguṇasaṃcayagāthā.[67] The Buddhist idea of docetism seems to involve a host of topics related to Buddhology (i.e., in the sense of the Buddhist conceptions of the Buddha's or a *buddha*'s body, speech, mind, qualities, and activities), including the idea of "non-fixed *nirvāṇa*" (*apratiṣṭhitaṃ nirvāṇam* = *apratiṣṭhitanirvāṇa: mi gnas pa'i mya ngan las 'das pa*), which reveals a balancing act of saṃsāric existence and nirvāṇic quiescence by means of discriminating insight (*prajñā: shes rab* = *shes pa*) and compassion (*kṛpā* = *karuṇā: snying rje*).[68] There seems to have been a clash between the Buddhist teaching of the karmic mechanism of (unawakened) sentient beings and of the salvific mechanism of awakened beings. According to the general Buddhist teaching of karmic mechanism, only those who have committed and accumulated volitional deeds (*karman: las*) propelled by one's cognitional-emotional defilements (*kleśa: nyon mongs pa*) can be born in *saṃsāra*. Those who have cut or burnt the roots of *kleśa*s cannot be born in *saṃsāra*. But then, how can those awakened *buddha*s and *bodhisattvas*—and in the case of the one-vehicle (*ekayāna: theg pa gcig*) theory, also *arhants*—remain in or return to *saṃsāra* and be active in it? Various Buddhist traditions (i.e., Yogācāra, Madhyamaka, Tathāgatagarbha, and Mantranaya) seem to have offered various solutions to solve this doctrinal problem, a discussion of which is, however, beyond the present scope. What I do wish to mention here is that the solution offered by the *Mahāyānasūtrālaṃkāra* extends the causes of a *bodhisattva*'s birth in *saṃsāra*.[69] It mentions four causes of a *bodhisattva*'s birth (*utpatti/upapatti: skye ba*) distributed according to four different levels of spiritual progress, namely, the power of volitional deeds (*karmādhipatya/karmavaśa: las kyi dbang*), the power of aspirational resolution (*praṇidhānavaśa: smon lam gyi dbang*), the power of meditative concentration (*samādhyādhipatya: ting nge 'dzin gyi dbang*), and the power of absolute command/mastery (*vibhutvādhipatya: dbang 'byor pa'i dbang*). The most important underlying motive, however, seems to be compassion, which enables a *bodhisattva* to maintain a continuity of existence (*bhavasaṃtati: srid mtshams sbyor* [*ba*] = *srid pa'i rgyun*).[70] In sum, the basic idea is that in whatever form the *prākṛtaloka* can be benefited best, in

stanza that both Candrakīrti and dPal-brtsegs cite is the *zhig pa med* verse and the only difference is that the Tibetan translation of the *Madhyamakāvatārabhāṣya* reads *brjod mdzad pa* instead dPal-brtsegs's *ston mdzad pa*. The Sanskrit text of the *zhig pa med* verse is as follows (Seyfort Ruegg 2010: 129; Uryuzu and Nakazawa 2012: 66 n.587): *avināśam anutpannaṃ dharmadhātusamaṃ jagat | sattvadhātuṃ ca deśeti eṣā lokānuvartanā ||*.

67 *Ratnaguṇasaṃcayagāthā* 8.2 (Yuyama 1976: 38, 167; cf. Obermiller 1937: 38): *traidhātukaṃ samatikrānta na bodhisattvāḥ kleśāpanīta upapatti nidarśayanti | jaravyādhimṛtyuvigatāś cyuti darśayanti prajñāya pāramita yatra caranti dhīrāḥ ||*.

68 See, for example, Maitreya (ascribed), *Abhisamayālaṃkāra* 1.10ab (Stcherbatsky and Obermiller 1929: 3): *prajñayā na bhave sthānaṃ kṛpayā na śame sthitiḥ* |; Tibetan in Stcherbatsky and Obermiller 1929: 4.

69 Maitreya (ascribed), *Mahāyānasūtrālaṃkāra* 20–21.8 (Lévi 1907: 177): *karmaṇaś cādhipatyena praṇidhānasya cāparā |samādheś ca vibhutvasya cotpattir dhīmatāṃ matā ||*; Tibetan in P, fol. 40b6–7; D, fol. 36b1–2.

70 Nāgārjuna, *Ratnāvalī* 4.66 (Hahn 1982: 118): *bodhisattvo 'pi dṛṣṭaivaṃ saṃbodhau niyato mataḥ | kevalaṃ tv asya kāruṇyādā bodher bhavasaṃtatiḥ ||*; Tibetan in Hahn 1982: 119.

that form would the *yogiloka* manifest. If necessary, according to the *Vimalakīrtinirdeś asūtra*,[71] also cited by Śāntideva in his *Śikṣāsamucya*, even as a courtesan.[72]

What I have attempted to do in this chapter is to examine the *prākṛtaloka–yogiloka* dichotomy proposed by Śāntideva in terms of six related perspectives, namely, (1) communication, (2) methodology, (3) ontology, (4) epistemology, (5) axiology, and (6) relations. There is an enormous amount of material that I would still need to explore and assess so as to enable me to corroborate the claims I made in this paper. Nonetheless, I hope I could convey what I believe is Śāntideva's idea of the yogic and non-yogic worlds and their complex and complicated relationship.[73]

Abbreviations

D Hakuju Ui, Munetada Suzuki, Yenshō Kanakura, and Tōkan Tadaet, *A Complete Catalogue of the Tibetan Buddhist Canons (Bkaḥ-ḥgyur and Bstan-ḥgyur)*, Sendai: Tōhoku Imperial University (aided by Saitō Gratitude Foundation) 1934.

P Daisetz T. Suzuki, *The Tibetan Tripitaka, Peking Edition: Catalogue & Index*. 2 vols., Tokyo: Suzuki Research Foundation 1962.

T Tadeusz Skorupski, *A Catalogue of the sTog Palace Kanjur* (Bibliographia Philologica Buddhica Series Maior 4), Tokyo: International Institute for Buddhist Studies 1985.

Primary Sources (Autochthonous Tibetan)

bSlab gsum rgyan gyi me tog bCom-ldan Rig(s)-pa'i-ral-gri, *bSlab pa gsum gyi rgyan gyi me tog = bDe bar gshegs pa'i shākya'i bstan pa'i bslab gsum rgyan gyi me tog*. In *Rig(s) ral gsung 'bum*, vol. 1, pp. 258–439.

dBu ma rgyan 'grel Mi-pham rNam-rgyal-rgya-mtsho, *dBu ma rgyan gyi rnam bshad 'jam dbyangs bla ma dgyes pa'i zhal lung*. In *'Jam mgon 'ju mi pham rgya mtsho'i gsung 'bum rgyas pa sde dge dgon chen par ma. The Expanded Redaction of the Complete Works of 'Ju Mi pham. Reconstructed and reproduced from the surviving prints at the order of H. H. Dilgo Chhentse Rimpoche*. 27 vols. Paro: Lama Ngodrup and Sherab Drimey, 1984–93, vol. 13 (Nga).

[71] *Vimalakīrtinirdeśa(sūtra)* §7.32 (Study Group 2006: 82; cf. Study Group 2004: 318): *saṃcintya gaṇikā bhonti puṃsām ākarṣaṇāya te | rāgāṅkuśena lobhetvā buddhajñāne sthapenti te* ||; Tibetan in T, fol. 366a7–b1; P, fol. 225b2 (Study Group 2004: 318). For an English translation, see Gómez et al. 2022: 90.

[72] Śāntideva, *Śikṣāsamuccaya* (Bendall 1897–1902: 326). For an English translation, see Bendall and Rouse 1922: 291.

[73] The present contribution is based on the lecture with the same title held on 25 May 2023 on the occasion of the International Workshop at the Cluster of Excellence with the title "Śāntideva and the Dynamics of Tradition" (25–7 May 2023, University of Münster) organized by Stephen E. Harris (University of Leiden) and Perry Schmidt-Leukel (University of Münster). Without their generosity, patience, encouragement, and editorial help, I would not have managed to submit my contribution even in this imperfect form. My thanks are thus due to the organizers. I am, of course, solely responsible for all the imperfections that abound.

'Dod don lam khyer	Kaḥ-thog-pa Ye-shes-rgyal-mtshan, *dPa' bo tshogs kyi rnam rol zhes bya ba'i ṭikka (sic) 'dod don lam khyer*. In *sNga 'gyur bka' ma shin tu rgyas pa*. 133 vols. Chengdu: Si-khron-dpe-skrun-tshogs-pa and Si-khron-mi-rigs-dpe-skrun-khang, 2009, vol. Ma (16), pp. 111–67.
Grub mtha' rgyan gyi me tog	bCom-ldan Rig(s)-pa'i-ral-gri, *Grub mtha' rgyan gyi me tog*. In *Rig(s) ral gsung 'bum*, vol. 5, pp. 102–425.
gSung thor bu	Bu-ston Rin-chen-grub, *Thams cad mkhyen pa bu ston rin po che'i gsung thor bu*. In *Gangs can mkhas grub kun gyi cod paṇ thams cad mkhyen pa bu ston lo tsā ba rin chen grub dpal bzang po mchog gi bka' 'bum* [Reprint of Zhol xylographic edition]. 26 vols. New Delhi: International Academy of Indian Culture, 1965–71 [BDRC: W22106], vol. 26, pp. 143–346.
gSung rab rin po che'i gtam	sKa-ba dPal-brtsegs, *gSung rab rin po che'i gtam rgyud dang shākya'i rabs rgyud* (P5844; D4357).
Klu sgrub dgongs rgyan	dGe-'dun-chos-'phel, *dBu ma'i zab gnad snying por dril ba'i legs bshad klu sgrub dgongs rgyan*. In *mKhas dbang dge 'dun chos 'phel gyi gsar rnyed gsung rtsom*, compiled by rDo-rje-rgyal. Hong Kong: Zhang-kang-gyi-ling-par-skrun-khang, 2002, pp. 172–269.
mTsho ṭīk	mTsho-sna-ba Shes-rab-bzang-po, *'Dul ṭīk nyi ma'i 'od zer legs bshad lung gi rgya mtsho*. Xining: Krung-go'i-bod-kyi-shes-rig-dpe-skrun-khang, 1993.
Nges shes sgron me	Mi-pham rNam-rgyal-rgya-mtsho, *Nges shes rin po che'i sgron me*. In *'Jam mgon 'ju mi pham rgya mtsho'i gsung 'bum rgyas pa sde dge dgon chen par ma. The Expanded Redaction of the Complete Works of 'Ju Mi pham. Reconstructed and reproduced from the surviving prints at the order of H. H. Dilgo Chhentse Rimpoche*. 27 vols. Paro: Lama Ngodrup and Sherab Drimey, 1984–93, vol. 9 (Shrī).
rDo rje'i lu	dPal-sprul O-rgyan-'jigs-med-chos-kyi-dbang-po, *mTsungs don man ngag rdo rje'i thal glu spros bral sgra dbyangs*. In *dPal sprul o rgyan 'jigs med chos kyi dbang po'i gsum 'bum*. 8 vols. [Xining]: mTsho-sngon-nang-bstan-rig-gnas-sgyu-rtsal-zhabs-zhu-lte-gnas-zhabs-zhu-khang, n.d., vol. 8, pp. 260–371.
rDzogs chen chos 'byung	sMyo-shul-mkhan-po 'Jam-dbyangs-rdo-rje, *Rang bzhin rdzogs pa chen po'i chos 'byung rig 'dzin brgyud pa'i rnam thar ngo mtshar nor bu bai ḍūrya'i phreng ba (= rDzogs chen chos 'byung)*. 2 vols. (E and Waṃ). Thimphu: Shanti Ashram, Moti Thang, n.d.
Rigs pa'i mtshon cha	bCom-ldan Rig(s)-pa'i-ral-gri, *Tshad ma bsdus pa rigs pa'i mtshon cha = Tshad ma'i bstan bcos gzhan phyogs zil gnon rigs pa'i mtshon cha = Grub mtha' sna tshogs bshad pa bde bar gshegs pa'i bstan pa'i sgron me. Sa skya'i dpe rnying bsdus sgrig khang, gsum rgyan gyi me tog*, edited by Sa-skya'i-dpe-rnying-bsdu-

	sgrig-khang. [Lhasa: Bod-ljongs-bod-yig-dpe- rnying-dpe-skrun-khang, 2010?].
Rig(s) ral gsung 'bum	*Id., bCom ldan rigs pa'i ral gri'i gsung 'bum*. 10 vols. [Lhasa: Khams-sprul bSod nams-don-grub], 2006.
Shes bya mdzod	Kong-sprul Yon-tan-rgya-mtsho alias Blo-gros-mtha'-yas, *Theg pa'i sgo kun las btus pa gsung rab rim po che'i mdzod bslab pa gsum legs par ston pa'i bstan bcos shes bya kun khyab [rtsa 'grel]*. Beijing: Mi-rigs-dpe-skrun-khang, 2002.

References

Almogi, O. (2009), *Rong-zom-pa's Discourses on Buddhology: A Study of Various Conceptions of Buddhahood in Indian Sources with Special Reference to the Controversy Surrounding the Existence of Gnosis (jñāna: ye shes) as Presented by the Eleventh-Century Tibetan Scholar Rong-zom Chos-kyi-bzang-po* (Studia Philologica Buddhica Monograph Series 24), Tokyo: International Institute for Buddhist Studies.

Almogi, O. (2010), "Māyopamādvayavāda versus Sarvadharmāpratiṣṭhānavāda: A Late Indian Subclassification of Madhyamaka and its Reception in Tibet," *Journal of the International College for Postgraduate Buddhist Studies* 14: 135–212.

Anālayo, B. (2009), "Vivāda," *Encyclopaedia of Buddhism* 8: 718–20.

Bendall, C., ed. (1897–1902), *Çikshāsamuccaya: A Compendium of Buddhist Teaching Compiled by Çāntideva Chiefly from Earlier Mahāyāna-sūtras* (Bibliotheca Buddhica 1), St. Petersburg: The Russian Academy of Sciences.

Bendall, C. and W. D. Rouse, trans. (1922), *Śikṣā Samuccaya: A Compendium of Buddhist Doctrine Compiled by Śāntideva Chiefly from Early Mahāyāna Sūtras*, London: John Murray.

Bernhard, F., ed. (1965), *Udānavarga. Band I: Einleitung, Beschreibung der Handschriften, Textausgabe, Bibliographie* (Sanskrittexte aus den Turfanfunden 10), Göttingen: Vandenhoeck & Ruprecht.

Bhattacharya, V., ed. (1960), *Bodhicaryāvatāra* (Bibliotheca Indica), Calcutta: The Asiatic Society.

Bodhi, Bhikkhu, trans. (2000), *The Connected Discourses of the Buddha. A Translation of the Saṃyutta Nikāya*, Boston: Wisdom Publications.

Conze, E., trans. (1975), *The Perfection of Wisdom in Eight Thousand Lines & Its Verse Summary*. 2nd rev. edn., Bolinas, CA: Four Seasons Foundation.

Devi, S., ed. (1958), *Samantabhadracaryā-praṇidhānarāja* (Śatapiṭaka 4), New Delhi: International Academy of Indian Culture.

Gómez, L. and P. Harrison (with the Mangalam Translation Group), trans. (2022), *Vimalakīrtinirdeśa: The Teaching of Vimalakīrti. An English Translation of the Sanskrit Text Found in the Potala Palace, Lhasa*, Berkeley: Mangalam Press.

Hahn, M., ed. (1982), *Nāgārjuna's Ratnāvalī. Vol. 1: The Basic Texts (Sanskrit, Tibetan, Chinese)*. (Indica et Tibetica 1), Bonn: Indica et Tibetica Verlag.

Higgins D. and M. Draszczyk (2016), *Mahāmudrā and the Middle Way: Post-Classical Kagyü Discourses on Mind, Emptiness and Buddha-Nature* (Wiener Studien zur Tibetologie und Buddhismuskunde 90.1), Vienna: Arbeitskreis für Tibetische und Buddhistische Studien Universität Wien.

Hokazono, K., ed. (1994), *Raritavisutara no Kenkyū Jōkan [Jōkan = vol. 1 = Lalitavistarasūtra: Chapters 1–14]*, Tokyo: Daitō Shuppansha.

Ichigo, M., ed. (1985), *Madhyamakālaṃkāra of Śāntirakṣita with His Own Commentary or Vṛtti and with the Subcommentary or Pañjikā of Kamalaśīla*, Kyoto: Buneido.

Kritzer, R. (2014), *Garbhāvakrāntisūtra: The Sūtra on Entry into the Womb* (Studia Philologia Buddhica Monograph Series 31), Tokyo: The International Institute for Buddhist Studies.

Kuan, T. (2013), "Legends and Transcendence: Sectarian Affiliations of the Ekottarika Āgama in Chinese Translation," *Journal of the American Oriental Society* 133 (4): 607–34.

de La Vallée Poussin, L., ed. (1901–14), *Bodhicaryāvatārapañjikā: Prajñākaramati's Commentary on the Bodhicaryāvatāra of Śāntideva*, edited with indices, 7 fascicules, Calcutta: The Asiatic Society.

de La Vallée Poussin, L., ed. (1931), "À propos du *Cittaviśuddhiprakaraṇa* d'Aryadeva," *Bulletin of the School of Oriental Studies* 6 (2): 411–15.

Lang, K., ed. (1986), *Āryadeva's Catuḥśataka: On the Bodhisattva's Cultivation of Merit and Knowledge* (Indiske Studier 7), Copenhagen: Akademisk Forlag.

Lasic, H., Li, X., and A. MacDonald, eds. (2022), *Candrakīrti's Madhyamakāvatārabhāṣya: Chapters 1 to 5: Critically and diplomatically edited on the basis of preparatory work by Helmut Krasser (†)* (Sanskrit Texts from the Tibetan Autonomous Region 22), Vienna: China Tibetology Research Center. Austrian Academy of Sciences Press.

Lévi, S., ed. and trans. (1907), *Mahāyāna-Sūtrālaṃkāra, Tome I: Exposé de la doctrine du Grand Véhicule selon le système* Yogācāra, Paris: Librarie Honore Champion.

Li, S. (2012), *Candrakīrti's Āgama: A Study of the Concept and Uses of Scripture in Classical Indian Buddhism* (Doctoral Dissertation), Michigan: University of Wisconsin–Madison.

Li, S. (2019), "Dimensions of Candrakīrti's Conventional Reality," *Journal of Indian Philosophy* 47: 49–72.

Li, X., ed. (2015), "Madhyamakāvatāra-kārikā: Chapter 6," *Journal of Indian Philosophy* 43: 1–30.

Li, X. and S. Ye, eds. (2014), *Yuktiṣaṣṭikākārikā: Editions of the Sanskrit, Tibetan and Chinese Versions, with Commentary and a Modern Chinese Translation*, Shanghai: Zhongxi Book Company.

Lopez Jr., D. S., trans. (2006), *The Madman's Middle Way: Reflections on Reality of the Tibetan Monk Gendun Chopel* (Buddhism and Modernity), Chicago: University of Chicago Press.

Negi, J. S. et al. (1993–2005), *Bod skad dang legs sbyar gyi tshig mdzod chen mo: Tibetan-Sanskrit Dictionary*. 16 vols, Sarnath: Central Institute of Higher Tibetan Studies, Dictionary Unit.

Nor-bu (mKhan-po Chos-'phel-nor-bu) et al., eds. (2022), *Shes rab kyi le'u'i tshig don go sla bar rnam par bshad pa nor bu ke ta ka*, Jeerango, Gajapati: Ārya-pa-lo'i-rtsom-sgrig-khang, Rigon Thubten Mindrolling Monastery.

Obermiller, E., trans. (1932), *History of Buddhism (Chos-ḥbyung) by Bu-ston II. Part: The History of Buddhism in India and Tibet*, (Heidelberg) Leipzig: Harrassowitz (in Kommission).

Obermiller, E., ed. (1937), *Prajñā Pāramitā-Ratna-Guṇa-Saṃcaya-Gāthā: Sanscrit & Tibetan Text* [*sic*] (Bibliotheca Buddhica 29), Leningrad: USSR Academy of Sciences Press.

Patel, P. B., ed. (1949), *Cittavisuddhiprakarana of Aryadeva. Sanskrit and Tibetan texts* (Visva-Bharati Studies 8), Calcutta: Visva-Bharati.

Rahula, W. (1956), *History of Buddhism in Ceylon: The Anuradhapura Period, 3rd Century BC – 10th Century AC*, Colombo: M. D. Gunasena.

Roloff, C. (2020), *The Buddhist Nun's Ordination in the Tibetan Canon: Possibilities of the Revival of the Mūlasarvāstivāda Bhikṣuṇī Lineage* (Hamburg Buddhist Studies 15), Bochum-Freiburg: Projekt Verlag.

Sad-mi-mi-bzhi (2018), mKhan-po bKra-shis-rdo-rje, mKhan-po O-rgyan-rig-'dzin, mKhan-po dPal-bzang-dar-rgyas & Slob-dpon-ma [now mKhan-mo] Karma-dbyangs-can, *sNang ba lhar sgrub pa'i tshul la brtag pa | rong zom pa'i mdzad rnam dang | snang ba lhar sgrub chen mo'i zhib dpyad zhu dag | de'i brjod bya rjod byed la brtag pa |* (Ngagyur Nyingma Research Centre Publication Series 1), Bylakuppe, Mysore: Ngagyur Nyingma Research Centre.

Scherrer-Schaub, C., ed. and trans. (1991), *Yuktiṣaṣṭikāvṛtti: Commentaire à la soixantaine sur le raisonnement ou du vrai enseignement de la causalité par le Maître indien Candrakīrti*, Brussels: Institut belge des hautes études chinoises.

Schmidt-Leukel, P. (2019), *Buddha Mind – Christ Mind. A Christian Commentary on the Bodhicaryāvatāra.* With a new translation by E. Steinkellner and C. Peck-Kubaczek, Leuven: Peeters.

Seyfort Ruegg, D. (1981), *The Literature of the Madhyamaka School of Philosophy in* India (A History of Indian Literature 7), Wiesbaden: Otto Harrassowitz.

Seyfort Ruegg, D. (2010), *The Buddhist Philosophy of the Middle: Essays on Indian and Tibetan Madhyamaka* (Studies in Indian and Tibetan Buddhism), Boston: Wisdom Publications.

Stcherbatsky, T. and E. Obermiller, eds. (1929), *Abhisamayālaṅkāra-Prajñāpāramitā-Upadeśa-Śāstra: The Work of Bodhisattva Maitreya. Part 1: Introduction, Sanskrit Text and Tibetan Translation*, Leningrad: USSR Academy of Sciences Press.

Study Group, ed. (2004), *Vimalakīrtinirdeśa: Transliterated Sanskrit Text Collated with Tibetan and Chinese Translations*, Tokyo: Taisho University Press.

Study Group, ed. (2006), *Vimalakīrtinirdeśa: A Sanskrit Edition Based upon the Manuscript Newly Found at the Potala Palace*, Tokyo: Taisho University Press.

Tillemans, T. J. F. (2019), "Mādhyamikas Playing Bad Hands: The Case of Customary Truth," *Journal of Indian Philosophy* (*Special Issue on Words, Concepts, and the Middle Way: Language in the Traditions of Madhyamaka Thought*) 47: 635–44.

Uryuzu, R. and M. Nakazawa, eds. (2012), *Tibetan edition of the Madhyamakāvatārabhāṣya*. Online: http://kishin-syobo.com/index.php?%E8%B3%87%E6%96%99.

Wangchuk, D. (2009), "A Relativity Theory of the Purity and Validity of Perception in Indo-Tibetan Buddhism," in E. Franco and D. Eigner (eds.), *Perception, Meditation, and Altered States of Consciousness*, 215–37, Vienna: Austrian Academy of Sciences.

Wangchuk, D. (2020), "Secrecy in Buddhism," in O. Almogi (ed.), *Birds as Ornithologists: Scholarship between Faith and Reason: Intra- and Inter-disciplinary Perspectives* (Indian and Tibetan Studies 8), 7–177, Hamburg: Department of Indian and Tibetan Studies, Universität Hamburg.

Watanabe, K. (1912), *Die Bhadracarī: Eine Probe buddhistisch-religiöser Lyrik, untersucht und herausgegeben*, Leipzig: G. Kreysing.

Yotsuya, K. (1999), *The Critique of Svatantra Reasoning by Candrakīrti and Tsong-kha-pa: A Study of Philosophical Proof according to Two Prāsaṅgika Madhyamaka Traditions of India and Tibet* (Tibetan and Indo-Tibetan Studies 8), Stuttgart: Franz Steiner Verlag.

Yuyama, A., ed. (1976), *Prajñā-pāramitā-ratna-guṇa-saṃcaya-gāthā (Sanskrit Recension A): Edited with an Introduction, Bibliographical Notes and a Tibetan Version from Tunhuang*, Cambridge: Cambridge University Press.

Zongtse, C. T., ed. (1990), *Udānavarga Band III: Der tibetische Text unter Mitarbeiter von Siglinde Dietz* (Sanskrittexte aus den Turfanfunden 10 [3]), Göttingen: Vandenhoeck & Ruprecht.

6

Mockery, Sarcasm, and Irony in the *Bodhicaryāvatāra*

Perry Schmidt-Leukel

Today, our knowledge about the author of the *Bodhicaryāvatāra* (hereafter BCA) has significantly advanced. For, now, we *do know* that we know next to nothing about the person to whom tradition gave various names (such as Śāntivarman, Acalasena, Bhusuku, Akṣayamati, Śāntideva), among which "Śāntideva" finally prevailed.[1] Analyzing the different versions of the accumulating legend reveals that these versions are better understood not as memories of his life but as reflections of the growing reputation and shifting perception of the text and its various facets mirrored in the different hagiographic personae that the alleged author assumed (Schmidt-Leukel 2019: 15–52). It seems that, initially, Śāntideva was presented as a simple monk, ignorant of the *sūtras* yet, according to some versions, skilled in meditation, ideal to serve as a mouthpiece for Manjuśrī's *ipsissima vox*, the supernatural inspirer and therefore true author of the celebrated text, with Nālandā functioning as the stage and its highly learned monks as the baffled witnesses of this miraculous revelation. Legend then turned Śāntideva into a wise scholar who out of humility merely disguised his intellectual caliber by pretending to be a dunce, before legend soon presented him as one of Nālandā's most eminent *paṇḍita*s. Further features of the developing narratives showed him, in different phases of his imagined life, as a compassionate, politically influential *bodhisattva* and as a powerful miracle-working *siddha*, indeed even as a mighty wizard engaging in a Harry Potter-like magical battle with Śaṅkara not hesitating to destroy the temples and cities of the heretic's followers in order to re-establish Buddhism—though the violence was softened to some extent in other versions of the legend. The transformation of Śāntideva's image, and thus of the perception of the text, continues into the present where he is displayed, for example, as an eccentric but skillful poet (as in Kachru 2019) or as someone much akin to a sober contemporary analytic philosopher providing moral guidance suitable for a secular age (as sometimes in the writings of "The Cowherds").[2]

1 *Pace* Williams 1995, Gold 2019, and many others, we do not know that he was a scholar at Nālandā, which is most likely a later fabrication.

2 "The Cowherds are an international collective of scholars in Buddhist Studies … united by a commitment to rigorous philosophical analysis as an approach to understanding Buddhist metaphysics and epistemology" (backcover text of The Cowherds 2016).

The following observations offer a still different image. They do not show a person with a serene, detached, and rational position above life's existential struggles but someone with a rather pessimistic view of human nature, seeking refuge in supernatural protection. He oscillates between an unsurpassably high ideal of altruistic perfection and the awareness of his own substantial failure leaving no other choice than trusting in what later forms of Buddhism called "other power" (*tariki*).[3] As Sonam Kachru states, "Śāntideva ... internalizes an exemplary ideal and increasingly comes to a sense of his distance from it and the recalcitrance of his embodied life to the ideals he has committed to, and for which he tasks himself to provide reasons" (Kachru 2019: 75). Śāntideva exhibits a mind "subject to all the confusions that change and self-reflection can involve" (69). In addition, his "work is composed in a way that we might find ourselves to be among his subjects" (68). This certainly more human and probably more realistic image may take us nearer to the personality of the unknown author of at least the presumably earliest form of the BCA.[4] It reflects character features that seem to shine through several remarks which can be best characterized along the spectrum of mockery, sarcasm, and irony.

1. Sarcasm

Sarcasm is a form of mockery with usually a rather negative or pessimistic tone. In its ironic form, a positive, appreciative, or sympathetic statement is made while meaning the opposite. As such, it may express some mild and satiric but often also bitter humor. A typical example of harsh sarcasm from a Buddhist text is found in *Abhidharmakośa bhāṣya* (commentary on verse 2:64d) criticizing the theist with the words:

> ... do you say that God finds satisfaction in seeing the creatures that he has created in the prey of all the sufferings of existence, including the tortures of the hells?
>
> Homage to this God! Well said, in truth, is the popular stanza, "He is called Rudra because he burns, because he is excited, ferocious, terrible, an eater of flesh, blood, and marrow."[5]

"Homage to this God!" is clearly intended as meaning the opposite. And it ridicules the theist for his inappropriate veneration of a being that in no way deserves such praise. A somewhat similar case is found in the BCA, which ridicules Sāṅkhya teachings by saying, "If the fruit were present in the cause, then one who eats rice would be eating excrement, and then one should buy cotton seed for the price of a dress and wear it"

[3] Those developments are especially (though not exclusively) connected to the so-called Pure Land Tradition (Foard et al. 1996) and find one of their most radical expressions in the writings of Shinran Shōnin (Ueda and Hirota 1989).

[4] This earliest form of the BCA seems to be lost, but according to Akira Saito's strong arguments, the Dunhuang version might be a translation of it. For a summary of the text-critical issues regarding the genesis of the BCA, see Schmidt-Leukel 2019: 3–12.

[5] Pruden 1991: 307. The verse quoted is from the *Śatarudrīya (Vyākhyā), Mahābhārata*. I am grateful to Chris Vic Jones who alerted me to this example.

(9:136–7).[6] While this example does not operate by ironic contrasts, the similarity to the sample from the *Abhidharmakośabhāṣya* consists in making rather drastic polemical fun of someone else's religious or philosophical beliefs. It lacks, however, a feature which is prominent in most (if not all) of the other mockeries, sarcasms, and ironies in the BCA, that is, the emphasis on the general blindness or foolishness of human beings, admittedly and intentionally including the author himself.[7] Śāntideva is aware that the "worldly ways" he criticizes (8:185) are still very much part of his own mind.

Sarcastic mockery may be hurtful, but it may also be an attempt to evoke self-critical reflection. As psychological experiments suggest "sarcasm, used with care and in moderation, can … trigger some creative sparks. … Because the brain must think creatively to understand or convey a sarcastic comment, sarcasm may lead to clearer and more creative thinking" (Gino 2015).

Indeed, sarcastic humor can be complex and complicated. Consider, for example, the following slate I once spotted outside a Scottish pub. On the one hand, in saying

[6] All translations from the BCA are taken from the new translation by Erich Steinkellner (with Cynthia Peck-Kubaczek) in Schmidt-Leukel 2019.

[7] Verses 9:136–7 belong to the material not contained in the Dunhuang version of the BCA. Hence it remains unclear whether these verses are from the same author as of the presumably earlier version of the text. Moreover, verses 9:136–7 ridicule an attitude that Śāntideva himself assumes when he, for example, says that the lover embraces a body which is nothing else than the bones that this body will be reduced to after death (8:41–3).

"Come In" it seems to mean the opposite, namely to prevent people from visiting the pub by warning them that in the long run such socializing will lead to the unpleasant experience of divorce. Yet simultaneously, and in contrast, it actually does invite visitors to step in as an act of accepting life as it is, despite any pessimistic perspectives, and thus let themselves not be discouraged from (and make them even curious on) living it. At least it sends the subliminal message that this pub is an honest place. This gets close to a kind of sarcasm which is not a one-way mockery about others but is self-deprecating and self-ironic and points to some non-sarcastic truth—something we find in the BCA at several places. The BCA "might show us of what we are like" (Kachru 2019: 68), but the author makes his mostly negative picture of our ordinary existence more acceptable by including himself in the mockery.

2. Satirical mockery, biting irony, and self-deprecating sarcasm

The BCA is replete with negative and pessimistic utterances about the state of the "world" (*jagat*), usually meaning here the "world of sentient beings." In 8:69, for example, Śāntideva says, "the world is full of crazy people zealously deceiving themselves." People behave like fools in that they create their own suffering even though they abhor suffering. And he does not exclude himself from this assessment: "I do not long for suffering, but in my foolishness I long for the cause of suffering" (6:45). Such foolishness is presented as part of the defilements (*kleśa*). And "this world is totally subject to the defilements, incapable of accomplishing its own benefit" (7:50). These statements do not match easily with the image of Śāntideva as an optimistic philosopher and moral educator. According to Śāntideva himself, "the good is always weak," while "the power of evil is great and terrible" (1:6).

In illustrating the world's and his own foolishness, Śāntideva uses examples that deride and make fun of the most common forms of ordinary and innocent conduct, as, for example, caring for one's body: "Knowing that he will not stay, one does not give a servant clothes or other things. After eating, the body will leave. Why do you bear the costs?" (5:68). Or: "You cannot eat the impure flesh nor drink the blood, cannot slurp the guts. So what will you do with the body?" (5:65). Or: "You do not take a clean wooden doll for yourself; why do you protect this stinking machine that has been forged with filth?" (5:61). In other words, we would not waste money for a servant who leaves. But this is what we do with our body which will perish. We cannot even eat our own body, so what is its use? And why do we consider our transient and unsavory body as our self, when we would not even do this with a nice and clean doll? There is hardly anyone who would spontaneously agree with Śāntideva in that caring for one's body is foolish. It is only by his comparisons that Śāntideva puts such ordinary behavior in a different and negative light thereby performing his sarcastic mockery. Indeed, no one would pay an unreliable servant, waste money on an inedible meal, and identify with an ugly and stinking machine. But, says Śāntideva, we all show this kind of foolish behavior when it comes to the body. It is our blindness to the deeper truth that prevents us from seeing the appropriateness of the comparisons and the foolishness of our conduct. By sarcastically pointing out the incongruity between what we would normally consider as crazy in the said examples, yet take as reasonable in relation our body, Śāntideva apparently wants to trigger the sarcasm-induced "clearer and more creative thinking."[8]

Let us take a further look at Śāntideva's remarks on body-related enjoyments: "Of course you are terrified by the sight of some skeletons at the charnel ground; in the charnel ground of the village, where walking skeletons crowd, you are cheerful" (8:70; similarly, 8:48). We would find it insane to enjoy the company of skeletons but nevertheless rejoice in them if they are still moving around. This satirical mockery exhibits the same structure as the previous examples: the ordinary habit of enjoying social company is compared to a kind of behavior that usually everyone would reasonably abhor, the company of dead bodies. Similar mockery is directed against the two Vedic goals of life: wealth/power (*artha*) and sensual pleasure (*kāma*)—which indicate what many if not most people pursue in their lives. Śāntideva's judgment is brief and succinct: "Realize that a fortune is a misfortune" and "the wants of the lecherous are great, small in contrast the pleasures" (8:79–80). Regarding the pursuit of *artha*, Śāntideva argues that the distress in acquiring and protecting it with the sure prospect of losing everything at death bears no proportion to any reward. Similarly, the short moments of sensual pleasure are not worth the trouble coming along with them. But note again the satirical mockery that turns ordinary views upside down: "fortune is a misfortune" and pleasure is linked to unfulfilled "wants."

In deriding *kāma*, Śāntideva draws again on the unclean and transient nature of the body. On kissing, he has to say: "Spit and faeces … come from the same food. Of these you find the faeces disgusting. Why are you fond of drinking the spittle?" (8:49). Spending money on matchmakers and risking one's reputation only for the sake of embracing female bodies is foolish, because these bodies are actually nothing but the bones of the skeletons. "Why don't you embrace them [the skeletons] lustfully and find bliss?" (8:41–3). In this context Śāntideva ventures into the probably worst and most disgusting sarcasm of his text (8:44–5, 51):

> The face which you once saw as it was hardly lifted, lowered in modesty, or did not see when covered by a veil, this face has now been exposed by vultures, as if they had pity on your distress. Look at it! Why don't you flee now?
>
> About what you are passionate even when covered why is it not dear when uncovered? If it brings you nothing, why do you caress what is covered?

The comparison here is between the cover of the veil or dress of a woman's body and the cover that is her skin. The lover is eager to see the face (and body) of the woman uncovered, without veil or dress, but is repulsed when the body is fully uncovered, that is, without skin. In other words: You want to see the woman naked? Why don't you want to see her fully naked, without the cover of her skin? To Śāntideva, sexual attraction is a major part of the world's foolishness. He depicts sex as deeply deceiving in as much as it binds us to what is transient, making us cling to what we actually abhor and causing far more suffering than pleasure.

Like many Buddhist texts and their authors, Śāntideva uses sexual attraction as one of the key samples to illustrate greed, which, along with hate and delusion, is one of the

[8] On the role of incongruity in Śāntideva's humor, see also Harris 2024.

three cardinal defilements. He does not spare his sarcasm either when it comes to anger or hate. He ridicules anger by once more employing the comparison with nonsensical behavior: "If the nature of fools is pestering others, it is inappropriate for me to be angry at them as at a fire whose nature is burning. And if this fault is accidental and all beings are pleasant by nature, even then being angry at them is just as unjustified as being angry at the air when it is filled with biting smoke" (6:39–40). It would be foolish to be annoyed by the fact that fire is hot as it would be foolish to be angry with the air when it is polluted by smoke. But, he says, this is how we behave when we are angry with other people. Anger, as he wants to show by this derision, is nothing but foolishness.

A harsher scoff is found in 5:12 where he writes: "How many evil beings, infinite as the sky, could I kill? But when the angry mind is killed, all enemies are killed." Here Śāntideva satirically seems to admit to the hateful person that he wants to kill only evil people. But as Śāntideva sarcastically argues, unfortunately their number is infinite and therefore it is actually impossible to kill them all. Hence it is better to kill one's angry mind, then all enemies are killed at once (because only anger perceives them as "enemies"). Here the satirical element is rooted in that Śāntideva gives a positive sense to what Buddhism usually considers as negative. In this case "killing." Killing becomes good when it is the killing of anger. Or as he says in a different place, hate is good if it is "hate for hate" (6:41; see also 4:43). Similarly, jealousy and pride are great if they are practiced by putting oneself in the other's shoes (8:140). And greed, even as passionate lust, is good if directed toward the compassionate activity of the bodhisattva (7:15, 31–2, 62–4). In fact, the key defilement of delusion (*moha*) is good if it serves compassion (9:76–7). And, above all, "thirst" or "desire" (*tṛṣṇa*), usually the Buddhist root of all evil, is good if it is the bodhisattva's "thirst/desire" for the welfare of others (8:109). Such an inversion of values, even Buddhist values, is characteristic of a form of sarcastic humor that one might call "inverted sarcasm" and is found at various places in the BCA.

3. Inverted sarcasm

Often sarcasm consists in saying something positive but actually expressing a negative meaning as in the following example: "'Pat, don't work so hard!', a boss might say upon catching his assistant surfing the Internet" (Gino 2015). Conversely, in inverted sarcasm, a statement that to ordinary ears sounds negative and sarcastic is taken as actually having a positive sense exactly in what it says. As if someone would wish to say to Pat that surfing the Internet is—from some other perspective—indeed hard work.

A good example of this is found in BCA 6:14–15: "By practicing mild pains, great agony becomes tolerable as well. Mosquitoes, gnats, flies, hunger, thirst and other painful sensations and afflictions such as severe itching, why do you disregard these as useless?" This sarcasm is much like black humor in the ears of ordinary "worldly" beings. For, what Śāntideva is saying here is that we should welcome small sufferings because they prepare us for the greater sufferings still to come. However, he gives this sarcastic statement a non-sarcastic, non-ironic meaning. Small sufferings are indeed a benefit to the bodhisattva in various ways, not just by preparing him for the greater sufferings that the bodhisattva path will inevitably imply, but also in making the bodhisattva more empathic and compassionate regarding the suffering of others. The worldly ways of thinking just do not recognize this.

Other examples are found in the same context. In 6:12, we read: "Happiness is attained with difficulty, suffering remains easily. Yet only through suffering do we escape." The first line sounds much like sarcastic proverbial sayings, widespread in common parlance, such as "If it weren't for bad luck, I'd have no luck at all," or on a bad experience, "That's just what I needed today!" or in the German saying, "Be comforted, it will get worse."[9] But the second sentence of the verse gives it a very different touch in saying that for the bodhisattva this is not a bad situation at all, because suffering is indispensable for liberation—which is even (or especially) for Buddhist ears a rather uncommon assertion.

Again: "An enemy is as welcome as a treasure found in your home" (6:107). To common ears this can only be a highly ironic and sarcastic statement. An enemy is far from welcome; it is just the opposite of the truly welcome discovery of a hidden treasure. But Śāntideva decidedly goes for the literal meaning. The enemy is indeed welcome to the bodhisattva because he gives the bodhisattva the opportunity to practice the virtue of *kṣānti*, that is, endurance, forbearance, forgiveness.

A further example is found in 7:25–6: "Initially the Guide prescribes the giving of vegetables and the like. Then he gradually impels one, so that later one would give away even one's own flesh. When also in regard to one's own flesh comprehension dawns as in regard to vegetables, is it then difficult for him who gives up flesh and bones?" Taking the first two sentences on their own, they sound like the typical pessimistic warning against exploitative and dishonest conduct of religious teachers: initially they tell you to donate only something small, but in the end, they will demand from you to give everything. Yet again Śāntideva gives this a positive sense: the Buddha will give you a different kind of perspective and this will make your life easier even in relation to its hardest bits such as self-sacrifice.

By inverted sarcasm Śāntideva triggers creative thinking in an even more radical way, because it challenges ordinary standards. If one realizes that a statement which clearly appears to be sarcastic might indeed have a non-sarcastic—that is, true and positive—meaning, one is automatically forced to question the ordinary presuppositions that give the statement its initial sarcastic note. Thus, behind Śāntideva's inverted sarcasm lies his inversion of worldly standards and usual ways of thinking. Consider the following example in 8:125: "'If I give, what will I eat?' Such concern for the sake of oneself is the character of a men-eating demon. 'If I eat, what will I give?' Such concern for the sake of others is the character of a king of gods." Of course, Śāntideva is fully aware that we are normally inclined to think, "If I give, what will I eat?" Even if I am a generous person, if I only have what I need for my own subsistence, I cannot give this away. Yet for Śāntideva such consideration is part of the "worldly ways" for which he shows severe dismissal by calling it demonic. The true and godly standard is the direct opposite: "If I eat, what shall I give?"

9 "Nur getrost, es kommt noch schlimmer."

This inversion of standards is found in various other places. As, for example, when he (again in the mode of inverted sarcasm) recommends as the right kind of self-confidence the thought, "Why does someone else do menial work when I am around?" (7:51)—which is just the opposite of what self-confident people usually think. Or when he makes sarcastic fun of using perfumes by praising bad body smells: "Is it not fortunate if one has no passion for a body because of its natural bad smell? Why do people, with their penchant for what is worthless, smear it with scent?" (8:66).

Inversion of ordinary standards and norms is not unusual in the religious field. In the New Testament, Paul famously declares that the wisdom of the world is foolishness in the eyes of God (see 1 Cor. 1:20–5; 2:6; 3:18–20). And in Acts 20:35, Paul is reported to quote Jesus with the words, "Giving is more blessed than receiving," which is astonishingly similar to what Śāntideva says on giving.[10] Amber Carpenter captures this feature of the BCA quite well when she presents the BCA as an example of protreptic writings. For, it is part of this genre to provoke a gradual transformation of standards, a "shifting appreciation of what counts as a reason" (Carpenter 2019: 47). This program is clearly spelled out by Śāntideva himself when he interprets the traditional Madhyamaka teaching of the two truths/two realities in terms of a gradual transformation of understanding through which the views of people at different stages of insight "are invalidated by ever more advanced ones through their higher level of understanding" (9:4).

4. Why Śāntideva violates his own instruction

In BCA Chapter 5, which is largely on behavioral instructions, Śāntideva recommends: "When the mind is ... scornful [or: 'sarcastic', *sopahāsa*] ... then one should remain like a wooden log" (5:49–50). Why does Śāntideva not comply with this, his own instruction? How shall we interpret the frequent mockery, sarcasm, and irony in the BCA? Is this merely revealing a trait of his character or his skill in protreptic writing? Or is there something more behind it? I suggest that in addition Śāntideva's sarcasm can also be seen as reflecting a particular tendency or dynamic within the development of the Buddhist tradition.

It is evident that Śāntideva uses mockery and sarcasm to underline the foolish or crazy nature of ordinary thinking and conduct. Yet, in so doing he partly employs worldly wisdom. That is, he tries to persuade his audience, and presumably also himself, that even according to generally accepted standards certain attitudes and ways of thinking are ridiculous. Wasting money for a servant who is not going to stay is foolish on ordinary standards. This kind of rhetoric aims at making some Buddhist teachings plausible even according to worldly ways of thinking. But as has been shown, Śāntideva

[10] Paul, too, could be quite sarcastic as can be seen in Gal. 5:12, where he says about the preachers of circumcision that they should go all the way and castrate themselves. There are various striking analogies in Śāntideva and Paul, most startling perhaps the analogy of the tension between defilements and bodhicitta in Śāntideva and the tension between flesh and spirit in Paul. For this and further examples, see Schmidt-Leukel 2019; 2021; 2025.

goes further when he uses inverted sarcasm. What appears to be negative or false from an ordinary point of view may turn out to be good or right from a different—that is, Buddhist—perspective. This amounts to a paradoxical move: worldly rationality reveals certain ways of ordinary thinking as crazy. But what counts as reasonable in ordinary life is itself unreliable. Śāntideva draws on ordinary thinking in order to overcome it. The overall goal of this paradoxical move is itself a paradox, namely, to present selfless altruism as being in the best self-interest (e.g., 8:129, 136, 173, and throughout).

This paradox lies behind his inverted sarcasm. Views such as "selflessness is in your best self-interest" or "loss is a gain" or "small sufferings are good because they prepare us for the greater sufferings still to come" undermine worldly reasoning while simultaneously employing it: protecting the self is what we all naturally wish to do, but it can be done only by not protecting it (8:173). Śāntideva regards the ones following the course toward awakening, including himself, as people in transition from worldly ways of thinking to Buddhist wisdom. He uses sarcastic rhetoric to foster the kind of creative thinking that this rhetoric can trigger. Yet Śāntideva's view that foolishness can be exposed as such even on ordinary standards is only part of a more radical view. To him, such foolishness is evidence of a thoroughgoing delusion, which in the end even makes worldly standards unreliable. Delusion is so deep that it not only makes it difficult to see the truth but prevents one from living according to the truth even if one sees it.

This is particularly clear in BCA Chapter 4. Śāntideva begins by putting unbearable pressure on the person who has entered the bodhisattva path. If the person following the bodhisattva path would not fulfill his or her bodhisattva vows, he/she would deceive the Buddhas, the high bodhisattvas, and the whole world of beings whose liberation depends on the work of the bodhisattvas (4:4, 6, 8). Moreover, impeding the work of a bodhisattva is the most horrible sin. If one "impedes the meritorious work of a bodhisattva even for a moment, there will be no end to his bad destinies, since he has damaged the goal of all beings" (4:9). But exactly such impeding is done by the person on the bodhisattva path if he or she does not live up to the bodhisattva vows. Because then this person impedes the bodhisattva that he or she is going to become. This pressure is further aggravated (if this is possible at all) in verses 4:21–2 by threatening that in the case of such failure there is no hope of escape.[11] And Śāntideva continues

[11] According to dominant strands of the Buddhist tradition, rebirth in the many hells is of extremely long durations (sometimes many multiples of world periods) but not literally everlasting. In 4:9, however, Śāntideva declares that for him who impedes the work of a bodhisattva hell will be without end. In 4:22, he even seems to make hell irredeemable for everybody because one will commit further sins (presumably by feelings of hate) while experiencing the pain of hell. This is how Gómez and others understand the verse: "What is more, you will not escape this merely by suffering the pains of the evil destinies, for even as you suffer you commit new sins" (Gómez 2015: 1087). However, the translation of 4:22 is ambiguous because *vedayitvā* and *vedayan* could also be translated as "confessing" instead of "experiencing [punishment in hell]." Therefore, Steinkellner translates: "And one will not be liberated if one confesses merely this single sin, because even if one is confessing it, a new sin is committed." See on this Schmidt-Leukel 2019: 187–8, including notes 14 and 15. I'm inclined to prefer the first interpretation. Because the idea of making hell eternal seems to be a further example of Śāntideva's conviction that we can achieve liberation only with the support of the Buddhas and bodhisattvas and not on our own.

through his literary "I" by confessing that he finds himself precisely in this situation: although now being aware of the truth, "I am being led to the same hells" (4:26), because the defilements "have penetrated my mind" and he is deluded by them as by magical spells (4:27–9). So Śāntideva can speak of himself as "a deluded fool" of "abysmal blindness" (2:64, 57). In 7:33–6, he confesses:

> I must do away with innumerable faults, my own and those of others, among which effacing even a single fault takes streams of eons.
>
> Yet there is nothing in me to begin the extinction of these faults. If immense suffering is my destiny, why does my heart not burst?
>
> And I must secure many virtues, my own and those of others. In this, the cultivation of every single virtue might well take streams of eons.
>
> I have never cultivated even a trifling virtue.

Even at the end of Chapter 9, in which Śāntideva expounds his understanding of *prajñā*, the highest wisdom, he admits that he himself has not yet realized wisdom in such a way that he might transmit it successfully to others (9:167–8).[12] The negative and pessimistic tone present in Śāntideva's sarcasm seems to be ultimately rooted in his recognition that he himself partakes in that foolishness or delusion for which he has so much scorn and derision. In a sense, he sees himself as belonging to the yogic-people striving for awakening, while at the same time still participating in the ways of thinking and feeling of the ordinary, worldly people.[13] So why, in the end, can he nevertheless take things somewhat lightly giving them even a sense of humor which is more than gallows humor though being at times rather close to it? What are the antidotes? What gives hope in the face of the "great" and "terrible" power of the defilements (1:6, 4:31) that dominate the world to such an extent that by itself, by its own power, the world cannot achieve liberation: "This world is totally subject to the defilements, incapable of accomplishing its own benefit" (7:50)?

5. Sources of confidence and ease

According to BCA 1:6 there is no other means to overcome the power of evil than *bodhicitta* or, more precisely, *saṃbodhicitta*, "the spirit of complete awakening." According to 4:46, "the miserable defilements can only be defeated .... by *prajñā*." And according to 4:7 (see also 2:57), only a Buddha can bring liberation to those for whom there is otherwise no hope whatsoever.[14] These statements indicate a close relation

[12] Note that BCA 9:168 has a parallel in the Dunhuang version, but one that—like the Dunhuang parallel to 9:1—even more strongly expresses Śāntideva's admission of not yet having achieved the goal. See Saito 1994: 5.

[13] See on this distinction Chapter 5 in this volume.

[14] Steinkellner translates: "Only the Omniscient One knows the inconceivable course of acts (*karman*) so that only he liberates these people, even if they have abandoned the spirit of awakening" (Schmidt-Leukel 2019: 181). Gómez understands the respective verse in the same way: "Only the All-knowing One knows the unfathomable course of actions and their fruits. He alone brings liberation even those who have abandoned the thought of awakening" (Gómez 2015: 1086).

between *bodhicitta*, the "spirit of awakening," *prajñā*, the highest "wisdom" achieved by awakening, and the *Buddhas* as the "fully awakened ones."

Śāntideva, in his famous distinction between two kinds of *bodhicitta*, compares *bodhicitta* to a journey. The first kind of *bodhicitta* is the initial resolution to embark on the journey of the bodhisattva path and the second kind of *bodhicitta* is the ongoing motivation to continue the journey until the goal is reached (1:15–17). The journey's goal is Buddhahood, marked by the perfection of *prajñā*. *Prajñā* can thus be understood as the fulfillment of *bodhicitta*. This is also true in relation to the most significant characteristic of *bodhicitta*, that is, the altruistic "wish to remove evil from all beings" (1:8). The *Buddhas* have perfected that wish, so that their perfection of *prajñā* is intrinsically linked with their perfection of compassion (*mahākaruṇā*, or *mahākṛpā*, as mostly in BCA). In their perfection of compassion, the *Buddhas* have identified with the whole world of beings as their own self (6:126).

Especially with the last view, Śāntideva takes the altruistic ideal of Mahāyāna to its unsurpassable climax. It seems to be virtually impossible to realize this attitude and put it into practice. But trusting that this is exactly what the Buddhas have accomplished makes it possible to rely on their support. In BCA Chapter 6, Śāntideva argues that doing harm to any being is in fact doing harm to the Buddhas because they have made all beings their own self (6:122–6). And according to the Buddhist tradition, harming a Buddha belongs to the five grave offenses. However, the same belief offers the solution, because it implies that all the evil and deluded beings with whom the Buddhas compassionately identify include also oneself. Hence, relying on the Buddhas' compassion one can turn to them for forgiveness (6:124), ask them for protection (e.g., 2:22, 33, 51, 63–6), and count on their support in one's own striving for Buddhahood (2:8–9). With the belief that the goal of *bodhicitta* consists in making all beings one's own self, as the Buddhas did, the maximal demand on self-power coincides with the maximal support by other-power.[15] Śāntideva's desperate cry for a savior in 1:29–30[16] is swiftly answered by pointing to the highly developed bodhisattvas and accomplished Buddhas (1:31–6), "against which even wrong doing results in happiness" (1:36). Therefore, he can say: "Right now I take refuge in the mighty Lords of the world, the Victors who strive to save the world and who take all fear" (2:48).

This is not only true for the beginning of the bodhisattva path. It applies to each single day and night of this unfathomably long journey. The bodhisattva-ritual that Śāntideva performs(!), not describes, in BCA Chapters 2 and 3 (*anuttarapūjā*), is not merely meant for a first initiation. Toward the end of Chapter 5 Śāntideva firmly recommends: "Three times per night and per day he should perform 'the three components' (*triskandha*) [that is, confession of sins, approval of goodness, ripening of awakening]. He thereby wipes away the rest of his sins, because he relies on the spirit

[15] I am grateful to Fabian Völker who suggested this way of phrasing it in the discussion of my paper during the initial conference.

[16] "Whence shall come a good person who likewise procures satisfaction in every happiness for those manifold tormented beings starving for happiness, who eases all pain and even removes delusion? Whence is such a friend to come? Or whence such merit?"

of awakening (*bodhicitta*) and on the Victors" (5:98).[17] Note the importance Śāntideva gives to reliance "on the Victors," i.e. the Buddhas. The *triskandha* ritual contains the key elements of the *anuttarapūjā*, which thus permeate the complete journey toward Buddhahood (see also 2:26). I agree with Huntington's view that the whole BCA "can be read within a ritual framework" (Huntington 2019: 133) and that the specific "rituals employ faith in higher powers and repletion to bolster the practitioner at critical moments" (132).

But how precisely do the Buddhas and highly developed bodhisattvas help? Given the Mahāyāna tradition, the most obvious answer would be by their transference of merit (*pariṇāmanā*). In 2:6–7 Śāntideva combines the confession that he is "without merit" with his prayer that the Buddhas and bodhisattvas may "in their great compassion take pity on me." And in response to such confidence, he surrenders himself to them as their servant out of "loving devotion" (*bhakti*) (2:8). The protection he seeks from them seems to consist in transferring their karmic merit to him in order to protect him from the negative—that is, infernal—consequences of his own lack of merit. Yet apparently this protection is not just a purely external mechanism. According to 1:14, it is the arousal of *bodhicitta* "that burns up major sins instantly and completely" and, as said in 1:13, it is *bodhicitta* that grants the protection by which one escapes the infernal punishments, "just as one escapes great dangers when protected by a hero." Thus, when Śāntideva prays to the Buddhas and bodhisattvas, "Protect me quickly! Let not a quick death overtake me *before my sins have been erased*!" (2:33; my emphasis), he may actually ask them to inspire *bodhicitta* in him before he dies, because it is *bodhicitta* that erases all negative karma. Directing their merit to him may thus mean to kindle *bodhicitta* by means of their own karmic merits.

This interpretation of supernatural protection seems to be supported by what Śāntideva has to say about the redeeming work of bodhisattvas in hells. For what they do there is to let *saṃbodhicitta* and compassion (*dayā*), "the mother of deliverance for all beings," (10:13) arise in the denizens of hell. Bodhisattvas get people out of hell by inspiring *bodhicitta* in them, the opposite of hate, which burns up their bad karma and thereby sets them free. In 1:25, Śāntideva wonders how the origination of *bodhicitta* in one's mind is possible at all (see also 3:27). And here too he points to the Buddhas and bodhisattvas who by their example and their compassionate deeds evoke a sense of praise and inspire a devote disposition (1:32–6). In that disposition one recognizes that the *bodhicitta* manifested by the Buddhas and bodhisattvas is the highest good. And, according to 7:19, the capacity "to know good from bad" belongs to those features of human existence which makes it so suitable for moving toward awakening.[18] The persistent repetition of the *triskandha* ritual,

[17] The *triskandha* refers to a ritual formula (already mentioned in the early proto-Mahāyāna *Ugraparipṛcchā* [16b]) that exists in several variants. Steinkellner's interpolation follows Prajñākaramati. For more, see Schmidt-Leukel 2019: 239 n.106.

[18] Compare this to Shinran Shōnin's even more radical view of his own delusion that makes him declare: "I know nothing at all of good or evil" (Tannishō, Postscript; Hirota 1997: 679). Accordingly, Shinran understands *bodhicitta* as complete trust (*shinjin*) in Amida's liberative power: "Shinjin … is none other than the mind aspiring for great enlightenment" (Jōdo wasan 107; Hirota 1997: 354), a trust that is given to the deluded people by Amida himself. In fact, it is nothing but Amida's own mind: "This is the great thought of enlightenment of the Pure Land. This aspiration for Buddhahood

which is essentially about the awareness and confession of one's own shortcomings in conjunction with the turn to the Buddhas and bodhisattva for their protection, serves the continuous and ever fresh arousal of the protecting and liberating *bodhicitta* by means of taking refuge to the Buddha's and bodhisattva's merit during one's own long journey to awakening. Such continuous practice is essential. For, without turning to the higher forces for their help, their help might not reach the deluded individual despite the compassionate striving from their side (see 4:13). This coalescence of the utmost demand on self-power with the strong awareness of one's inability and the necessary persistent reliance on the other-power of higher beings allows us retrospectively to place Śāntideva within those dynamics of the evolving Buddhist tradition that gave increasing prominence to the liberating forces coming from outside oneself. This development is most evident in those Buddhist formations that circle around the idea of Pure Buddha Lands expressive of the Buddhas' will and power to save. Hence, it is no surprise to find traces of Pure Land Buddhism at some places in the BCA.[19]

In all his mockery, sarçasm, and irony, Śāntideva expresses a rather pessimistic view about the ordinary human state. He seems to do so in order to give momentum to his conviction that we depend on the spiritual help/protection of higher beings. Or, more precisely, that we depend on the *bodhicitta* that these beings manifest and are capable to ignite in those who take their refuge to them. Śāntideva paints the night of human existence pretty dark so that the work of the Buddhas shines even brighter (see 1:5). Thus, despite all his pessimist sarcasm, in the end his message is one of hope, which explains why his sarcasm is often combined with a sense of humor that is more than just gallows humor (see also Harris 2024: 259–60). Such hope with a dose of humor is evident, for example, when he reminds the dejected one that even the great Buddhas and bodhisattvas once were just "gnats, mosquitoes, flies, and worms" but nevertheless made it (7:18)—presumably by the support of other Buddhas and bodhisattvas (see 3:22). So where does the light of *bodhicitta*, the only power of good in this world, stem from? I do not see any other possible source than that ultimate reality (*paramārthasatya*),[20] which is veiled by the world of defilements, but in which all beings are already liberated (9:151).[21]

References

Carpenter, A. (2019), "Reason and Knowledge on the Path. A Protreptic Reading of the Guide," in J. Gold and D. Duckworth (eds.), *Readings of Śāntideva's Guide to Bodhisattva Practice*, 45–59, New York: Columbia University Press.

is none other than the wish to save all beings. [...] This shinjin is the aspiration to bring all beings to the attainment of supreme nirvana; it is the heart of great love and great compassion. This shinjin is Buddha-nature and Buddha-nature is Tathagata" (Yuishinshō mon'I; Hirota 1997: 463).

[19] Sukhāvatī, the pure land created by Buddha Amitābha, is explicitly mentioned in BCA 10:4 and referred to in 7:44. It is also mentioned in the Hymn on Samantabhadra's Vows, on which the Bodhisattva ritual seems to be modeled. Moreover, Nāgārjuna, the founding figure of Madhyamaka, takes it for granted (see *Suhṛllekha* 121).

[20] On the translation of *paramārthasatya* as "ultimate reality" instead of "ultimate truth," see Steinkellner 2019: xxiii.

[21] Also contained in the Dunhuang version as 8:84.

Foard, J., Solomon, M., and R. K. Payne, eds. (1996), *The Pure Land Tradition: History and Development*, Berkeley: University of California.
Gino, F. (2015), *The Surprising Benefits of Sarcasm*. Online: https://www.scientificamerican.com/article/the-surprising-benefits-of-sarcasm/.
Gold, J. (2019), "Introduction. Participatory Authorship and Communal Interpretation: The *Bodhicaryāvatāra* as a 'World Classic,'" in J. Gold and D. Duckworth (eds.), *Readings of Śāntideva's Guide to Bodhisattva Practice*, 1–25, New York: Columbia University Press.
Gómez, L. O., trans. (2015), "Introduction to the Practice of the Bodhisattva Path," in J. Miles et al. (eds.), *The Norton Anthology of World Religions*. Vol. 1, 1077–123, New York: W. W. Norton & Co.
Harris, S. E. (2024), "The Joke is *Saṃsāra*. Humor as a Means in Śāntideva's Bodhisattva Path," in M. Barbato, M. Schneider, and F. Völker (eds.), *Beyond Boundaries. Essays on Theology, Dialogue, and Religion in Honor of Perry Schmidt-Leukel*, 253–60, Münster: Waxmann.
Hirota, D., ed. and head trans. (1997), *The Collected Works of Shinran*. Vol. I: The Writings, Kyoto: Jōdo Shinshū Hongwanji-ha.
Huntington, E. (2019), "Ritual Structure and Material Culture in the *Guide to Bodhisattva Practice*," in J. Gold and D. Duckworth (eds.), *Readings of Śāntideva's Guide to Bodhisattva Practice*, 132–45, New York: Columbia University Press.
Kachru, S. (2019), "On Learning to Overhear the 'Vanishing Poet,'" in J. Gold and D. Duckworth (eds.), *Readings of Śāntideva's Guide to Bodhisattva Practice*, 60–83, New York: Columbia University Press.
Pruden, L., trans. (1991), *Abhidharmakośabhāṣyam of Vasubandhu*. Vol. I, Berkeley: Asian Humanities Press.
Saito, A. (1994), *On the Difference between the Earlier and the Current Versions of Śāntideva's Bodhi(sattva)caryāvatāra, with special reference to Chap. 9(/8) entitled: 'Perfection of Wisdom (prajnāpāramitā)'*. Research paper presented at the IXth World Sanskrit Conference held on 9th to 15th January, 1994, in Melbourne, Australia.
Schmidt-Leukel, P. (2019), *Buddha Mind – Christ Mind. A Christian Commentary on the Bodhicaryāvatāra*. With a new translation by E. Steinkellner and C. Peck-Kubaczek, Leuven: Peeters.
Schmidt-Leukel, P. (2021), "Śāntideva and Paul—An Unexpected Encounter," *Journal of Buddhist-Christian Studies* 41: 195–205.
Schmidt-Leukel, P. (2025), "The Image of the Body's Unity in Christianity (Paul) and Buddhism (Śāntideva)," in A. Lohwasser, A. Lichtenberger, and H. Strutwolf, eds., *The Body in Religion: Images and Practices*, 25–41, Baden-Baden: Ergon Verlag.
Steinkellner, E. (2019), "A Word on the Translation," in P. Schmidt-Leukel, *Buddha Mind – Christ Mind. A Christian Commentary on the Bodhicaryāvatāra*. With a new translation by Ernst Steinkellner and Cynthia Peck-Kubaczek, Leuven: Peeters, xix–xxiii.
The Cowherds (2016), *Moonpaths: Ethics and Emptiness*, Oxford: Oxford University Press.
Ueda, Y. and D. Hirota (1989), *Shinran. An Introduction to his Thought*, Kyoto: Honwanji International Center.
Williams, P. (1996), "General Introduction: Śāntideva and his World," in *Śāntideva, The Bodhicaryāvatāra*. Translated with Introduction and Notes by Kate Crosby and Andrew Skilton, vii–xxvi. Oxford: Oxford University Press.
Figure 1

7

A Feminist Buddhist Perspective on Śāntideva's *Bodhicaryāvatāra*

Carola Roloff (Bhikṣuṇī Jampa Tsedroen)

1. Introduction

The *Bodhicaryāvatāra*, a seminal Mahāyāna Buddhist text, is justly regarded as a component of the world's cultural heritage and a cornerstone of Buddhist literature. It was composed in Sanskrit verse by Śāntideva (*c.* eighth century), who, according to legend, was a Buddhist monk at Nālandā Monastic University in India.[1] He is considered one of the greatest mystics of the Mahāyāna tradition, and a great philosopher of the Prāsaṅgika-Madhyamaka school. Does a feminist view add a new aspect to his work?

Historically, the foundations of feminist Buddhist studies can be traced back to the late nineteenth century, notably through the work of scholars like Caroline Augusta Foley Rhys Davids. In 1892, she participated in the Ninth International Congress of Orientalists in London, where she presented a seminal paper, "The Women Leaders of the Buddhist Reformation. As Illustrated by Dharmapāla's Commentary on the Therīgāthā" (Foley 1893). This work, published in 1893, marked an important early contribution to the study of women in Buddhism. While the 1893 World's Parliament of Religions in Chicago is often recognized for its groundbreaking role in interreligious dialogue, it conspicuously lacked a focus on gender issues and had limited representation of women. Today, the field of feminist Buddhist studies continues to evolve, paralleling the broader struggle for women's rights in religion—rights that are crucial for maintaining the relevance of religions in contemporary society.

For the analysis presented in this chapter, I have chosen a textual interpretation that confronts the text of Śāntideva quasi-unhistorically or super-historically with today's situation and way of questioning: Where are the sticking points from a feminist-Buddhist perspective in the *Bodhicaryāvatāra* (hereafter BCA)? Where and how do women or the feminine appear in the text? Is the power of interpretation in Buddhism, as in other world religions, exclusively male? Does Śāntideva set narrow limits for women, representing outdated gender roles or can the text also provide religious inspiration from a feminist perspective?

[1] Here, I follow the dating provided by David Seyfort Ruegg 1981: 82 vs. 1977: 88.

In section 2, I will show by example that it is often a question of translation how the text comes across to its readership. Does one use philological leeway to reach the broadest possible audience through gender-sensitive language in order to convey Buddhism sympathetically? Or does one instead try to reconstruct the author's intention? Can we understand a foreign mind at all? To what extent can and maybe should the translator put him or herself in the author's place and empathize with the author's mind?

In section 3, I will look for possible female role models in the text. In section 4, I will examine examples from existing translations, taking into account that the Sanskrit term *manuṣ(y)a* can mean both "human" and "male" or "man." In English, the term "man" can ambiguously refer to either *Mensch* (human) or *Mann* (male person) in German, depending on the context. In contrast, German uses two distinct terms—*Mensch* (human) and *Mann* (male person)—making it necessary for translators to choose a specific interpretation, as an ambiguous rendering like "man" in English is not possible in German. Section 5 refers to the images of women and women's roles that become visible in the text, and section 6 deals with the code of conduct of ascetics in the seventh/eighth century in relation to women. After this, I will present my conclusion.

It will become clear that the author as well as the translator and the reader, with their respective horizons, are actively involved in constructing meaning. Such an empathic reading can lead to a re-creation or contemporary feminist interpretation of the text without—in the sense of eisegesis—reading something into the text that is not there.

With the help of some examples, I put forward the hypothesis that Śāntideva was not only a scholar and poet but also a mystic or *yogin* who thought in a multiperspectival and all-participatory way, entirely in the sense of the Mahāyāna teachings and that his basic principles can serve us as a hermeneutical key when teaching the text today to Buddhists.

2. Feminist translation perspectives

The question which translation is correct or better, and whether a feminist might immediately close the book or continue reading, already arises in the very first verse, where the Sanskrit[2] *sugatān sasutān* can be translated as either: "Buddhas with their [spiritual] sons" or "Buddhas with their children" (BCA 1:1).

The English translation by Ernst Steinkellner and Cynthia Peck-Kubaczek[3] chooses the first gender-exclusive reading "Buddhas with their [spiritual] sons," as it specifically

[2] All citations from the Sanskrit are taken from Śāntideva, *Bodhicaryāvatāra* (Göttingen Register of Electronic Texts in Indian Languages [GRETIL], SUB Göttingen, 2020).

[3] This translation by Ernst Steinkellner and Cynthia Peck-Kubaczek is part of the 2019 book, *Buddha Mind – Christ Mind. A Christian Commentary on the Bodhicaryāvatāra* by Perry Schmidt-Leukel. All citations from this translation are taken from the online resource Steinkellner and Peck-Kubaczeck 2019 and compared to the translation given in Schmidt-Leukel 2019.

references "buddhas" and "sons," historically and linguistically associated with male offspring. In Sanskrit, both terms are grammatically masculine:

> After reverent obeisance before the Buddhas with their [spiritual] Sons and their Body of Truth (*dharmakāya*) and before all those worthy of praise, I would briefly like to describe according to the tradition how one resorts to the discipline of the Sons of the Buddhas.
>
> BCA 1:1[4]

Vesna A. Wallace and B. Alan Wallace (1997: 17) also translate from Sanskrit, but opt for the second more inclusive reading "Sugatas with their children":

> Reverently bowing to the Sugatas, who are endowed with the Dharmakāya, together with their children and all who are worthy of veneration, I shall concisely present a guide to the discipline of the Children of the Sugatas in accordance with the scriptures.
>
> BCA 1:1

Similarly, the English translation of Chapter 2, verse 1 reads in the translation by Steinkellner and Peck-Kubaczek (2019; Schmidt-Leukel 2019: 139):

> … I properly worship the Buddhas, the flawless jewel of the True Teachings, and the Sons of the Buddhas, the oceans of virtues.
>
> BCA 2:1

And in the translation by Wallace and Wallace (1997: 24):

> … I make offerings to the Tathāgatas, to the stainless jewel of the sublime Dharma, and to the Children of the Buddhas, who are oceans of excellent qualities.
>
> BCA 2:1

In Sanskrit, this translation is based on three different terms: *sugata sasuta*, *sugatātmaja*,[5] and *buddhātmaja*.[6] Philologically, the masculine translations for all three terms "Sugatas and their sons," "sons of the Sugatas," and "sons of the Buddhas," as found verbatim in the translation by Kate Crosby and Andrew Skilton (1996: 5, 14), are reasonable because here *sugatān sasutān* is doubtless the accusative plural form of

4 Steinkellner and Peck-Kubaczeck 2019; Schmidt-Leukel 2019: 111. All English translations from the BCA are taken from the translation by Steinkellner and Peck-Kubaczeck in Schmidt-Leukel 2019, otherwise stated for comparison with other translations.

5 *sugatān sasutān sadharmakāyān praṇipatyādarato 'khilāṃśca vandyān / sugatātmajasaṃvarāvatāraṃ kathayiṣyāmi yathāgamaṃ samāsāt* // BCA 1:1.

6 *taccittaratnagrahaṇāya samyak pūjāṃ karomyeṣa tathāgatānāṃ / saddharmaratnasya ca nirmalasya buddhātmajānāṃ ca guṇodadhīnāṃ* // BCA 2:1.

sugata sasuta.[7] According to Monier-Williams and Böhtlingk, however, Skt. *sasuta*, f. *sasutā* can either mean "having a son" or "together with sons or children," German *nebst Söhnen* or *nebst Kindern*, depending on the context.

Not only Vesna and Alan Wallace, who compare the Sanskrit text with the Tibetan translation and note deviations in the footnotes, but also Diego Hangartner (2005: 21, 33) and Christof Spitz (2014: 9, 15), both of whom translate solely from Tibetan, have opted for the translation "children" (German: *Kinder*) or "descendants" (German: *Nachkommen*) instead of "sons."[8]

According to the Tibetan–English dictionary by Heinrich August Jäschke, Moravian missionary and excellent linguist, published in 1881, *sras* or *sras po* is honorific for *bu*, son, child. He translates *thugs sras* as "spiritual son or daughter"; and remarks: "in this sense, *sras* may be applied to females: *sangs rgyas kyi sras dag pa'o* 'she has become a spotless child of Buddha.'" In addition, in Tibetan, like in Sanskrit, there is a female form *sras mo*.

From this, we can conclude that in both the Tibetan translation and, apparently, the Sanskrit, the masculine form can be interpreted as either specifically male or gender-neutral, depending on the context.

A similar question of gender-appropriate translation arises in BCA 2:43, where the term *nāthāḥ* is used. Steinkellner and Peck-Kubaczek (2019; Schmidt-Leukel 2019: 146) render this term as "oh Lords":

> Out of fondness for the vagrant life, besotted I have accumulated many sins without realizing the peril, oh Lords.
>
> BCA 2:43

In contrast, Wallace and Wallace (1997: 28, here 2:42) opt for "O Protectors":

> O Protectors, I, negligent and unaware of this danger, have acquired many vices out of attachment to this transient life.

In this passage, *nāthāḥ*—a vocative plural form of *nātha*, meaning "protector" or "refuge"—is traditionally translated as "oh lords," as seen in Steinkellner's German and English translation, where he uses *ihr Herren* (2005: 35) and "oh Lords" (Schmidt-Leukel 2019: 146), respectively. However, Vesna Wallace and Alan Wallace (1997: 28, here 2:42) offer a gender-neutral alternative "O Protectors," which avoids the explicitly masculine connotation of "oh lords."

[7] The neuter accusative plural would be *sugatāni sasutāni*, the feminine accusative plural *sugatāḥ sasutāḥ*. The Sandhi rule does not apply here. When a word ends in *-āḥ* and the following word begins with a vowel or a voiced consonant, the ending *-āḥ* changes to *-ā*. However, *ś*, *ṣ*, and *s* are voiced consonants (sibilants). Therefore, this can be excluded in this case.

[8] It could also be a matter of the spirit of the times (zeitgeist) or the extent to which the translators follow the interpretation of their respective Tibetan teachers. For example, Stephen Batchelor (1981: 3, 10) as well as Kalsang Gyaltsen and Kunga Chodron (2006: 3, 19), who translate solely from Tibetan, use "Sons."

As we will see in the following section, Śāntideva mentions only male *bodhisattva*s in the BCA. One could argue, therefore, that "Lords" is accurate in this context, as the confession is addressed to *buddha*s and *bodhisattva*s, none of whom are explicitly female. However, it is also possible that Śāntideva, following societal conventions of his time, names only male *bodhisattva*s explicitly but implicitly includes female *bodhisattva*s and *buddha*s. Furthermore, within the framework of non-duality, he may ultimately conceive of *buddha*s and *bodhisattva*s as neither male nor female.

This exploration of gender-neutral language in translating Buddhist texts opens a path for a deeper inquiry into gender representation in Buddhist role models.

3. Gender representation in Buddhist role models

In the following section, we turn our attention to the question: Does the *Bodhicaryāvatāra* present us with only male figures, or do we also encounter female role models?

I will discuss this question in three sections:

1. Śāntideva explicitly mentions male *bodhisattva*s by name, while also referring to *sura-vanitāḥ* (Tib. *lha mo rnams*, "celestial women," "goddesses," or "female deities"). Is there room for female *bodhisattva*s?
2. Besides monks, Śāntideva also mentions nuns. Why does he leave female teachers unmentioned?
3. In Śāntideva's thought, does "Bodhisattva-nature" and "Buddhahood of all creatures" include attaining Buddhahood in a woman's body?

3.1 Male-centric bodhisattva narratives: Space for female inclusion?

If you wear feminist glasses when reading the BCA, you will notice that Śāntideva explicitly praises only male but not female *bodhisattvas*. He mentions Samantabhadra, Ajita, Mañjughoṣa, Lokeśvara, and the other *bodhisattva*s (BCA 2:13), and Samantabhadra and Mañjughoṣa (BCA 2:50), Avalokita (BCA 2:51), and in addition Kṣitigarbha (BCA 2:52). The same applies for Chapter 10, in which the *bodhisattva*s Vajrapāṇi (BCA 10:11), Kamalapāṇi (BCA 10:12), Mañjughoṣa (BCA 10:14 and 10:58), Samantabhadra (BCA 10:15), Avalokiteśvara (BCA 10:18), and Gaganagañja (BCA 10:28) are mentioned by name.

A further notable reference to female figures appears in BCA 10:10, where Śāntideva speaks of *suravanitāḥ* (Tib. *lha mo rnams*), translated as "celestial women," "goddesses," or "female deities." The verse describes a compassionate wish for those submerged in the hell-river Vaitaraṇī to be transformed through the power of Śāntideva's wholesome deeds. They are envisioned as divine beings, dwelling in joy and purity alongside celestial women in the heavenly river Mandākinī:

> May those drowned in the hell-river Vaitaraṇī, with its fire-like waters, all their flesh fallen off and their skeletons the color of white jasmine, find themselves

> through the power of my wholesome works as celestial beings with celestial women in the celestial river Mandākinī![9]
>
> BCA 10:10

While *suravanitāḥ* could be interpreted as heavenly companions akin to *apsarās* (cf. Schmidt-Leukel 2019: 69), literally "daughters of the gods" (Tib. *lha'i bu mo*), Śāntideva does not explicitly identify them as such. The use of this more general term suggests a symbolic role rather than a personalized depiction. These celestial women appear as part of an idealized heavenly realm, representing joy, purity, and liberation from suffering.

This raises a further question: Could *suravanitāḥ* also hint at female *bodhisattvas* or even female Buddhas in a broader sense? While Śāntideva does not explicitly draw this connection, the verse's depiction of divine transformation leaves room for such interpretations. Whether read as conventional imagery or as a subtle acknowledgment of women's spiritual potential, this passage adds a new dimension to the representation of gender in the BCA.

Tibetan *lha mo* (goddess) as the counterpart to *lha* (Skt. *deva*) appears in the Mahāvyutpatti (Mvy 3167) for Sanskrit *devī*. The term *lha mo* or *devī* is highly nuanced within Buddhist and Indo-Tibetan iconography, carrying various meanings depending on its specific context. In addition to its general usage to denote celestial or divine women, *lha mo* can also refer to protective deities (*dharmapālas*), whose roles are central to Tibetan Buddhist ritual practices. A prominent example is Śrīdevī (Palden Lhamo, Dpal ldan lha mo), a wrathful and highly venerated protector deity. As Cabezón (2010: 10) notes, while Palden Lhamo is widely regarded as the protector goddess of the Dalai Lamas, she appears to be of Tibetan origin but has been retroactively given an Indian pedigree by amalgamating her with Indian goddesses such as Rematī and Ekajaṭī. This blending reflects a broader tradition within Tibetan Buddhism, where indigenous Tibetan deities are integrated into the Indian Buddhist pantheon, lending them greater scriptural authority and legitimacy. Śrīdevī exemplifies this dynamic: though wrathful and locally Tibetan in origin, she is elevated to the status of a *dharmapāla*, illustrating the complex interplay between local traditions and pan-Indian Buddhist frameworks.

A deeper exploration of *lha mo* reveals another layer of meaning within tantric traditions. Tsongkhapa, in *The Brilliantly Illuminating Lamp of the Five Stages*, discusses the classification of tantras according to male and female deities, aligning *art* (symbolizing method) with male deities and *wisdom* with female deities. He writes:

> Thus, separate "art" and "wisdom" tantras were set up according to male deities established as art from the symbolically purified aggregates and female deities

[9] Sanskrit: *patitasakalamāṃsāḥ kundavarṇāsthidehā dahanasamajalāyāṃ vaitaraṇyāṃ nimagnāḥ mama kuśalabalena prāptadivyātmabhāvāḥ saha suravanitābhiḥ santu mandākinīsthāḥ* // BCA 10:10. Tibetan: *chu bo rab med me dong 'dra nang bying ba dag/ sha kun zhig gyur rus gong me tog kunda'i mdog/ bdag gi dge ba'i stobs kyis lha yi lus thob nas/ lha mo rnams dang lhan cig dal gyis 'bab gnas shog.*

> established as wisdom from the purified elements … The way of establishing the two tantras through male and female deities is intended as a matter for changing emphasis and not as a fixed [classification] …
>
> Blo-bzang-grags-pa 2019: 62

This passage highlights a conceptual shift where male and female deities (*lha* and *lha mo*) play roles that are not fixed but symbolically fluid, depending on the emphasis placed on method (*art*) or wisdom. In tantric contexts, *lha mo* can thus signify not only celestial goddesses or protectors but also active participants in profound symbolic rituals representing wisdom and nonduality.

Śāntideva's use of *suravanitāḥ* (*lha mo rnams*) in BCA 10:10 may be read in light of these broader meanings. While the immediate context points to celestial women within an idealized heavenly sphere, the term's multivalence in Buddhist thought opens the door for deeper interpretations. Could Śāntideva's choice of language inadvertently echo this tantric understanding, where the female form represents ultimate wisdom? This possibility invites a more expansive reading of *lha mo* that transcends its conventional role, aligning with the Mahāyāna emphasis on wisdom (*prajñā*) as essential for liberation.

Accordingly, the question arises whether Śāntideva excludes female *bodhisattva*s or takes them implicitly into account. Is there room for such consideration here? The only possibility seems to lie in the phrase "and the other bodhisattvas" (*ādīn api* in BCA 2:13). Does this wording leave space to include female *bodhisattva*s? And if so, whom could Śāntideva have in mind? Bhagavatī Prajñāpāramitā? Or Bhagavatī Tārā? Did the Tārā-Tantra already exist in Śāntideva's lifetime? And if not, when did the image of Prajñāpāramitā occur first in history? Together with the *Prajñāpāramitāsūtras*? About first century, or later?

Conze (1960: 88), in his "Annotated Bibliography" on Tantric Texts, section CD "Rituals" describes our first dated source for the iconography of the Bodhisattva Prajñāpāramitā, translated into Chinese by the monk Atigupta (阿地瞿多), *c.* 653–4.[10] Therefore, it seems possible that Śāntideva was aware of this image or the idea of a female Bodhisattva or Buddha. Despite Tārā's uncertain origins in Indian sources, her cult was well-established by the seventh century (Landesman 2020: 28).

While Śāntideva's BCA predominantly highlights male *bodhisattva*s, the *Śikṣā-Samuccaya* (*Compendium of Training*), another work attributed to Śāntideva, provides a rare instance of a female *bodhisattva* narrative. In this text, we encounter the *bodhisattva* Candrottārā in the *Candrottarādārikāparipṛcchā*, who is depicted as highly advanced in her spiritual practice and capable of supernatural feats. However, her portrayal is not without complexity. Despite her elevated status, Candrottārā's physical

[10] Atigtupta also known as Atikūṭa arrived in Chang'an, the capital of the Tang Dynasty (present-day Xi'an), in 652 and was active in several monasteries, primarily translating Buddhist texts and introducing tantric Buddhism. His involvement in a translation project is specifically mentioned for 654. See also the entries in Chinese Wikipedia and Baidu for further biographical details (no exact birth or death years are available). I am grateful to Dr. Carsten Krause (University of Hamburg) for bringing this information to my attention.

beauty becomes a source of distraction for men, which is framed as an obstacle to their spiritual progress. This depiction reflects the broader male-centric orientation of the *Śikṣā-Samuccaya*, where female bodies are seen as potential distractions, reinforcing a dichotomy between female beauty and spiritual development (Bendall and Rouse 1922: 83–4; Mrozik 2007: loc. 766–9).

This portrayal raises critical questions about the inclusion or exclusion of female *bodhisattvas* in Śāntideva's work. While BCA makes no explicit mention of female *bodhisattvas*, the implicit potential for their inclusion, as indicated in the phrase "and the other *bodhisattvas*," opens the door to consider whether Śāntideva might have had figures like Prajñāpāramitā or Tārā in mind. Given the well-established cult of Tārā by the seventh century and the iconographic representations of Prajñāpāramitā dating to the mid-seventh century, it is conceivable that Śāntideva was aware of these female *bodhisattva* figures. Nevertheless, their exclusion from explicit mention in his texts reflects a broader trend within Mahāyāna literature, where female *bodhisattvas*, while present in iconography and ritual contexts, often remain marginal in doctrinal narratives.

3.2 Monks and nuns in Śāntideva's work: The absence of female teachers

Before exploring why Śāntideva omits female teachers, it is important to note that he does explicitly mention both monks (*bhikṣus*) and nuns (*bhikṣuṇīs*) (BCA 10:43–4), which is noteworthy in itself. In the context of Buddhist history, the highest ordination or full ordination (*upasaṃpadā*) for nuns, known as the *bhikṣuṇī* ordination, has been one of the most debated topics in modern Buddhist discourse, especially from a feminist perspective, beginning in the 1960s.[11] The fact that Śāntideva explicitly references *bhikṣuṇīs* in his BCA suggests the existence of a flourishing order of nuns during his time, which further supports the idea that female monasticism was still well-established.

However, the absence of female teachers (*upādhyāyikā*) raises intriguing questions about gender roles and representation in Śāntideva's work. While Śāntideva does explicitly mention male teachers, or *upādhyāya*, he omits any reference to female teachers. Consider the following verse:

> I greet all the shrines and all the abodes of the Bodhisattva. I bow before the venerable teachers and ascetics.
>
> BCA 2:25, Schmidt-Leukel 2019: 140

In this verse, Śāntideva specifically uses the term *upādhyāyān* for "teachers" and *ānyatīn* for "ascetics," both of which are commonly interpreted in masculine terms, supporting a reading focused on male figures of spiritual authority.

[11] In Buddhism, ordination (*upasaṃpadā*) traditionally refers to the highest consecration within monastic communities, understood as ordination in accordance with the Vinaya (monastic code). In more recent literature, the term *upasaṃpadā* is also rendered as "full ordination," to distinguish it from the initial entry into the monastic community (*pravrajyā*) and the female novice ordination (*śrāmaṇerikā*). The minimum age for entering the monastery is seven years, and for full ordination, it is twenty years. For women, there is an additional two-year probation and training period as a *śikṣamāṇā* before receiving the highest ordination.

In contrast, Wallace and Wallace (1997: 26) render these terms differently:

> Likewise, I pay homage to all the shrines and to the resting-places of the Bodhisattva. I prostrate to the preceptors and to the praiseworthy adepts as well.
>
> BCA 2:25

Thus, in this case both English translations opt for a gender-neutral language, although Śāntideva himself, in Sanskrit, uses the masculine. While he acknowledges the presence of nuns, it remains unclear why he does not explicitly include female teachers, which may be related to the Vinaya tradition to which he belonged.[12] Rules governing nuns' education and authority vary across different Buddhist schools, and it remains uncertain which specific Vinaya Śāntideva followed, warranting further research.[13]

This brings us to our next question: Why does Śāntideva mention both monks and nuns, yet remain silent about female teachers? In his Dedication, Chapter 10, Śāntideva explicitly mentions both, *bhikṣus* and *bhikṣuṇīs*, as follows (Schmidt-Leukel 2019: 504):

> May the monks find solitude and love the precepts! May they meditate with pliable minds, free of all distraction!
>
> BCA 10:43

> May the nuns receive support free of quarrels and troubles, and may all who renounce the world likewise be of unbroken morals!
>
> BCA 10:44

There seems to be a problem with the one line dedicated to nuns. Again, the various translations differ at this point. While Steinkellner and Peck-Kubaczek read that the nuns may "receive support free of quarrels and troubles," Wallace and Wallace (1997: 143) read that the nuns may "receive provisions and be free of quarrels and troubles." Therefore, let us take a look to the Sanskrit and Tibetan.

The first line of the verse for the nuns reads: "May the nuns receive support, free from quarrels and troubles" (*lābhinyaḥ santu bhikṣuṇyaḥ kalahāyāsavarjitāḥ*). While most translations interpret the phrase "free from quarrels and troubles" as a compassionate wish for the well-being of nuns, it is important to consider the nuances brought out by the Tibetan translation.

The Tibetan rendering reads: *dge slong ma rnams rnyed sldan zhing // 'thab dang gnod pa spang bar shog* (Vidhuśekhara Bhaṭṭācārya 1960: 241), which translates as: "May the fully ordained nuns find the necessities, and abandon all quarreling and

[12] School affiliation in the Vinaya tradition typically depends on factors such as place, time, language, and the presence of specific teachers or preceptors (Tib. *mkhan po*, Skt. *upādhyāya*) as well as instructors (Tib. *slob dpon*, Skt. *ācārya*) (Roloff 2020: 308).

[13] On Śāntideva's ordination, see Schmidt-Leukel 2019: 17 and 20. I will return to this question below in section 6.1.

harm" (Gyaltsen and Chodron 2006b: 455). This interpretation emphasizes both the provision of material necessities for the nuns and the encouragement to avoid conflict and harm. The Tibetan translation seems to more clearly underscore the importance of the nuns' well-being, both materially and socially.

From a gender perspective, the distinction between the Sanskrit and Tibetan versions highlights the broader social and economic conditions in which nuns lived. Historically, nuns have often faced greater economic hardships than monks, as laity frequently prioritized monks in their offerings, believing it to generate more merit. The Tibetan phrasing reinforces the idea that nuns required material support, but it also reflects the ongoing expectation for nuns to maintain harmony, which may subtly indicate societal pressures on women to embody peace and obedience. While the text falls short of directly addressing these inequalities, it at least acknowledges the need for the nuns' support, even if the exact nature of that support remains somewhat ambiguous.

While Śāntideva acknowledges the presence of both monks and nuns, his references to teachers in BCA raise further questions about gender inclusion. In contrast to the early Vinaya texts, which explicitly mention both male and female teachers, BCA 2:25—as shown above—refers solely to male teachers, potentially reflecting a gender bias in his portrayal of monastic authority.

The line literally reads: I bow before the *upādhyāyas* (Tib. *mkhan po*), i.e., the male teachers/preceptors and others worthy of praise (*namaḥ karomyupādhyāyān abhivandyānyatīṃstathā* // BCA 2:25). If there was a *bhikṣuṇī* order (*bhikṣuṇīsaṃgha*), there must also have been female teachers (Skt. *upādhyāyikā*, Tib. *mkhan mo*). Does Śāntideva ignore them deliberately? Has he blind spots? Or does he, as a monk, hesitate to bow to female teachers? In general, the four assemblies (Skt. *catvāraḥ pariṣad*, Tib.*'khor rnam bzhi*) of the Buddha consists of male and female householders, and male and female monastics, namely, monks (*bhikṣus*), nuns (*bhikṣuṇīs*), laymen (*upāsakas*), and laywomen (*upāsikās*).[14] This concept is central to the composition of the Buddhist community as envisioned by the Buddha. The idea of the four assemblies ensures that both monastic and lay members, as well as both genders, are represented and contribute to the spiritual and social life of the community.

Another possibility is that, as with the use of "sons/children of the Buddha" discussed above, Śāntideva may use masculine terms to refer to people or groups regardless of their actual gender, i.e., the masculine form used here intended to encompass both genders. Today, the use of the generic masculine is a subject of linguistic and social debate. While it limits the visibility and equality of women and non-binary individuals in language, we cannot exclude the possibility that—depending on the context—the

[14] In Sanskrit, the term "four assemblies" is *catvāraḥ pariṣad*. (Roth 1970: 12 and 14). In Tibetan, the term for the four assemblies is *'khor rnam bzhi*, which corresponds to the definition given in Zhang Yisum 1984: *ston pa'i 'khor rnma pa bzhi ste/ kyim pa pho mo gnyis dang/ rab tu byung ba pho mo gnyis te/ dge slong dang/ dge slong ma/ dge bsnyens/ dge bsnyen ma bcas so/*. This translates to: "The four assemblies of the teacher, i.e., the Buddha, are as follows: male and female lay followers, male and female monastics; consisting of monks, nuns, male lay followers, and female lay followers." For further analysis, see Krey 2010: 53, Anālayo 2010: 66.

masculine in Tibetan and Sanskrit in early Buddhist texts was used as a generic masculine. Śāntideva even may think that the four assemblies belong to the same Vinaya ordination lineage, and that there is no separate female Vinaya ordination lineage. I tend to think that the lineage of nuns, probationers, male or female novices, or Buddhist lay people are all part of the lineage of the male *upādhyāya*s, the holders of the Prātimokṣa lineage (Tib. *so sor thar pa'i sdom brgyud*), because the male *saṃgha* is considered paramount (Roloff 2020: 297).

Lastly, it is possible that Śāntideva had nuns in mind when referring to "others who are worthy of praise" (BCA 2:25). This opens the door for contemporary interpreters of the BCA to offer gender-sensitive translations and commentaries that reflect current perspectives.[15]

Now, let us come back to Bhagavatī Prajñāpāramitā and Bhagavatī Tārā and turn our interest toward the question of women's potential to attain Buddhahood (*buddhatva*) or Sugatahood (*sugatatva*).

3.3 Does bodhisattva-nature and Buddhahood of all creatures include the attainment of Buddhahood as a woman?

In BCA 3:2 Śāntideva says:

> I find pleasure in delivering all creatures from the sufferings in the cycle of existences. I find pleasure in the bodhisattva-nature and Buddhahood (buddhatva) of the Saviors.
>
> Schmidt-Leukel 2019: 153

Finding pleasure in Buddhahood and wanting to liberate all living beings does not necessarily mean that the beings can reach this state directly from their present form. The prerequisite for the practice of Dharma is usually a birth as a human being. Śāntideva wishes all sentient beings (*sarvasattvāni*) to be free from suffering. In BCA 3:6 he dedicates all the goodness he has gained to allay all the suffering of all "sentient beings" (*sarvasattva*):

> Through the goodness I have gained in this way, may I be able to allay all the suffering of all sentient beings.
>
> Schmidt-Leukel 2019: 153

That Śāntideva trusts in the potential of all sentient beings to become enlightened and to attain Buddhahood is clear from BCA 3:33, where he says:

15 Compare Gyaltsen and Chodron (2006b: 80), who translate here: "I prostrate to the abbots, and likewise to the masters, and also excellent practitioners." This refers to "the abbots who bestow the transmission of vows; to the masters who taught the path to liberation; and to those who maintain pure moral conduct." However, just one page later, they offer a translation that is less conducive to interreligious dialogue and more exclusivist: "By taking refuge in the Sangha, do not associate with heretics" (Gyaltsen and Chodron 2006b: 81).

Verily, in front of all the Saviors, the world is today invited by me to Buddhahood,[16] in the meantime, to worldly happiness.

Schmidt-Leukel 2019: 176

But does Śāntideva believe that a woman can attain Buddhahood as a woman? As Schmidt-Leukel (2019: 507) points out: "While earlier canonical texts confirm that women can achieve awakening (as *arhats*) in their female bodies (which was the main reason why the Buddha finally agreed to establish the order of nuns), it is also affirmed that a Buddha always has to be a male." This is conventionally true for "historical" *buddhas* like Buddha Śākyamuni and future *buddhas* like Maitreya. On the other hand, in Chapter 7, first, Śāntideva postulates "the sameness of the others and oneself" (*parātmasamatā*), and describes the practice of "the exchange of the others and oneself" (*parātmaparivartana*) (BCA 7:16):

Lack of dejection (*aviṣāda*), all of the powers (*balavyūha*), full dedication (*tātparya*), self-control (*ātmavidheyatā*), the sameness of the others and oneself (*parātmasamatā*), and the exchange of the others and oneself (*parātmaparivartana*) [are the aids of vigor].

Schmidt-Leukel 2019: 310

Based on this, Śāntideva states:

Even those who by virtue of efforts have attained supreme, almost unattainable awakening have once been gnats, mosquitoes, flies and worms.

BCA 7:18; Schmidt-Leukel 2019: 310

Śāntideva elaborates on this in BCA 8:111–58, explaining the meditation on "the exchange of others and oneself." The main goal of this practice is to cultivate universal responsibility and *bodhicitta*—the awakened mind or the mind of enlightenment. This practice encourages the meditators to develop deep compassion and empathy by reversing their usual self-centered perspective. Instead of prioritizing their own well-being, the practitioner learns to place the needs and suffering of others on par with or even above their own. This practice is based on equanimity (*upekṣā*), not in the sense of impartiality, but in the sense of multi-partiality. In this context, "multi-partiality" captures the idea of being equally supportive or empathetic toward all sides, much like its application in contemporary conflict mediation.

Through this meditation, one aims to overcome self-cherishing, which is seen as a root cause of suffering, and to develop a sense of equanimity, compassion, and altruism. By imagining oneself in the place of others, practitioners gain insight into the shared experience of suffering, fostering greater compassion and the wish to benefit all beings, ultimately aiming for the realization of full enlightenment for the sake of others. This exercise involves empathizing with all individuals, including women.

However, this does not answer the question: Can women attain Buddhahood as women? Is being human enough to achieve enlightenment, or is being born male a

[16] Synonymous with "sugatahood" (*sugatatva*). Cf. Wallace and Wallace 1997: 37.

requirement to become a Buddha? To explore this, as we will see from the next section, all translators have opted to render the Sanskrit term *manuṣ(y)a* in verse 20, Chapter 4 of BCA as "human being." The Buddha spoke about the preciousness of human birth, not specifically male birth.

4. Reevaluating "precious human birth"

The concept of "precious human birth" in Buddhist teachings emphasizes the rarity of human rebirth and its potential for spiritual progress, but it is important to reassess this idea in light of gender-neutral interpretations, particularly in Śāntideva's BCA.

4.1. Beyond male-centric interpretations

Precious human birth is not just about precious male birth:

> This is why the Exalted One (Bhagavan) has said: to attain the human state is as difficult as for a [blind] turtle to stick its neck through the opening of a yoke [floating in the] vast ocean.
>
> BCA 4:20; Schmidt-Leukel 2019: 185[17]

The Sanskrit has here *manuṣa* or *manuṣamati durlabha*— "human being" or "the human state which is difficult to attain." As mentioned above, *manuṣa* means "human being," but can also mean "man." Nevertheless, here, all translators agree and translate "human state" or "human existence," not "male state" or "male existence." To this day, this remains the traditional Tibetan way of commenting on this text. See also Gyaltsen and Chodron (2006b: 136): "Likewise among the categories of other beings, the likelihood of finding a human birth is very small."

This interpretation aligns with the Pāli canon, *Aṅguttaranikāya* (hereafter AN) 8:29, where the Buddha explains eight inopportune moments that are not the right occasions for living the spiritual life. For living the spiritual life, it is important to be born in the central provinces.[18] A central province is—among others—a place to which monks, nuns, male and female lay followers travel:

[17] Sanskrit: *ata evāha bhagavān mānuṣamatidurlabhaṃ mahārṇavayugacchidrakūrmagrīvārpaṇopamaṃ* (BCA 4:20).

[18] In the Pāli Canon, the phrase used for "central provinces" is *majjhimesu janapadesu* (locative plural) referring to the "central country" where the fourfold assembly of four assemblies of the Buddha's community—monks, nuns, male lay followers, and female lay followers—are present. The corresponding term in the nominative singular is *majjhimapadesa*, denoting this "central region." The Sanskrit equivalent is *madhyadeśa* or *madhyamopadeśa*, and in Tibetan, the corresponding term is *'khor gyi yul dbus ma*. These terms across the three languages all refer to the culturally central region that is crucial for the presence and flourishing of the Buddha's community. "In fact, according to a discourse in the *Aṅguttara-nikāya* and its *Madhyama-āgama* parallel, as well as a quotation in Nāgārjuna's *Sūtrasamuccaya* preserved in Tibetan, being reborn in a border country of the type where the four assemblies, including the nuns, are not found is a most unfortunate condition" (Ānalayo 2010: 69).

> Again, a Tathāgata has arisen in the world … and the Dhamma leading to peace, *nibbāna*, and enlightenment is taught as proclaimed by a Fortunate One. But a person has been reborn in the outlying provinces among the uncouth foreigners, a place to which *bhikkhus*, *bhikkhunīs*, male lay followers, and female lay followers do not travel. This is the fifth inopportune moment that is not the right occasion for living the spiritual life.
>
> AN 8:29[19]

To conclude, there are only a few places in the BCA where Śāntideva explicitly speaks of women. He does not question whether women can attain Buddhahood. He neither affirms nor denies it. However, he implicitly seems to assume that all sentient beings—including women—can attain Buddhahood, and he takes responsibility for it.

While Śāntideva acknowledges the spiritual potential of both male and female practitioners, his reference to teachers in masculine terms may prompt questions about gender inclusivity in his portrayal of monastic authority. However, canonical texts suggest that the requirement for achieving enlightenment rests on attaining a human birth, not specifically a male birth.

Furthermore, the example of Tārā in the *Tārā Tantra* directly challenges gender-specific assumptions about Buddhahood. When Tārā was advised by monks to aspire to enlightenment in a male form, she resolutely vowed to pursue the path as a woman, highlighting the lack of intrinsic significance in male or female form from the standpoint of ultimate reality (Landesman 2020: 27-8). Her commitment to remain in female form for the benefit of all beings led to her revered status as "Bhagavatī Tārā," an honorific that mirrors the masculine title "Bhagavan," reserved for Buddhas and other enlightened beings. Tārā's example thereby underscores the Buddhist view that the potential for Buddhahood is not contingent upon a male body, but a human body. This narrative supports the interpretation that Śāntideva's masculine terminology in the BCA may have been conventional rather than exclusionary.

5. Depictions of women and their roles

The following section explores various representations of women and their roles as depicted in the *Bodhicaryāvatāra*. I have identified four key images: (1) the positive portrayal of the mother; (2) the negative archetypes of Ḍākinī witches and women who torment adulterers in hell; (3) women as objects of sensuality and the associated dangers they pose to the Śramaṇa; and (4) the contrast between the ideal wife and the prostitute.

[19] PTS 4.226—4.228. English translation based on the 2012 work *The Numerical Discourses of the Buddha*. Available online: https://suttacentral.net/an8.29/en/bodhi?lang=de&reference=none&highlight=false.

5.1 Maternal imagery in Śāntideva's writings

The more positive image of the mother appears when showing respect for parents. The mother is mentioned in at least two or three verses. BCA 1:23 reads: "Whose mother and father" (*kasya mātuḥ piturvāpi*). In Sanskrit, the mother (*mātṛ*) is mentioned first. In Tibetan, the father (Tib. *pha*, Skt. *pitṛ*) is mentioned first *(pha 'am yang na ma yang rung*). Another traditional depiction of the wife as a mother, from the husband's and father's perspective, is found in BCA 8:74:

> Others, suffering the hardship of being away on military campaigns, even for years do not see the sons and wives for whom they long.
>
> Schmidt-Leukel 2019: 363

The mother figure emerges as both a source of respect and a symbol of familial longing, reflecting the conventional societal role of women.

Śāntideva's writing touches on the experience of birth, highlighting both the physical and symbolic significance of the mother's womb. In BCA 7:38, he describes birth from the mother's womb: "I became a thorn in the womb of the mother, causing nothing but pain." This birth is contrasted with two symbolic forms: first, birth from a lotus in the pure land of Sukhāvatī, where "beautiful bodies … came forth from the lotus blossoms unfolding through the radiance of the Wise Ones" (BCA 7:44, Schmidt-Leukel 2019: 316); and second, without the throes of labor, as seen in the verse, "may the pregnant give birth without throes as queen Māyā [i.e., Māyādevī] did!" (BCA 10:19; Schmidt-Leukel 2019: 503).

This portrayal of motherhood and birth offers a complex view of women's roles. However, Śāntideva also presents more negative depictions of women.

5.2 Negative archetypes: Dākinī witches and tormentors in hell

In addition to maternal imagery, Śāntideva introduces negative archetypes of women, such as Ḍākinī witches and women who torment adulterers in hell. In BCA 5:4, the term "Ḍākinī" is used, but due to the context, Steinkellner and Peck-Kubaczeck translate it as "Dākinī witches" (Schmidt-Leukel 2019: 203) while Crosby and Skilton (1995) suggest "ogresses," and Wallace and Wallace (1997: 47) retain *ḍākinī*s but note that the Tibetan version reads "evil spirits" (*byad ma*) instead of Ḍākinī.

Another striking negative portrayal is found in BCA 5:7, where women are described as tormentors of adulterers in hell, drawing from a broader Buddhist motif. For instance, the image of the "sword-leaved forest," with seductive women tempting adulterers to climb trees with sharp leaves, reflects karmic punishment for sexual misconduct (cf. BCA 6:46, 10:6).[20] Śāntideva asks: "And whence do those women [who torment adulterers] come?" The answer is implied in the preceding verse (BCA 5:6):

[20] See Schmidt-Leukel 2019: 341 for an in-depth discussion of the "men of flames" and other symbolic representations of punishment in the Buddhist hells.

"For all kinds of peril and boundless suffering arise from nothing but the mind" (Schmidt-Leukel 2019: 203).

While these depictions present women as instruments of suffering, Śāntideva, writing primarily for a monastic audience, may be subtly critiquing his readers rather than women themselves. By pointing out that the source of suffering lies not in women but in the mind of the perceiver, Śāntideva seems to mock the ascetic's struggle with desire, highlighting the internal nature of the problem.

This leads us to Śāntideva's portrayal of women as objects of sensuality, and the challenges this poses for the ascetic.

5.3 Women as objects of sensuality: Challenges for the ascetic

Śāntideva also frames women as objects of sensuality and a potential danger to the Śramaṇa (ascetic). In Chapter 8, the section on "The Passion of the Flesh" addresses the practice of *smṛtyupasthāna* (mindful contemplation) of the body as a means to overcome attachment to women (Schmidt-Leukel 2019: 362):

> The face which you once saw as it was hardly lifted, lowered in modesty, or did not see when covered by a veil, this face has now been exposed by vultures, as if they had pity on your distress. Look at it! Why do you flee now?
>
> BCA 8:44–5

> What was well protected even from the gaze of others is meanwhile being devoured.
>
> BCA 8:46

When considering AN 1:1 and AN 7:48 from the Pāli Canon, one could ask whether Śāntideva, if he had been addressing an audience of nuns rather than monks, would have framed the contemplation of the body differently. In AN 7:48, the Buddha speaks of the mutual attraction between men and women, and although the *sutta* lists the attractive qualities of women, it also notes that men are similarly objects of attraction. This mutuality suggests that the contemplation of the body's impermanence is not inherently gendered, but can be applied to both men and women. The teaching in AN 1:1, which emphasizes mindfulness and detachment from sensory pleasures, further supports this interpretation. The practice of *smṛtyupasthāna* is ultimately about transcending all forms of attachment, regardless of whether the object of desire is male or female.

Thus, while Śāntideva's verses reflect the male-centered perspective of his monastic audience, they do not preclude the possibility that, in a different context, he could have highlighted the same bodily impermanence and unattractiveness in relation to men's bodies. This underscores the universality of the Buddhist teaching on impermanence and detachment, suggesting that Śāntideva's framing is more a reflection of his intended audience than an inherent gender bias in the practice of contemplation itself (cf. AN 1:1, AN 7:48).

Furthermore, in these verses BCA 8:44-6, Śāntideva simultaneously presents the ideal of a wife—beautiful, modest, bashful, reserved, and well-protected.

5.4 The ideal wife vs. the prostitute

Śāntideva juxtaposes the image of the ideal wife with that of a prostitute giving birth in the wilderness. In BCA 8.166, he describes a newlywed girl as "bashful, timid, and withdrawn," adhering to the qualities of modesty expected of women in traditional roles.

Both before and after his reflection on the impermanence and unappealing nature of the dead female body in BCA 8:44-6, Śāntideva presents contrasting images of women. In BCA 8.166, he portrays the traditional ideal of a virtuous wife—bashful, timid, and reserved—reinforcing societal expectations of modesty and propriety for women. This image is further juxtaposed with the depiction of women in BCA 8:76, where he contrasts the virtuous wife with women living outside the bounds of society, such as those giving birth in the wilderness. Through these contrasting depictions, Śāntideva both reinforces and critiques the societal roles expected of women:

> The wives of others, who have sold themselves and carry out errands [of their masters], give birth beneath the trees of the jungle and other [rough places].
>
> BCA 8:76; Schmidt-Leukel 2019: 363

These women, living on the fringes of society, embody a stark opposition to the idealized wife. One might wonder if Śāntideva is implicitly drawing a connection between prostitutes and nuns.

This association of the nun with the prostitute reflects a recurring motif in Buddhist and Hindu literature, where both figures occupy roles outside the conventional family structure. As Diana Paul (1979: 79) observes, the nun and the prostitute share a symbolic parallel as women detached from familial roles, existing on the peripheries of societal expectations. In her analysis of the *Gaṇḍavyūhasūtra*, Paul highlights how a nun directs a pilgrim to a "good friend," Vasumitrā, who, while appearing as a prostitute to those unenlightened, serves a spiritual purpose (96). This parallel, Paul suggests, represents a deeper metaphysical union between the sensual and spiritual realms, illustrating how these seemingly incongruous figures transcend traditional female roles (105 n.21).[21]

Nuns, unlike monks, are not supposed to live in the wilderness. As I have shown in my book on Buddhist Nuns' Ordination (Roloff 2020: 240-4), at the end of the ordination ritual, nuns are instructed to rely on the Three Supports of Life (Tib. *gnas gsum*, Skt. *trayo niśrayāḥ*): clothing, food, and medicine. They are required to make their robes from rags, take alms food (*piṇḍapāta*), and use herbal decoctions as medicine. However, the instruction to live under trees, as some monks sometimes do, was deemed too dangerous for nuns, given the risk of sexual violence, including cases of rape. Now I come to my sixth and final set of findings on the female.

[21] For the relation drawn between the nun and the courtesan, see Vimalā, The Former Courtesan, Vimalātherīgāthā Thig 5.2 Verse 72–6, https://suttacentral.net/thig5.2/en/sujato?lang=de&layout=plain&reference=none&notes=none&highlight=false&script=latin.

6. Asceticism and gender dynamics

This section examines how ascetics engage with gender dynamics, focusing on three key aspects: (1) the influence of social conventions and Vinaya rules on gendered interactions; (2) the challenges of lust for forbidden women in ascetic practice; and (3) the presence of androcentrism and misogyny, or potential traces of gender deconstruction in the BCA.

6.1 Social conventions and Vinaya rules: Gendered interactions

Consideration of social conventions and Vinaya rules is expressed in two verses: "He should not recite the teaching to women not accompanied by a man" (BCA 5:89), and "he may not travel with someone else's wife if she is alone, nor may he sleep or sit with her" (BCA 5:93).[22]

Wallace and Wallace (1997: 57) translate that one should not teach the profound and vast Dharma "to those who are inadequate, nor to women in the absence of a man" (BCA 5:89) and "one should not travel, lie, or sit alone with someone else's spouse" (BCA 5:93). It seems that this passage refers to the monks' Vinaya rules such as not to teach more than five or six sentences of Dhamma/Dharma to a woman, except in the presence of a man who understands (Pacittiya 7), and not to sit in private, alone with a woman or a nun (Pacittiya 30 and 45).[23]

For comparison, see the *Bhikṣu Prātimokṣa Sūtra* of the Mahāsāṃghikas, Pācattika Dharmas 5, 26, and 27, alongside the corresponding Pāyantika Dharmas 5, 26–8 in the Mūlasarvāstivāda tradition (Prebish 1975: 74–5, 78–9). Despite Akira Yuyama's analysis (2003), which highlights textual references to the Mahāsāṃghika-Lokottaravādins in Śāntideva's *Śikṣāsamuccaya*, the comparison of these Sanskrit sources suggests a closer alignment with the Mūlasarvāstivādins.

Both texts (BCA 5:89 and PrMoSū Mū-Banerjee Pāy. 5) warn against teaching Dharma to women unless proper conditions are met (such as accompaniment or a proper audience). BCA 5:93 parallels PrMoSū Mū-Banerjee Pāy. 26–8 in warning monks against traveling or sitting with women (or nuns) alone, as it might cause public scandal or inappropriate behavior.[24]

[22] Schmidt-Leukel 2019: 237. Sanskrit: *gambhīrodāramalpeṣu na strīṣu puruṣaṃ vinā hīnotkṛṣṭeṣu dharmeṣu samaṃ gauravamācaret* // BCA 5:89; *naikayā'nyastriyā kuryād yānaṃ śayanamāsanam lokāprasādakaṃ sarvaṃ dṛṣṭvā pṛṣṭvā ca varjayet* // BCA 5:93.

[23] https://suttacentral.net/pli-tv-bu-pm?view=normal&lang=en.

[24] Pāy. 5 (PrMoSū Mū-Banerjee) *yaḥ punar bhikṣur mātṛgrāmasyottari ṣaṭpaṃcikayā vācā dharmaṃ deśayed anyatra vijñapuruṣāt pāyantikā* /; Pāy. 26 (PrMoSū Mū-Banerjee) *yaḥ punar bhikṣur bhikṣuṇīsārtheṇa sārdham adhvānamārgaṃ pratipadyeta ato grāmāntaram api pāyantikā / tatrāyaṃ samayaḥ sārthagamanīyo mārgo bhavati sāśaṅkasaṃmataḥ sabhayasaṃmataḥ sapratibhayabhairavasaṃmato 'yaṃ tatra samayaḥ* / Pāy. 27 (PrMoSū Mū-Banerjee) *yaḥ punar bhikṣur bhikṣuṇīsārtheṇa sārdhaṃ saṃvidhāya ekanāvam abhirohed ūrdhvagāminīṃ vā adhogāminīṃ vānyatra tīryakpārasantaraṇāt pātayantikā* / Pāy. 28 (PrMoSū Mū-Banerjee) *yaḥ punar bhikṣur mātṛgrāmena sārdham eka ekayā rahasi praticchanne āsane niṣadyāṃ kalpayet pāyantikā* /.

While Śāntideva's BCA is not a Vinaya text, these parallels indicate that Śāntideva might have drawn on monastic codes of conduct in his ethical verses, which align closely with the Mūlasarvāstivāda Vinaya, though there are also references to Mahāsāṃghika practices in the *Śikṣāsamuccaya*. However, further philological investigation is necessary to fully assess the extent of Śāntideva's affiliation with this monastic tradition.

From a gender perspective, it is important to note that comparable rules exist for nuns, regulating their conduct toward both monks and laymen, ensuring appropriate boundaries in monastic settings.

6.2 Lust for the forbidden: Gendered desires in ascetic practice

The ascetics' dealings with women become clear from this verse on lust for "forbidden" or "inappropriate" women:

> Out of rashness, anger, lust for unattainable women and so on, they torment themselves with beds of thorns and other tortures, with food deprivation and other punishments.
>
> BCA 6:35

As Schmidt-Leukel (2019: 271) explains, Śāntideva here delves into the deeper nature of defilements, which he identifies as the main cause of aggressive behavior. Although people do not wish to suffer, they often torment their bodies and minds due to delusion, driven by defilements such as lust and anger. This self-inflicted suffering can manifest as auto-aggression or harm toward others. In this context, Śāntideva reminds us that those driven by such delusions deserve the Bodhisattva's compassion rather than anger, as their destructive behavior stems from ignorance and self-inflicted harm. In the broader discussion of defilements (BCA 6:34–41), Śāntideva addresses both the personal suffering caused by attachment and the aggressive tendencies that arise from it, making the Bodhisattva's response one of understanding and empathy.

6.3 Androcentrism, misogyny, or gender deconstruction?

The former two examples in sections 6.1 and 6.2 of the ascetics' dealing with women can either be seen as examples of androcentrism and misogyny or as traces of gender deconstruction, especially when we read them against the very different background of the following two verses:

> Thus everything depends on something else: also that upon which it depends is dependent. If in this manner, things do not move on their own like magic creations, what is one angry about (or hostile against)?
>
> BCA 6:31

> The destinies [in the cycle of existences] are like a dream. When examined, they are like the stem of a plantain tree [without a core]. In ultimate reality there is no difference between the released and the non-released.
>
> BCA 9:151

Based on this understanding, Śāntideva offers insights that lend themselves to gender deconstruction:

> Who would, when examining in this way, cling to the physical form, which resembles [the image in] a dream? Now, if in this way a body does not exist, then what is a woman (*strī*) and what a man (*pumān*)?
>
> BCA 9:88

As Perry Schmidt-Leukel points out in his commentary: "The result of the insight is non-attachment. Whoever is still attached to objects has not yet abandoned the false belief in their reality" (2019: 455–6). The verses Schmidt-Leukel refers to are composed from a Madhyamaka point of view:

> How then do the defilements cease, even if one has recognized that [the world] is like an illusion, when passion for a conjured woman stirs even in her creator?
>
> BCA 9:31

> Because the latent impression in her creator for attributing existence has not worn out, thus, when he sees her, the latent impression of her as empty is feeble.
>
> BCA 9:32; cf. also 9:48

But why then, in the final chapter of the Dedication, do we encounter this seemingly awkward verse:

> May whatever women there are in the world become men! May the lowly attain high positions but still not be arrogant.
>
> BCA 10:30[25]

While this verse may appear awkward or even troubling to modern readers, it can be interpreted within the context of Śāntideva's time and the prevailing socio-religious assumptions. The premise that Buddhahood required a male body, and thus the wish for women to be reborn as men, reflects a conventional and contingent understanding rather than an ultimate truth. As I have discussed in section 4.1, texts such as the *Tārā Tantra*, which were well-established in Śāntideva's era, emphasize that the potential for Buddhahood is not tied to a male body but to the human condition. This narrative suggests that Śāntideva's use of masculine terminology in the BCA may have been a reflection of convention rather than an intention to exclude.

[25] Sanskrit: *yāḥ kāścana striyo loke puruṣatvaṃ vrajantu tāḥ/ prāpnuvantu ca tāṃ nīcā hatamānā bhavantu ca //* BCA 10:30. Tibetan: *'jig rten bud med ji snyed pa/ de dag skyes pa yid gyur cig/ ma rabs rnams ni mtho thob cing/ nga rgyal dag kyang bcom par shog*. Cf. Schmidt-Leukel 2019: 507, who argues that while Śāntideva acknowledges the lower social status of women, it would be unjustified to label his view as typical Buddhist misogyny. Instead, the author suggests that the main motive behind this belief lies in the Bodhisattva ideal itself and the notion that a Buddha must always be male, a view affirmed by canonical texts.

From a feminist liberation-theological perspective, however, this verse cannot serve as an ultimate aspiration. Instead, it highlights the enduring struggle of women who, even today, face systemic inequalities and might, understandably, yearn for an existence free from these burdens. Yet, the solution lies not in reinforcing these conventions but in challenging them. The world does not need fewer women but more courageous women who, like Tārā, are determined to attain Buddhahood in the form of a woman—despite the challenges this path may entail.

In this light, BCA 10:30 can be reimagined as an opportunity for critical engagement with gendered assumptions in Buddhist texts. Rather than accepting the conventional worldview it reflects, we are called to reinterpret it in ways that inspire gender justice and transformative action. Śāntideva's own insights into emptiness and the deconstruction of identity offer the tools for such a reimagining. By questioning fixed categories, including those of gender, we can draw from the BCA a vision not only of personal liberation but of societal transformation.

A similar sentiment regarding the transformation of women appears in Nāgārjuna's *Ratnāvalī* 5:72, a text likely composed in the late second to early third century CE—several centuries before Śāntideva's *Bodhicaryāvatāra*. While Śāntideva's BCA 10:30 wishes for women (Skt. *striyaḥ*, Tib. *bud med*) to become men (Skt. *puruṣatva*, Tib. *skyes pa*), Nāgārjuna envisions women becoming "the best of men" or "the supreme beings." The Tibetan translation of *Ratnāvalī* avoids gendered language altogether. Instead, it aspires for all women to become *skyes mchog*—"the best of men" or "supreme persons." While the Sanskrit original of *Ratnāvalī* 5:72 is no longer extant, different interpretations of the Tibetan term *skyes mchog* provide insight into the line's meaning:

> At all times may all women become the best of men. May all beings be endowed with knowledge and good conduct.
>
> 5:72; McClintock and Dunne 2024: 177[26]

Jeffrey Hopkins (1998: 160) translates the passage as:

> May all women at all times become supreme persons. May all embodied beings have the intelligence [of wisdom] and the legs [of ethics].

In his accompanying note, Hopkins explains that Ajitamitra reads *skyes mchog* as *skyes pu'i mchog* ("supreme person"), in Sanskrit *puruṣottama*, referring to Buddhas as the highest among all sentient beings. He further suggests that the line could more inclusively refer to other supreme persons who are not yet Buddhas. But Hopkins also

[26] Tibetan: *bud med thams cad dus kun du/ skyes mchog nyid du 'gyur bar shog/ lus can thams cad rig pa dang / rkang par ldan pa nyid du shog* || (5.72; McClintock and Dunne 2024: 312). The Sanskrit text for Ratnavali 5:55–5:78, including verse 5:72, is missing in the current edition of McClintock and Dunne. This analysis is therefore based solely on the Tibetan rendering of the text.

points out that in contrast, Gyel-tsap[27] interprets *skyes mchog* as *skyes pa mchog* ("supreme men"), introducing a gendered reading that reflects a sexist bias. However, as Hopkins notes, Nāgārjuna's philosophical framework, particularly in his exposition of Highest Yogatantra, upholds the equality of male and female beings. This non-dual perspective undermines any strict necessity for women to undergo transformation into men in order to attain spiritual perfection.

It is significant that the Tibetan rendering *skyes mchog* avoids gender-specific language altogether, pointing instead to the supreme spiritual potential of all beings. This suggests that Nāgārjuna envisions women as capable of achieving the highest realization—Buddhahood—without requiring transformation into a male body. Such an interpretation aligns with Nāgārjuna's rejection of essentialist distinctions and underscores the inclusivity of the Buddhist path, where gender does not constitute an impediment to the attainment of ultimate awakening.

Furthermore, this comparison highlights a significant divergence in emphasis. While Śāntideva's BCA reflects the androcentric norms of his time by envisioning gendered transformation, the *Ratnāvalī*, as preserved in its Tibetan form, transcends such distinctions. By rendering the aspiration as "the best of men" or "the supreme persons," it reframes the goal as one of universal spiritual perfection, applicable to all beings (*lus can thams cad*) regardless of gender or birth—whether human or otherwise.

The shift from "men" (*skyes pa*) to "supreme persons" (*skyes mchog*) in the Tibetan text reflects a more inclusive worldview—one that aligns closely with the Mahāyāna ideal of universal liberation. This broader vision serves as a reminder that Buddhist texts, even when shaped by specific cultural contexts, often contain the seeds of a more egalitarian interpretation.

By juxtaposing Śāntideva's BCA 10:30 with Nāgārjuna's *Ratnāvalī* 5:72, we observe both the persistence of gendered assumptions and an alternative, more inclusive aspiration. This dialogue between texts invites a critical reexamination of gendered hierarchies, emphasizing the universal potential for liberation.

Nevertheless, it is essential to acknowledge that texts like Nāgārjuna's *Ratnāvalī* also carry elements of gender bias, reflective of their historical and cultural context. As McClintock and Dunne point out, passages in the *Ratnāvalī*—such as the description of women's bodies in 2:64[28] as inherently impure—demonstrate a rhetoric that disproportionately targets women in ways that are far more negative and extreme than comparable references to men. While the ultimate aim of such meditations is to reduce

[27] Gyel-tsap Darma Rinchen (rGyal tshab Dar ma rin chen, 1364–1432) was initially a student of Red mda' ba gzhon nu blo gros (1348–1412), an influential scholar and teacher whose legacy shaped the early development of the *dGe lugs* tradition. Red mda' ba taught scholastic philosophy to many prominent figures, including Tsongkhapa Blo bzang grags pa (1357–1419), Gyel-tsap Darma Rinchen, and mKhas grub dGe legs dpal bzang (1385–1438)—who are often regarded as the "three main founders" of the *dGe lugs* tradition. Gyel-tsap, in particular, played a critical role in transmitting and systematizing Tsongkhapa's teachings (Roloff 2009).

[28] Nagarjuna's *Ratnāvalī* 2:64 presents a reflection on the body's impurity as a basis for renouncing attachment: "Your own body is just as filthy as the body of a woman. So doesn't it make sense to be unattached to both other and self?" (McClintock and Dunne 2024: 125). An alternative translation by Jeffrey Hopkins reads: "Since your own body is as unclean as a woman's, is it not suitable to part from desire for self and other?" (1998: 116).

attachment to all bodies, they nonetheless reveal the androcentric assumptions embedded within the text (cf. McClintock and Dunne 2024: 64–5).

This gendered framing is further evident in Ratnāvalī 5:72, where the aspiration for women to become "the best of persons" (*puruṣottama*) can be read as reinforcing the notion that manhood represents spiritual or social superiority. Even in the Tibetan rendering as *skyes mchog*—a term that avoids gendered connotations—this aspiration remains rooted in a context where the male body was seen as normative for spiritual advancement.

Recognizing these tensions does not negate the potential for liberative readings of such texts but underscores the importance of approaching them critically. By doing so, we can identify both the limitations of their socio-historical frameworks and the seeds of a more egalitarian vision—one that aligns with the Mahāyāna emphasis on universal liberation and transcends fixed gender hierarchies.

Can the BCA, then, serve as a source of inspiration for gender justice? The answer lies in our willingness to read it critically and expansively, transcending the limitations of its historical context while honoring its deeper liberative potential.

7. Conclusion

At this point, it is undeniable that Śāntideva's writings reflect the androcentric worldview of his time, where being born as a woman (*striyaḥ/bud med*) was seen as a disadvantage, and becoming a man (*puruṣatva/skyes pa*, specifically male) was presented as a prerequisite for spiritual progress (BCA 10:30). It remains unclear whether Śāntideva considered a change of gender—either through magical transformation or rebirth—a necessary condition for women to pursue the Bodhisattva path toward Buddhahood without barriers, or whether he believed that only men could ultimately attain this goal. As Schmidt-Leukel points out, Śāntideva's perspective in the BCA may primarily stem from the Bodhisattva ideal itself, with its ultimate goal of attaining Buddhahood, which was, in his time, largely framed in male terms.

This does not mean, however, that such a view is acceptable today. Regardless of Śāntideva's specific intent—whether rooted in cultural convention or doctrinal interpretation—it is clear that contemporary readers must engage critically with such passages to make them relevant and liberative for today's context. Constructive theology is essential here, as the question is not primarily what Śāntideva may have thought (something we cannot definitively know), but rather how we, as readers today, can interpret the text in ways that uphold the principles of gender justice and inclusivity. By drawing on Śāntideva's own philosophical tools, such as the deconstruction of fixed identities and the emphasis on ultimate over conventional truth, we can challenge the androcentric assumptions embedded in his time.

The Vajrayāna tradition, particularly in Highest Yoga Tantra, offers an important counterpoint. As Yael Bentor highlights, Tsongkhapa explicitly affirms that women can attain enlightenment in their female form, stating: "The fruit women attain by means of this practice in no way differs from the fruit men attain" (Bentor 2008: 129).

Similarly, the Dalai Lama (1995) emphasizes in Highest Yoga Tantra: "The possibility of a female practitioner becoming fully enlightened in her lifetime in female form is stated explicitly and unambiguously [...] From the point of view of possessing the fundamental innate mind of clear light, there is no difference between men and women" (Dalai Lama XIV 1995, 2015: 114).

These affirmations challenge androcentric assumptions directly and demonstrate that gender is ultimately irrelevant to spiritual attainment. By drawing on such later Buddhist teachings, we can expand Śāntideva's liberative vision to be more inclusive and equitable.

Śāntideva's own text already hints at a radical inclusivity. His conviction that even worms and mosquitoes can attain Buddhahood (BCA 7:18) underscores the Mahāyāna ideal that all sentient beings—regardless of form—have the capacity for awakening. While this is not a literal endorsement of rebirth as lower beings, it reflects a commitment to universality that invites us to transcend both androcentrism and anthropocentrism.

I have focused on issues related to the representation of the feminine in Śāntideva's work. From the outset, I have demonstrated that translators disagree on key points regarding how the feminine is portrayed, highlighting a certain ambivalence.

What do I expect from a gender-conscious translation? As a reader of world literature, I want to understand what the text says, and if I don't speak the language of the original, I want to know the different translation possibilities—and, perhaps, why a translator has chosen one over another. In this context, it seems essential that gender considerations are integrated constitutively from the very beginning of the translation process.

I have come to the conclusion that Śāntideva was not only a great scholar and poet but also a mystic or *yogin* who, as early as the seventh/eighth century, may have thought in a multiperspectival and inclusive way, in line with Mahāyāna teachings. To fully understand Śāntideva, we must take his core principles as a hermeneutic key. He writes:

> Merely desiring the benefit [of all beings] is more meritorious than worshipping the Buddhas; still more so is striving for the perfect happiness of all beings.
>
> BCA 1:27

> Verily, in front of all the Saviors, the world is today invited by me to buddhahood, and in the meantime, to worldly happiness. May the gods, the antigods and all other beings rejoice!
>
> BCA 3:33

A defining feature of a classic work of world literature is its timelessness. Thus, an important question arises: How can we methodologically approach the ambiguity of this text, particularly in the context of a Buddhist or interreligious hermeneutics? Empathy and intuition are essential tools for grasping the core essence of the text, which may lead to a re-creation or rereading of its meaning. In conclusion, Śāntideva's BCA is not timeless because it is free from historical limitations, but because it empowers us to address those limitations creatively.

It is quite possible that Śāntideva, in crafting his masterpiece, intuitively adopted a multiperspectival approach that includes all living beings—women included. Some passages are indeed ambivalent; from a modern perspective, they may even appear misogynistic. However, they might also simply reflect the social dynamics and conventional reality of his time. In that context, the belief that powerful roles—whether as Buddhas embodying ultimate goodness, Māra representing ultimate evil, or Cakravartins symbolizing political dominance—had to be male was deeply entrenched. This reflects not only the gendered worldview of Śāntideva's era but also the broader limitations of conventional reality.

In my interpretation, Śāntideva reveals his blind spots, but in doing so, he also hints at a path forward for socially engaged Buddhism and the pursuit of gender justice when he writes:

> If there is remedy, then why be dejected? And why be dejected, if there is no remedy?
>
> BCA 6:10

This verse, while ambiguous, can be understood as a call to action when a remedy exists—and as an invitation to accept and transcend what cannot be changed. From a feminist perspective the situation of women throughout history demonstrates that remedies for injustice are often uncovered or created through persistent resistance. The progress made in gender equality over centuries is a testament to the fact that what once seemed insurmountable can indeed be changed through collective effort and resilience.

Ultimately, the question is not what Śāntideva may have thought—something we cannot definitively know—but how we, as readers today, interpret his work to meet the ethical challenges of our time. By taking Śāntideva's principles seriously, we can transform his text into a resource for socially engaged Buddhism and the pursuit of gender justice. This requires us to critically examine the cultural biases of his era while remaining open to reinterpretations that resonate with contemporary values.

Buddhism has always evolved, adapting to the cultural contexts in which it finds itself. The key is to examine the core teachings of the text while remaining open to reinterpretations that resonate with contemporary values. Were Śāntideva alive today, I am convinced that he—at least in Europe—would express himself differently. By challenging the androcentrism of his time and embracing the inclusive potential of Buddhist liberation, we are invited to reimagine a path that transcends gender, species, and human boundaries—a path toward awakening that is truly universal.

In the end, there is no reason to despair: the core insights of the BCA offer hope and inspiration, not because they are free from the biases of their time, but because they empower us to reimagine and expand their liberative potential in light of today's challenges.[29]

[29] I am grateful to Monika Deimann-Clemens, Stephen Harris, and Perry Schmidt-Leukel for their insightful editorial comments and valuable suggestions on an earlier draft of this chapter. Their feedback has been immensely helpful in refining my arguments.

References

Anālayo (2010), "Women's Renunciation in Early Buddhism: The Four Assemblies and the Foundation of the Order of Nuns," in T. Mohr and J. Tsedroen (eds.), *Dignity and Discipline. Reviving Full Ordination for Buddhist Nuns*, 65–97, Boston: Wisdom Publications.

Bendall, C. and W. H. D. Rouse (1922), *Śikṣāsamuccaya: A Compendium of Buddhist Doctrine Compiled by Śāntideva Chiefly from Earlier Mahāyāna Sūtras*, London: John Murray.

Bentor, Y. (2008), "Can Women Attain Enlightenment through Vajrayāna Practices?" in D. Shulman and S. Weil (eds.), *Karmic Passages. Israeli Scholarship on India*, 125–40, New Delhi: Oxford University Press.

Blo-bzang-grags-pa, Thurman, R. A. F., and Yarnall, T. F. (2019). *Tsong Khapa Losang Drakpa: Brilliantly Illuminating Lamp of the Five Stages: (rim lnga rab tu gsal ba'i sgron me): Practical Instruction in the King of Tantras, the Glorious Esoteric Community* (2nd edition), American Institute of Buddhist Studies. Kindle Version.

Cabezón, J. I. (2010), *Tibetan Ritual*. Oxford: Oxford University Press.

Conze, E. (1960), *The Prajñāpāramitā Literature*, 's-Gravenhage: Mouton.

Crosby, K. and A. Skilton, trans. (1995), *Śāntideva. The Bodhicaryāvatāra*, Oxford: Oxford University Press.

Dalai Lama XIV (1995, 2015). *The World of Tibetan Buddhism: An Overview of Its Philosophy and Practice* (English edition), Somerville, MA: Wisdom Publications (Kindle Version).

Foley, C. A. (1893), "The Women Leaders of the Buddhist Reformation. As Illustrated by Dharmapala's Commentary on the Therigatha," in E. D. Morgan (ed.), *Transactions of the Ninth International Congress of Orientalists. (Held in London, 5th to 12th September 1892)*. Vol. I Indian and Aryan Sections, 344–61, London: Printed for the Committee of the Congress.

Fletcher, J. H. (2013), *Motherhood as Metaphor. Engendering Interreligious Dialogue*, New York: Fordham University Press.

Gyaltsen, L. K. and A. K. Chodron, trans. (2006), *Engaging in the Conduct of the Bodhisattvas by Shantideva*, New York: Tsechen Kunchab Ling.

Gyaltsen, L. K. and A. K. Chodron, trans. (2006b), *A Commentary on Shantideva's Engaging in the Conduct of the Bodhisattvas. Written by Sazang Mati Panchen*, New York: Tsechen Kunchab Ling.

Hangartner, D., trans. (2005), *Shāntideva. Anleitungen auf dem Weg zur Glückseligkeit. Bodhicaryāvatāra.* Vollständige zweisprachige Ausgabe Deutsch / Tibetisch, Frankurt: O. W. Barth.

Hopkins, J. (1998), *Buddhist Advice for Living and Liberation: Nāgārjuna's Precious Garland*. Ithaca, NY: Snow Lion.

Krey, G. (2010), "Some Remarks on the Status of Nuns and Laywomen in Early Buddhism," in T. Mohr and J. Tsedroen (eds.), *Dignity and Discipline. Reviving Full Ordination for Buddhist Nuns*, 39–63, Boston: Wisdom Publications.

Landesman, S. A. (2020), *The Tārā Tantra: Tārā's Fundamental Ritual Text (Tara-mūla-kalpa)*, Somerville, MA: Wisdom Publications.

McClintock, S. and J. Dunne (2024), *Nāgārjuna's Precious Garland: Ratnāvalī* (Classics of Indian Buddhism) (English edition). Boston: Wisdom Publications (Kindle Version).

Mrozik, S. (2007), *Virtuous Bodies: The Physical Dimensions of Morality in Buddhist Ethics.* AAR Cultural Criticism Series: Kindle Version.

Prebish, C. S. (1975), *Buddhist Monastic Discipline. The Sanskrit Prātimokṣa Sūtras of the Mahāsāmghikas and Mūlasarvāstivādins*, Dehli: Motilal Banarsidass.
Roloff, C. (2009), *Red mda' ba. Buddhist Yoga Scholar of the Fourteenth Century. The Forgotten Reviver of Madhyamaka Philosophy in Tibet*, Contributions to Tibetan Studies, 7, Wiesbaden: Dr. Ludwig Reichert Verlag.
Roloff, C. (2020), *The Buddhist Nun's Ordination in the Tibetan Canon, Possibilities of The Revival of the Mūlasarvāstivāda Bhikṣuṇī Lineage*, Hamburg Buddhist Studies 15, Bochum/Freiburg: Projektverlag.
Roth, G., ed. (1970), *Bhikṣuṇī-Vinaya: Including Bhikṣuṇī-Prakīrṇaka and a Summary of the Bhikṣu-Prakīrṇaka of the Ārya-Mahāsāṃghika-Lokottaravādin*, Tibetan Sanskrit Works Series 12, Patna: K. P. Jayaswal Research Institute.
Ruegg, D. S. (1977), Review of *Entering the Path of Enlightenment, The Bodhicaryāvatāra of the Buddhist Poet Śāntideva*, by M. L. Matics & Śāntideva. *Journal of the American Oriental Society* 97 (1): 88–9. https://doi.org/10.2307/600299
Ruegg, D. S. (1981), *The Literature of the Madhyamaka School of Philosophy in India*, Wiesbaden: Otto Harrassowitz.
Śāntideva (7th century) (2020), *Bodhicaryāvatāra*. Data entry by Richard Mahoney. Göttingen Register of Electronic Texts in Indian Languages (GRETIL), SUB Göttingen. Available online: http://gretil.sub.uni-goettingen.de/gretil/corpustei/transformations/html/sa_zAntideva-bodhicaryAvatAra.htm.
Schmidt-Leukel, P. (2019), *Buddha Mind – Christ Mind. A Christian Commentary on the Bodhicaryāvatāra*. With a new translation by E. Steinkellner and C. Peck-Kubaczek, Leuven: Peeters.
Spitz, C., trans. (2014), *Śāntideva. Anleitung auf dem Weg zum Erwachen (Bodhicaryāvatāra)*. Aus dem Tibetischen übersetzt für die Unterweisungen des Dalai Lama in Hamburg 2014. Mitarbeit: Sonam Spitz; Hamburg: Tibetisches Zentrum.
Steinkellner, E. and C. Peck-Kubaczek, trans. (2019), *Śāntideva's Bodhicaryāvatāra*. An extract from the book *Buddha Mind – Christ Mind. A Christian Commentary on the Bodhicaryāvatāra* by Perry Schmidt-Leukel, Leuven: Peeters 2019. Available online: https://www.oeaw.ac.at/fileadmin/Institute/IKGA/PDF/digitales/Steinkellner_and_Peck-Kubaczek_2019.pdf.
Vidhuśekhara Bhaṭṭācārya, ed. (1960), *Bodhicaryāvatāra of Śāntideva*, Calcutta: Asiatic Society.
Wallace, V. A. and B. A. Wallace, trans. (1997), *A Guide to the Bodhisattva Way of Life (Bodhicaryāvātara)*. Translated from the Sanskrit and Tibetan, Ithaca, NY: Snow Lion.
Wille, K., ed. (2020), *Prātimokṣasūtra of the Mūlasarvāstivādins*. Göttingen Register of Electronic Texts in Indian Languages (GRETIL), SUB Göttingen. Based on the edition by Anukul Chandra Banerjee, *Prātimokṣa-sūtra (Mūlasarvāstivāda)*, Calcutta 1954. Reprinted in *Two Buddhist Vinaya Texts in Sanskrit: Prātimokṣa Sūtra and Bhikṣukarmavākya*, ed. Anukul Chandra Banerjee, Calcutta 1977, 1–56. Available online: https://gretil.sub.uni-goettingen.de/gretil/corpustei/transformations/html/sa_prAtimokSasUtra-of-the-mUlasarvAstivAdins.html.
Yuyama, A. (2003), "The Bhikṣu-Prakīrṇaka of the Mahāsāṃghika-Lokottaravādins Quoted by Śāntideva in His Śikṣāsamuccaya," *ARIRIAB* 6: 3–17.
Zhang Yisum, ed. (1984), *Bod rgya tshig mdzod chen mo (Great Tibetan-Chinese Dictionary)*. 3 vols., Beijing: Mi rigs dpe skrun khang (Nationalities Publishing House).

8

Hierarchy Versus *Charism*

Śāntideva's Hagiography as an Exemplar of the Tension in Buddhism Between Ecclesiastical Status and Spiritual Attainment

Andrew Skilton

Those who cannot remember the past are condemned to repeat it.

Santayana 1906: 284

1. Hierarchy and charisma: A personal experience

The subject of the following is a historical review of issues relating to hierarchies in Buddhism but is rooted in a personal practice context and I will be exploring the links between the two. I began to regard myself as a Buddhist in the mid-1970s, ultimately taking formal ordination in 1979 into the Western Buddhist Order, a modernizing ecumenical Buddhist organization based in the UK.[1] My own identification with and participation in the activities of this group waned after time. By the early 1990s I was only peripherally involved with it, but despite that—probably because of my involvement in the academic world—I was commissioned by the editor in 1994 to write a 2,500-word article, to be titled "Buddhism and Hierarchy: a historical perspective" for a special issue of *Golden Drum*, the organization's regular newsletter or magazine, on the subject of "Buddhism and Hierarchy," to be published in April 1995. This magazine was published several times a year for insider and public consumption and expressed the ideas and values of that Buddhist group. In the event, my article was rejected by the editorial board (rather than the commissioning editor), having been deemed unsuitable and subversive of the group's values. Despite this rejection, the article itself had an afterlife. It continued to circulate in samizdat fashion—even ten years later I received a private request for a copy, and I know that others passed copies around, although I do not think it had any substantive effect on attitudes or policy within that organization, a topic to which I shall now turn.[2]

[1] Subsequently renamed the Triratna Buddhist Community.
[2] Although at one stage I lost track of that article, in recent years I found a file containing several drafts, plus the correspondence relating to its rejection and the magazine as eventually published.

That rejection deserves some explanation. My piece was seen as challenging, even undermining, the main theme of the planned special issue, although I had not been involved in the planning for it. That theme was the presentation of the position that the capacity to take leadership responsibility within the organization reflected spiritual attainment and hence spiritual status on the Buddhist Path.[3] Put a little reductively, the taking of organizational and leadership responsibility was an expression of "spiritual responsibility" and was therefore a measure of one's stature as a spiritual being. This position had been evolving within the organization for a year or so and, looking back now, had evolved out of a somewhat ambiguous emergent leadership situation. The charismatic founder, whose leadership was undisputed, had a core of senior disciples who also exercised what might be described as degrees of charisma. I use the term here more in its contemporary sense of a compelling personal persuasiveness based on (non-sexual) attraction, and differentiate it from the original theological sense of *charism*—i.e., of possessing "spiritual gifts" or spiritual stature—which, in the Buddhist context, I see as the possession of the primary virtue, or perfection, of wisdom. In the Buddhist context the latter is usually understood as a matter of direct insight rather than scholarly learning.[4] While the founder was regarded as also possessing *charism*, the exact status of the cohort of senior disciples—i.e., the proportions of their personal influence vs. spiritual attainment recognized by the group at large—was disputable, and I suspect at a certain level was an uncertain matter even in their own minds. However, I would now suggest that the emergence of the hierarchy issue at this point in time should mainly be seen as part of a strategy for managing the transition away from the leadership of its founder, who was aging, to a successor leadership from among those pupils. I did not articulate this in my article, but I note on rereading that the lead article in the special issue, "Ascending the Spiritual Hierarchy," indirectly makes that connection in passing: "All this is especially relevant at the moment … for [*the founder*] is now handing on his remaining responsibilities for its direction . . ." (Golden Drum 1995: 9).

The idea was seen by those propounding it as a matter of "spiritual truth." This is asserted in the rejection letter: the "conflation of spiritual and institutional hierarchy represents the fruits of a spiritual insight"; it is "a spiritual principle, presumably good for all time and place, and not our response to the particular conditions of the modern

[3] The idea had been "launched" in a lecture, which I had not attended, by a senior disciple earlier in the year. He was also the author of the lead article in the magazine. I did not offer the present ideas in a polemical sense, but just tried to articulate what I found in the tradition. I do not know the currency or status of this strategy in the contemporary organization.

[4] I would extend this notion of *charism* to include all the so-called perfections, *pāramitā*, of the bodhisattva in Mahāyāna Buddhism, but for present purposes find it simpler to use it with this restricted referent. There is a disjunction between the Christian sense of *charism* as "spiritual gifts given by God," and any potential Buddhist application of the term, since all spiritual virtues are, in most parts of Buddhism, not given but rather "earned" or accumulated through one's practice of the Path. Nevertheless, the possession of high-order virtues in Buddhism is reasonably denoted by the term, not least because of the similarity with which their possessors are regarded in both religious traditions.

world."[5] Rephrasing this, the leaders of the organization had come to see the idea that organizational leadership roles reflected spiritual development was not a temporal construction or strategy, as I have just suggested, but an aspect of reality or "of the way things truly are" (*yathābhūta*), as discovered under the impact of insight (*vipassanā*) arising from Buddhist practice—i.e., understanding this was an expression of their *charism*. Making this claim, of course, gives it an unassailable status—the lowly individual practitioner hardly dares dispute "the way things truly are." Quoting again the lead piece, the author—seen by many at the time as the most likely successor to the founder of the organization, and who regularly spoke and wrote in a mode of authoritative mouthpiece for him—said:

> One's position in the spiritual hierarchy is a question of one's ability to take genuine spiritual responsibility for others, not of what office one holds. Thus it corresponds, at least to a large extent, to one's genuine spiritual attainment. Naturally, there is always a potential for a true hierarchy of responsibility to decay into a hierarchy of status and power.
>
> Golden Drum 1995: 9

Why revisit this episode some thirty years on? I do so because it provides the context for my original thinking on the matter (also prompted at the time by translating, together with Kate Crosby, the *Bodhicaryāvatāra*) but also because it underlines the topicality of the issue. Issues of hierarchy and charisma have played and continue to play powerful roles in Buddhist communities, and the Buddhist tradition's resolution of their interaction is deeply significant for Buddhist communities in the present day. That said, in what follows I do not reproduce verbatim the text of the article I wrote in 1994. That was written in a different voice for a different audience, and in a different state of my own perspective on Buddhist tradition and on my personal practice environment. It went through several drafts and was never published in definitive form. My understanding of the issue has not changed, but only deepened, so I have not here changed the substance of the original. Instead, I reuse the data as reordered and augmented for this chapter. In particular, in the interim I had been able to incorporate reflections on lived Buddhism outside India. The article had originally focused on Śāntideva as one of several case studies embodying important attitudes about hierarchy, but under editorial pressure to reduce my word total in 1994, I had for reasons I no longer recall edited him out of later drafts. I now reinstate him and take him as my starting point.

2. The case of Śāntideva

Śāntideva is rightly respected as the author of the *Bodhicaryāvatāra* (BCA), and the importance of his text in a number of Tibetan lineages has led to the publication of

5 Private correspondence, 23 December 1994, p. 3. Despite its clear pejorative sense in contemporary British English, I think the author used the term "conflation" in a consciously neutral mode, although a skeptical reading might detect an unconscious admission of the problem I had addressed.

multiple translations and commentaries. As part of this exposure, people who read or study BCA are more or less familiar with a version of Śāntideva's "story." I use inverted commas because there are in fact multiple stories. Fortunately, Perry Schmidt-Leukel (2019: 13–37) has given us an account of them in his *Buddha Mind - Christ Mind*. There he identifies a total of eight versions which demonstrate a development through three stages of growth. A core "scene" concerns Śāntideva's residence at the monastic university of Nālandā, my account of which will be based on the earliest versions of the story, those of Vibhūticandra and Abhayadatta (17–18).

Śāntideva, it seems, was not the "ideal" monk in that he did not participate in the expected monastic activities. Instead he spent his time engaged in meditation in his cell (*kuṭi*), otherwise reputedly just eating, sleeping, and defecating. This in turn gave rise to a spiteful nickname given to him by the Nālandā monks—Bhusuku—seemingly derived from the initial syllables of the words for eating, *bhuñj*, sleeping, *sup*, and the place of defecation, the *(vacca-)kuṭi*.[6] Devising a scheme to humiliate Śāntideva publicly, he was challenged to recite from memory at an upcoming assembly. Śāntideva attempted to decline the challenge, claiming ignorance of the Tipiṭaka, but was presented with a fait accompli—the elevated recitation platform in the midst of the assembly. Śāntideva agreed to perform, offering a choice to the auditors—"new or old" material? In a mood of derisory skepticism the assembly asked for something "new" and so Śāntideva sang (it is a verse text with elegant poetry) his *Bodhicaryāvatāra* for them. As he reached a key verse from his section on *prajñā*, Mañjuśrī appeared above him and they both levitated in the air:

> When neither entity nor non-entity remains before the mind, since there is no other mode of operation, grasping no objects, it becomes tranquil.
>
> BCA 9:35[7]

At this point in the early versions they disappeared, although in Buston's version Śāntideva's disembodied voice continued the recitation until the BCA was finished—another 190 verses in the long recension. The key point in this is that, while some versions describe a post-Nālandā life for Śāntideva, his (non-)career at Nālandā is over after this episode. Vibhūticandra has him go away at verse 9.35, never to be seen again, whereas Abhayadatta describes his levitation and then allows that he spent a little more time at the temple-university, during which the monks begged him to become the Abbot. At this request he simply disrobed and left, never to return. My proposition is that this story offers to us a narrative demonstration of the contrast between

6 The subversive and scatological tone of this anecdote has all the marks of authenticity to anyone who has read much of the Vinaya, in which poor monastic behavior is described all the time. Nevertheless, while the interpretation of the -*ku* of Bhusuku as referencing the toilet, *vacca-kuṭi* (literally "feces-room"), fits this tone, I cannot help suspecting that it may originally have been coined in relation to his keeping to his monastic cell, his *kuṭi*, rather than using the toilet. This in turn explains alternative exegeses of "Bhusuku" as connected with meditation rather than toileting, because it was in his *kuṭi* that he meditated. This is the natural reading of the Sanskrit text, which describes him being *kuṭiṃgata*, which literally means, "in his cell." Taking this to refer to the *vacca-kuṭi* is probably just a sarcastic tweak in some versions.

7 *yadā na bhāvo nābhāvo mateḥ saṃtiṣṭhate puraḥ tadānyagatyabhāvena nirālambā praśāmyati*

organizational engagement and status, on the one hand, and possession of wisdom and its preferred arena of deployment, on the other. Implicitly, it contrasts Śāntideva's evident *charism* with the "professional" world of the monks at this high-status institution—a world of institutional involvement, corporate responsibility, public performance, reputation, and even career advancement, the pinnacle of which would be to occupy the primary organizational position of Abbot. Crucially, this story depicts the wise person, the one who has *charism*, as rejecting that world of organizational activity and responsibility, going so far as to disrobe. The implication is that those who occupy (or are preoccupied by?) the organizational monastic environment have difficulty recognizing Śāntideva's genuine spiritual advancement—until it becomes blatantly evident through Mañjuśrī's endorsement. Śāntideva has made spiritual progress while at Nālandā through his meditation and while "at odds" with his fellow monks over his organizational participation, but he leaves the monastic world clearly deeming it unappreciative of his true achievements and spiritual status and an inappropriate field for the expression of these "gifts."

3. Hierarchies in Buddhism

It is useful at this point to reflect on the nature of hierarchies in Buddhism. It is a pervasive yet sometimes misunderstood feature of the Buddhist tradition. I have heard people express the conviction that hierarchy is antithetical to the spirit of Buddhism. However, not only has hierarchy been a significant preoccupation throughout Buddhist history but, like other major religious traditions, Buddhism has formed and expressed itself through hierarchies. Hierarchy is also multifaceted and deserves careful analysis to differentiate its different modes and functions.

This anti-hierarchy view could stem from an episode in the *Vinaya-piṭaka* in which the Buddha declares that he will not appoint a successor as head of the Saṅgha. Among Western converts this is sometimes seen as "enlightened" anti-establishmentarianism, in positive contrast to the hierarchically oppressive institutional regimes of other traditions. Whatever the broader intention of the Buddha, the context of this declaration is the attempt by the Buddha's cousin, Devadatta, to secure this status for himself—the Buddha was rebuffing what is depicted as an over-weening career move by a close relative (Horner 1963: 264–5).[8] It is also plain to see that, whatever the Buddha's wishes in life, after his death various senior monks appear to have functioned in this role, or have been regarded in ways analogous to it.[9]

For the Theravāda tradition it was the formidable Mahākassapa who seized the lead role in arranging the First Council at which, traditionally, the canon was compiled and fixed (Horner 1963: 393–406). The denigration of Ānanda as non-arhat in this account perhaps reflects an attempt to deflate the obvious claim to seniority that may have been made—either by Ānanda or on his behalf—as a close relative and long-standing

[8] My references here and hereafter are to the *vinaya* of the Theravāda school preserved in Pali language.

[9] For example, the lineages of *vinayadhara* recorded in the *Dīpavaṃsa* (v.55–107).

companion of the Buddha and acknowledged recorder of the *Sutta-piṭaka* (Findly 1992). This speculation is confirmed by the position of the later Sautrāntika school which claimed Ānanda as the head of its own lineage (Bareau 2013: 209)—a position that gave symbolic expression to its rejection of the Abhidhamma as "the word of the Buddha" *buddhavacana*, which other schools made into a third *Piṭaka*. The elderly monk Purāṇa only arrived just after the First Council had concluded (Horner 1963: 401–2). Invited to add his endorsement to the "authentic" canon of teachings that had been defined there, he declined. Informing Mahākassapa that he knew the Buddha's teachings well enough for himself and thereby not subordinating his understanding to Mahākassapa's organizational arrangement, he withdrew taking his own following of disciples. These narrative events reflect the interaction between the perception of authority, leadership, and hierarchy in the formation of the Saṅgha.

Even casual reading of the early discourses reveals that the Buddha inspired considerable faith and respect from his disciples and possessed considerable charisma. One might also say that, as Buddha, he possessed absolute *charism*. His personal influence was accepted and respected throughout the early Buddhist community. Even though he relinquished exclusive responsibility for ordination early on, there is little doubt that all monks regarded him as the spiritual head of their community. The Vinaya—the record of monastic regulations—puts each rule in a narrative context explaining how the Buddha came to devise it. While it is unlikely that the Buddha was personally responsible for every rule, there is no doubt that he was concerned to establish a community that could sustain itself after his death. His effort to devise regulations which could facilitate the smooth functioning of the community, both internally and within the surrounding society, suggest this. We can see that the Buddha functioned not only as spiritual leader to the Saṅgha which he had initiated, but as its organizational head too. Yet, after the Buddha's *parinirvāṇa*, this simplicity of structure finished and we can reasonably assume that, in the absence of an official successor to the Buddha, there were a number of prospective and even competing institutional leaders.

This process contributed, in the long run, to two distinct forms of sectarianism—on the one hand, the various mutually exclusive ordination lineages based on distinctive accounts of Vinaya and known as *nikāya*, and on the other, different schools of doctrine, distinctive articulations of teaching—Sarvāstivāda, Sautrāntika, Darṣṭāntika, etc. This divergence is significant for two factors: the need for the Saṅgha to be sure that it is transmitting "the true Dharma," implicitly a teaching rooted in *charism*; and the need for there to be a sufficiently stable and reputable institutional base for any lineage of the Saṅgha to flourish from one generation to the next. The latter might preferably be guarded by those with *charism*, but it is not clear that that was or has been thought absolutely necessary.

Aside from leadership of the monastic community as a whole, how did the individual monastic experience spiritual and institutional hierarchy? At the simplest level precedence between individuals was established by chronological seniority—the monk or nun who had been ordained the longest would be the senior-most member of their community. This established a purely formal hierarchy of precedence which was expedient for ritual and other collective activities but made no explicit statement of spiritual status. Alongside this arrangement, individuals were appointed to serve a community by holding organizational posts such as "quartermaster" or "supervisor of buildings or sleeping quarters" through which they could exercise a kind of control over others, but this was understood as a matter of personal competence and organizational need rather than spiritual hierarchy.

More pertinent than those arrangements are the preceptor, *upajjhāya*, and instructor, *ācariya*, allotted to each ordinand and described as one of the five *nissaya*, reliances, allowed to a monastic (Horner 1951: 57–9).[10] It is clear that the newly ordained person looks to these figures as spiritual guides. It is they who give guidance on proper conduct, practice, and understanding. In this sense, the preceptor and instructor are immediate spiritual superiors, the two individuals who have formally accepted responsibility for that person's practice of the Teaching and growth within the Path, and these appointments constitute a rather flat formal spiritual hierarchy of just two levels, although they are not based on *charism* so much as personal competence, time served, and organizational need. An individual monastic would be expected to remain in reliance on their spiritual instructors for at least ten years, although formal freedom from this *nissaya* was also reliant on demonstration of personal competence, and a dull person might spend their entire monastic career under the formal guidance of their preceptor. By contrast, a highly competent individual might have the term reduced to five years or even less. Only after the point of formal release from the fifth *nissaya* might one function as either preceptor or instructor oneself—not a measure of *charism* as much as competence and "time served" (Horner 1951: 101–3).

What then of discipline? The most grievous lapses in observance of Vinaya, committing any of the *pārājika* offenses (four for men and eight for women), were met by expulsion from the Saṅgha. A few "less grievous" infringements resulted in suspension from participation in the life of the Saṅgha, while the majority could be expiated by proper confession of one's fault. All these regulations were enacted at a full meeting of the local Saṅgha, this being the only legally valid meeting for this purpose, and their proper enactment was agreed by consensus. There was no use of power to correct or punish an individual for wrongdoing, although this does explain why at some periods the Saṅgha was happy to rely on the power of the secular authority to enforce some form of "purification" of the Saṅgha, when factional monks did not cooperate with this system. It should be noted that Vinaya is concerned solely with behavior rather than "views," and that in the early Saṅgha there is no monastic disciplinary procedure to control or penalize how individuals interpret doctrine. Genuine ethical lapses, where distinct from infringements of the Vinaya rules, and wrong views were matters for private confession.

This arrangement was not free of difficulties. The most obvious and possibly most consequential was outside interference, when the political powers of the day attempted to regulate the internal affairs of the monastic institutions within their jurisdiction. The earliest and most famous instance of this was the episode in which the emperor Asoka "purified" the local Saṅgha in Pātaliputta, thereby providing a precedent for numerous

[10] For a summary discussion of these roles and the mutual duties falling on the *upajjhāya*, *ācariya*, and the ordinand, see "Chapter 2 Nissaya," in Ṭhānissaro 2013: 43–9.

later monarchs and governments to "purify" or "reform" the Saṅgha when they deemed such action necessary. Among the most radical of such interference must be the reform of the twelfth-century Sri Lankan monarch, Parakkamabāhu I, which led to the institution of a government-appointed Saṅgharāja, King of the Saṅgha, who was responsible to the monarch for the activities of all monastic communities in the realm. This pattern was exported throughout Southeast Asia, and the institution still exists in Thailand, Laos, and Cambodia.[11]

Thus an average monk in Thailand experiences a world of hierarchy or authority that has at least three dimensions. First, there is the formal hierarchy of the Saṅgha. He individually is responsible to his "section head" (larger temples are usually subdivided into sections, *khanā*), and via him to the abbot of his monastery, who is in turn responsible to the Mahāthera Samāgama, a national body of the twenty currently highest ranking monks. That body is in turn responsible to the Saṅgharāja. Allied to this is a network of monastic administrative divisions (Na-rangsi 2002). However, the Saṅgharāja is himself implicated in a second order of hierarchy, that of the secular state—in the case of Thailand, this is primarily embodied in the King and the royal court but also, in symbiosis with them, the government (elected or otherwise). A Saṅgharāja cannot be appointed who is not acceptable to either the royal court or secular authorities, as recent events preceding the appointment of the current Saṅgharāja illustrate.[12]

A third frame of hierarchy is perhaps a kind of inverse authority—the laity. It is universally understood that in religious terms the monastic community is regarded as superior to the lay community, the latter showing considerable deference to the former. But in recent academic discussion, a senior monk commented that the monastic community is also subject to the control of the laity, in respect of its expectations. While I understood this in part to be a reference to the burdensome nature of lay demands on a monk's time in terms of his duties (the monk who made the comment has a high degree of organizational responsibility in his temple), I am also aware that the laity to some extent also "police" the behaviors of monks, and, whether or not they know the details of *vinaya* regulations, exert a normative pressure on monks regarding daily activities and etiquette, particularly in regard to matters of food consumption after the noontime deadline, interaction with members of the opposite sex, receiving (excessive) donations, etc.[13]

[11] A modern example of state intervention is the State Saṅghamahanayaka Committee in Myanmar (established 1980) which tries and imprisons monastics and lay teachers for *dhamma* and *vinaya* misdemeanors (see Ashin and Crosby 2017).

[12] After the demise of the last Saṅgharāja, Vajirañāṇasaṃvara, in 2013, the next in line of seniority, Somdet Chuang Varapuñño, was considered by the military government to be unsuitable because of his opposition to the violent protests that had led to the military coup in 2014. It refused to forward his nomination to the King for approval. In the event Varapuñño withdrew.

[13] Regarding the theme of lay "policing" of the monastic community, accusations of sexual and financial misdemeanors are a common part of the play of the politics of influence in Thai society. The highest stakes include the loss of government and royal support, not to mention diminution of one's popular lay support, along with threats of official harassment in the form of "investigations," forced disrobing, and/or jail time if the government deems key regulations have been infringed. In a different mode altogether, in traditional Cambodia a lay *achar wat* is responsible for the annual cycle of temple activities and may outrank the resident monks who might be considerably younger and have less knowledge or experience of their full ritual and pastoral obligations.

Finally, I cannot move on from discussion of the Saṅgha's internal hierarchies without mentioning the most explicit and generally immutable hierarchy, that of gender, in which all nuns are subordinate to the most junior monk by force of Vinaya regulation.[14] In those countries which no longer accept female ordination, women have evolved quasi-monastic renunciate roles—as *maechi* in Thailand, *thilashin* in Myanmar, *dasasīlamātā* in Sri Lanka—or express their spirituality as laywomen: e.g., as *zale* in traditional Shan State or even as online teachers and guides in modern Thailand.

We should also consider forms of hierarchy outwith the Saṅgha. Monks and nuns usually function within a setting that is in part secular or non-monastic, including the immediate lay support for a given temple but extending beyond that too into broader society. In a recent lecture on the topic of the "mechanisms of power" in Thai Buddhism, Thomas Borchert (2023) suggested that there are three bases on which a monk can exert influence in and beyond the Saṅgha.[15] It is useful to draw on the emic terms of reference for these hierarchies of power or authority used by him in the discussion that follows. First, there is the realm of *barami (pāramī)*, spiritual authority or charisma. This is a reflection of the individual monk's spiritual stature and implicitly is an assessment of his status on the Path. There is, of course, a fuzzy boundary between being actually possessed of certain qualities (*charism*) and being seen as possessing them (charisma), and Borchert clearly wants to exclude *barami* from a simple equation with the Weberian idea of charisma. In using *barami* he makes it clear that the Thai Buddhist tradition itself has terminology that points to this important factor but not necessarily in a neat equivalence to our Western usages for discussing the same area. My understanding of *barami* is that it straddles both *charism* and charisma, in the sense that, for example, a senior monk may be considered to possess *barami*, on the one hand, because of the perception by those around him that he possesses *charism*—i.e., is endowed with high-order virtues (real or imagined) such as wisdom—and/or, on the other, possesses a charismatic personality and manner. My understanding is that within the faith community setting it is impossible to determine objectively the ontological status of any individual's "gifts," and that the influence of those gifts within the community is directly proportionate to the community's *belief* in that person's *charism*.[16] The degree of influence of that *barami* within the community is not itself a direct measure of actual *charism* or the possession of high-order religious virtues.

[14] The legal requirement is stated as the first of the eight "important rules," *garudhamma*, through observance of which women were allowed to become nuns: "A nun who has been ordained (even) for a century must greet respectfully, rise up from her seat, salute with joined palms, do proper homage to a monk ordained but that day. And this rule is to be honored, respected, revered, venerated, never to be transgressed during her life" (Horner 1963: 354). At the Münster workshop I was pleased to be reminded of this hierarchy by Carola Roloff (see Chapter 7 in this volume). We should note that people with non-normative or non-binary gender identities are excluded from ordination altogether. The initial exclusion of persons with non-normative gender identities is expressed in the Vinaya (Horner 1951: 108–9) and elaborated in the commentary to that passage.

[15] I hope I do not misrepresent Borchert's analysis with this interpretative account, and take full responsibility for errors here.

[16] Of course, individuals may claim the capacity to determine by direct perception whether or not another possesses certain spiritual virtues (I have met plenty of such people), but the claim to possess this capacity (*yogi-pratyakṣa*) on the part of the observer/judge is just as problematic and subject to the same determinants as the virtues of the person observed.

Either way, I have observed this "mechanism" in many Buddhist practice communities, both Asian and Western, where what I believe Thais would term *barami* is often a status or authority that is imputed for or projected on the teacher of the temple or group (plus sometimes a cohort of senior disciples). In a Mahāyāna context s/he might be regarded as a bodhisattva.[17] In a Theravāda context the attributed status might be from among the categories of the *ariya-saṅgha*. *Barami* is a matter of the person's spiritual reputation, as it has emerged among the broader practice community. It is not a matter of formal status, and significantly, Borchert suggests, is also undermined if the individual is seen to seek it. Thinking of Śāntideva, we can see that at Nālandā he did not have *barami*. His contemporaries there had no respect for him, even as a *confrère*, let alone in terms of his progress on the path. This changed after his endorsement by the appearance of Mañjuśrī during his recitation, accompanied by his own demonstration of *ṛddhi*, supernatural power, and in one account he was offered high organizational status as a marker of this new regard in which he was held.

The second mechanism in Borchert's analysis is *amnat*. This is easier to understand, and is roughly akin to institutional authority or power. It is the influence that an individual monk can wield through institutional roles and status, and the interactions he can have with secular society on that basis. In Thailand the Saṅgharāja has a very high level of *amnat*, being part of the highest level of the national establishment, while sitting at the top of a pyramid of organizational networks within the Saṅgha through which he wields ecclesiastical influence. At temple level the Abbot occupies the position of highest *amnat*, although obviously he may be considered as also possessing *barami*, and may have great influence on both counts. But I have also met or know of abbots who appear to perform their *amnat* "duties" in a spirit of humble service, with a sense that they do "this" work because they do not have the talent for other, "higher" work; and yet others who do it because it was just "their turn,"—i.e., the position came to them because of their chronological seniority. Again, we can see that Śāntideva had no *amnat* at Nālandā—if anything he was despised for his non-participation in the organizational structures and activities of the temple. In one version the offer of the abbacy, the highest degree of *amnat*, prompted him to disrobe.

The third mechanism in Borchert's analysis is *saksit* or supernatural power—*ṛddhi* or *iddhi*. While this is not accessible to empirical ratification, the belief that advanced meditation practitioners can manipulate the world with their mind is universal in traditional Buddhist circles. In contemporary Thailand this is not so much witnessed directly as experienced through reputation—i.e., anecdotes verging on hagiography—of an individual's performance of some "miracle" at some other time and in some other place. The spread and influence of such stories are proportional to the audience's willingness or desire to believe that they are true. This is the only dimension explicitly

[17] I am aware that in Thailand *maechi* and female lay teachers can possess (or be seen to possess) considerable *barami* and thus exert influence within a community and society—e.g., the *maechi* Thongsuk and Candra, and the lay preacher/lifestyle guru Dhitinart (Kru Oi). In Myanmar the female *zale* Nang Kham Ku and Pa Mule have been well-renowned teachers. Whether the issues discussed later in this chapter are replicated, nuanced, or even avoided in the *bhikkhuni saṅgha* or in women's orders deserves exploration.

acknowledged in the story of Śāntideva. It is through his *ṛddhi* or *saksit* acquired through his meditation that he rises into the air and then vanishes from sight.

To summarize, we can describe the Saṅgha as a community in which clear differentiations are made between areas of status, activity, and responsibility, such that in effect there were, and are, multiple hierarchies:

1. a deferential and ritual absolute hierarchy established by chronological precedence—i.e., date of ordination;
2. a pragmatic organizational or institutional hierarchy established by consensus, aptitude, and appointment (Borchert's *amnat*);
3. a one-step training-cum-spiritual hierarchy established by collective appointment at ordination;
4. a one-step hierarchy of gender, with all nuns subordinated to all monks;
5. a hierarchy between monastic and lay status, with the latter nuanced further by social standing;
6. a hierarchy of supernatural power that is usually based on reputation but supposedly originates in practical demonstration (Borchert's *saksit*);
7. a hierarchy of spiritual authority, again based on reputation, but referring to the individual's status on the Path (Borchert's *barami*).

My understanding of this situation is that the differentiation of these hierarchies within the monastic tradition is intentional and understood to ease the functioning of the Saṅgha in a number of respects, especially with regard to internal factionalism, but also to protect it from a variety of confusions that might occur were these hierarchies not clearly differentiated. The Vinaya, both with *saṅghādisesa* rules and in the *Saṅghabhedakkhandhaka*, addresses how to resolve factionalism once it has emerged.

If the interference in Saṅgha life by secular authority on the basis of power is another kind of problem, as I suggested above, then yet another complication, which undoubtedly undermines the manifold differentiated hierarchies described above, is the conflation of the spiritual hierarchy, particularly the community perception of spiritual status (7) with any of these others but especially the organizational (2). This kind of problem is not usually recorded in the history of external events—i.e., chronicles, *vaṃsa*, but more often in spiritual biography. There are stories from the lives of famous Buddhist figures which clearly demonstrate that this could and did happen. This brings us to our case studies.

4. The cases of Huineng and Nāropa

Before returning to Śāntideva's case there are two others at which we can profitably look and which support the interpretation I am making of Śāntideva's. The first of these concerns the Chan monk Huineng who lived in China in the seventh to eighth century. He was both the Sixth Patriarch of the Chan School and also the First Patriarch of the Southern Chan School. His story, and the reason for the double status, is explained in a quasi-historical hagiography compiled by a personal pupil of his called Fahai, and based on Huineng's own words.[18] In that text Huineng describes himself as a young peasant who happened to overhear the recitation of the *Vajracchedikā Sūtra* while delivering firewood to a customer. Being told that the text came from a monastery far to the north, in Huangmei, Huineng traveled there and requested admission from Hongren, the Abbot and Fifth Chan Patriarch. He was admitted but, as a foreigner from "down south" and illiterate, he was put to menial work in the kitchen.

Later that year the Abbot had decided to determine the leadership succession in the monastery and initiated a contest that involved candidates writing a poem that expressed the highest insight they could understand. Only one candidate, Shenxiu the chief disciple of the Abbot and presumed successor, even attempted to compete, and wrote his verse anonymously on a corridor wall. Privately the Abbot thought it insufficient and though he required the other monks to show it respect (presumably he was protecting the anticipated succession by doing this), he spoke privately to Shenxiu giving him the chance to compose a second verse. Meanwhile Huineng had asked for the poem to be read to him and in spontaneous response composed his own, asking someone present to write it on the wall. The Abbot deemed this one expressive of a higher insight, but wiped it from the wall to protect Huineng. The next day, Huineng tells us, the Abbot met him secretly, transmitted the *Vajracchedikā Sūtra* to him, gave him the symbols of the Patriarchate—his bowl and robe—ordering him to leave the monastery and teach the Dharma elsewhere. Huineng, though pursued by people who wanted to steal the symbols of his status, eventually returned to the south of China where he established his own tradition of which he was the First Patriarch, even as he was still the Sixth Patriarch of the Northern School.

Here again we see a contrast being drawn between insight and organizational status. The *Platform Sūtra* wants to present the highest office as a position held by the most spiritually developed person—thus Hongren is depicted by Huineng as only transmitting the Patriarchate to him once he has attained Awakening (*bodhi*). At the same time, everyone (including Hongren) had expected his successor to be his most senior disciple, and he had already made this known. Thus, Shenxiu's lackluster performance was something of a problem in the smooth working of this transfer of the organizational succession. Huineng recalled Hongren saying to him (McRae 2000: 24):

> The robe [however] has become the focus of conflict, and beginning with you it should not be transmitted. If you transmit this robe, your life expectancy will be like a hanging thread. You should go quickly! I fear people will harm you!

Even in a system where the attempt is made to equate organizational status with spiritual status, the impossibility of achieving it is expressed by this well-known story.

Huineng does not employ *saksit*, and he has no *amnat*—he is the lowliest kitchen boy and cannot even read. He is not regarded as possessing *barami*, but the text itself is his own account of how he comes to be seen as possessing it. Crucially in this respect, Huineng declares he does not seek status: "I wish only to achieve buddhahood and do

[18] Quasi-historical not just in the sense of being hagiography but also in acknowledgment that Huineng's very historical existence has been queried (see Nagashima 1978).

not seek anything else" (McRae 2000: 18). Hongren is depicted as recognizing his *charism* and endorsing Huineng's status. So this is also a story of succession—the text is Huineng's account of why he himself should be accepted as the legitimate heir to the Patriarchate, but this is expressed in terms of how Hongren can ensure that his successor is the right person, and this is made into an "objective" matter of Hongren formally, but secretly, recognizing and endorsing Huineng's *charism*—i.e., his possession of wisdom, etc. On the allied issue of the community's acceptance of his choice, Hongren judges that the community will not be able to agree with him, a judgment that is validated by events—Huineng's life is in danger and Hongren sends him away out of the organization altogether.

Now both the Śāntideva and Huineng stories can be seen as "outsider" narratives in which an unlikely candidate with low organizational status, and who is held in low regard by the organizational members, comes to be revealed as the individual at the top of the spiritual hierarchy. In both cases the organization—using this term to denote the temples or monasteries involved and their members—and its opportunities for status are absolutely rejected, even if they had also functioned as a context for the development of high-order virtues. It is therefore useful and salutary to look at a case study where the "hero" is an *insider*. This brings us back to Nālandā, the great educational temple complex of Bihar, but some two or three centuries after Śāntideva was supposed to have been there. The same issues are explored and the resolution—rejection of the conflation of organizational and spiritual status—is depicted. This story concerns Nāropa aka Abhayakīrti, a tenth- to eleventh-century Mahāsiddha in the Vajrayāna tradition. The narrative comes from a hagiography of Nāropa written in the late twelfth century. He is described as training at a monastery in Kashmir as a lay student but then succumbing to parental pressure to marry. Divorced after eight years, and after another three years in Kashmir where he finally became a *bhikṣu*, he entered Nālandā at the age of 28. He was already attributed with authorship of many learned commentaries on various tantric cycles, and the biography makes it clear that in Nālandā he was moving in a highly competitive environment filled with the most illustrious individuals of the day. Particular emphasis is given to the "gatekeepers,"—i.e., those monks whose learning was the greatest and whose job was to filter those allowed to the enter the complex. The four highest-ranking individuals each had responsibility for one gate, and it so happened that Jetarī, the head of the "northern department,"—i.e., the northern gate—passed away. He was renowned for "his realization that rejection and attainment are the same when all obstacles have been overcome"—a matter of *charism* (Guenther 1963: 20). The five hundred scholar monks of Nālandā by consensus requested Nāropa to take Jetari's position.

After decorous hesitation, he accepted the post. Tradition was that new incumbents must engage all-comers in debate. A grand contest was arranged, a throne set up, this time for the king who acted as chairman, and after a month of wide-ranging debate with Buddhists and non-Buddhists alike, Nāropa was declared unbeaten. Such was his absolute eminence that he was unanimously invited to become the Abbot of Nālandā and he agreed. He composed a suite of self-congratulatory verses, seven hundred Hindu teachers converted to Buddhism, the monks of Nālandā beat the big drum, the king placed his head on Nāropa's feet saying that he was happy to be his patron. With this absolute organizational and establishment approval, Nāropa continued as Abbot for another eight years. Until one day he was seated consulting some texts outdoors. A shadow fell over his manuscripts as an elderly woman stood over him. She asked could he read all this stuff, and when he said "yes," she asked if he understood the words or the meaning (*artha-vyañjana*). He replied, "the words"—at which she smiled—but then he added "and the meaning too," at which she wept. Initially delighted to hear the great scholar tell the truth by admitting he could read the words, she was dismayed to hear him "lie" by claiming to understand them. He asked who *could*, to which she replied, "My brother!" and left. Nāropa, galvanized by the encounter, resolved to leave his "dream job" at Nālandā to seek understanding, true spiritual status on the Path—*charism*.

In this story, once again *saksit* appears to be irrelevant, but the hero has abundant *amnat*, in that he has won, by reputation and through vigorous public encounter, the highest organizational status. He was also regarded as possessing great *barami* as the community's spiritual guide and protector (Guenther 1963: 27–8):

> Sublime and glorious sage, Abhayakīrti [i.e. Nāropa],
> We should have no physician, Dharma's embodiment,
> 'Gainst the diseases of our blindness and ignorance,
> So, saint Abhayakīrti, stay for our sake,
> And look with mercy on Nalanda.

But he realized that he was not what he and everyone else had thought he was—he did not truly have insight knowledge of the doctrines he so eloquently and effectively articulated. He did not really have *charism*. In fact, we could summarize these three case studies by saying that, whereas Śāntideva and Huineng are depicted as having *charism* but no charisma, Nāropa is shown as having charisma but no *charism*.

5. Concluding reflections

We have now reviewed a body of information about monastic hierarchies and three stories about iconic Buddhist figures that demonstrate a conflict between organizational status and spiritual status, each of which performs in narrative terms the rejection of the former in favor of the latter. This discussion has employed materials from a wide range of Buddhist contexts—from Theravāda sources, both ancient and modern, from Mahāyāna and Vajrayāna, from India, China, and Thailand, from *vinaya* regulations, from sociological observation, from the early history of the Saṅgha, and from narrative hagiography.

We can now close the circle and look back at the strategy of the equation of institutional responsibility with spiritual status that I encountered in the mid-1990s. Retrospectively, I can see that we can unpack it employing the terms used by Borchert in his analysis of the Thai Saṅgha. I have already suggested that it was a strategy for managing the leadership succession, but how did this work, or rather, why was it necessary? In order for that transition to be successful it was necessary to be able to draw on "objective,"—i.e., collectively agreed—parameters by which the successors could be unambiguously identified within the practice community as the "real" successors to the founder. The founder, as always, was held in very high regard by all members of the organization.[19] He had had the highest level of *amnat*—i.e, institutional status or authority—but had gone some way to divesting all of that as he moved into his later years of retirement. He was, in a low-key fashion, attributed with *saksit* on the basis of stories circulating privately about minor incidents in which it was deemed he had exercised some kind of supernatural agency—typically these amounted to a claim that he "knew the mind" of individual disciples—but also based on stories he told about himself in his extensive memoirs and seminars. Most of all, and overwhelmingly, he was attributed with what Borchert terms *barami*. He was regarded as highly advanced on the Path, regularly described as a bodhisattva and attributed with insight (*vipassanā*) or wisdom (*paññā*), etc. Although he was supported by a gradually enlarging cohort of senior disciples who ran the organization and took over the duties of the founder's *amnat*, there were (and are) no indisputable markers of spiritual status and authority. As well as posing an organizational problem, this transition crisis exposed an awkward frailty in respect of members' sense of their own progress on the Path.[20] In the absence of clear measures of spiritual progress—"Is anyone getting anywhere on the Path?" "How do we know if person 'x' is a bodhisattva or arhat yet?" "Have I just got older while performing a 'Buddhist' identity?"—the issue of "responsibility" filled a very useful role, in fact fitted the empty gap that completed a magic circle of wish fulfillment.

Alan Coles's exegesis of the Huineng story offers a relevant observation. Commenting on the *Platform Sūtra* as a literary device to convince Chan followers that the succession has been legitimately passed from Hongren to Huineng, he writes (2015: 171):

> we need to remember that claims of inheritance, however private, are really public affairs. Thus, Huineng can only be Hongren's truth-son if the public takes him to be such, based on the "publication" of a plausible-looking narrative. In this sense, claims to sonship are just like claims to owning property—they only mean something when they are accepted by the public at large.

If the equation of organizational responsibility with spiritual status on the Path worked, then here there was a clear measure, that could be objectively and publicly verified, of the spiritual status and hence the spiritual *fitness* of the senior disciples to succeed the founder in leadership. Several of them had been "taking organizational responsibility" for a couple of decades by this time. The equation outlined in their magazine allowed them to cash in this service as "spiritual attainment" and thus secure the validity of their succession, and, as an additional perk, gain some sense of an objective measure of their own personal spiritual growth.

[19] Those who did not hold him in this regard were either marginalized or expelled.

[20] This is my own observation. Assessment of spiritual "progress," in Buddhism no less than other religions, is another topic that deserves exploration in its own right.

This kind of analysis also accounts for the deemed subversiveness of my original article. I did not critique, nor even mention, in my own piece the theory being outlined in the rest of the special issue—I had seen no other contribution and was the first author to submit—but I had raised significant questions about it by drawing on issues pertaining to hierarchy in the administrative and organizational arrangements of the historical Saṅgha and on narratives from the hagiography of well-regarded "saints" of the Buddhist tradition. I had cited key stories relating to high-status figures from the Buddhist lineage, all well known and highly revered within this particular organization—Śāntideva, Nāropa, Huineng—whose stories expressed a profound suspicion of this equation. In retrospect I now realize that I had, unwittingly, pitted the *barami* of these great historical figures against that of the senior disciples who were promulgating the equation, and ultimately against that of the founder who had devised and endorsed this strategy. Ironically, as I have already pointed out, the key article that was published in the special issue, acknowledged that "there is always a potential for a true hierarchy of responsibility to decay into a hierarchy of status and power" (Golden Drum 1995: 9). At face value this statement suggests that there should have been no problem with what I had written, although retrospectively I wonder if that sentence had been an afterthought added by its author after reading my unpublished contribution.

The managing editor wrote, on behalf of the editorial board, that the key problem was my statement that the separation of the various hierarchies I had identified was *intentional* and was a *safeguard* implemented by the Saṅgha, to ignore which could be *problematic* [their italics]. Putting those concerns aside, what interests me here is that the stories, the case studies that reflected the *barami* of these three great iconic figures, were ignored in their judgment. My conclusion is that they were simply too weighty and decisive to be questioned, and therefore were best dealt with by being ignored. The closest they came to being acknowledged was in the paragraph asserting the insight status of the problem equation (Private correspondence 1994: 3):

> Believing as I do that we are in the arena of spiritual insight, I also find it hard to imagine that there are not a good few stories and incidents that you couldn't have dug out to support an opposite case at least as plausibly.

I was struck by the assumption expressed here that I had presented a selective reading of Buddhist "history," and that, while my correspondent believed that counter-examples existed, he could not cite any even though asked to do so in my reply. Of course the key term is the word "believing," and indeed we are moving in the deep and dangerous waters of personal and collective belief. The bottom line is that the author(s) of the letter wanted to believe—the word used in the letter was "imagine"—that an opposite reading of Buddhist history on this topic was possible, and must be out there waiting to be "dug out." It was *necessary* for their beliefs that it was out there. Perhaps it was *so* necessary for them that they could not take the risk of checking whether or not it *was* there? I thus understood two things: that the claimed insight had been formulated without any reference to the organizational or narrative history of the Buddhist tradition; and that I had been recruited to provide historical backing for their strategy, on the assumption that *any* account of the matter would automatically support their claim.

The implication of the editorial committee's attitude to history seemed to be that history is at the service of belief, and maybe postmodern historiographers would agree. In a way I do myself, as indicated by my free use of the term "hagiography." The stories about Śāntideva, Nāropa, and Huineng are undoubtedly hagiography, by which I understand "any biography that idealizes or idolizes its subject" to quote a dictionary definition. But I also see a significance to such idealized stories, in that they are the expressions of un- or partially conscious ideals, truths, or aspirations held by the compiling and transmitting communities. Such stories are not transmitted if they are *not* meaningful. Buddhist (as indeed Indic) tradition has been criticized by Western historians as weak on recording the past as historical data. By contrast stories are enthusiastically transmitted and elaborated, but they are stories that have a trajectory and a meaning. The three I discussed in that original article share a concern with the conflation of spiritual and organizational hierarchy, and this theme was transmitted over many centuries and in a variety of contexts and cultures because it was meaningful.

It turns out then that this aspect of the hagiography of Śāntideva does not have just devotional or quasi-historical interest, but can perform a role in a very contemporary debate in a modern Buddhist community. The debate concerned issues of authority and succession and was expressed in terms of hierarchy. Śāntideva's story, as also those of Nāropa and Huineng, spoke to the very concerns of a group of late-twentieth-century Western Buddhists, and highlighted the very problem with which they sought to overcome and another problem which they courted. While doctrinal expositions were a part of the stuff of training and study in that contemporary group, it was ecclesiastical regulations and hagiographical narrative that made the most powerful and relevant statements addressing their views on hierarchy. It is no coincidence that such a powerful figure as Śāntideva, endowed with such great *barami*, should be used to transmit the truth about "the conflation of spiritual and institutional hierarchy."

References

Ashin, J. and K. Crosby (2017), "Heresy and Monastic Malpractice in the Buddhist Court Cases (Vinicchaya) of Modern Burma (Myanmar)," *Contemporary Buddhism* 18: 199–261.

Bareau, A. (2013), *The Buddhist Schools of the Small Vehicle*. Translated from the French by Sara Boin-Webb, Honolulu: University of Hawai'i Press.

Borchert, T. (2023), "Barami and Bureaucracy: Mechanisms of Monastic Power in Contemporary Thailand," *Glorisun Lecture Series*, University of Oxford, 1 May 2023 (unpublished).

Cole, A. (2015), "Conspiracy's Truth: The Zen of Narrative Cunning in the Platform Sutra," *Asia Major* 28 (1): 145–75.

Findly, E. B. (1992), "Ananda's Hindrance: Faith (*saddhā*) in Early Buddhism," *Journal of Indian Philosophy* 20: 253–73.

Golden Drum – Buddhism and Hierarchy (1995) February–April, Windhorse Publications.

Guenther, H. v. (1963), *The Life and Teaching of Nāropa*, Oxford: Oxford University Press.

Horner, I. B. (1951), *The Book of Discipline Vol. IV*. London: Luzac.
Horner, I. B. (1963), *The Book of Discipline Vol. V (Cullavagga)*. London: Luzac.
McRae, J. R. (2000), *The Platform Sutra of The Sixth Patriarch*, Berkeley: Numata Center for Buddhist Translation and Research.
Nagashima, T. S. (1978), *Truth and Fabrications in Religion: An Investigation from the Documents of the Zen (Ch'an) Sect*, London: A. Probsthain.
Na-rangsi, S. (2002), "Administration of the Thai Saṅgha: Past, Present and Future," *Chulalongkorn Journal of Buddhist Studies* 1 (2): 1–28.
Private correspondence (23 December 1994) from the managing editor of *Golden Drum* to the present author.
Santayana, G. (1906), *The Life of Reason Vol. 1: Reason in Common Sense*, London: Constable.
Schmidt-Leukel, P. (2019), *Buddha Mind – Christ Mind, A Christian Commentary on the Bodhicarāvatāra*. With a new translation by E. Steinkellner and C. Peck-Kubaczek, Leuven: Peeters.
Ṭhānissaro, B. (2013), *Buddhist Monastic Code: The Pāṭimokkha Rules. Translated & Explained* (3rd edition). Available online: https://www.accesstoinsight.org/lib/authors/thanissaro/bmc1.pdf.

III

Interreligious Dynamics

9

Śāntideva's Twofold *bodhicitta* in Light of Comparative Spirituality

Francis Brassard

1. Status quaestionis

It is said in verse 15 of the first chapter of Śāntideva's *Bodhicaryāvatāra* (BCA) that the spirit of awakening (*bodhicitta*) is to be known as twofold: as a mental resolution to strive for awakening and the actual striving for awakening (Schmidt-Leukel 2019: 127). Although this distinction has simply been explained by highlighting the difference between someone who decides to leave for a destination and someone who is actually traveling to that destination, that pillar of the path of the bodhisattva is not without ambiguities as to what this path exactly consists of. For example, based on the descriptions of the spiritual experiences provided by various religious traditions, one may ask whether we are dealing with two different states of mind with their specific modes of operation. Assuming a plurality of such states, one may more specifically examine the functions we normally attribute to the activity of the mind like that of sensation, desire, cognition, or awareness. Thus, if one wishes to better understand Śāntideva's twofold *bodhicitta*, one needs to figure out the nature and role of one's motivation and activity, be it physical or mental.

I have dealt with those questions in my doctoral dissertation, which has been published under the title, *The Concept of Bodhicitta in Śāntideva's* Bodhicaryāvatāra (Brassard 2000). The answers I suggested all assumed that the arising of *bodhicitta* (*bodhicitta-utpāda*) refers to the emergence of a specific state of mind in which one's view of the world and one's actions are fused as one reality so that, within that newly generated state of mind, the mental strength or the constant renewal of one's commitment that is usually required to perform an activity or to accomplish specific goals, especially spiritual goals, is no longer necessary. One major implication of this affirmation is to say that, because the desire for awakening is intrinsic to that state of mind, the desiring subject, as initiators of actions, is also no longer necessary. In fact, I argued that clinging to such a dynamic of action dominated by a sense of being responsible for one's own fate is likely to inhibit the operations of the acquired state of mind. Indeed, since I presupposed that the arising of *bodhicitta* must be characterized by a dissolution of the distinction between a subject and an object, an act of the will can only reinforce that distinction, thus making it more difficult for the experience of *bodhicitta* to occur. It is a paradoxical situation. It could be argued here that the desire for a desireless state of mind is comparable to a stick that is consuming itself by kindling a fire. To some extent, this explanation does resolve the paradox, but at the expense of reducing *bodhicitta* to a mere instrument—that is, a concept devoid of any ontological and ethical connotations. Although the instrumental aspect of *bodhicitta* is important, I argued that it is also comprised of a metaphysical as well as a moral aspect. Wangchuk (2007), in Chapter 7 of his comprehensive study of the history of the concept of *bodhicitta*, seems to confirm that point. However, irrespective of this discussion on the paradoxical nature of one's desire for a desireless state of mind, the problem with my suggestion regarding the redefinition of the nature of one's motivation, as Schmidt-Leukel (2019: 129) pointed out, is that it "finds almost no support in the BCA, where Śāntideva appeals repeatedly to acts of will and commitment."

While developing my idea about the meaning of *bodhicitta*, I was aware of the fact that the BCA abundantly featured an individual, an "I" that is actively engaged with himself—that is, a "me" as well as with projections of others, whether they are Buddhas, Bodhisattvas or simple mortals. I assumed that all this mental activity centered around a thinking subject would fall within the purview of the first type of the twofold *bodhicitta*, the one responsible for strengthening one's mental resolution to strive for awakening. Recognizing the importance of this stage in any spiritual endeavor, as well as any secular enterprise, I believed that *bodhicitta* could not rely exclusively on the strength of one's will power, as D. T. Suzuki seems to contend (Brassard 2000: 18–22). If it were the case, there would then be no need to mention the second type of *bodhicitta*. Instead, I was inclined to follow the lead suggested by Sangharakshita in his discussion on the act of Going for Refuge (Brassard 2000: 22–5). According to the founder of the Friends of the Western Buddhist Order, this fundamental decision, that transforms any individual into a Buddhist aspirant, can be done at five different levels of commitment. The first three levels—the Cultural, the Provisional, and the Effective—rest on a type of commitment similar to that of the first type of *bodhicitta*. At the fourth level, the Real Going for Refuge, also referred to as the Cosmic Going for Refuge, an aspirant undergoes a spiritual transformation that brings him on a transcendental path in which he is carried off by some kind of cosmic force that transcends the powers of one's individual will. That crucial event would be the arising of *bodhicitta*, "the entry into the path of the aspirant to awakening" (*bodhicaryāvatāra*) according to the Mahāyāna tradition, an event that has been described in various ways in other Buddhist traditions—for example, the Stream Entry of the Opening of the Dhamma-Eye in Theravāda, the attainment of the eighth *bhūmi* called *Acalā*, also in Mahāyāna, or the entering of the Path of Vision in Tibetan Buddhism. We can also add the experience of rebirth into the Pure Land where one is, so to speak, carried by the Buddha Amida toward the final destination which would be, still according to Sangharakshita, the Absolute or Ultimate Going for Refuge.

There is another idea that influenced my suggestion favoring two types of motivation or force of the will, one emanating from an individual and the other intrinsic to a transcendent reality in which the subject has to let go of his tendency to control his own destiny. It is the idea of non-action (*wuwei*) as described in Daoism. It refers to a state of mind where actions are naturally flowing in instantaneously and, most importantly, in a non-premeditated manner. This mode of action seems to have been known by Śāntideva when he described *bodhicitta* as a source of merits and benefits that "quite easily causes the vast flood of beings to leap out [of the ocean of suffering]" (BCA 1:7; Schmidt-Leukel 2019: 116). We are also told that "even if one has committed terrible sins, in its protection one escapes instantly, just as one escapes great dangers when protected by a hero" (BCA 1:13; Schmidt-Leukel 2019: 117) and "it burns up major sins instantly and completely, like the fire at the end of the eons" (BCA 1:14; Schmidt-Leukel 2019: 117). The impression we get from those passages is that another force seems to be at work or comes to assist our initial commitment as an earlier passage seems to imply: "First of all this reinforces in me the strength of mental clarity that brings forth what is wholesome [for final release]" (BCA 1:3; Schmidt-Leukel 2019: 111).

As alluded to above, this mode of action is possible on account of having one's actions emanating from a view of reality that has been fully integrated by a subject. It is as if a person is possessed by an all-encompassing view of the phenomenal world. Not only this view redefined that world, but it also serves as a trigger mechanism for one's actions in it. A famous Buddhist theme of one's meditation to develop empathy toward the others best illustrates that relation between a view and actions. It is based on the idea that every individual in the world—past, present, future—has been at least once one's mother. The meditation does not merely consist in providing a justification to act in a compassionate manner toward all beings—that would be an example of the first type of *bodhicitta*—but rather to bring about a transformation of one's mind so that we naturally and instantaneously relate to other people as a son would do toward his mother. Thus, I assumed that, because this mode of action is known within other Buddhist traditions, it could apply to our understanding of the second type of *bodhicitta*.

I will sum up my suggestion regarding the meaning of the twofold *bodhicitta* by using the analogy of rafting. First, the mental resolution to strive for awakening corresponds to the commitment to bring the raft to the bank of a river. Because that raft is pushed on dry land, there is a direct correspondence between the efforts put in and the distance traveled by the raft. Secondly, the actual striving for awakening consists in having the raft carried by the current of the water, a force that is independent of the subject who pushed the raft in the river. This analogy, however, assumes that there is a qualitative rift between the first and second types of *bodhicitta*. Considering Schmidt-Leukel's previous observation, I wonder if that drastic change has somehow not been inflated or rather, that the distinction I suggested between the two types of *bodhicitta* is true insofar as it only takes into account the extremities of a spectrum of experience regarding the contribution of a desiring subject in the process of his spiritual transformation. To use the raft analogy again, anyone familiar with rafting would know that going down the rapids of a river has its share of dangers. Obstacles are to be constantly avoided. One should be very attentive to the situations at hand. Skills have to be acquired to stay on course, to avoid capsizing, etc. In the case of the BCA, those obstacles are the three defilements (*kleśa*) of greed, hate, and delusion (Schmidt-Leukel 2019: 55).

There is another reason why I am questioning my original suggestion regarding *bodhicitta*. Since the publication of my study of this concept, I have moved away from a dualistic model distinguishing exclusively two modes of being and acting. I believe that there is a third alternative to understand the relation between one's vision of reality and activity, an alternative that would explain the dynamic of the second type of *bodhicitta* without having to exclude a thinking and acting subject.

2. Modes of resolution

In a recently published book (Brassard 2021), I developed a model to understand the structure of the major religious discourses with the hope of establishing a basis for the comparative study of religions. This model assumes that, despite the wide variety of religious, spiritual as well as philosophical traditions, it is possible to classify their respective discourses within four categories. Each of these categories is defined by a founding event that presents itself as a solution to a given problematic situation, whether individual or social. This founding event brings its own set of presuppositions about the nature of the individual, the world, and the relations between these two realities, presuppositions that are explicitly or tacitly articulated in beliefs and rituals. In other words, each of these categories of discourses deals with a specific type of individual or social problematic situation for which there is one general approach at solving it. I called such an approach *mode of resolution*. I have identified four distinct modes that articulate the connection between knowledge and actions.

2.1 Ritual mode

The first mode is the *ritual mode of resolution* and its founding event is the discovery or the creation of an object which is endowed with the power to solve a specific problem. That object could simply be a stone to crack open a coconut or a mathematical formula that allows us to harness the energy contained within matter. In a pre-scientific culture, where the forces of nature are often connected to supernatural realities, magic and divination are the most common practices that identify and create the objects of the present mode of resolution. Once the proper course of actions has been established, one simply need to repeat it to solve a given problem. It is on account of such repetition that the first mode is called the *ritual mode of resolution*. Good examples of a tradition issued from this first mode are Brahmanism in India, Shintoism in Japan, and most indigenous shamanistic religions.

For the purpose of the present discussion on *bodhicitta*, I will only mention the most important implications of the ritual mode of resolution. The first implication is the belief that the world of objects is real and that it exists apart from a knowing and acting subject, who is also believed to be real. Doubting the existence of the world would inhibit the ability of that subject to act efficiently as its objects are the supports of his actions. Secondly, as alluded to above, because efficient actions will be ritualized, they are likely to be fully integrated into the psychological structure of the acting subject. That fusion between an object and an action also implies a fusion between the source of the problem to be solved and the object itself. Put differently, an object is the concrete manifestation of a subjective desire or need. We can now see how the attempt at eradicating a desire and its emanating actions or habits will be made possible by destroying, deconstructing, or simply negating the reality of its corresponding object. This brings me to the second mode of resolution.

2.2 Mystical mode

As long as the problems facing an individual or a community are fragmented, one would expect a plurality of solutions with their corresponding objects and ritualized actions. Within the confinement of a view dominated by the ritual mode of resolution, we navigate through our existence with the hopes that the gods will be favorable by responding to our entreaties. If not, the only avenue left is a sense of fatalism that could only be countered, at this point, by the virtue of stoicism. Or we can reject the world as a whole with the hope that there is a way to escape it. Escaping the world—more particularly, one's social environment—seems to have been understood, at first, exclusively in a literal way. The creation of semi-autonomous communities of mendicants and the culture of ascetics roaming by themselves that developed parallel to the urbanization of society are indications to that effect. However, when it was realized that living outside the social environment does not necessarily mean to live physically apart from it, that the entire experience of being free from it rests above all on a distinct state of mind, a state that is devoid of attachment toward that environment, one started to look for that state of mind. Giving the new nature of the problem—all our existential problems are now reduced to one fundamental predicament—the founding event of this second mode of resolution is the appearance of an individual embodying that state of mind. Because that new state of mind always presents itself as a kind of mystery for those individuals still stuck in the world of objects/desires, I call this second mode the *mystical mode of resolution*.

That new state of mind, which implies an entirely new way of relating to the phenomenological world, is more than an existential experience of detachment or aloofness. It also comes with an ontological revelation that encompasses in one single vision the entirety of whatever can be perceived with the senses. This revelation could be compared to the discovery of the center of gravity of a material structure. It is also interesting to point out that such a center of gravity is also a mystery from the point of view of the material structure as it requires no material support for an observer to be aware of its existence. We simply feel its presence by manipulating material objects. It is also by being aware of it that we can instrumentalize those objects in an optimal way. More interesting is to understand how it is possible to say that those objects do not really exist. Similar to the fact that all the mass of an object is condensed at its center of gravity, seizing the entire phenomenological world by a vision revealing its foundation makes it "invisible." The cognitive process at work here is, however, not mysterious. To give a simple example of this process, we could say that the moment one seizes the meaning of a word, one automatically loses sight of the individual letters that form that word.

The mystical mode of resolution not only redefines the status of the phenomenological world, but also that of the individual as well as the nature of the relation between the subject and the objects of the world, including the other subjects. Still using the analogy of the center of gravity, we could imagine how an individual occupies that center by being fused with an all-encompassing view of reality. This privileged position now gives him full autonomy to act in a manner that appears unpredictable, spontaneous, or mysterious from the point of view of those who are still entangled in the realities generated by their respective non-centered position. But, that acquired autonomy does not mean that an awakened subject can do whatever he wants. Since we are dealing with states of mind, the actions that emanate from them, although not directly determined by external factors, do follow a certain logic. Thus, similar to a cat having a cat-like behavior, individuals identifying themselves with the mystery behave in an expected manner as a whole—still mysterious as for their individual actions—so that they could be, to some extent, recognized as witnesses of that mystery. That is why it is said that "a Buddha is perfect in both wisdom *and compassion*" (Schmidt-Leukel 2019: 92).

Going back to my original discussion on the meaning of the twofold *bodhicitta*, the mystical mode of resolution would correspond to the actual striving for awakening—that is, the state of mind making that striving possible whereas the mental resolution to strive would be a characteristic of the ritual mode of resolution. If all religious and spiritual discourses were only to be articulated by these two modes of resolution, we would again find ourselves in an either/or situation. To refuse that alternative between two states of mind, we have to find an intermediary state or a space in which a subject can operate as an individual—that is, with partial knowledge and a will to act, while being somehow under the influence of a reality that is encompassing or possessing him. One might find that intermediary space by exploring what both the ritual and the mystical modes, in their own way, have left out—namely, the other subjects. Indeed, following only the logic of the ritual mode of resolution, the others can only be seen as objects while, in the mystical mode, the others disappear with the disappearance of one's own awareness of being a distinct subject. However, no matter how the others are perceived or made invisible, they are always there. How to deal with the others within the context of a path of transformation is what the next mode of resolution is going to resolve.

2.3 Relational mode

A religion whose main purpose is to regulate the relations among autonomous and, to some extent, unpredictable subjects will fall, according to my model, under the category of the *relational mode of resolution*. We know that any group of individuals, to manage possible conflicts, will create laws and rules. However, what makes those laws an integral part of a religious system is that they find their source in a transcendent reality. In addition to how the mystics may describe that transcendent reality, the religious discourses of the relational mode of resolution always attribute a Will to it. The first communities regulated by religious laws seemed to have relied on the presence of a witness of the mystery, a sage or a mystic who has taken the responsibility to organize the society he has distanced himself from or, as social structures evolved, above which he now positioned himself. The Pharaohs of Egypt and the ancient emperors of Japan are good examples of the later stages of development of a society ruled by intermediaries having, so to speak, one foot in the transcendent world and the other in the world of the common people. However, history has shown that such a social structure is very unstable.

The first cause of this instability is related to the problem of succession. Wisdom or the experience of the transcendent, the source of the laws, is not hereditary despite the efforts to make the common people believe so. Degradation in the quality of rulership is deemed to occur with time. This first reason is about the physical medium of the Will of the transcendent reality. A second reason, which is probably more important, deals with the very nature of the laws itself. The laws that are transmitted by a witness of the mystery are, from a certain point of view, dead laws. Their only purpose is to regulate the behavior of people. The only responses expected of those people is to obey or face the consequences of disobedience. Within such a system of laws, an individual has no autonomy and no space to grow or mature. Such an individual is constantly in a state of infantilization.

Again, history tells us that the stability of a community has been greatly improved when the medium of transmission of the Will of the transcendent reality has passed from an "inspired" leader to a sacred book revealing that Will. This is the founding event of the relational mode of resolution. Whether written in stone or on carefully preserved documents, the revealed laws are in a better position to withstand the passage of time. But this is the least of the benefits in this change of medium of transmission. More important is the fact that the book, being now the source of the laws in this world, is at the center of the community. Although still shrouded in mystery, it has nevertheless become the center of gravity, a center that connects the transcendent reality with all the autonomous centers of gravity—that is, the individuals of that community. This change also implies that the community itself has become autonomous. It no longer needs a dictator. One may ask, at this point, since the laws are fixed in a book, how can a society adapt to a changing environment? A benevolent sage rule would be more flexible to provide new laws. Not necessarily. This is why we have to look at the transformation of the nature of the laws.

The laws that have been revealed are no longer reduced to simple prohibitions of certain actions, but rather are framed in such a way that they are better viewed as boundaries or guidelines of one's behavior. For example, to dress in a modest way does not specify what one should wear, or to honor one's parents does not specifically tell us what I should or shouldn't do. However, the interpretation of what is expected of us by following those guidelines will evolve with time. In short, we have here the principle of jurisprudence at work by which a community is able to adapt regardless of the fact that those guidelines are fixed. In fact, one could argue that the dynamic of jurisprudence works best when its foundations are fixed. It is also on the basis of this dynamic that an individual finds the space to grow and transform himself.

That transformation can occur along two distinct, but interrelated, planes of reality. The first plane is connecting the individual with the transcendent reality which, in the present context, is conceived as a person on account of the fact that it has a Will. I will show later that this view does not directly contradict the conception of an impersonal reality that is mainly found in the discourses of the mystical mode of resolution. Thus, by exploring and enacting new ways to submit to the Will of the transcendent reality, an individual can develop his creativity and truly enjoy his sense of autonomy. Moreover, any action, performed within the boundaries of the law, is a witness of the mystery for the individual as well as the community. We can also say, through such actions, which are in the present context acts of submission, that there is an instantaneous transfer of merits from the mystery to the phenomenological world. In other words, contrary to what is expected with the mystical mode of resolution, the source of merits is no longer a person, but rather an action—more specifically, an act of submission.

The second plane is connecting a person with another person. As every person is defined by or even reduced to specific roles within a society—for example, being a father or a son, a husband or a wife—the space in which one can develop one's creativity and fully exert one's autonomy is now the unlimited ways of being a better father, etc. The newly found ways also exert an influence on the development of the person and his community. Similar to the situation where doctors strive to become better doctors and, by the same token, raise the standards of their profession, the quality of life within a community increases by having more and more people living up to the role they have been assigned temporarily or permanently within the framework of the revealed laws. What are then the implications of this third mode of resolution for our understanding of the twofold *bodhicitta*?

The first, and probably the most significant, is the fact that creativity is the engine that drives one's transformation. In the context of the mystical mode of resolution, the experience of synthesizing a transformative vision of reality is presented as a one-time event. For example, the experience of *satori* in Rinzai school of Zen Buddhism which is the outcome of an arduous mental struggle with a *kōan*. Other traditions mention the idea of stages like the three stages of awakening leading to Arahant (the awakened person) in Theravāda or the ten *bhūmi* a bodhisattva has to go through on the Mahāyāna path toward awakening. In the relational mode of resolution, the experience of creativity is spread over a larger spectrum of actions—simple actions like blessing a meal, expressing gratitude, remembering God, extending help to someone in need, or just welcoming a guest. These simple actions may be done automatically, but that would be missing out on their potential to transform us. What is needed is an inquiring mind ready to find new and more significant ways to perform those actions. And finding more significant and engaging ways to act requires an assessment of the conditions responsible of our previous ways. In short, a subject is constantly in a problem-solving mode of experience. This is a point I will explore later. For the moment, I would like to consider what exactly is being created within the context of this third mode of resolution.

As the name of this mode of resolution indicates, what is being created are relations or, more precisely, ways to relate a person with other persons. Although we speak of ways of relating two entities, it is important to remember that only the relation is real and manifested. The entities are just the limit of the relations and as such, like the limits of a line, have no dimensions. We assume their existence on the basis of our experiences of the relations, although they are not directly perceived. Using again the analogy of the center of gravity as a reality not dependent on a material support for its existence, the two persons of a relation are mysteries to each other. Thus, because they are, so to speak, objectless objects, there is no contradiction with the claim, found in most discourses of the mystical mode of resolution, that objects and, to some extent, persons, are illusions. By the same token, the negation or relativization of the event of creation is true insofar as it applies to the static world of objects and objectified persons from which we seek to liberate ourselves. In the discourses articulated by the presuppositions of the relation mode of resolution, creation is real, not only because it is a way to describe a dynamic world, but also because it is at the heart of one's transformative experience. It is also the means to experience God, a God who is not only *innominabile* and *omninominabile* (Meister Eckhart), but who has also made Himself known through His own creative activity. The structure of this activity is going to be revealed by the next and last mode of resolution.

2.4 Mode of the cross

From a certain point of view, the mode of the cross is not a separate mode of resolution distinct from the previous three modes. Because the discovery or the fabrication of a new object, the realization of a new state of mind, or the enactment of a new relation are all experiences of creation, I would argue that the discourse that makes explicit the process of those events of creation possesses a universal character without—this is important—negating the particularities of the discourses it explains. Notwithstanding its universal character, the fourth mode of resolution comprises one distinctive discourse because of the specificity of its funding event—namely, the crucifixion and resurrection of Jesus of Nazareth as an historical fact that gave rise to Christianity. Let's first look at the universal dimension of this discourse.

The emergence of a new structure, which consists in creating new relations and integrating them into existing ones, is made possible if the ancient structure goes through a moment of crisis. That moment has been described by Henri Laborit (1974), a French surgeon, biologist, and philosopher, as an experience of inhibition of action. It is a moment in which a person is incapable of any action on account of not possessing the necessary information. A typical depiction of this moment in religious literature is certainly the case of Arjuna who, at the beginning of the Bhagavadgītā, standing between the two armies, is having an existential crisis, so strong that he is experiencing such acute physical symptoms as loss of strength, having his mouth drying up, and his skin burning all over. Another example of this moment of crisis, which this time plays itself out at the social level, is when the Israelites, led by Moses, stood between the Red Sea and the advancing Egyptian army. In both cases, these moments of inhibition of actions, or, from the point of view of the Christian discourse, these experiences of the cross, were preludes to a transformative experience. In the case of Arjuna, it precedes the revelation of the Bhagavadgītā and the manifestation of Kṛṣṇa's divine nature. For Moses and the Israelites, it was the experience of liberation through YHWH's power. Even scientific discoveries seem to have always been the results of an experience of inhibition of action, if we trust the account given by Henri Poincaré in his essay *Science et méthode*, as reported by Polanyi (1975: 60). There it is said that the first stage of discovery consists in racking one's brains by successive sallies of the imagination, while the second, which may be delayed for hours after one has ceased one's efforts, is the spontaneous appearance of the idea one has struggled for. In this regard, D. T. Suzuki (1970: 72), who introduced Zen to the West, summarized the entire process of spiritual transformation by the following law: *accumulation*, *saturation*, and *explosion*. The moment of saturation would correspond to the situation of inhibition of action or the experience of the cross, while the explosion—that is, the spontaneous creation of a new idea made possible by a personal transformation—could certainly be viewed as a kind of resurrection.

If the experience of the cross, when understood as a moment of inhibition of action, is a universal component of human existence and the event of resurrection is viewed as symbolic of all human transformations, what remains specific to the Christian discourse is the idea that salvation is by grace through faith in Jesus Christ. Indeed, as taught in Eph. 2:8–9, "For it is by grace you have been saved, through faith—and this not from yourselves, it is the gift of God—not by works, so that no one can boast." Despite this view of salvation, which would put the Christian approach at odds with most of the spiritual paths articulated along the presuppositions of the mystical mode of resolution—that is, those approaches that rely on one's ability to achieve liberation or awakening through one's own efforts—I believe it is nevertheless possible to identify in this affirmation a universal component that can help us understand the twofold *bodhicitta*. For that, we need to explore some of the anthropological implications of the notions of salvation, grace, and faith.

If we were to rely on my original suggestion to explain the twofold *bodhicitta*, we would have to assume that a powerful commitment and perseverance are necessary to bridge the gap between the decision to embark on the bodhisattva path and the actual striving, which would be, in the present context, equivalent to fulfilling its purpose. It is a deferred reward that may take a very long time, even a lot of rebirths as it is assumed in many spiritual traditions of the mystical mode of resolution. Similar to the attainment of excellence in sports or the acquisition of a highly specialized skill, it seems that only very few people are capable of bridging the gap between "Crossing the Red Sea" and "Entering the Promised Land." Or maybe this gap is, in normal conditions, impossible to overcome and those exceptional people who did it by their respective endeavor did so because they knew something which ordinary people did not know. Like Christopher Columbus who knew that it was possible to cross the Atlantic faster than expected on account of the sea currents, those achievers of excellence know about something that would sustain their commitment and multiply the impact of their efforts.

What they seem to know is that, at some point, in their endeavor, a new type of experience called *flow* is being generated, an experience that nourishes their efforts and makes the constant renewal of their commitment or resolution unnecessary. That experience has been identified and scientifically studied by the psychologist Mihaly Csikszentmihalyi. I would thus argue that the second type of *bodhicitta*, the actual striving to awakening, is precisely that experience of flow, and that it could also be described as a state of grace. It is that experience or state that allows one to achieve difficult goals. The scope of the present article does not allow me to provide a detailed description of the research dealing with the experience of flow. I would nevertheless highlight its main characteristic and show how it may help us understand the experience of *bodhicitta*. I will also analyze the conditions of its arising as an attempt to elucidate the notion of faith as well as its anthropological implications—that is, what it means, as human beings living in this world, to be saved.

3. The experience of flow

The most relevant characteristic of the experience of flow is probably the fact that it is autotelic, a concept composed of the Greek words *autos* (self) and *telos* (goal). An autotelic experience or activity is one that is performed for its own sake. When we say that a spiritual path is a means to an end, and the end itself, as mentioned (Brassard 2000: 70) with regards to *bodhicitta*, we simply mean that it is autotelic. What Csikszentmihalyi (1997: 116–30) has shown is that this experience is not limited to spiritual experiences, but to an entire range of activity. In fact, although people engaged in highly creative activity are more likely to experience flow, when asked about the conditions in which usual tasks or activities have been performed, many more people reported an autotelic experience. Three of those conditions are worth noting. The first one is the experience of well-being or feel-good. As such, it is always a positive experience. The second condition is the fact that people said that they were highly focused on the task at hand. Their state of absorption made them even oblivious of their physical needs—that is, less concerned about themselves. A third condition of their experience of flow was their ability to process new information on the spot to a point where some had the impression that time had slowed down. Such slowing down of time usually occurs, without being fully aware of it, when we are paying attention to something we are quite familiar with, like a lecture in our area of expertise, a conversation in our mother tongue, etc. We are thus able to be aware of and to process more information, something we completely missed when we are not familiar with a given environment. I believe that this third condition is related to what is happening to our mental structure, something that concerns what we mean by salvation. Before exploring that point, I would like to look at the dynamic of the experience of flow to elucidate the notion of faith and its universal purpose.

What seems to be unique to the experience of flow, in contrast to other types of experiences, like the feeling of awe one may get from seeing a beautiful landscape or even the ones induced by drugs, is the fact that the mind is engaged in a problem-solving activity. Not just one major problem to be solved—here the experience of inhibition of action could be painful—but a continuous series of problems with a minimum level of difficulty to mobilize one's attention. In fact, without that minimum level, one gets bored. Thus, the experience of flow appears to be sustained only within a certain margin of difficulty. This is why I believe that a spirituality articulated along the presuppositions of the relational mode of resolution—that is, one that focuses on improving one's relations with others—is a very good candidate for sustaining such an experience of flow. I would also argue that the popularity and the universality of the BCA lie in the fact that it depicts a mind fully engaged in perfecting such relations. Given the current nature of the world, one can be sure that any altruism-based project would rank quite high as an activity to sustain an experience of flow. Consequently, the desire to help others is likely to trigger such an experience. It is so, because the main function of a desire to change an existing state of affairs is to intentionally put us in a situation of inhibition of action by forcing upon us an influx of new and yet to be processed information. There is another way of purposely exposing us to an influx of information: an act of faith.

Many Western apologists of Buddhism argued that, in contrast to the notion of blind faith of the Abrahamic traditions, the ideas constitutive of the spiritual path advocated by the Buddha are to be accepted critically. More precisely, the teachings of Buddhism should be tried out for ourselves, their validity confirmed by our own experience as opposed to accepting them as valid just because a religious authority has decreed them to be true. In a way, those apologists resituated the mystical discourses of Buddhism within the purview of the ritual mode of resolution, a mode that is, incidentally, that of modern science. It goes without saying that this pragmatic interpretation of Buddhism was well received by the scientifically minded generations of the West. But from the point of view of the experience of flow and the factors that are triggering it, this diluted form of faith appears to be inefficient.

An act of blind faith, or the experience of "being sure of what we hope for and certain of what we do not see" (Heb. 11:1), surely induces a situation of inhibition of action that triggers the creative process. For example, in a society where people are obsessed by their self-image, to be told that there is no self has a greater impact for the creative process when we accept it at face value than when we rationalize its meaning. In fact, looking more closely at the nature of the act of faith, one can see that its rational component is not directly related to its content, but rather to its effect on us. The situation of inhibition of action or the experience of shock—the cross—is a strong sign of the validity of a new idea. But precisely because such an idea is, on first contact, disturbing and unappealing, its acceptance has to be an act of free will. This also means that an act of faith is always a response to an event loaded with a surplus of information.

It is therefore the free acceptance of the validity of an event, even if not understood or rather, because it is not understood, that triggers an experience of flow. Such an event could be an idea, but also the experience of being in contact with an extraordinary person. That would explain why many people upon meeting Gautama Buddha would decide to take refuge in him, his teachings, and his newly formed community. When a living witness of the mystery is no longer present, it is quite natural to portray him through statues, images, icons, etc. It is an attempt at maintaining the conditions that triggers an experience of flow. In this regard, I agree with Wangchuk (2007: 22) when he says that "the psychological need of the Buddhists to make up in one way or another for the demise of the historical Buddha may have been one of the principal internal factors that contributed to the formation of the idea of the resolve to become a *buddha*." I would just add that the psychological need is existentially quite significant as it refers to the experience of flow. From a comparative perspective, it would also mean that, in the case of the twofold *bodhicitta*, the mental resolution to strive is the equivalent of an act of faith.

Although a comparative and scientific evaluation of religious events is doing its best to avoid qualitative judgments, it is nevertheless important to appreciate differences when they are justified. For example, we may consider Moses, Muhammad, and Gautama Buddha as equally extraordinary people, but we have to concede that the point of impact has shifted, in the case of the founders of Judaism and Islam, away from the persons to rest on the revelation of a book. It is precisely on account of this shift that the traditions and discourses that emerged from those extraordinary persons are quite different. Similarly, with Christianity, we see that the point of impact has further shifted away from the revelation of a scripture—the only miracle according to Islam—to the event of the resurrection of Jesus. That event, which appears to have revealed the transformational potential of the experience of flow, has exerted a major impact in the consciousness of humanity. One can thus understand why most Christians insist that salvation be through faith in the resurrected Jesus. It is not to value one means of salvation over another, but rather to choose what type of salvation one aspires to.

I suspect that the study of comparative spirituality and, to some extent, interreligious dialogue have been dominated by the presuppositions of the mystical mode of resolution in which it is quite plausible to affirm that several means lead to the same goal. Religious and spiritual discourses would have, according to the expression of Raimon Panikkar, a "homeomorphic equivalence" in the sense that their symbols play an equivalent role within their respective system, but only to express this mystery which is not exhausted by any name while being capable of receiving it all (Panikkar 1978: xxi–xxiii; see also Bergeron 2004: 215–16). The discourses of this mode of resolution have a strong tendency to overvalue the importance of the *innominabile* and *omninominabile* over the world which, in many cases, is viewed as something negative or illusory. Because of this tendency, there is often an ambiguity as to the nature of the actions of the witness of the mystery. Since the entire process of transformation plays itself out within the mind, we may ask whether the cultivation of altruism ultimately translates itself into concrete acts of charity. Put differently, we can say that the very nature of the mystical experience and the means to achieve it both make it tempting to completely withdraw from the world and to refuse any engagement with it.

The religions whose discourses are mainly articulated according to the presuppositions of the relational mode of resolution—that is, religions that define the world in terms of relations and whose spirituality is based on the possibility of improving those relations—have no choice but to be fully engaged with the world. Moreover, an analysis of the experience of flow (Kotler 2014) reveals that it contributes to an increase of intimacy with the environment in which it occurs. If the mystical mode of resolution seems to favor a retraction or even an annihilation of the self, the relational mode proposes an approach that results in the expansion of the boundary of the self as well as the reach of our senses. Using again the analogy of the center of gravity, I would say that the self becomes more centered and autonomous the more it reaches out to the world and becomes intimate with it. It is this increase in intimacy that would account for the dilation of time. As the process of transformation consists in creating more relations or, from another point of view, to consume more and more experiences of meaning, the resulting mental structure is able to process more information in a given frame of time. The passage of time is thus relative to the complexity, as defined in terms of integrated information or relations, of the mental structure of an active observer.

I believe that more research is needed to better understand the parallels between religious discourses, on the one hand, and the creative process and its conditions, on the other. More importantly, it would be necessary to translate in a common language the symbolic descriptions of spiritual experiences as found in various religious and spiritual traditions. The formulation of the model of the mode of resolution and, more specifically, the notion of flow is such an attempt which has been suggested in the present chapter to make sense of the twofold *bodhicitta*. At this point, one may ask for whom this enterprise is interesting. Should the scientific explanation always have the last word? What if the arising of *bodhicitta* or the resurrection of Jesus, taken at face value, would force a complete reinterpretation of the nature or structure of man as well as a complete reassessment of his potentialities?

References

Bergeron, R. (2004), *Hors de l'Église plein de salut : Pour une théologie dialogale et une spiritualité interreligieuse*, Montréal, Paris: Médiaspaul.

Brassard, F. (2000), *The Concept of Bodhicitta in Śāntideva's Bodhicaryāvatāra*, Albany, NY: State University of New York Press.

Brassard, F. (2021), *Meeting the Others in their Differences: Toward a Christian Approach to the Scientific Study of Religions*, Kalamazoo, MI: Ekpyrosis Press.

Csikszentmihalyi, M. (1997), *Finding Flow: The Psychology of Engagement with Everyday Life*, New York: Basic Books.

Kotler, S. (2014), *The Rise of Superman: Decoding the Science of Ultimate Human Performance*, Amazon Publishing.

Laborit, H. (1974), *La nouvelle grille : Pour décoder le message humain*, Paris: Éditions Robert Laffont.

Panikkar, R. (1978), *The Intrareligious Dialogue*, New York: Paulist Press.

Polanyi M. and H. Prosch (1975), *Meaning*, Chicago: University of Chicago Press.

Schmidt-Leukel, P. (2019), *Buddha Mind – Christ Mind. A Christian Commentary on the Bodhicaryāvatāra*. With a new translation by E. Steinkellner and C. Peck-Kubaczek, Leuven: Peeters.

Suzuki, D. T. (1970), *Outlines of Mahayana Buddhism*, New York: Schocken Books.

Wangchuk, D. (2007), *The Resolve to Become a Buddha, A Study of the Bodhicitta Concept in Indo-Tibetan Buddhism*, Studia Philologica Buddhica, Monograph Seris XXIII, Tokyo: The International Institute for Buddhist Studies.

10

Śaṅkara and Śāntideva on Consciousness and Ultimate Reality

A Field Guide to Identify the Buddhist Advaitin

Fabian Völker

Apart from the legends, we know next to nothing on the basis of firm historical evidence about Śāntideva, the imagined author of the universally acclaimed *Bodhicaryāvatāra* and *Śikṣāsamuccaya*. Was his proper name even Śāntideva or was his name actually Akṣayamati? Did a Buddhist named Akṣayamati write the Dūn-huáng version of a markedly different and substantially shorter text called *Bodhisattvacāryavatāra* in the early eighth century and another Buddhist named Śāntideva compose the *Śikṣāsamuccaya* a few decades later? Did the original author of the Dūn-huáng version continuously revise and rework the text himself or was the Sanskrit text of the larger canonical version composed by the author of the *Śikṣāsamuccaya*? Indeed, it could well be the product of yet another, a third Buddhist, or even several more anonymous redactors who omitted, supplemented, and changed the contents of the older edition during its transmission (see Saitō 2010: 22; Schmidt-Leukel 2019: 3–52). Until new historical or literary sources are adduced, it remains "pointless to try and demythologize the traditional Life of Śāntideva in order to find some historical core," as Paul Williams (1995: ix) compellingly argued.

When we turn to Śaṅkara (seventh/eighth century),[1] the situation is similarly bleak. According to the most prominent narratives of the contemporary living tradition of Advaita Vedānta that are widely circulated by comics, popularized by movies, and now firmly entrenched in Indian culture, it was Śaṅkara who in the course of his "conquest of the (four) quarters (of Bhārata)" (*digvijaya*) organized the Daśanāmi Saṃnyāsīs into the first Brahmāṇical order of ascetics (*saṃpradāya*), established four cardinal monasteries (*āmnāya maṭhas*) known as "thrones" (*gaddī*) or "seats of knowledge" (*vidyāpīṭha*) under the direct authority of his four chief disciples Toṭaka, Padmapāda, Sureśvara, and Hastāmalaka in the north, east, south, and west of India, and inaugurated

1 Tilmann Vetter (1979: 11) argued that we can claim only that Śaṅkara lived sometime between 650 and 800. However, by identifying personal names that appear in Śaṅkara's Brahmasūtrabhāṣya with historic persons, Kengo Harimoto (2006) placed the composition of the Brahmasūtrabhāṣya between 756 and 772.

a lineage of knowledge transmitted from guru to disciple (*guruśiṣyaparaṃparā*) that connects the contemporary Śaṅkarācāryas ("abbots") of these *maṭhas* in one continuous and unbroken line of succession with Śaṅkara. However, an examination of the extensive collection of Śaṅkara hagiographies (*śaṅkaravijayas*), none of which can legitimately claim to be composed prior to the fourteenth century, reveals that the first mention of four *maṭhas* and the founding of the Daśanāmi order of ascetics appears briefly and not until the late sixteenth century in Cidvilāsa's *Śaṅkaravijayavilāsa*.[2] Even though Śaṅkara's genuine works illustrate that he was almost certainly an avowed Vaiṣṇava (see Hacker 1995), the plethora of conflicting hagiographies conveniently ignored the evidence and subsequently projected him as a fully divine or partial incarnation (*aṃśāvatāra*) of Śiva, who vanquished teachers of heterodox sects and rival orthodox schools in debate, resuscitated the orthodox Brahmāṇical tradition, and reunited a divided India under the banner of absolute non-dualism (*kevalādvaita vedānta*). Thus, again, apart from the profusion of various miraculous accounts and mythic images cast by the hagiographers, we do not know anything specific about Śaṅkara, who remains elusive to the impartial historian and continues to be veiled behind a curtain of fictional reappropriations and arbitrary fabrications. However, there is a certain consensus among scholars that he lived around the seventh or eighth century and was contemporary with Śāntideva, who is generally thought to have flourished in the same centuries, although the reasoning behind Śāntideva's dating is by no means conclusive either.

Now, unless we are willing to accept Buston Rinchen Grub's (1290–1364) and Sabzang Mati Paṇchen's (1294–1376) accounts of Śāntideva's debate with a Hindu *paṇḍita* named Śaṅkaradeva (Buston) or Śaṅkānanda (Sabzang) as allusions to Śaṅkara and actual evidence of a historical event, we can safely infer that Śaṅkara and Śāntideva never met and didn't know of each other (see Stein and Zangpo 2013: 260–1; Chodron 2013). Thus, if it is argued that any comparison should be legitimized either historically or systematically, we have at least no historical reason to compare them. Fortunately, however, there is a long history of dynamical interaction between the rival, at times hostile Buddhist and Brahmāṇical traditions in general, and a long-standing philosophical competition and feud between Mādhyamikas and Advaitins in particular that provides us with countless systematic reasons to compare both thinkers (see Nakamura 1990: 131–265). Śaṅkara and Śāntideva lend themselves particularly well to comparative elucidation of both traditions, especially since both grew up in basically the same historical and cultural milieu and moved in circles where philosophical rivalry with Vijñānavāda Buddhism spurred the creation of their specific dialectics (see Todd 2013: 18). However, while the salient features of Śaṅkara's "doctrine of non-difference" (*abhedadarśana*; *Brahmasūtrabhāṣya* 3:2:13, in: Panoli 2011: 891) and "denial of dualism" (*dvaitavādapratiṣedha*; *Brahmasūtrabhāṣya* 1:3:19, in: Panoli 2011: 288) are comparatively unambiguous and clear, Śāntideva's Madhyamaka is notoriously obscure and has occasioned protracted scholarly debate that again resulted

[2] For a survey of this literature, its political entangelements, and conflicting accounts of Śaṅkara's life in line with the partisan claims of rivaling *maṭhas* and their power struggles, see Bader 2000, Clark 2006: 148–76, and Sundaresan 2003.

in numerous competing and highly disputed explanations. In order to identify the key philosophical issues at stake and establish clear parameters necessary for enabling a meaningful comparison, it is therefore advisable to yield a preliminary exposition of the central points of contention that structure the general debate between Mahāyāna Buddhists and Advaita Vedāntins and examine the apparent similarities and basic differences between the doctrines of Buddha-nature (*tathāgatagarbha*) and Self (*ātman*). While an exhaustive survey and detailed account is precluded, I will restrict myself to those recurring patterns of these inter- and intrareligious debates that lie at the heart of the contested views on consciousness and ultimate reality. It is within this mutually illuminating context that I will try to determine, in exclusively Buddhist terms, what it means to be a Buddhist Advaitin before critically engaging the wisdom chapter of Śāntideva's *Bodhicaryāvatāra* from Śaṅkara's perspective.

1. Mahāyāna Buddhism and Advaita Vedānta: Irenics and polemics, conundrums and confusions

Following Dignāga's (480–540) *Pramāṇasamuccaya*, that critically examines opposing philosophical schools, but omits Vedānta, Bhāviveka's (490/500–70) *Madhyamakahṛdayakārikā* along with its auto-commentary (*Tarkajvāla*) is the earliest extant Buddhist source to recognize Vedānta (*vedāntadarśana*) as an independent school of Brahmāṇical thought.[3] Its eighth chapter (*vedāntatattvaviniścaya*) is entirely devoted to an examination and critique of the doctrines held by pre-Śaṅkara Vedāntavādins containing among largely unidentifiable Vedāntic sources several quotes that substantially resemble or are even virtually identical to verses from the *Gauḍapādīyakārikā* traditionally ascribed to Śaṅkara's *paramaguru* Gauḍapāda (fifth/sixth century) (see King 1995: 35–49). However, many of the allegedly Vedāntic characterizations of the Self (*ātman*) effectively criticized by Bhāviveka, like agency (*kartṛtva*) and enjoyment (*bhoktṛtva*), do not apply to Gauḍapāda (or Śaṅkara) and are either strategic misrepresentations or representative of some of the variegated and multifarious views held by dissenting Vedāntins.[4] Yet, Bhāviveka readily acknowledges that Vedānta is not entirely without merit. He famously counters the contention of non-Mahāyāna Buddhist Śrāvakas that Mahāyāna is not Buddhism, because it teaches either Vedānta or nihilism (*nāstikadarśana*), by stating that "whatever is well said in the Vedānta has [already] been said by the Buddha" (*Madhyamakahṛdayakārikā* IV:7–8:56,

[3] The earliest Jain sources treating Vedānta as a separate school are Siddhasena Divākara's (sixth century) *Dvātriṃśikā* and Haribhadrasūri's (700–70) *Śāstravārtāsamuccaya*, which both include a chapter on Vedānta (*vedavāda, brahmādvaitavāda*). See Qvarnström 2003, 2015: 24–6. Even though Mallavādin's (sixth–seventh century) *Dvādaśāranayacakra* uses the term *puruṣavāda*, Siṃhasūri's (seventh century) commentary (*Nyāyāgamānusāriṇī*) identifies the doctrine under discussion as *advaitavāda*. See Timalsina 2017.

[4] Several of these pre-Śaṅkara Vedāntins are known by name. However, beside various fragments, the only texts of early Advaita Vedānta that are still extant are Bhartṛhari's (*c.* 450–510) *Vākyapadīya*, Gauḍapāda's (fifth/sixth century) *Gauḍapādīyakārikā*, Ādiśeṣa's (sixth century) *Paramārthasāra*, and Maṇḍanamiśra's (seventh/eighth century) *Brahmasiddhi*. See Nakamura 1990: 369–408; 2004: 3–208.

in: Eckel 2008: 110–11, 199). The uncomfortable proximity is thus resolved in one bold stroke by condescendingly dismissing the cardinal doctrines of Vedānta that correspond far too closely to essential features of Mahāyāna teachings to be all derivative to the Buddha-dharma (see *Madhyamakahṛdayakārikā* 8:86, in: Qvarnström 2015: 185). If we follow Richard King (1995: 47), who suggested that the last of the four *prakaraṇas* of the *Gauḍapādīyakārikā* was initially a separate treatise postdating the *Madhyamakahṛdayakārikā*, its penultimate verse (4:99) may be construed as a direct response to Bhāviveka's claim: "The gnosis of the enlightened holy man (*buddha*) does not proceed toward *dharmas*. All *dharmas* are like gnosis [in this respect]. This was not stated by the Enlightened One [*naitad buddhena bhāṣitam*]" (King 1995: 257–8).

Beginning with the *Gauḍapādīyakārikābhāṣya*, this verse has been traditionally read as an attempt to differentiate the teachings of the Buddha from those of Vedānta and stress the superiority of the latter.[5] While the attribution of the *Gauḍapādīyakārikābhāṣya* to Śaṅkara has not been uncontested throughout Indian intellectual history, the *bhāṣyakāra* "Śaṅkara" gives the following explanation: The Buddha came only close to the non-dual reality (*advayavastu*) of Vedānta by negating external objects (*bāhyārtha*) and imagining everything to be mere knowledge (*jñānamātra*). Absolute reality (*paramārthatattva*), however, which, like space (*ākāśa*), is unchanging (*acala*), immutable (*avikriya*), partless (*niravayava*), eternal (*nitya*), non-dual (*advitīya*), unattached (*asaṅga*), invisible (*adṛśya*), ungraspable (*agrāhya*), and free of the difference of knowledge, known, and knower (*jñāna-jñeya-jñātṛ-bheda-rahita*) can only be known from the Upaniṣads (see Gambhīrānanda 1992: 402–3). At least Bhāviveka's *Madhyamakahṛdayakārikā* provides ample evidence to justify Śaṅkara's assessment. Even though Bhāviveka's elaborate account of the "ultimate Buddha" (*paramārthabuddha*) is at times astonishingly reminiscent of Śaṅkara's predicateless and partless *nirguṇa brahman*, he is sufficiently clear and free of ambiguities in his outright repudiation of any superficial resemblance and propinquity between Mahāyāna Buddhism and Vedānta. While discussing the notion of an all-pervasive and permanent Tathāgata and the intention of the teachings on Buddha-nature (*tathāgatagarbha*), he states:

> To say that there is "pervasion by [the essence of] the Tathāgata" means that [the Tathāgata's] knowledge encompasses all objects of cognition, not that he is omnipresent like Viṣṇu. To say that [sentient beings] have the essence of the Tathāgata means that emptiness (*śūnyatā*), signlessness (*animitta*), wishlessness (*apraṇihita*), and so forth, are present in the continuum of all sentient beings, but this [essence of the Tathāgata] is not like an all-pervasive, eternal, inner soul (*puruṣa*).
>
> *Madhyamakahṛdayakārikā-Tarkajvāla* 4:36, in: Eckel 2008: 154[6]

[5] According to Vidhuśekhara Bhaṭṭācārya (1878–1958), however, *naitad buddhena bhāṣitam* refers to the Buddha's silence in a manner reminiscent of the thunderous "silence" (*tūṣṇīṃ*) of Vimalakīrti. See Bhaṭṭācārya 1943: 213–16. Thus, the Buddha didn't say what in principle cannot be verbalized or spoken of, only experienced personally (*pratyātmavedanīya*) and expressed by silence.

[6] Given Bhāviveka's fundamental criticism of a singular (*eka*), all-pervasive (*sarvatraga*), eternal (*nitya*), inexpressible (*avācya*), and inconceivable (*nirvikalpa*) self in his *Vedāntatattvaviniścaya* (73–7), his unprecedented identification of the *dharmakāya* with the supreme Brahman (*paraṃ brahma*) of the Upaniṣads was evidently not intended to facilitate a rapprochement, but to evince the superiority of Buddhism to the competing Vedāntic notion of the Absolute that can only be meaningfully interpreted, if at all, from the vastly superior standpoint of Madhyamaka. See *Madhyamakahṛdayakārikā-Tarkajvāla* III:288, in: Eckel 1992: 169.

While Dharmapāla's (sixth century) commentary on Āryadeva's (third century) *Catuḥśataka* mentions only a group of heretics that holds the inner self to be all-pervading, formless, and actionless (see Nakamura 1990: 219–20), Śāntarakṣita (725–88) endeavored to give another elaborate exposition of the *ātman* as postulated by the followers of the Upaniṣads, who rely on the "view of non-duality" (*advaitadarśana*). According to his *Tattvasaṅgraha* (328–32), there is only a "slight fault" (*alpāparādha*) in their view (*darśana*) that earth, fire, water, etc. are "transformations of consciousness" (*vijñānaparināma*) and "false appearances" (*vivarta*) of "eternal knowledge" (*nityajñāna*). Like Mahāyāna Buddhism, Vedāntins assert "knowledge-only" (*jñānamātra*), which, according to Kamalaśīla's (740–95) commentary, is quite reasonable. The error, however, lies not only in asserting its "eternality" (*nityatā*). Advaitins are also seriously mistaken in claiming consciousness to exist in a state of pure, undifferentiated awareness "distinct" (*bhinna*) from its constantly changing mental contents (see Goodman 2022: 176–8).

By the time of Avalokitavrata's (eighth/ninth century) *Ṭika* on Bhāviveka's *Prajñāpradīpa*, Śaṅkara was known to the Buddhists by name.[7] It was, however, not until Maitrīpa (986–1063) that another crucial aspect was contributed to the discussion. In his *Tattvaratnāvalī* (25), he went even further than Bhāviveka or Śāntarakṣita by asserting that for Buddhist Nirākāravādins, "who cultivate a permanent [*nitya*], self-aware consciousness [*svasaṃvedana-vijñāna*] which is devoid of both appearances [*nirābhāsa*] and mental fabrication [*niṣprapañca*], there is the undesired consequence of following (another) tenet of the proponents of Vedānta," (Mathes 2015: 69, 358) here identified with the tradition of Śaṅkara's adversary Bhāskara (eighth/ninth century). According to Maitrīpa, these Vedāntins maintain that pure consciousness is *brahman*, devoid of properties and entirely free from all names and forms (*vyapagatasakala-nāmarūpa*), completely purified of the confusion of mental fabrication (*prapañca-upaplava-viśuddha*), clear (*prakāśa*), without limit (*ananta*), uninterrupted (*ghana*), and permanent (*nitya*) (see Mathes 2015: 69, 358).[8] Thus, the "stain of the meditative stabilization" (*samādhimala*) of Nirākāravādins is to cling to this ultimately existing and permanent consciousness like Vedāntins, while realizing true reality depends upon not abiding in anything (*amanasikāra*).

Turning to the Vedāntic critique of Mahāyāna Buddhism, it suffices to confine the exposition to Śaṅkara and Śrīharṣa (twelfth century), who embody two opposing approaches to Buddhism. Since Daniel H. H. Ingalls (1916–99) presented *Saṁkara's Arguments against the Buddhists* (1954), there has been a surge of publications analyzing the various facets of Śaṅkara's criticism that has traditionally been credited as major cause for the decline and virtual demise of Buddhism in India. In fact, according to the chronicles (*vaṃśāvalī*) of Nepāl, Śaṅkara did not only defeat the

7 "Tīrthikas are those who reach the shore for their religion, such as Vāsudeva [Kṛṣṇa], Kubera, Mahādeva [Śiva], Brahmā, Kapila, Kaṇāda, Akṣapāda, Śaṅkara, and Jaiminiputra" *Prajñāpradīpaṭika* (I: Toh 3859, 15b; *Dpe bsdur ma* 58:893, in: Jinpa 2022: 75).

8 According to Bodhibhadra's (tenth/eleventh century) *Jñānasārasamuccayanāmanibandhana*, there are two kinds of Yogācārins, who differ regarding the ultimate nature of consciousness. Sākāravādins maintain that consciousness is always endowed with images (*sākāra*), while Nirākāravādins contend that consciousness is ultimately without images (*nirākāra*). See Kajiyama 1998: 154.

"Bauddhamārgīs" in debate, but put some of them to death, ordered others to sacrifice animals despite their unwavering commitment to non-violence (*ahiṁsā*), forced Buddhist nuns (*bhikṣuṇī*) to marry, prohibited the performance of Buddhist rites and ceremonies, destroyed 84,000 Buddhist scriptures, and forcibly introduced the Śaiva religion: "Shankarāchārya thus destroyed the Buddhist religion, and allowed none to follow it" (Wright 1877: 120).

Beside these readily dismissable myths, Śaṅkara's actual critique of Buddhism strikes at the heart of the matter. The primary focus of much of Śaṅkara's scathing appraisal is that the Vijñānavādin's doctrine of momentariness (*kṣaṇabhaṅgavāda*) cannot account for the phenomena of memory (*smṛti*), remembrance (*anusmṛti*), recollection (*pratisaṃdhāna*), and recognition of similarity (*pratyabhijñā*), whereas the Mādhyamika's wholesale denial of an unconditioned Absolute is self-defeating and tantamount to nihilism. In brief, unless there exists an unchangeable principle (*kūṭastha*) and foundational consciousness akin to Immanuel Kant's (1724–1804) transcendental unity of apperception, which "sees" everything (*sarvārthadarśini*), neither memory nor recognition can take place eventually undermining our everyday experience. Both necessarily presuppose a stable subject that is able to span a series of momentary and fleeting experiences, recognize successive cognitions, and relate them to itself as the selfsame perceiver (*draṣṭṛ*, *jñātṛ*, *upalabdhṛ*). If, however, even the perceiver is said to be momentary and in a state of constant flux, the phenomena of (*anu-*)*smṛti*, *pratyabhijñā*, and *pratisaṃdhāna* become completely inexplicable and unintelligible, as Śaṅkara persistently emphasizes.

Thus, the Vijñānavādin's conception of momentary consciousness including the *ālayavijñāna* notion of an individual and insubstantial mindstream that serves as subliminal substratum of residual impressions needs to be resolutely opposed and consistently rejected as explanatory model of experience and reality (see Darling 1987: 259–64). Furthermore, Mādhyamikas cannot possibly negate the everyday world (*lokavyavahāra*), which is firmly established by all valid means of knowledge (*sarvapramāṇaprasiddha*), without necessarily affirming another reality (*anyatattva*) as subjacent ground based upon which they could impugn its existence in the first place (see *Brahmasūtrabhāṣya* 2:2:31, in: Panoli 2011: 628). The precise import of this brief statement becomes immediately clear when read alongside Śaṅkara's *Praśnopaniṣadbhāṣya* (6:2), where he challenges the Mādhyamika with retorsive arguments to explain "how he would argue away the presence of that knowledge by which he imagines the non-existence of that knowledge; for the non-existence of the knowledge being itself a knowable object, it cannot be cognized unless there is knowledge of it." Upon closer examination, it follows that transcendental knowledge cannot be disputed without committing a performative self-contradiction, "because the non-existence of knowledge becomes essentially a knowledge" (Gambhīrānanda 1992: 484). Thus, if the Mādhyamika says anything at all, he cannot deny the *ātman* as the inescapable presupposition of all philosophical discourse without performative self-contradiction; if the Mādhyamika prefers to remain silent, he is "like a vegetable," as Aristotle (384–322 BCE) put it in book *Gamma* of his *Metaphysics* (1006a, in: Reeve 2016: 54). Naturally, the Mādhyamika would repudiate both being a vegetable and denying consciousness while simultaneously being conscious. Only Śaṅkara's claim that ultimate reality can be consistently defined as pure consciousness is resolutely rejected. Ultimately, however, any possible position contains insoluble contraditions which would, of course, also pertain to any position presented by a Mādhyamika. Thus, what the Mādhyamika says, if he/she says anything at all, is that Mādhyamikas do not have any thesis (*pratijñā*), so there is indeeed no fault (*doṣa*) for them (see *Vigrahavyāvartanī* 29, in: Westerhoff 2010: 29).

For Śaṅkara, however, this pure, irrefutable knowledge or consciousness is completely devoid of all phenomenal content and utterly lacking in self-conscious subjectivity. It has been continuously communicated and represented by the transcendental symbol of light ever since the *Bṛhadāraṇyakopaniṣad* (4:3:7), where the unseen seer (*adṛṣṭaṃ draṣṭr*) is referred to as the "light within the heart" (*hṛdy antarjyotiḥ*). Just as pure light cannot be perceived by our eyes and appears as an apparent dark void of nothingness until it is reflected off something, the intelligble light of pure consciousness requires a reflecting medium to manifest. In the absence of a reflected image, the unobjectifiable consciousness does not fade, however, but shines on ceaselessly illuminating *nothing* in its numinous transparency. Thus, pure consciousness is not even extinguished during deep sleep (*suṣupta*) and cannot coherently be doubted, as Śaṅkara persistently claims:

> In so far as knowledge (*jñāna*) that reveals its objects is an illuminator of its object just like light (*āloka*), the absence of knowledge during deep sleep cannot logically be inferred, just as the absence of light (*ālokābhāva*) cannot be inferred from the absence of the thing to be lighted up. Certainly, the nihilist (*vaināśika*) cannot imagine the absence of the eye when it fails to perceive colour in darkness.
>
> *Praśnopaniṣadbhāṣya* 6:2, in: Gambhīrānanda 1992: 483

Hence, according to Śaṅkara's analysis, we must inevitably draw the conclusion that the Buddhist is ensnared in a hopeless contradiction, because the self-luminous (*svayaṃjyotiḥ*) and pre-reflectively self-evident (*svataḥsiddha*, *svapramāṇaka*) self (*ātman*) is indispensably presupposed by even the most comprehensive negation and indeed that from which even the most ardent advocate of emptinesss is utterly unable to abstract.

Modern scholars have repeatedly ventured to substantiate the claim that Śaṅkara invariably misunderstood Buddhism, that he obviously failed to grasp the full significance of its subtle doctrines, or even willfully misrepresented them as nihilism in a hideous attempt to hide his own "crypto Buddhism" in the garments of orthodox Vedānta and cover his great propensity toward Madhyamaka behind the cloak of outward vituperation and contempt. Frank Whaling (1934–2022), like so many others, claimed that Śaṅkara was "either unfair or lacking in understanding" (Whaling 1979: 9), while more recently Gregory Darling has charged Śaṅkara with "deliberate misinterpretation" (Darling 1987: 373). However, Śaṅkara's accusation of nihilism cannot be dismissed out of hand as "sectarian animosity" or "extreme hatred" (Stcherbatsky 1994: 22) confined to the realm of interreligious polemics. On the contrary, it was also frequently voiced and elaborately developed among fellow Buddhists. Even though these intrareligious disputes were at times no less polemical than interreligious debates, the frequency with which this accusation occurred on both sides seems to indicate an actual problem of doctrinal importance rather than stale polemics. Vasubandhu (fourth/fifth century), for instance, saw nothing but nihilism in the teaching of the Mādhyamikas, who "cling to the non-existence of everything (*sarvanāstitāgrāha*)" (see Pruden 1991: 1338, 1373). Again, according to Asaṅga's (fourth century) *Tattvārthapaṭala* of the *Bodhisattvabhūmi*, there cannot possibly be conceptual designation (*prajñapti*) without underlying substratum (*adhiṣṭhāna*), but that is exactly what complete nihilists (*sarvavaināśika/pradhānanāstika*) like the Mādhyamikas claim: "Everything is nothing but a (verbal) designation [*prajñaptimātra*] and this represents (ultimate) reality [*tattva*]" (Engle 2016: 82).

Thus, describing Madhymaka as nihilism is not, as Jan Westerhoff (2016: 340, 356) recently claimed, "the result of a fairly profound conceptual and historical confusion" that is "easily resolved." In his attempt to exonerate the Mādhyamikas from this charge, he distinguishes five different conceptions of nihilistic positions that are explicitly rejected. According to Westerhoff, Mādhyamikas are no nihilists, because (1) they are resolute travelers of the "middle path" (*madhyamā-pratipad*) between all extremes, whereas nihilism is an "extreme view"; (2) Mādhyamikas do not teach annihilationism (*uccheda-dṛṣṭi*), that is, the destruction of anything previously held to exist substantially, because they never subscribed to the inherent existence of anything in the first place; (3) Mādhyamikas do not deny efficacy as things can perform their respective functions notwithstanding their insubstantiality (*niḥsvabhāvatva*); (4) Mādhyamikas do not reify emptiness as non-existence or metaphysical meta-truth, but declare it to be empty itself (*śūnyatāśūnyatā*); and (5) Mādhyamikas do not reject the law of karma and the idea of rebirth tantamount to ethical nihilism (see Westerhoff 2016: 362–7).

However, none of these rejected "nihilisms" addresses the problem as originally charged. Mādhyamikas are accused of nihilism, not because they allegedly entertain the ludicrous idea that absolutely nothing—not even self-contradictory appearances of *nothing*—exist. The nihilism in question concerns rather the acceptance of a conventional world "without recognizing any reality upon which convention might be built." In this way, the Mādhyamika's notorious refusal to affirm an unconditioned substratum turns the world into a "hallucination that rises from nothing, that is, from the absence of any objective or subjective foundation from which (or in which) this hallucination might be produced," as Giuseppe Ferraro (2013: 214) appropriately framed it. Thus, to claim, as Mādhyamikas like Bhāviveka and Candrakīrti clearly do, that Madhyamaka is not susceptible to the charge of nihilism (*nāstikadṛṣṭi*), because the empty phenomenality of dependently arisen *phantoms-in-themselves* is accepted, is no answer, but a simple restatement of the problem conceding legitimacy to the critics of "Madhyamaka Chimerism" (see *Madhyamakahṛdayakārikā-Tarkajvāla* 5:82–4, in: Eckel 2008: 281–3; *Prasannapāda* 368, in: Burton 2004: 96).

While Śaṅkara's attitude toward the Buddhists was rather intransigent, once Buddhism gradually dwindled in India and eventually disappeared for the most part around the twelfth century, Advaitins came to be more appreciative of Buddhism. As Śrīharṣa states in his *Khaṇḍanakhaṇḍakhāḍya* (1:89): "The difference between the Bauddha and the Vedāntin comes to this: The Bauddha regards everything, without exception, as *anirvachanīya*, *i. e.* undefinable [...] The Vedāntins on the other hand declare that this entire Universe, *with the exception of Cognition or Consciousness*, is neither absolutely real nor absolutely unreal" (Jhā 1986: 40). In his epic poem, the *Naiṣadhacarita* (21:88), even this last crucial difference seems to be discarded in favor of a genuine recognition of congeniality acknowledging the virtual identity of both teachings. The Buddha is characterized as both *vidhūtakoṭicatuṣka*—one who has rejected the tetralemma (*catuṣkoṭi*)—and *advayavādin*, one who affirms the ineffable Absolute beyond the *catuṣkoṭi* as unconditioned substratum underlying the empty appearance of the world:[9] "Thou exponent of monistic being, the stream of consciousness is the only reality for thee. Thou art wise, even without being learned in the three Vedas" (Handiqui 1956: 319).

Thus, according to Śrīharṣa, both Advaitins and Mādhyamikas affirm the same non-dual reality (*advaitatattva*) as the ineffable "fifth lemma" (*pañcamakoṭimātra*) beyond the fourfold *catuṣkoṭi* (see *Naiṣadhacarita* 13:36, in: Handiqui 1956: 201), which seems to be confirmed, at least prima facie, by Buddhists like Prajñākaramati, who in his commentary to Śāntideva's Bodhicaryāvatāra refers to the "reality of absolute truth" (*paramārthasatyatattva*) as "essentially liberated from all phenomenality" (*prapañcavinirmuktasvabhāva*) (*Bodhicaryāvatārapañjikā* 9:2, in: Oldmeadow 1994: 26). According to Maitrīpa, who succinctly summarizes this quintessential feature of Buddhist philosophy in his *Tattvaratnāvalī* (27), "Mādhyamikas know reality as being free from the tetralemma (*catuṣkoṭivinirmuktaṃ tattvaṃ mādhyamikā viduḥ*)" (Mathes 2015: 359). It remains to be seen whether Śrīharṣa is right or the ineffable Absolute beyond the *catuṣkoṭi* is just another instance of Hegel's night of the Absolute, in which all Advaitins and Mādhyamikas are black, while in truth they are not.

2. Tathāgatagarbha and ātman

In his introduction to his extensive commentary on the *Ratnagotravibhāgavyākhyā*, the famous Tibetan historian and scholar Gö Lotsāwa (1392–1481) succinctly enunciates the basic hermeneutical possibilities to understand Buddha-nature of which the first two mark the most crucially different and significant interpretations (see Mathes 2008: 163). According to Gö Lotsāwa, *tathāgatagarbha* can be construed either as emptiness that has the character of being a non-implicative negation (*prasajya-pratiṣedha*) or as the luminous nature of the mind (*prakṛti-prabhāsvara-citta*), where emptiness is explained as implicative negation (*paryudāsa-pratiṣedha*). While a non-implicative negation expresses simply a commitmentless negation without implying any affirmative alternative, the connotative force of an implicative negation or privation points beyond itself and entails a countervailing affirmation. Proponents of the former typically consider Buddha-nature (*tathāgatagarbha*) as a preliminary doctrine of provisional meaning, written with a didactic and propaedeutic purpose, and requiring further

[9] The *catuṣkoṭi* or tetralemma encompasses the following four propositions: (1) "x exists"; (2) "x does not exist"; (3) "x both exists and does not exist"; and (4) "x neither exists nor does not exist."

explanation (*neyārtha*), while proponents of the latter usually regard Buddha-nature to be of definitive meaning (*nītārtha*).[10]

The *Mahāparinirvāṇamahāsūtra*, that may in fact provide us with the earliest-known occurrence of the ambiguous expression *tathāgatagarbha* (see Jones 2024), suggests that the teachings on *anātman* and *śūnyatā* are skillful means (*upāyakauśalya*) to disclose the nature of worldly phenomena as appearances, cut attachment to everyday reality (*lokasaṃvṛtisatya*), and clear away the host of false beliefs, dogmatic convictions, and soteriologically deleterious notions, while *tathāgatagarbha* is of definitive meaning and the culmination of the Buddha's teaching. By contrast, the *Laṅkāvatārasūtra* (2:136) proclaims the reverse: the Buddha teaches the *tathāgatagarbha* as an intrinsically pure (*prakṛti-pariśuddha*) and luminous (*prakṛti-prabhāsvara*) mind (*citta*) concealed within the conditioned *dharmas* (*skandhas*, *āyatanas*, and *dhātus*) as skillful means in order to alleviate the fear of emptiness, attract teachers and adepts of rival religious doctrines (*tīrthakaras*) to Buddhism, and eventually lead them to the ultimate truth (*paramārthasatya*) of emptiness.

Thus, according to one strand of Mahāyāna Buddhism, the *tathāgatagarbha* teachings are provisional rhetorical devices (*neyārtha*) only and eventually to be dispensed with, while *anātman* remains the Buddha's ultimate and most profound teaching (*nītārtha*) that frees us from worldly fetters. From this perspective, there is no underlying substratum to discover beyond empty phenomena that could possibly ground the mental events that constitute the subject (*pudgala-nairātmya*) and those representing an object (*dharma-nairātmya*). Both are utterly without foundation and thus no distorted appearances of something ultimately real, but unsupported illusions or mere appearances of *nothing*. The "triple realm" (*traidhātuka*) may arise from the mind, but this very mind (*citta*) is itself not substantially real (*adravyasat*), as Bhāviveka argues: "Just as a stream of leaves and flowers comes from a powerful lotus root, the different streams of [rebirth] come from the mind, even though it is not substantially real" (*Madhyamakahṛdayakārikā* 5:48, in: Eckel 2008: 258).

This brief foray should suffice to show that in order to identify a Buddhist Advaitin we need to side with those Buddhists who interpret emptiness as *paryudāsa-pratiṣedha*, determine the teachings on Buddha-nature to be *nītārtha*, and identify the *tathāgatagarbha* with the luminous nature of a fundamentally worldless mind as the innermost core of the human subject and its intelligible essence. In fact, we need to distinguish still further between distinctly different interpretations that hold Buddha-nature to be merely a potential to achieve enlightenment and those that see Buddha-nature as primordially enlightened reality. Proponents of the latter view may be further divided into Buddhists that invariably confine the unconditioned (*asaṃskṛta*)

[10] According to Mark Siderits, who published *A Field Guide* in 1997 (republished in Siderits 2016) to distinguish the Mādhyamika from the Advaitin, the use of the commitmentless negation—and its concomitant interpretation of Buddha-nature as *neyārtha*—marks "the real difference between Madhyamaka and Advaita" (Siderits 2016: 300). Conequently, Śrīharṣa was seriously mistaken in conflating both traditions and reading Advaita metaphysics into Buddhism for Mādhyamikas ultimately aim "to extirpate all remaining vestiges of metaphysical realism" and hold that "there is only conventional truth that is grounded in the exigencies of our worldly practices": "The ultimate truth is that there is no ultimate truth" (Siderits 2016: 290, 297–8).

tathāgatagarbha to the mindstreams (*citta-santāna*) of sentient beings and those that equate it with the universally present and true nature of all phenomena (*dharmadhātu*) (see Schmidt-Leukel 2008: 110–11).

According to the largely underappreciated *Anūnatvāpūrṇatvanirdeśaparivarta* that surives in a single Chinese translation, Buddha-nature (*tathāgatagarbha*; *rúláixìng*) pervades everywhere and is omnipresent like space. There is, in fact, only one single unitary reality (*ekadhātu*; *yíjiè*) differently termed as "true nature of phenomena" (*dharmatā*; *fǎxìng*), "single sphere of phenomena" (*ekadharmadhātu*; *yìfǎjiè*), "sphere of *nirvāṇa*" (*nirvāṇadhātu*; *nièpánjiè*), *tathāgatagarbha* (*rúláixìng*), or *dharmakāya* (*fǎshēn*) that underlies all subjective interiority as "intrinsically pure mind" (*prakṛtipariśuddhacitta*; *zìxìng qīngjìng xīn*) and all objective exteriority as "absolute *ground* of being" (Silk 2015: 34). This identification of Buddha-nature with space is also repeatedly emphasized in the influential *Ratnagotravibhāga* (1:49): "Just as being of indiscriminative nature (*nirvikalpātmaka*), space (*nabha*) pervades everywhere, similarly all-pervading (*sarvatraga*) is the essence, the immaculate nature of the mind (*cittaprakṛtivaimalyadhātu*)" (Takasaki 2014: 229).

Yet, as is readily apparent, the metaphor of space is intrinsically vague and open to multiple, mutually antagonistic metaphysical interpretations. Whereas Bhāviveka limits the pervasion by the essence of the Tathāgata to the single continuum and experiential field of a Buddha, Śaṅkara affirms the indwelling essence of sentient beings as spacelike "witness of all intellects" (*aśeṣabuddhisākṣitva*, *Upadeśasāhasrī* 1:7:3, in: Mayeda 2006: 81) and unified "witness of all that is seen" (*sarvadṛśyasākṣitvāt*, *Brahmasūtrabhāṣya* 3:2:23, in: Panoli 2011: 916). This ambiguity extends beyond "space" and applies equally to other crucial terms like "permanence," insofar the permanence of the *dharmakāya* may refer to either a "static permanence" (*kūṭastha-nityatva*) akin to Śaṅkara's *nirguṇa brahman* or the "permanence of a continuous flow" (*pravāha-nityatva*). Thus, we must certainly countenance the possibility that "space" and "permanence" are terms that followers of Vedānta and Buddhism and even partisans of different Buddhist schools understand quite differently.

While these distinctions may be subtle, they are evidently far-reaching. If taken literally, however, the all-pervading Buddha-nature is of exceeding metaphysical importance. For if Buddha-nature were discretely limited to the mindstreams (*citta-santāna*) of sentient beings and not ubiquitously present, we would inevitably end up with "The Many Finite Minds Principle" (Wood 1991: 172), according to which the external world (*bhājanaloka*) is a "collective hallucination" based on common (*sādhāraṇa*) *karma* and projected by a multiplicity of telepathically connected (*adhipatipratyaya*) mindstreams (*ālayavijñāna*).[11] To be precise, although we might interpret emptiness as implicative negation, regard Buddha-nature teachings to be of definitive meaning, and strive toward the "realization of the perfection of the supreme

[11] When the *ālayavijñāna* is "shared" (*sādhāraṇa*), it becomes the seed of the "world-receptable" (*bhājanaloka*); when it is "unshared" (*asādhāraṇa*), it is the seed of the "individual bases of consciousness" (*prātyātmikāyatana*). Shared, it is the "seed of the insensate" (*nirveditotpattibīja*) world; unshared, it is the seed of the sensate (*saveditotpattibīja*) world. *Mahāyānasaṅgraha* 1:60. See Lamotte 1973: 82.

self" (*paramātma-pāramitādhigama*) (*Ratnagotravibhāgavyākhyā* I:36, in: Takasaki 2014: 229) as the pinnacle of the Buddhist spiritual path, we might be still clearly beyond the conceptional framework of Advaita Vedānta. Thus, "the *ālayavijñāna* pluralism of minds" must "collapse into a form of mentalistic monism" or "Buddha-nature Absolutism" (Williams 2008: 310) to arrive at a philosophical position that reflects a greater proximity to the ontological and systematic concerns of Advaita Vedānta.

3. Toward a Buddhist Absolute

As previously discussed, this tendency toward an absolute idealism can be clearly discerned in the *Anūnatvāpūrṇatvanirdeśaparivarta*, the *Ratnagotravibhāga*, and other seminal Buddhist texts. In China, these ideas led to the formation of the "doctrine of the Buddha-nature of the insentient" (*wúqíng fóxìng*), which presumed that even grasses and trees, tiles and pebbles were endowed with Buddha-nature and that suchness extends to all *dharmas*.[12] In Tibet, these tendencies were fully evolved and developed in all their bearings in the ingenious writings of Dölpopa (1291–1361), who is generally credited with establishing the philosophical tenets of "Great Madhyamaka" (*dbu ma chen po*), devising an elaborate system of "ultimate mind-only" (*don dam pa'i sems tsam*), and asserting the superiority of "other-emptiness" (*gzhan stong*) over "self-emptiness" (*rang stong*). His most profound insights rely heavily on the *Bṛhaṭṭīkā*, a commentary on the long *Prajñāpāramitāsūtras* attributed to Vasubandhu or Daṃṣṭrāsena (eighth century), in which the ultimately existent perfected nature (*pariniṣpanna-svabhāva*) of the standard three-natures (*trisvabhāva*) Yogācāra model is not the dependent nature (*paratantra-svabhāva*) empty of the imagined (*parikalpita-svabhāva*), but empty of both the *paratantra* and *parikalpita* natures and thus utterly beyond dependently arisen phenomena (see *Bṛhaṭṭīkā* 6:41, in: Sparham 2022: 614). Across his strikingly apophatic writings, Dölpopa repeatedly identifies the ultimate remainder of *pariniṣpanna* with a wide variety of leading Buddhist concepts. The living presence of the Absolute within conditioned existence is unapogetically and unrelentingly affirmed as truly established "universal-ground primordial awareness" (*kun gzhi ye shes*), pure self (*dag pa'i bdag*), *paramārthadhātu* (*don dam dbyings*), *dharmatā* (*chos nyid*), *dharmakāya* (*chos sku*), and mind's unobscured natural luminosity (*rang bzhin gyi 'od gsal ba*) that impels us toward awakening and renders us receptive to the ubiquitous but otherwise hidden Absolute as a prearticulate awareness of its immanent transcendence. In *The Categories of the Possible and the Impossible* (*Srid mi srid kyi rab dbye dbu phyogs legs par bzhugs so*), Dölpopa explains the relation between gnosis (*ye shes*; *jñāna*) and ordinary consciousness (*rnam shes*; *vijñāna*) as *asymmetric non-duality*, that is, the "undefiled buddha-nature can exist without defilements, but there can be no defilements without that buddha-

[12] An overview of the further developments of the *wúqíng fóxìng*-doctrine in Chinese and Japanese Buddhism would exceed the scope of this chapter. For a discussion of Dàoshēng (360–434), Sēngzhào (374–414), Jìngyǐng Huìyuǎn (523–92), Jízàng (549–623), Fǎzàng (643–712), Zhànrán (711–82), Annen (ninth century), Ryōgen (912–85), and the "Buddha-nature Manifestation Theory" of "Critical Buddhism" (*hihan bukkyō*), see Völker 2020: 683–92.

nature" as there can be "wisdom without consciousness," but "no consciousness without wisdom" (Duckworth 2015: 487).

Similarly, Śaṅkara's "*brahman* is the essential nature (*svabhāva*) of this phenomenal universe (*prapañca*), even though this phenomenal universe is not the essential nature of *brahman*" (*Brahmasūtrabhāṣya* 3:2:21, in: Panoli 2011: 903). As opposed to Dölpopa's and Śaṅkara's *asymmetric non-dualities*, there is no immanent transcendence and substantially unchanging reality accepted in *symmetric non-duality* (see Völker 2023), as the famous verse from the *Heart Sūtra* makes abundantly clear: "Form is emptiness and emptiness is form" (*rūpaṃ śūnyatā śūnyataiva rūpaṃ*). According to Mipham's (1846–1912) commentary on Śāntarakṣita's *Madhyamakālaṃkāra* (72cd), there is ultimately nothing beyond the inconceivable unity of emptiness and form, which is this empty world seen with complete penetration: "The appearance itself does not exist, but it is still apparent all the while. Such an inseparability of appearance and emptiness remains inexpressible, and as the final meaning is thus free from negation and affirmation it transcends the mind" (Doctor 2004: 523).

Given the wide range of Buddhist positions already excluded, we are ineluctably drawn toward the conclusion that Dölpopa is the last man standing to share a deeper affinity or even common ground with Śaṅkara. It is with him and the distinctive way he portrays the Absolute that we are evidently closest to identifying a Buddhist Advaitin, although there are undeniably important differences between him and Śaṅkara, which I cannot fully address here, like their opposing views on the necessity of yoga as a means of apprehending ultimate reality or the way in which Śaṅkara's *brahman* is utterly formless and without determinate quality (*nirguṇa*), whereas Dölpopa's Buddha-nature is essentially endowed with a host of exalted qualities pertaining exclusively to a Buddha (*bodhipakṣadharmas*), etc.

4. How to identify the Buddhist Advaitin: A preliminary list

From this necessarily brief and inevitably incomplete survey, we can identify a limited number of significant criteria in exclusively Buddhist terms that must be necessarily met in order to legitimately identify a Buddhist as Advaitin: (1) emptiness is set forth as implicative negation (*paryudāsa-pratiṣedha*); (2) *tathāgatagarbha* is of definitive meaning (*nītārtha*); (3) *tathāgatagarbha* is identified with the intrinsically pure and luminous mind (*prakṛti-prabhāsvara-citta*); (4) consciousness is ultimately without images (*nirākāra*); (5) the subject–object dichotomy of intentional consciousness (*rnam shes*; *vijñāna*) is differentiated from its pre-reflective and pre-relational ground (*ye shes*; *jñāna*); (6) *tathāgatagarbha* refers to a static permanence (*kūṭastha-nityatva*); (7) *tathāgatagarbha* is omnipresent and pervades all phenomena undividedly (*sarvatraga*) like space (*ākāśa*); (8) *tathāgatagarbha* is equated with the universal immanence of the Absolute beyond individual mindstreams (*dharmakāya*, *dharmatā*, *dharmadhātu*, etc.); (9) *parinispanna-svabhāva* is empty of both *paratantra-* and *parikalpita-svabhāva*; (10) the non-duality between the Absolute and its appearance is *asymmetric*.

However, even this account needs to be refined further before it could function as a complete list of necessary conditions and I am sure that additional criteria could easily be discerned. Yet, this rather long preamble provides us with the background necessary to thoroughly scrutinize Śāntideva's *Bodhicaryāvatāra* and these controversial points in question.

5. An Advaitic reading of the Wisdom Chapter (BCA 9) of the *Bodhicaryāvatāra*

Considering the vast amount of literature pertaining to both Śaṅkara and Śāntideva as two of the preeminent thinkers of India, coming anywhere near a comprehensive comparison within the limits of this chapter is impossible. For my Advaitic reading, I will focus on the ninth chapter of the *Bodhicaryāvatāra*, engaging critically with Śāntideva's views on consciousness and ultimate reality from Śaṅkara's perspective and apply the criteria developed in the previous part of this essay. Of pivotal importance is Śāntideva's dismissal and refutation of rival Mahāyāna schools, where the disputed views on consciousness and ultimate reality between Mādhyamikas and Yogācāras are one of the central targets of his polemical thrust (see BCA 9:16–30). Śāntideva's imagined interlocutor is basically in line with Śaṅkara here. Both argue that the most fundamental and inalienable feature of consciousness is its self-luminosity (*svayaṃprakāśatva*) and pre-reflective self-evidence (*svataḥsiddhatva*). This transcendental consciousness does not require a conscious-making act of self-objectification or other means of valid cognition to know itself but is itself immediately and non-inferentially known and as such inevitably presupposed in all reflective activity. In contrast, a reflection-based account of self-consciousness would inevitably end in an infinite regress (*anavasthā*), for if consciousness depends upon a second-order consciousness that takes the original first-order consciousness as its intentional object to be self-conscious, this second-order consciousness would itself depend on a third-order consciousness for being conscious, and this again on a fourth, and so on, ad infinitum. Thus, consciousness must be intrinsically self-aware and as such essentially free of the difference of knowledge, knower, and known. As Tāranātha (1575–1634) argues in line with Śaṅkara, intellectual intuition or "self-knowing timeless awareness" (*rang rig ye shes*; *svasaṃvid*) is not really a subject–object relationship at all. It is "without division between the subject and object of consciousness" and needs "neither an object of awareness nor someone who is aware" (*Dbu ma theg mchog*, in: Joos 2022: 362).

Śāntideva, however, unequivocally rejects both models of self-consciousness: Neither can the mind see itself (*cittaṃ cittaṃ na paśyati*), just like a sword cannot cut itself, nor can the mind illuminate itself (*saṃprakāśa*) like a lamp (*dīpa*): "Lamplight is surely not illuminated since it has not been covered by darkness" (9:19, in: Schmidt-Leukel 2019: 426). In response to this rather unconvincing attempt to dismiss a pre-reflective account of self-awarenesss, Śāntideva's opponent introduces another argument that, again, figures prominently in Śaṅkara's criticism of Vijñānavāda Buddhism: an enduring subject that is pre-reflectively aware of itself is necessary as an explanatory device to fully account for the occurrence of memory and recognition. The viability of this argument is again sharply contested by Śāntideva in a terse and somewhat cryptic rebuttal: "When something other [than cognition] has been perceived, one remembers [the cognition] on account of a connection [with its object], as in the case of rat poison [which takes effect later]" (9:24, in Schmidt-Leukel 2019: 427).

According to Matthew T. Kaptstein (2019: 91–3), who devoted an entire essay to Śāntideva's "rat poison" (*ākhuviṣa*), Śāntideva seeks to establish an alternative, causal theory of memory formation without recourse to the discredited notions of "reflexive awareness" (*svasaṃvitti, svasaṃvedana*) or a persisting self. The example is meant to show that someone who had been bitten and poisoned by a rat would have forgotten about the encounter altogether until the remaining venom would be reactivated and with it the memory of having been bitten. To make sense of how this example is meant to refute the necessity of *svasaṃvedana*, Kapstein alludes to Vasubandhu's theory of memory (*smaraṇā*) and recognition (*pratyabhijñā*) from the *Abhidharmakośabhāṣya* (9, in: Pruden 1991: 1340–1). Memory or recognition of objects experienced long before can occur in the absence of an unchanging substratum, as Vasubandhu maintains, because the object initially experienced and the object subsequently remembered are instantaneous mental events linked and associated with each other in one causally connected, unbroken, and single stream of consciousness (*citta-santāna*). Whereas Śāntarakṣita's and Kamalaśīla's explanation of remembrance and recognition is somewhat similar (see *Tattvasaṅgrahapañjikā* 542, in: Goodman 2022: 227–8), Candrakīrti does not even bother with such an attempted explanation. According to his *Madhyamakāvatārabhāṣya* (6:75), the identity of the one who originally experiences an event and the one who remembers it afterwards is unhesitantly accepted at the level of conventional truth (*saṃvṛti-satya*). But this does in no way commit the Mādhyamika to accept anything inherently existing at the level of ultimate truth (*paramārtha-satya*), like an apperceptive faculty of reflective awareness or a single unifying perceiver, as Candrakīrti insistently claims. The Prāsaṅgika-Mādhyamika simply goes along with "empirical experience," as Mipham explains in his commentary *The Word of Candra* (*zla ba'i zhal lung*): "However, if an analysis is made of the recalled object and the experiencing consciousness, both are found to be without true existence" (Padmakara Translation Group 2004: 248).

Now, we can safely conclude that Śāntideva substantially departs from Śaṅkara in all crucial respects and reveals a sharp contrast between them when he addresses the pivotal question of consciousness. The notion of a transcendental unity of apperception or unencumbered "witness-consciousness" (*sākṣi-caitanya*) is evidently anathema to Śāntideva's view about which I must express some rather strong reservations. For present purposes I limit myself to adducing one particularly clear statement of his unfortunate dismissal of a pure, non-referential consciousness:

> If cognition is what does not cognize, it follows that also a log of wood is cognition. Thus it is certain that there is no cognition without a cognizable object at hand [. . .] Also the consciousness [of the soul] and the unconsciousness [of primordial matter] would be one and the same [. . .] In this way one might also conceive of the unconscious and inactive space as being the self.
>
> *Bodhicaryāvatāra* 9:62, 68, 70, in: Schmidt-Leukel 2019: 444–5

As Śāntideva consistently argues, on the level of conventional reality intentionality is the fundamental and irreducible feature of consciousness highlighted by the interdependence and interrelation of the cognizing subject and the cognizable object both of which are simultaneously constituted in the act of knowing as the stream of consciousness unfolds. However, as Śaṅkara would certainly demur, both are correlative limbs of a disjunction, which in its doubleness yearns toward a higher unity, for all differences necessarily presuppose a unity and are themselves expressions of that unity. Pure "otherness" and "alterity" without recourse to unity is literally unthinkable. The transcendental *unity* of identity and difference is logically anterior and independent of all conceptual dichotomies. It bridges the fundamental distinction between subject and object and "illuminates" the flux of brute phenomenality. As such the undifferentiated unity of complete self-identity of pure consciousness is an ineliminable feature of the Advaitic framework of experience and given to itself through an act of intellectual intuition or self-illumination (*svaprakāśatva*), defined by Citsukha (thirteenth century) in his *Tattvapradīpikā* as *jñānāviṣayatva* (Saha 1997: 106), that is, that which is not an object of knowledge (*nirviṣayaka*), for whatever becomes an object is conditioned and ceases to be absolute.[13]

Moreover, this transcendentally refined notion effectively prevents the Advaitin from succumbing to the "subreption of hypostatized consciousness (*apperceptionis substantiatae*)" (A 402). According to Kant's critique of rational psychology, the four paralogisms of substantiality, simplicity, personality, and ideality arise because we mistakenly take the unity of consciousness, which grounds the categories, for an intuition of the subject as an object and apply the category of substance to it. But "the subject of the categories cannot, by thinking them, obtain a concept of itself as an object of the categories; for in order to think them, it must take its pure self-consciousness, which is just what is to be explained, as its ground" (B 422, in Kant 1998: 452). Accordingly, Śaṅkara's *ātman* is not a monad or simple substance as, for instance, in Viśiṣṭādvaita Vedānta, but a substrate-less (*nirāśraya*), changeless, and eternal (*kūṭasthanitya*) consciousness (*caitanya*): "The perceiver is indeed nothing but eternal perception. And it is not right that perception and perceiver are different" (*Upadeśasahasrī* 2:2:79, in: Mayeda 2006: 241).

Despite Śaṅkara's and Śāntideva's irreconcilable approaches to consciousness which seem to reflect deep insuperable differences with regard to their metaphysical visions of ultimate reality, we may still inquire whether there is an underlying common ground of the Absolute that ultimately reconciles the antagonism. If we follow Mipham's commentary, this is an altogether futile attempt at reconciliation, for there is no radically acosmic Absolute beyond conventional consciousness and empty phenomena to be discovered. When placed under critical examination, all phenomena are found to be non-existent. Still, they miraculously appear, and their empty phenomenality is

13 Unlike Śāntideva, pure consciousness was no particularly strange and unsettling idea for at least some circles within early Buddhism who maintained *nirvāṇa* as an objectless (*anārammaṇa*), unsupported (*appatiṭṭhita*), non-manifestive (*anidassana*), infinite (*ananta*), unconstructed (*asaṅkhata*), and stopped (*niruddha*) consciousness and unconditioned sphere (*nirvāṇa-dhātu*). According to Peter Harvey (1986: 44), in the "timeless experience of arahantship, *viññāṇa*, schooled so as not to be taken in by *nimittas* and worldly objects, does not even take *nibbāna* as object, but, objectless, transcends conditions and is the unconditioned."

all there is: "Whatever appears *is empty*; whatever is empty *appears*." To attain the perfection of wisdom (*prajñāpāramitā*), then, is tantamount to realize the *symmetric non-duality* of the *dharmadhātu* as "the *union of appearance and emptiness*" (*Norbu Ketaka* on *Bodhicaryāvatāra* 9:2, in: Padmakara Translation Group 2017: 83).

In contrast, Schmidt-Leukel (2019: 420) argues in line with apophatic mysticism that Śāntideva's recognition of the "illusory character of all conceptually constructed reality [...] inevitably implies the corresponding idea of a non-illusionary and ultimately true reality." As I have shown above, this would only be the case if sufficient textual evidence could be adduced to convincingly show that Śāntideva indeed interprets emptiness as implicative negation. Moreover, just like "sky" and "permanence," Śāntideva's reality (*tattva*) can be interpreted almost arbitrarily within the given constraints of the undoubtedly wide range of Buddhist philosophy. As Paul Williams's (2000: 1–28) rigorous perusal of the extant Indian and Tibetan commentaries has conclusively shown, the *Bodhicaryāvatāra* was claimed from almost all competing and mutually antagonizing Buddhist schools and at times interpreted by the Tibetan exegetical traditions with reference to philosophical notions that were either unknown or considered irrelevant by Śāntideva and his Indian commentators. Whereas Prajñākaramati treats *tattva* in his *Bodhicaryāvatārapañjikā* (9:1, in: Oldmeadow 1994: 4) from a Prāsaṅgika perspective, according to which wisdom (*prajñā*) is the discriminating comprehension (*pravicaya*) of the reality of dependently arisen phenomena just as they are (*yathāvasthita pratītyasamutpanna-vastutattva*), Sabzang Mati Paṇchen commented upon the *Bodhicaryāvatāra* from a decidedly *gzhan stong* perspective in line with Dölpopa. By quoting the famous and widely cited verse from the *Aṣṭasāhasrikā-prajñāpāramitāsūtra* according to which "mind is not mind; the nature of mind is clear-light" (*taccittamacittam. prakṛtiścittasya prabhāsvarā*), he suggests that Śāntideva never intended to negate a primeval and supramundane gnosis, but only intentional consciousness, as can supposedly be confirmed by verse 35 (among others): "If neither existence (*bhāva*) nor non-existence (*abhāva*) stands in front of the mind (*mati*), then, with no objective support (*nirālamba*), it finds rest (*praśāma*), for there is no other way" (BCA 9:35, in: Schmidt-Leukel 2019: 427).

Even though Śāntideva quotes from the *Śrīmālādevīsiṃhanāda-* and *Tathāgatakośasūtra* in his *Śikṣāsamuccaya* (42; 172) and explicitly states that the Buddhas "in their compassionate nature" have made "this whole world their own self (*ātmīkṛta*)" (BCA 6:126, in: Schmidt-Leukel 2019: 296), there is no single reference to the doctrine of Buddha-nature in the *Bodhicaryāvatāra*. Moreover, given his explicit rejection of the notion of pure consciousness, we can safely infer that he would have regarded the Buddhist doctrines of an intrinsically pure and luminous mind and Buddha-nature at best as preliminary and of provisional meaning only. Thus, regardless of my sympathies for Dölpopa's *gzhan stong* and his overall commentarial project, Sabzang's rather bold attempt to read an inherently existing clear-light nature of the mind and "ultimate gnosis body" (*paramārthajñānakāya*) into the *Bodhicaryāvatāra* is thoroughly unconvincing. Rather unsurprisingly, Gyaltsab Jé (1364–1432), one of the chief disciples of Tsongkhapa (1357–1419), emphatically and rightfully denied that Śāntideva affirmed anything like an enduring and truly existing mind as remaining substratum to the cessation of subject and object.

If, however, Śāntideva is no nihilist (and let's assume he isn't), for whom the "veil of the conventional" is not "only veiling its own illusory nature" (Schmidt-Leukel 2019: 421), but grounded in a strictly ineffable Absolute, like Śrīharṣa and Schmidt-Leukel claim, why did he abstain from any unequivocal affirmation of an unconditioned substratum and positive conceptualization of the Absolute thereby fostering misunderstanding, along with the subsequent charge of nihilism? I suspect that Śāntideva's deep reticence, almost anxiety, tacitly rests on the excessively hyperbolic view that every affirmation (however lofty) necessarily and invariably involves a pernicious reification (*samāropa*) and must be relentlessly dismissed as eternalist substantialization (*śāśvatānta*). Even the ontological commitment to a transcategorial Absolute, that is necessary to yield a non-nihilist understanding of the phenomenal world that is otherwise suspended in nothingness and unreality, is generally repudiated by Mādhyamikas.

The *Madhyamakārthasaṅgraha*, whose attribution to Bhāviveka is controversial, contains an especially clear and carefully developed theory of the two truths (*satyadvaya*) that might aid us here in providing a more profound answer (see Lindtner 1981: 200–1). According to this short treatise, *paramārthasatya* is of two kinds, that is, there is an "inexpressible Absolute" (*aparyāya-paramārtha*) or the Absolute as it is *in itself* (*prapañcaśūnya*) and an "expressible Absolute" (*saparyāya-paramārtha*) or the Absolute as it is *for us* within the medium of reflective concepts (*saprapañca*) and its inherent boundaries. Now operating with this distinction between the unutterable actuality of the Absolute and the absolute appearance of the Absolute, I suggest that there is no harm in explicitly affirming ultimate reality as *saparyāya-paramārtha* or concept-bound appearance of the Absolute as long as we insist, at the same time, that "ultimate reality (*in itself*) is not a domain of cognition" (*buddheragocarastattvaṃ*) (BCA 9:2, in: Schmidt-Leukel 2019: 415). Being mindful of the emptiness of all concepts, one may allow the Absolute to emerge as affirmation in an image that expressly gives itself as mundane linguistic convention (*lokavyavahāra*) or conceptual approximation, albeit as the best, and not at all as the "thing" itself. Thus, when the inconceivable Absolute is conceptually conceived as pure consciousness, as in Śaṅkara's case, or as *nirvāṇa* and all-encompassing compassion (*karuṇā*) of the Buddhas and higher Bodhisattvas, as in Śāntideva's case, it is its absolute appearance *for us*. If, however, we want to conceptually grasp the Absolute as it is in *itself*, we necessarily fail, for even the distinction between reality *itself* and its appearance *for us* is part of conventional reality (see BCA 9:107–8). The strictly indescribable Absolute always eludes the linguistic medium in every form and can only be indicated by negations and the negation of negations that function evocatively rather than descriptively. As both Śaṅkara and Śāntideva intimately know, we cannot realize the transcategorial Absolute speculatively in a consistent and non-contradictory way, but only existentially by the remainderless cessation (*prapañcopaśama*, see *Mūlamadhyamakakārikā* 25:24) and complete dissolution (*prapañcapravilaya*, see *Brahmasūtrabhāṣya* 3:2:21) of our conceptual representations of the Absolute and the conceptually constructed phenomenal world of becoming (*prapañca*). Consequently, its affirmation as *paramārthasatya* or *nirguṇa brahman* is just another empty concept of relation. Ultimately, however, as Fichte (2005: 42–3, 81) tellingly puts it, the unthinkable beyond of all thinking will "remain *zero* (= 0)" for philosophy, which has its "essence in concepts," and "only becomes an affirmation in living." In truth, "we in no way *conceive* it, but rather we *are* it."

Now do all differences between Śaṅkara and Śāntideva finally prove to be merely superficial and ultimately reconciled in a common Absolute beyond *prapañca*, as Śrīharṣa originally claimed? Not quite. For neither Śaṅkara (see *Bṛhadaraṇyakopaniṣadbhāṣya* 1:4:7; *Brahmasūtrabhāṣya* 2:1:3) nor Śāntideva (see BCA 9:49) consider a "cessation of mental activity" (*cittavṛttinirodha*) or "unconscious absorption" (*asaṃjñisamāpatti*) to be a sufficient means of liberation, because "the bound mind will return" after these death-like trance states. Both consistently claim that a non-conceptual gnosis (or experience) of the absolute truth is indispensable for a lasting and irreversible liberation. According to Śaṅkara, the highest good (*niḥśreya*) can be achieved only by the Upaniṣadic knowledge of the unity of the self (*vaidikādātmaikatvavijñānāt*) and its steady recollection (*smṛtisantāna*); in contrast, Śāntideva maintains that awakening is dependent entirely on the existentially internalized insight into the ultimate truth of universal emptiness. Thus, the philosophical gap between Śaṅkara and Śāntideva can only partially be closed, for the abiding and irreconcilable point of contention resides in the crucial question of whether the absolute appearance of the Absolute may be consistently conceived in terms of pure consciousness or not. For if both unwaveringly insist that a correct understanding of the "expressible Absolute" at the level of conventional truth is imperative in order to intuit the "inexpressible Absolute", then it inevitably follows that both must necessarily deny the salvific efficacy of the other's teaching.

References

Bader, J. (2000), *Conquest of the Four Quarters. Traditional Accounts of the Life of Śaṅkara*, New Delhi: Aditya Prakashan.

Bhaṭṭācārya, V. (1943), *The Āgamaśāstra of Gauḍapāda*, Calcutta: University of Calcutta.

Burton, D. (2004), *Buddhism, Knowledge and Liberation. A Philosophical Study*, Aldershot and Burlington, VT: Ashgate.

Chodron, C. (2013), "Accounts of the Biography of Śāntideva: Some Observations concerning the Effect of Culture," in C. U. Rao, C. K. Chodron, and M. L. Dexter (eds.), *Śāntideva and Bodhicaryāvatāra (Images, Interpretations, Reflections)*, 14–52, Delhi: Eastern Book Linkers.

Clark, M. (2006), *The Daśanāmī-Saṃnyāsīs. The Integration of Ascetic Lineages into an Order*, Leiden and Boston: Brill.

Darling, G. J. (1987), *An Evaluation of the Vedāntic Critique of Buddhism*, Delhi: Motilal Banarsidass.

Doctor, T. H. (2004), *Speech of Delight. Mipham's Commentary on Śāntarakṣita's Ornament of the Middle Way*, Foreword by Chökyi Nyima Rinpoche, translated by T. H. Doctor, Ithaca, NY, and Boulder, CO: Snow Lion.

Duckworth, D. S. (2015), "Other-Emptiness in the Jonang School: The Theo-Logic of Buddhist Dualism," *Philosophy East and West* 65 (2): 485–97.

Eckel, M. D. (2008), *Bhāviveka and His Buddhist Opponents*, Cambridge, MA: Harvard University Press.

Eckel, M. D. (1992), *To See the Buddha. A Philosopher's Quest for the Meaning of Emptiness*, Princeton: Princeton University Press.

Engle, A. B. (2016), *The Bodhisattva Path to Unsurpassed Enlightenment. A Complete Translation of the Bodhisattvabhūmi. Ārya Asaṅga*, translated by A. B. Engle. Foreword by His Holiness the Fourteenth Dalai Lama, Boulder, CO: Snow Lion.

Ferraro, G. (2013), "A Criticism of M. Siderits and J. L. Garfield's 'Semantic Interpretation' of Nāgārjuna's Theory of Two Truths," *Journal of Indian Philosophy* 41: 195–219.

Fichte, J. G. (2005), *The Science of Knowing: J. G. Fichte's 1804 Lectures on the Wissenschaftslehre*, translated by W. E. Wright, Albany: SUNY Press.

Gambhīrānanda, S. (1992), *Eight Upaniṣads. Volume Two (Aitareya, Muṇḍaka, Māṇḍūkya & Kārikā, and Praśna). With the Commentary of Śaṅkarācārya*, Calcutta: Advaita Ashrama.

Goodman, C. (2022), *The Tattvasaṃgraha of Śāntarakṣita. Selected Metaphysical Chapters*, translated by C. Goodman, Oxford: Oxford University Press.

Hacker, P. (1995), "Relations of Early Advaitins to Vaiṣṇavism," in W. Halbfass (ed.), *Philology and Confrontation. Paul Hacker on Traditional and Modern Vedānta*, 33–9, Albany: SUNY Press.

Handiqui, K. K. (1956), *Naiṣadhacarita of Śrīharṣa*, translated into English by K. K. Handiqui, Poona: Deccan College.

Harimoto, K. (2006), "The Date of Śaṅkara: Between the Cāḷukyas and the Rāṣṭrakūṭas," *Journal of Indological Studies* 18: 85–111.

Harvey, P. (1986), "Signless Meditation in Pali Buddhism," *The Journal of the International Association of Buddhist Studies* 9 (1): 25–52.

Ingalls, D. H. H. (1954), "Śaṁkara's Arguments against the Buddhists," *Philosophy East and West* 3 (4): 291–306.

Jhā, G. (1986), *The Khaṇḍanakhaṇḍakhāḍya of Shri-Harṣa. Vol. I. Comprising Parichchheda I*, Delhi: Sri Satguru Publications.

Jinpa, T. (2022), *Science and Philosophy in the Indian Buddhist Classics. Volume 3: Philosophical Schools*, conceived and introduced by His Holiness the Dalai Lama, developed by the Compendium Compilation Committee, edited by T. Jinpa, translated by D. S. Lopez Jr. and H. S. Ham, introductory essay by D. S. Lopez Jr., Somerville: Wisdom Publications.

Jones, C. V. (2024), *The Buddhist Self. On Tathāgatagarbha and Ātman*, Honolulu: University of Hawai'i Press.

Joos, S. (2022), "The Role of the Ratnagotravibhāga in Tāranātha's *Great Madhyamaka Vehicle*," in K.-D. Mathes and C. Kemp (eds.), *Buddha Nature Across Asia*, 349–76, Vienna: Arbeitskreis für Tibetische und Buddhistische Studien Universität Wien.

Kajiyama, Y. (1998), *An Introduction to Buddhist Philosophy. An Annotated Translation of the Tarkabhāṣā of Mokṣākaragupta*, Reprint with Corrections in the Author's Hand, Vienna: Arbeitskreis für Tibetische und Buddhistische Studien Universität Wien.

Kant, I. (1998), *Critique of Pure Reason*, translated and edited by P. Guyer and A. W. Wood, Cambridge: Cambridge University Press.

Kapstein, M. T. (2019), "An Intoxication of Mouse Venom: Reading the *Guide*, Chapter 9," in J. C. Gold and D. S. Duckworth (eds.), *Readings of Śāntideva's Guide to Bodhisattva Practice (Bodhicaryāvatāra)*, 84–98, New York: Columbia University Press.

King, R. (1995), *Early Advaita Vedānta and Buddhism. The Mahāyāna Context of the Gauḍapādīya-kārikā*, Albany: SUNY Press.

Lamotte, É. (1973), *La Somme du Grand Véhicule d'Asaṅga (Mahāyānasaṃgraha). Tome 2, Traduction et Commentaire par É. Lamotte*, Louvain-la-Neuve: Institut Orientaliste, Université de Louvain.
Lindtner, C. (1981), "Atiśa's Introduction to the two Truths, and its Sources," *Journal of Indian Philosophy* 9 (2): 161–214.
Mathes, K.-D. (2008), *A Direct Path to the Buddha Within. Gö Lotsāwa's Mahāmudrā Interpretation of the Ratnagotravibhāga*, Boston: Wisdom Publications.
Mathes, K.-D. (2015), *A Fine Blend of Mahāmudrā and Madhyamaka. Maitrīpa's Collection of Texts on Non-conceptual Realization (Amanasikāra)*, Vienna: Österreichische Akademie der Wissenschaft.
Mayeda, S. (2006), *Śaṅkara's Upadeśasāhasrī. Volume I (Introduction, Text & Indices)*, translated, critically edited with Introduction and Indices by S. Mayeda. Foreword by W. N. Brown and H. Nakamura, Delhi: Motilal Banarsidass.
Nakamura, H. (1990), *A History of Early Vedānta Philosophy. Part One*, translated by Trevor Leggett, Sengaku Mayeda, Taitetz Unno, and others, Delhi: Motilal Banarsidass.
Nakamura, H. (2004), *A History of Early Vedānta Philosophy. Part Two*, edited by Sengaku Mayeda, translated by Hajime Nakamura, Trevor Leggett, and others, Delhi: Motilal Banarsidass.
Padmakara Translation Group (2004), *Introduction to the Middle Way. Chandrakirti's Madhyamakavatara with Commentary by Jamgön Mipham*, translated by the Padmakara Translation Group, Boston and London: Shambhala.
Padmakara Translation Group (2017), *The Wisdom Chapter. Jamgön Mipham's Commentary on the Ninth Chapter of 'The Way of the Bodhisattva'*, translated by the Padmakara Translation Group, Boulder, CO: Shambhala.
Panoli, V. (2011), *Prasthanathraya. Volume VI (Brahmasutra). With the complete text and Bhasyha in the original Sanskrit, English translation, explanatory notes and footnotes*, Kozhikode: Mathrubhumi Grandhavedi.
Pruden, L. M. (1991), *Abhidharmakośabhāṣyam of Vasubandhu. Volume IV*, translated into French by Louis de La Valleé Poussin. English Version by Leo M. Pruden, Berkeley: Asian Humanities Press.
Oldmeadow, P. R. (1994), "A Study of the Wisdom Chapter (Prajñāpāramitā Pariccheda) of the Bodhicaryāvatārapañjikā of Prajñākaramati." MA dissertation, The Australian National University.
Qvarnström, O. (2003), "Early Vedānta Philosophy preserved by the Jain Tradition: The Vedavādadvātriṃśikā of Siddhasena Divākara," in O. Ovarnström (ed.), *Jainism and Early Buddhism. Essays in Honour of Padmanabh S. Jaini*, 575–93, Berkeley: Asian Humanities Press.
Qvarnström, O. (2015), *Bhāviveka on Sāṃkhya and Vedānta. The Sāṃkhya and Vedānta Chapters of the Madhyamakahṛdayakārikā and Tarkajvālā*, Cambridge, MA: Harvard University Press.
Reeve, C. D. C. (2016), *Aristotle. Metaphysics*, translated with Introduction and Notes by C. D. C. Reeve, Indianapolis: Hackett Publishing Company.
Ruegg, D. S. (1963), "The Jo naṅ pas: A School of Buddhist Ontologists According tot he Grub Mtha' šel gyi me loṅ," *Journal of the American Oriental Society* 83 (1): 73–91.
Saha, S. (1997), "Translation and Elucidation of Definitions of Svaprakāśatva in Citsukha's Tattvapradīpikā," *Journal of Indian Philosophy and Religion* 2: 88–142.
Saitō, A. (2010), "An Inquiry into the Relationship between the *Śikṣāsamuccaya* and the *Bodhi(sattva)caryāvatāra*," *Studies in Indian Philosophy and Buddhism* 17 (3): 17–24.
Schmidt-Leukel, P. (2008), *Understanding Buddhism*, Edinburgh: Dunedin Academic Press.

Schmidt-Leukel, P. (2019), *Buddha Mind – Christ Mind. A Christian Commentary on the Bodhicaryāvatāra.* With a new translation by E. Steinkellner and C. Peck-Kubaczek, Leuven: Peeters.

Siderits, M. (2016), *Studies in Buddhist Philosophy*, edited by J. Westerhoff with the assistance of C. J. Jones, Oxford: Oxford University Press.

Silk, J. A. (2015), *Buddhist Cosmic Unity. An Edition, Translation and Study of the Anūnatvāpūrṇatvanirdeśaparivarta*, Hamburg: Hamburg University Press.

Stein, L. and N. Zangpo (2013), *Butön's History of Buddhism in India and Its Spread to Tibet. A Treasury of Priceless Scripture*, trans. by L. Stein and N. Zangpo, Boston and London: Snow Lion.

Sparham, G. (2022), *The Long Explanation of the Noble Perfection of Wisdom in One Hundred Thousand, Twenty-Five Thousand, and Eighteen Thousand Lines. Attributed to Daṃṣṭrasena (Diṣṭasena) or Vasubandhu*, translated by G. Sparham. Available online: https://84000.co/translation/toh3808.

Stcherbatsky, T. (1994), *Buddhist Logic. Vol. I*, Delhi: Motilal Banarsidass.

Sundaresan, V. (2003), "Conflicting Hagiographies and History: The Place of Śaṅkaravijaya Texts in Advaita Tradition," *International Journal of Hindu Studies* 4 (2): 109–84.

Takasaki, J. (2014), *A Study on the Ratnagotravibhāga (Uttaratantra). Being a Treatise on the Tathāgatagarbha Theory of Mahāyāna Buddhism*, Delhi: Motilal Banarsidass.

Timalsina, S. (2017), "Puruṣavāda: A Pre-Śaṅkara Monistic Philosophy as Critiqued by Mallavādin," *Journal of Indian Philosophy* 45: 939–59.

Todd, W. L. (2013), *The Ethics of Śaṅkara and Śāntideva. A Selfless Response to an Illusory World*, Farnham and Burlington, VT: Ashgate.

Vetter, T. (1979), *Studien zur Lehre und Entwicklung Śaṅkaras*, Vienna: Institut für Indologie der Universität Wien.

Völker, F. (2020), *Philosophie der Nondualität. Religionshistorische Einordnung und philosophische Kritik der Buddhismus-Interpretation David R. Loys*, Freiburg and Munich: Karl Alber.

Völker, F. (2023), "The Plurality of Nonduality. Toward a tripartite Typology," in J. P. Sydnor and A. J. Watson (eds.), *Nondualism. An Interreligious Exploration*, 51–70, Lanham, MD: Lexington Books.

Westerhoff, J. (2010), *The Dispeller of Disputes. Nāgārjuna's Vigrahavyāvartanī*, translation and commentary by J. Westerhoff, Oxford: Oxford University Press.

Westerhoff, J. (2016), "On the Nihilist Interpretation of Madhyamaka," *Journal of Indian Philosophy* 44: 337–76.

Whaling, F. (1979), "Śaṅkara and Buddhism," *Journal of Indian Philosophy* 7 (1): 1–42.

Williams, P. (1995), "General Introduction," in Śāntideva, *The Bodhicaryāvatāra*, translated with an Introduction and Notes by K. Crosby and A. Skilton, vii–xxvi, Oxford: Oxford University Press.

Williams, P. (2000), *Studies in the Philosophy of the Bodhicaryāvatāra. Altruism and Reality.* Delhi: Motilal Banarsidass.

Williams, P. (2008), *Mahāyāna Buddhism. The Doctrinal Foundations*, London and New York: Routledge.

Wood, T. E. (1991), *Mind Only: A Philosophical and Doctrinal Analaysis of the Vijñānavāda*, Honolulu: University of Hawai'i Press.

Wright, D. (1877), *History of Nepāl*, translated from the Parbatiyā by M. S. S. Singh and P. S. Gunānand, Cambridge: Cambridge University Press.

11

Learning To Be Empty

Śāntideva's Wisdom on Creaturely No Self

S. Mark Heim

Christian theologians have learned to seek the very best they can find in philosophy, history, and science for use in their work, whether or not authors in these disciplines accept Christian assumptions. The practice of comparative theology extends a similar principle to explore major texts from various religions as key sources for Christian reflection, with coordinate willingness to be instructed in the meaning of those texts by those at the heart of their relevant traditions (see Clooney 2010; Cornille 2019).[1] This exchange of religious wisdom among those ready to place themselves at least partially within other traditions' spheres of influence may be viewed as an element "of a global religious *ressourcement* and re-foundation" (Sheridan 2007: 8).

The form of this mutual influence may be modern, but its substance is ancient. Though Buddhism is the elder tradition, its Mahāyāna branches date roughly from the same time as the development of Christianity. Among the crucial areas for development of Mahāyāna were Northwest India (today's Pakistan and Afghanistan) and the Silk Road of Central Asia, areas of known interaction among Buddhists, Manichaeans, Zoroastrians, Christians, and (later) Muslims. During the same eighth century when Śāntideva lived and wrote, a stele was erected near Xian in Tang Dynasty China commemorating the arrival in 635 of a delegation of Christians from what is now Iraq and Iran. These established a monastery and began translating biblical scriptures and Christian texts into Chinese. Just some five years earlier than that arrival, the Chinese Buddhist monk Xuanzang traveled the same route in the opposite direction, headed to Central Asia and India on his famous search for Buddhist texts to bring back and translate (see Wriggins 2004). In the many monasteries Xuanzang visited, he encountered the rising tide of Mahāyāna thought that would soon be crystallized powerfully by Śāntideva in the *Bodhicaryāvatarā*.[2]

1 See also the series of Christian commentaries on non-Christian sacred texts published by Eerdmans and Peeters. In regard to Buddhism, see Keenan and Klepinger Keenan 2011; Lefebure and Feldmeier 2011; Schmidt-Leukel 2019.

2 There are two Sanskrit titles for the same work. The Tibetan version uses the longer Sanskrit title, *Bodhisattvacaryāvatāra*, or "The Entrance to the Way of the Bodhisattva." The shorter Sanskrit title (*Bodhicaryāvatāra*) is more widely used, with the sense of "Entrance to the Path of Awakening." See Śāntideva 2006: 195.

Just as the Qumran and Nag Hammadi discoveries cast new light on Jewish and Christian history, similar finds in Central Asia have had a similar (if much less publicized) impact on the histories of several traditions. Around 1900, a monk in Dun-huang, China, discovered a sealed cave with a rich collection of texts dating from the fifth to the eleventh centuries, mainly from Buddhist writers but including others. Among the others were Christian texts composed in China, reflective of a church there that was deeply transformed by engagement with Buddhism and Taoism.[3] These Dunhuang manuscripts include what may be the earliest known copies of the *Bodhicaryāvatāra*.[4] Śāntideva's texts and those Christian ones slumbered in neighborly anonymity for centuries. They represent a time of mutual awareness that our contemporary interreligious conversation may only be reinventing. "One could almost speak of a Christian-Buddhist dialogue being conducted in Central Asia one thousand years ago, Christians and Buddhists not only living together but being in constant interaction" (Gillman and Klimkeit 1999: 206). Comparative theological engagement with Śāntideva is not an alien imposition, but a renewed opportunity.

In this chapter I focus on one theme to illustrate how Śāntideva may be read as a constructive teacher for Christian theology. The example applies his explications of Mahāyāna emptiness to Christian understandings of creatureliness. These are often posed as contraries. Terrence Tilley, a prominent Roman Catholic theologian, summarized his own study of the *Bodhicaryāvatāra* with the conclusion that "Buddhists are not creatures. Christians are" (Tilley 2002: 2). To put it differently, we could say that Buddhists are empty and Christians are not. At every point it matters that Buddhists find selves to have no intrinsic nature and Christians find persons grounded in a divine interpersonal source. This is an enduring difference, but an often subtle one. We could say that it is the primary learning curve of Buddhists to learn to be empty and of Christians to learn to be creatures, against the strong resistant currents of ignorance and sin, respectively. The root teaching for this Buddhist learning includes the insights of no-self, emptiness, and impartial benevolence toward all beings, and the root teaching for the Christian learning includes the creator God, divine-human incarnation, and loving communion of all creation with God.

Of course, a flat view of selves that concludes "Buddhists, no; Christians, yes" oversimplifies.[5] Buddhist thinkers hedge the ultimate truth of *anātman*, the no-self teaching, with recognition of the significance of relative, impermanent persons. This phenomenal self is addressed and assumed throughout Śāntideva's writing. Indeed, the vivid personalism of his style exemplifies a bodhisattva's skillful technique, eloquently exploring what it is to be a self in order to wean us from captivity to the category.

[3] A recent translation of these texts can be found in Nicolini-Zani 2022.

[4] These three manuscripts of the *Bodhicaryāvatāra* preserve a version shorter than the later canonical text, and that shorter version may be closer to the original. See "Translators' Introduction," in Śāntideva 1996: xxvii–xlii.

[5] Buddhist interpretations of *anātman* are very nuanced about just what sort of self is denied, reflected in different schools of thought in the tradition. Christian tradition has engaged in a long interaction with other sources to shape its perspective on the self, a process addressed in different ways in John Zizioulas's contention that Trinitarian thought reshaped the understanding of the human person (Zizioulas 1985), Krister Stendahl's famous essay on Paul and the introspective conscience of the West (Stendahl 1976), and Charles Taylor's magisterial study *Sources of the Self* (Taylor 1992).

Though Śāntideva writes *from* the wisdom of the emptiness of the self, he writes with great sensitivity *to* the self and *about* selves.

Christian affirmation of the significance of persons has its own complexities. Some central Christian beliefs—the Trinity, the incarnational union of the divine and the human in Jesus, the union of Christ and the believer, the *koinonia* (communion) of Christians with each other—appear to violate common notions of the self. These convictions require at the least a porousness to persons, such that three of them in God are also one, such that Christ is one person with two natures, and such that the one that is me can also encompass Christ in me. Christian theology has an internal need to deconstruct the apparent self if it is to make sense of its central teachings. This complexity in selves and creatures means that Buddhist and Christian perspectives intersect in interesting ways, ways that can only fascinate a Christian reader of Śāntideva. Being a creature means to be empty in many important ways, ways where Christians have much to learn from Śāntideva.

I will consider three areas where Śāntideva's teaching can enrich a Christian reader's understanding. The first point reflects an agreement that creatures are not what Śāntideva's self is not: both lack essential being. Christians can learn in the vein of *diagnostic* emptiness. The second point has to do with a convergence in the understanding of the sinful creature and of the reified self Śāntideva describes. This clears a path for what may be the most pervasive form of learning for Christian creatures, the application of antidote or *therapeutic* emptiness. The third point is not quite an agreement, but a deep resonance between emptiness as part of the intrinsic goodness of creatures and emptiness as nirvanic bliss. Emptiness is a doorway, whether to non-dual realization or full communion, a *redemptive* emptiness.

1. Contingent creatures and empty selves

Śāntideva vividly expounds the manner in which selves do not exist. What selves lack is *svabhāva* or self-existence. According to Śāntideva, to have *svabhāva* would mean to be without any external causation and to be permanently existing. There is no such continuing, unchanged, single essence entity.[6] Selves may exist in many other ways, but not in this one. The way they *do* exist is as mental constructions, as the mutual falling together of causally conditioned, impermanent phenomena. This is true of the mind itself, which is not a "constructor" standing outside this condition but a particular aggregate of constructions.[7]

Śāntideva lays the foundation for a bodhisattva's unrestricted altruism on this teaching of no self, arguing that it is finally impossible to distinguish between one

[6] This is such a high bar for the reality of the self (it would have to come from no cause but itself and be eternal) that a Christian may wonder whether any thing but God is even a candidate for such existence. By the *svabhāva* criterion, either God/gods exist or nothing does.

[7] There are various schools of Buddhist thought on the vexed question of how to treat the special case of minds, so closely tied to the question of selves: "realist" views that the mind is empty but the elements that make it up are real, views that phenomenal awareness is real but a subject of awareness is not, views that mind is as empty as everything else. These are the sophisticated nuances at issue in Madhyamaka and Yogācāra perspectives.

person and another because they are all equally insubstantial. If selves have no inherent qualities by which they exist, there can be no distinction in how I treat them:

> All sufferings are without an owner, because they are not different.
> They should be warded off simply because they are suffering.
>
> BCA 8:102[8]

This means that there is no ontological distinction between persons. They are interdependent, and even our feelings and our consciousness cannot be fully contained within the boundaries of one entity. We are bound up with other people. Śāntideva drives this home in a matchless way, with humorous comments on our efforts to draw a line around one self separate from others:

> If I do not protect them because I am not afflicted by their suffering,
> why do I protect my body from the suffering of a future body, which is not my pain?
>
> BCA 8:97

For Christians, to be a creature is, by definition, to lack self-existence. Athanasius wrote that God granted humanity a share of the divine image, "seeing that by the principle of its [humanity's] own coming into being it would not be able to endure eternally" (Athanasius 2011: 57). Creatures are precisely those whose existence does not arise from their own power and whose continued existence is not in their control. What is more than impermanent in them is loaned from God, not an intrinsic possession. Creaturely life is conditioned on proximate causes and materials that are themselves contingent on a free act of divine will. This looks like chapter and verse from the Buddhist teaching of dependent co-origination. The Protestant theologian Karl Barth stated this emphatically. Humanity "without God is not; [and] has neither being nor existence." Humanity without God "is not an object of knowledge" (Barth 2004: 345). Barth was clear that the creature's true "nature" is, on its own terms, already empty. So, the falsification or "negation" of that nature lay only in a kind of reification, acting as though it had a solidity it lacks.

Interestingly, one of the pioneers of modern Buddhist–Christian dialogue, Thomas Merton, found himself stimulated on this path precisely by his reading of Barth (Merton 1966). Merton summarized what he found there that resonated so powerfully with his Buddhist learning: "The great joke is this: having a self that is to be taken seriously, that is to be proved, free, right, logical, consistent, beautiful, successful and in a word 'not absurd'" (quoted in Williams 2008). Merton is deeply moved by Barth's recognition that "the self before God is not *serious*, it is *groundless*. It is not something that exists in its own density and solidity"—as Williams (2008) summarizes Merton's views. Much of Śāntideva's most vivid writing in fact treats the self like a bad joke: "If

[8] Unless otherwise noted, all text citations from the *Bodhicaryāvatāra* are taken from the translation by Vesna and Alan Wallace (Śāntideva 1997).

even at a small danger fear arises on account of great attachment to oneself, why would one not abhor that self like a terrifying enemy?" (BCA 8:121).

According to Christian teachings, human selves lack the same kind of reality that Buddhism says they lack: autonomous self-existence. Buddhist analysis correctly concludes that any self-understanding constructed on such an assumption is mistaken and unsatisfactory. Creatureliness and no-self share this theme of impermanence. "All are from the dust, and to dust we shall return" (Ecclesiastes 3:20). On Ash Wednesday Christians carry the mark of the grave on their foreheads, just as Buddhist "corpse" meditations are steeped in this mortal transience. Śāntideva states it trenchantly:

> Seeing a few corpses in a charnel ground, you are repelled,
> Yet you delight in a village which is a charnel ground crowded with moving corpses.
>
> BCA 8:70

That Buddhist analysis discovers no self-existent, eternal entities in the entire phenomenal world comes as no surprise in this respect.[9] What Buddhists find nowhere, most Christians likewise find nowhere, except perhaps in God.[10] What would we expect to find in an instant of pure meditative awareness focused entirely on our mental contents? Śāntideva tells us we will find sensation, succession, distraction, emotion, intention . . . but no permanent thing doing the experiencing. There is no Christian reason that a creature contemplating its interiority in isolation would find anything else as the content of immediate awareness.[11] From this perspective, Buddhist wisdom has the deepest word on what it is to be a creature, standing alone and rigorously analyzed from the perspective of the emptiness of intrinsic existence.[12]

2. Sinful creature and reified self

Buddhists and Christians agree that there is nothing intrinsically wrong with the non-essential character of selves or creatures as just described. But something negative does follow from this, in which selves become sources of suffering, because mistakenly reified, and creatures become sinful, because their relations with others are broken and distorted. In either case, the perspectives of selves and creatures become a kind of

9 Indeed, for a full-scale argument about this one would have to turn to Zoroastrians, Manichaeans, or Gnostics who would hold that there are human souls that are in fact uncreated pieces of eternal spirit, permanent ontological entities.

10 God at first appears an obvious instance of *svabhāva* existence. But a Trinitarian God, a co-inherent communion, is resistant to that characterization as well. For further discussion of this, see Heim 2019: 82–124.

11 One area where this question is asked is in the monastic dialogue between Buddhists and Christians, and the similarities in contemplative experience described there would seem to support this perspective (see Mitchell and Wiseman 1997).

12 Similarly, Aquinas accepted Aristotle's philosophy as an account of our humanity in its natural state, derived from analysis of the teleology of our life in the world. To Aquinas, Aristotle had the nearly last word on what it was to be a creature and know one's self as a creature, by reference to nature and reason alone.

captivity. Christians hope to rectify this captivity by uniting the individual outlook with that of others, through communion with God, while Buddhists hope to rectify it by seeing through the supposed source of that outlook itself.

There is profound overlap in Buddhist and Christian takes on the difficulties created by the mistaken self, sinful or reified. Christians see our vision of the world as unsatisfactory not because there is an "I" that is doing the looking, but because selfishness, feelings of inferiority, and broken relations distort how we see, yielding twisted projections of ourselves and others. Buddhists see the problem in the location of the seer *as* an "I" among others, an assumption that produces the parallel impression of real selves and others which actually have no objective referents at all. Precisely because of the divergence in these accounts, Christians can benefit from distinctive Buddhist therapeutic approaches.

Take as an example our tendency to treat others in a highly reductive manner, to mutual harm. We take a few fleeting impressions—our knowledge of someone's job, their manner of dress, their name—and spin these into assumptions that become the basis for dismissive behavior: "That's only an old woman." Such highly limiting pictures of others correlate with an equally limited impression of who "I" am. Perhaps, in the case of the negative stereotype of the woman, this involves an "I" anxiously identified with an inevitably declining body, frightened to see the prospect of that decline reflected back to me in the person of the aged woman. This process leads me to reify this person as hostile or dangerous (because of the fear I associate with her) and treat her badly (perhaps evoking animosity in turn). This example illustrates how my mental life can become a constant play of phantoms, imaginations about what fabricated versions of other people may think, threaten, or promise for my imagined version of myself. Buddhist teaching would say this is unreality piled on unreality, starting with the unreality of the "I" that is the reference point for the whole exercise.

Remedy is sought at the source—the mind and its self-reification. In BCA 5:2, Śāntideva says, "Untamed, wild elephants do not inflict as much harm in this world as the unleashed elephant of the mind." For these harms, Śāntideva has many concrete prescriptions and antidotes. He tells us there is a tremendous leveling power in the no-self insight, which blurs not only the lines between people but the entire ownership of experience. Taking selves out of our stories allows a great sense of identification: all minds are the same. It also fosters clarification about what is happening phenomenally with us. We think, "that is anger talking," "this is the effect of a former trauma," "that is the expression of a false assumption," instead of attributing everything in our experience to the intentional orchestration of substantial agents. Giving up an obsession with blaming or changing other selves shifts energy to concrete management of emotions and more direct control over the suffering experienced as mine.

The introspective, meditative practices of Buddhism reflect this wisdom, whose most basic form might be the observational disjunction of our mind-generated projections from their immediate control over our behavior: "When one sees one's own mind to be attached or to be repulsed, then one should neither act nor speak, but remain still like a block of wood" (BCA 5:48). This apparently bland injunction from Śāntideva presupposes the extraordinary capacity to become aware of and suspend that very connection.

There is liberating effect in the analytical application of no-self as an antidote to our egocentrism. To directly see that the "I" whose dominance over others I have been laboriously asserting, or whose end I have been fearing in death, or whose inadequacies I am so ashamed of is literally an episodic phenomenon is a relief. To "let go" of the search for an independently existing self, whose reality I have honestly come to doubt is, likewise, freeing.[13] Buddhism is not just therapeutically helpful but analytically correct in a fundamental sense. Sometimes the shortest path to overcoming our mental and social ills is not sorting out what is bad or good, but dispelling illusions about what is real. Christianity and Buddhism agree there is value in practices that disrupt the presumed objectivity of the unreal selves we project, whether the disruption comes through confession and repentance or mental analysis. Śāntideva's application of emptiness as antidote to specific negative emotions, such as anger, are directly beneficial for Christians.

There are manifest goods that come from the capacity to accept the momentary emptiness of phenomena. This is particularly true, I believe, in dealing with moment-by-moment bodily and emotional suffering and pain. First, practice of immediate attention to inner mental processes helps diminish what we might call superadded pain. To whatever physical pain is experienced, the focus on selves can gratuitously project even more, adding fear and anxiety about suffering I imagine in the future to that I experience now. Second, it offers concrete bodily relaxation and feedback practices that mitigate the generation of physical pain. These practices today are increasingly detached from Buddhist settings and presented in a purely medical setting. They are also those for which it may be easiest to find direct Christian correlatives in forms of repetitive prayer. Third, for more extensive practice, this meditation further diminishes the felt or "received" pain, both by weakening our exclusive identification with the self that registers the pain and by disaggregating that pain into its smallest, momentary sensory phenomena.

The condition of captivity to a world of our own making, which we then further assume is objective reality, is a generative disposition the theological tradition calls original sin. Buddhism holds that ordinary people are born with "mental obscurations carried over from previous lives" and then compound these with "speculative distortions" acquired in the course of their lives (A. Wallace in Dalai Lama 1994: 140 n.2). Buddhism calls this state ignorance. It will never allow us to flourish until it is corrected. What Christians call sinners are creatures who have forgotten they are no-thing (in the *svabhāva* sense), whose desires are distorted because their constitutive relations are broken. Since Augustine, it has been common to hold that evil has nothing substantial to work with, that all we call evil is literal negation or else disordered good.[14] In this sense, the sinful is an offshoot of the unreal.

The sinful disposition of taking nothing for something manifests as pride, in which we give our individual selves priority over all others, or as abnegation, in which we

[13] Paul Knitter (2009: 74–91) writes affectingly of the way this approach freed his own thinking about the plausibility of life after death and mooted his discomfort with the presumptive selfishness of an interest in individual continuation.

[14] See Leo Lefebure's (1993: 115–40) fine discussion of Augustine and Buddhist emptiness.

deny the value of those same individual selves. Both abusive assertion and destructive abnegation rest on something more basic: the condition in which I simply take my eyes' view of the world as the true world. Whether that view exalts my ego or discounts it, it is the verdict rendered by my own perspective that I take to be unconditioned and determinative. There is nothing wrong with looking at the world from my perspective. But presuming an autonomous existence behind that perspective, and thereby validating its absolute direction of my behavior, is the source of much suffering and evil.[15]

Christians rarely resist importing into the Buddhist account of things something that is purposely not there. We think that our limited impressions lead us to have a false image of the other person, as opposed to an appreciation for *who they actually are*. But it is that notion also, the supposition of an authentic self, that the teaching seeks to dispel. We readily picture a contrast between a false me and a real me, an unreal image of my neighbor and one closer to the truth. But from Śāntideva's perspective any notion of a true self or actual neighbor is mistaken in a structural way (though one projection may be much better than another, because less destructive).

As I suggested earlier, there is a real divergence here, but it is not that a "true self" is hidden in the ontological separateness that Buddhism denies. The created person, with its authentic and enduring value, is not to be found locked in an eternal self-subsistence, within the boundaries of a self, but *among* and between others. The fecundity of creation and the continual outflow of new and unique persons is in Christian view a fundamental good, an overpouring of relational possibility, where each creature is constituted by relation (and so no-self in that sense) and fulfilled through relation (and so enduring in significance). Positive selflessness means curbing the priority of the self as compared to other selves or even giving away the self completely as a gift of solidarity with others, but not "losing it" in the sense of literally not being able to find it.

Śāntideva is noted among Buddhists for his willingness to "lean in" to self-projections for therapeutic or tantric purposes, despite the dangers that this may inflame the illusion of substantive selves. This makes him particularly accessible to Christian readers, for whom the approach is less paradoxical. For instance, one famous feature of the *Bodhicaryāvatāra* is the exercise of "exchanging self and others" in which the author invites readers to imagine themselves from the perspective of other persons:

> Take others—lower, higher, equal—as yourself,
> Identify yourself as "other."
> Then without another thought,
> Immerse yourself in envy, pride, and rivalry.
>
> BCA 8:140

For Śāntideva this practice of considering ourselves as an other, and giving vent to the grievances or dislike "we" evoke in those around us, fosters distaste for our supposed

[15] See the Orthodox writer Pavel Florensky who describes original sin as the failure to recognize the self's identity in the "participatory nexus" set by the Trinity, a failure that leads to the construction of a static self, discussed in Mitchell 1991: 47.

self and breaks down egocentric attachments. It is an engine for humility. Christians naturally extend it as a vision of positive communion as well. Indeed, the Jesuit missionary to Tibet, Ippolito Desideri, translated the second of the two great Christian commandments into Tibetan (with explicit awareness of Śāntideva) as a command to count "all other human beings worthy of being cherished like yourself, as if you exchanged [self and other]" (Lopez and Jinpa 2017: 237).[16] From this perspective, time out from filling our minds with our own limited projections is also "time in" to receive balancing input from others, and particularly from God.

We could sum this up by saying for creatures there is joy in being nothing. If Christians see no-self as mainly a preliminary insight, paving the way to deeper relations and more authentic personhood, they are taught by Śāntideva to appreciate the blessings of this insight itself, the way that it can eliminate at the source projections that cause suffering to us and to others. Creaturely emptiness is at base neither sin nor estrangement, but gift, the nothingness that makes space for freedom and creativity. To turn toward it is not necessarily an act of pride or even self-critique, but can reflect gratitude and grace. Our creaturely no-self, our nothingness-on-our-own, is a "very present help in trouble" (Psalms 46:1) as well as a source of mortification and humility.

3. Creaturely redemption: Nirvanic emptiness and divine immanence

A Buddhist would probably say that while Christians effectively grasp many of the negative implications of creaturely emptiness, their understanding of its benefits is severely limited. "Emptiness" is, in Buddhist telling, both a deconstructive insight, dispelling our reified projections (the emptiness of "realities") and a luminous, unconditioned ground realized in liberation from ignorance (the reality of emptiness). What Christian understanding seems to lack most is an expectation of emptiness as a radiant positive final end. In addition to a diagnostic emptiness (the non-essential being of creatures) with its therapeutic application of antidotes to misguided reifications of selves, Śāntideva commends a supreme, non-dual realization as itself the solution, final or transcendent liberation.

Chapter 9 in the *Bodhicaryāvatāra*, the "wisdom chapter," offers one long meditation on emptiness as the nature of enlightenment. Saṃsāric existence is not other than nirvanic realization. The mind

> which is not in the body nor anywhere else,
> neither intermingled nor somewhere separate, is nothing.
> Therefore, sentient beings are by nature liberated.
>
> BCA 9:103

[16] From Desideri's "Essence of the Christian Religion." The translator underlines that Desideri had Śāntideva clearly in mind in this phrasing. See Lopez and Jinpa 2017: 237. Lopez's commentary is found on pp. 184–5.

Non-dualism is a constant theme of Buddhist–Christian discussion, particularly the question of what, if anything, in Christian theology and faith might be thought similar to the nature of enlightenment or of reality itself by Buddhist accounts.[17] Christians tend to perceive Buddhist non-dualism as subtractive, remaining when all distinctions are peeled away, a unity achieved in negation. Christian non-dualism, by contrast, is framed as "excessive" interbeing, realized when boundaries between selves or between God and creatures are overflowed.

Buddhist non-duality has a "never was otherwise" character. Both creaturely emptiness and the immanence of the divine energies are dimensions that Christian theology affirms underlie existence at every moment. But Christian non-duality has a history (it stems from creation) and a model (the life of the Trinity). The doctrine of creation *ex nihilo* in this sense already expresses a kind of non-dualism, one Rowan Williams calls "non-dual non-identity" (Williams 2018: xiv).[18] The primordial model of non-dual non-identity is the Trinity, which while it does not obviously violate the Buddhist strictures on "being" yet does not fully meet Buddhist standards for unconditioned emptiness.

Despite these differences, Śāntideva prompts us to ask whether emptiness is part and parcel of what it means to be a creature, even in the creature's obedience and fulfillment, what we may call redemptive emptiness. The classical Christian itinerary of spiritual practice includes the stages of purgation, illumination, and mystical union with God. If the elements of diagnostic and therapeutic emptiness we have reviewed figure in purgation and illumination, may there also be a form of creaturely emptiness realized in union?

Buddhist meditation instruction makes clear that although the practice may occasion or be accompanied by insights for worldly affairs, even by the exercise of supernormal powers, these things are not the primary purpose of the practice. They are secondary to wisdom and enlightenment.[19] In a Christian context, elements like guidance or healing are legitimate primary aims for prayer or meditation. Christians tend to see our mind space almost exclusively as a site for encounter and communication. But Christian practitioners testify to stretches of contemplative practice that do not fit those forms. One can simply practice the presence of God, a state without any separate consciousness of God as an object of attention, because it lacks discursive consciousness *as* a self at all.

We are well aware of types of experience that are not communicative, that involve profound self-forgetfulness through unity with a wider process. Play, sexual ecstasy, athletic absorption, becoming "lost" in nature, attentive perception in making or contemplating art—these are all instances of intense awareness without either

[17] See, for instance Coob, Ives, and Abe 1990; Nishitani 1982; Panikkar 1989. See also Perry Schmidt-Leukel's (2019: 478–85) review of the different Buddhist and Christian approaches to emptiness in comparison with God.

[18] This is Williams's (2028: xiv) take on Nicholas of Cusa's designation of God as *non aliud*, the "non-other" or "not another thing."

[19] In some of its Western forms, Buddhist practice may be applied in a manner that reverses this principle: the effects on health, productivity, creativity are the primary purpose for the practice. See, for instance, Donald Lopez's (2008) critique of this from a Buddhist perspective.

contrasting identity or explicit communication of information. We can regard these as glimpses of, or analogies to, what Christians may regard as "bare awareness" of the divine or Buddhists as unconditioned, luminous mind.

By analogy to human pre-conscious awareness, we can imagine the divine mind having an immediate apprehension of the universe from within. At this level, God's perception would be a "view from everywhere," reflecting God's implicit presence in all of creation, a consciousness with no active separated subject (just as our non-conscious modes of awareness need have no explicit subject), but one permeated with beneficence and peace. This is a mode of God's presence in and to the world. A receptive sentient mind might commune with this awareness, which is always available underneath the business of communicative consciousness. This awareness could be likened to the kinds of sensitivity that exist in mental or physical processes below the plane of conscious thought, such as the implicit sense of location in space or an unconscious registering of internal bodily conditions. This participation in the divine presence or in the divine energies has the character of a non-dual identity, an identity only possible *through* the creaturely emptiness we have previously discussed.

It is the apophatic strand within Christian theology that most directly suggests a oneness with God that includes the dimension of emptiness. I am thinking particularly of the Eastern Orthodox Church's theological understanding of salvation as *theosis* or "divinization." That divinization is a union which is participation or sharing in the divine life. We become "by grace (that is to say, in the divine energies), all that God is by nature, save only identity of nature" (Lossky 1976: 87). The saved are "enlightened ones" who have realized the fullness of the divine image that overflows into their own life. This may be the closest Christian parallel to the non-dualism of Buddha-nature, which is an underlying oneness with emptiness. Yet the Christian non-dualism is a participation, not an exclusive identity.[20]

Deification is an overflowing of divine immanence, an immanence that is always in place within all of nature and every creature. Eastern Orthodox theological traditions characterize this immanence as the sharing of the divine energies. The divine energies are communicable aspects of God's life, distributed into creatures in the act of creation. These energies permeate all things, particularly all animate things. "All things are permeated and maintained in being by the uncreated energies of God, and so all things are a theophany that mediates" divine presence (Kallistos 1995: 118). This vision of the divine energies is simply a realization of what is always present, a removal of obstacles in our sight. As a blade of grass may be thought to have Buddha-nature, so it may be thought to be alive with the glory of God.[21]

[20] For a sophisticated exploration of this question, including elements in Tibetan Buddhist tradition that could draw the parallel more deeply, see Cattoi 2008.

[21] As a concrete expression of this, see the photography of Christopher Burkett at http://christopherburkett.com/ An Eastern Orthodox Christian, Burkett believes that as these divine energies manifest with the qualities of light, it should be possible under the right circumstances to capture something of them in photography. He writes: "All of our world, each living cell, every stone and drop of water, even the air and light around us, reflects and mirrors the glory and presence of the Creator and calls us to respond with wonder and praise . . . The purpose of my photography is to provide a brief, if somewhat veiled, glimpse into that clear and brilliant world of light and power" (Christopher Burkett, "Artist's Statement").

The uncreated energies are a universal immanence of God in all nature, a universal participation of all nature in God. These energies are particularly signified by light.[22] Representation of these energies usually takes non-personal form, as in the light surrounding Christ at the Transfiguration, the fire of the burning bush, or tongues of fire at Pentecost.[23] All creation, sentient or not, carries this charge of the divine presence. Orthodox theology directly refers unusual realizations of this reality to mystical experience, a wordless and non-conceptual unity with the divine life. This is a kind of bare awareness of divine immanence, a luminous consciousness without anything to be conscious of, because the creature is wholly one with the divine energies. "One must be raised above created being, and abandon all contact with creatures in order to attain to union with the 'rays of the Godhead'" (Dionysius the Areopagite, quoted in Lossky 1976: 89). Creaturely no-self is the prior condition that makes this participation possible.

Some Christian theologians see three steps on the apophatic way.[24] The first is an intellectual one, in which we recognize and affirm the inadequacy of our concepts to grasp the divine (and even, finally, nature). One could say we *know* the emptiness of our concepts. The second goes beyond cognitive recognition to something more existential, an operative stillness of our mind's projections, a form of prayer that does not use concepts. This is an apophatic *experience*, "a culminating state of prayer, as a feeling in the darkness of a presence of God and as a total quietness of the mind . . . The mind reaches the abyss which separates its knowledge from God but is still here, on the human side" (Stăniloae 2002: 242). In the third step, to continue the metaphor, the mind is "carried off by God, it goes over there, to the vision of the divine light" (Stăniloae 2002: 242). In the second step, one encounters God in emptiness, but in the third step one is suffused with the superabundance of the divine life in the emptiness of union, an apophatic *gift*. The one is a true grasp of the depths of one's incomprehension and the other a manifestation of the inexpressibility of what is received.

As therapeutic no-self meditative attainments are rooted in the true emptiness of the creature, so the unconditioned and non-conceptual nirvanic ideal points Christians toward the mysteries of divine immanence. In the nuances of the apophatic way we find something that can begin to engage the sophistication of Śāntideva's articulation of the various levels at which emptiness can be understood: the illusion of a dream compared to conventional truth, of conventional truth compared to wisdom, and of even Buddhist teaching compared to nirvanic attainment.

[22] The fourteenth-century theological controversy over *hesychasm*, mystical practices associated with the divine energies in the form of light, were as formative in Eastern Christianity as the Reformation in the West (see Meyendorff 1974: 76–7). In this connection, it is interesting that the Chinese Christian church of the Tang Dynasty adopted the self-designation "luminous religion." In that Buddhist and Taoist context, Christian thinkers appear to have explored the same themes of divine immanence that arise in contemporary dialogue with Buddhism. See "Text E: Book on Profound and Mysterious Blessedness" in Nicolini-Zani 2022.

[23] In many cases the word "glory" carries these overtones. For instance, in Romans 6:4, Jesus is said to have been raised from the dead through "the glory of the Father." This can be taken to mean by the power of God, but it also connotes a concrete medium for action through sharing the radiance or energies of God.

[24] For what follows, see Stăniloae 2002: 237–44.

I have briefly tried to indicate how a Christian reader may be affected by encounter with Śāntideva, in three modes of reflection on emptiness. I have reviewed ways Christians may learn to be empty *as* creatures lacking self-existence. I explored the therapeutic insights and practices that flow from learning to be freed *from* reified projections that produce harm. Finally, I considered what it might mean to be empty *for* the indwelling of divine immanence. These are ways Christians can be tutored by Śāntideva's teaching.

At the close of the ninth chapter, Śāntideva asks:

> When shall I respectfully teach emptiness and the accumulation of merit—in terms of conventional truth and without reification—to those whose views are reified?
>
> BCA 9:167

Śāntideva would no doubt find this paper, with its Christian terms, to be bound to reified views. I yet hope that it represents one fulfillment of his aspiration to teach emptiness to those with such views, a respectful response to his respectful teaching.

References

Athanasius (2011), *On the Incarnation*, translated by J. Behr. Yonkers, NY: St. Vladimir's Seminary Press.

Barth, K. (2004), *Church Dogmatics*, translated by T. F. Torrance, edited by G. W. Bromiley. Vol. III, Part 2, London & New York: T. & T. Clark.

Cattoi, T. (2008), "What Has Chalcedon to Do with Lhasa? John Keenan's and Lai Pai-Chiu's Reflections on Classical Christology and the Possible Shape of a Tibetan Theology of Incarnation," *Buddhist-Christian Studies* 28: 13–25.

Clooney, F. X. (2010), *Comparative Theology: Deep Learning across Religious Borders*, Malden, MA: Wiley-Blackwell.

Cobb, J. B., C. Ives, and M. Abe, eds. (1990), *The Emptying God: A Buddhist-Jewish-Christian Conversation*, Maryknoll, NY: Orbis Books.

Cornille, C. (2019), *Meaning and Method in Comparative Theology*, Hoboken, NJ: Wiley-Blackwell.

Dalai Lama (1994), *Transcendent Wisdom*, translated, edited, and annotated by A. Wallace (2nd edition), Ithaca, NY: Snow Lion.

Gillman, I. and H.-J. Klimkeit (1999), *Christians in Asia before 1500*, Ann Arbor: University of Michigan Press.

Heim, S. M. (2019), *Crucified Wisdom: Theological Reflection on Christ and the Bodhisattva*, New York: Fordham University Press.

Kallistos (Timothy Ware) (1995), *The Orthodox Way* (Revised edition), Crestwood, NY: St. Vladimir's Seminary Press.

Keenan, J. P. and L. Klepinger Keenan (2011), *I Am / No Self: A Christian Commentary on the Heart Sutra*, Grand Rapids: Eerdmans.

Knitter, P. F. (2009), *Without Buddha I Could Not Be a Christian*, Oxford: Oneworld.

Lefebure, L. D. (1993), *The Buddha and the Christ: Explorations in Buddhist and Christian Dialogue*, Maryknoll, NY: Orbis Books.

Lefebure, L. D. and P. Feldmeier (2011), *The Path of Wisdom: A Christian Commentary of the Dhammapada*, Grand Rapids: Eerdmans.
Lopez, D. S. (2008), *Buddhism & Science: A Guide for the Perplexed*, Chicago: University of Chicago Press.
Lopez, D. S. and T. Jinpa (2017), *Dispelling the Darkness: A Jesuit's Quest for the Soul of Tibet*, Cambridge, MA: Harvard University Press.
Lossky, Vladimir (1976) *The Mystical Theology of the Eastern Church*, Crestwood, NY: St. Vladimir's Seminary Press.
Merton, Thomas (1966), *Conjectures of a Guilty Bystander*, Garden City, NY: Doubleday.
Meyendorff, J. (1974), *Byzantine Theology: Historical Trends and Doctrinal Themes*, New York: Fordham University Press.
Mitchell, D. W. (1991), *Spirituality and Emptiness: The Dynamics of Spiritual Life in Buddhism and Christianity*, New York: Paulist Press.
Mitchell, D. W. and J. Wiseman, eds. (1997), *The Gethsemani Encounter: A Dialogue on the Spiritual Life by Buddhist and Christian Monastics*, New York: Continuum.
Nicolini-Zani, M. (2022), *The Luminous Way to the East: Texts and History of the First Encounter of Christianity with China*, translated by W. Skudlarek, New York: Oxford University Press.
Nishitani, K. (1982), *Religion and Nothingness*, Berkeley: University of California Press.
Panikkar, R. (1989), *The Silence of God: The Answer of the Buddha*, Maryknoll, NY: Orbis Books.
Śāntideva (2006), *The Way of the Bodhisattva. A Translation of the Bodhicaryāvatāra*, translated by the Padmakara Translation Group (2nd Revised edition), Boston: Shambhala.
Śāntideva (1996), *The Bodhicaryávatára*, translated by K. Crosby, and A. Skilton, Oxford: Oxford University Press.
Śāntideva (1997), *A Guide to the Bodhisattva Way of Life*, translated by V. A. Wallace and B. A. Wallace, Ithaca, NY: Snow Lion.
Schmidt-Leukel, P. (2019), *Buddha Mind – Christ Mind. A Christian Commentary on the Bodhicaryāvatāra*. With a new translation by E. Steinkellner and C. Peck-Kubaczek, Leuven: Peeters.
Sheridan, D. (2007), *Loving God: Krishna and Christ; A Christian Commentary on the Nārada Sūtras*, Leuven: Peeters.
Stăniloae, D. (2002), *Orthodox Spirituality: A Practical Guide for the Faithful and a Definitive Manual for the Scholar*, South Canaan, PA.: St. Tikhon's Seminary Press.
Stendahl, K. (1976), "The Apostle Paul and the Introspective Consciousness of the West," in K. Stendahl, *Paul among Jews and Gentiles, and Other Essays*, 78–96, London: SCM Press.
Taylor, C. (1992), *Sources of the Self: Making of the Modern Identity* (2nd edition), Cambridge: Cambridge University Press.
Tilley, T. W. (2002), "Santideva's Bodhicaryavatara: One Catholic Theologian's Inadequate Reactions Extended," in *Presentation to the Comparative Theologies Section of the Catholic Theological Society of America. June 2002* (unpublished manuscript).
Williams, R. (2018), *Christ the Heart of Creation*, London: Bloomsbury.
Williams, R. (2008), "Not Being Serious: Thomas Merton and Karl Barth." Available online: http://rowanwilliams.archbishopofcanterbury.org/articles.php/1205/not-being-serious-thomas-merton-and-karl-barth.html.
Wriggins, S. H. (2004), *The Silk Road Journey with Xuanzang*, Boulder, CO: Westview Press.
Zizioulas, J. (1985), *Being as Communion: Studies in Personhood and the Church*, Crestwood, NY: St. Vladimir's Seminary Press.

12

Compassionate Ethics and Contemplative Dynamics

Some Observations on Śāntideva's *Bodhicaryāvatāra* and Zayn al-ʿĀbidīn's *Makārim al-akhlāq*

Reza Shah-Kazemi

In a BBC radio interview with the Dalai Lama, on July 4 2009, Mark Tully said to His Holiness: "Obviously, in all the troubles you have been through, it must have been difficult for you always to live by your principles of compassion and forgiveness, for instance forgiving the Chinese for what they have just done in Lhasa"—referring to the massacres then taking place in Tibet. The Dalai Lama replied, in his characteristically childlike manner, with a chuckle at once charming and disarming: "That is not difficult—as a practitioner."[1]

Making an effort to understand the implications of the word "practitioner" will help us to enter into the theme of this chapter—namely, the ways in which the dynamics of contemplative praxis generate a spiritual energy which enlivens and empowers the quest for virtue in general, and compassionate ethics in particular. The practitioner, or *sādhaka*, is one who practices diligently a spiritual discipline, a *sādhana*, and is thereby rendered receptive to the grace which bestows upon the soul spiritual capacities that transcend the plane on which conventional—and all too often baneful—human responses take place. These energies, qualities, or capacities enable the sincere soul to surmount the plane of consciousness whence arise emotions such as desire for revenge, the instinct to "fight fire with fire," the reactions of bitterness and despair, hatred and rage. The spiritual practitioner, in other words, is one who practices, with remorseless regularity, the art of rendering oneself receptive to powers and values which transcend the ordinary ethical resources of the human soul: "With human beings this is impossible, but with God all things are possible," in the words of the Christ (Matthew 19:26).

Whereas it is understandable that a Tibetan monk—or any compassionate human being—should feel anger in the face of atrocious violence, and to find unforgivable those who perpetrate them, the Dalai Lama's response expresses well the spirit of

[1] https://www.bbc.co.uk/sounds/play/p003jht1 at 21 minutes into the interview.

Śāntideva's *Bodhicaryāvatāra*, a text which, in a quasi-alchemical fashion,[2] opens up to our vision that dimension of the human soul whence an attitude of forgiveness toward our enemies becomes not only morally and psychologically possible, but also existentially and spiritually irresistible, so that any response other than compassion is unthinkable. To move toward that dimension of the soul, to think and to live, to act and to react, in accordance with this enhanced spiritual dimension, is "not difficult," as the Dalai Lama puts it, for "the practitioner." The practitioner, in the Dalai Lama's worldview, is a person who not only reflects upon, or conceptually comprehends, the principles of mercy, love, and forgiveness; rather, the realized practitioner is one whose life—day after day—is dominated by an implacable current of rhythmic grace—that is, the methodic contemplation of the supra-human reality, the Void (*śūnyatā*) out of which flows the spiritual energy which enlivens and deepens one's capacity to live according to the selfless virtues inherent in the Reality of the Void.

Faithfully living according to the virtues of forgiveness and mercy is deemed by the Dalai Lama to be "not difficult" for the practitioner, because it is a question here *not* of striving with one's will to conform to ethical standards or moral imperatives being imposed from without, but of allowing the innate qualities of one's very being—one's "Buddha-nature" (*buddhadhātu*)—to flow forth spontaneously, effortlessly, and even, as the Dalai Lama exemplifies to perfection, joyously. One observes a refraction of the objective or metaphysical emptiness of the Void in the subjective or ethical selflessness of one who contemplates the Void. The ontological emptiness of the Void vis-à-vis alterity reverberates in the merciful altruism that flows from the realized selflessness of the "practitioner." These dynamics can be defined in terms of merciful grace—a theme to which we will return at the end of this chapter.

The moral agent of the actions and reactions pertaining to this deeper mode of compassion, is as it were, effaced in their "performance" of these virtues—that is, the formal manifestation of the spiritual essence of these virtues on the planes of morality and psychology. The sense of moral and psychological agency, however, is eclipsed by the ontological repercussions put in motion by awareness of the Void. The ego of the agent is radically transcended by the compassionate "exchange" with all sentient beings, by means of which the sufferings of "the other" become assimilated as one's own (see BCA 8:140ff.): the liberation from one's own suffering through contemplation of the Void is thus tantamount both to the transfer of merit (*pariṇāmanā*, see BCA10:2ff.), and to the liberation of all beings through bodhisattvic compassion. Contemplation of the Void—and not ratiocinative reflection thereupon, for "ultimate reality is not a domain of cognition" (BCA 9:2)—is therefore inseparable from that compassion which liberates the self and all other sentient beings.

As Schmidt-Leukel notes, in his monumental commentary on the *Bodhicaryāvatāra*, "Śāntideva leaves no doubt about his exclusivist position that perfect liberation can only be achieved by insight into universal emptiness" (Schmidt-Leukel 2019: 435). And he also refers to the principle expressed in the ancient Buddhist text, *Aṅguttaranikāya*

2 "Śāntideva compares *bodhicitta* to an alchemist substance, a 'penetrating healing elixir' (BCA 1:9) that transforms ordinary humans into Buddhas" (Schmidt-Leukel 2019: 51–2). BCA refers to the translation of the *Bodhicaryāvatāra* by Steinkellner and Peck-Kubaczek in Schmidt-Leukel 2019.

(8:39), that the ethical practice of the "noble disciple" bestows "freedom from fear, enmity, and affliction" upon "an immeasurable number of beings" (Schmidt-Leukel 2019: 397). The practice of compassion is therefore both cause and consequence of the Void: according to Śāntideva, the bodhisattva's compassion is "the fruit of emptiness" (BCA 9:53).

The spiritual practices and disciplines of Buddhism culminate in this liberating insight into the universal Void, out of which arises—in principle, at least—the perfect manifestation of compassion. The difference between one who really "practices" compassion and one who does not (or one who has a purely theoretical engagement with these principles) is clear: on the one hand, there is the aspiring soul spiritually enlivened and ethically empowered by regular contact with the graces cascading from that which transcends the human plane; on the other, there is the tortured human psyche struggling to overcome natural reactions, defensive instincts, subconscious atavistic drives, unacknowledged prejudices, doing so on the basis of its own fallible, feeble, and fragile resources. In this connection, His Holiness referred to the stark contrast between modern and traditional approaches to the soul: modern psychology, he said in the interview, was equivalent to a kind of "kindergarten" in relation to the vastness, depth, and subtlety of the Buddhist science of human consciousness.[3]

It is important to stress the extent to which this refined science of consciousness is the fruit of spiritual praxis, and not merely the consequence of philosophical reflection; as noted above, "ultimate reality is not a domain of cognition." This is a point which must be emphasized again and again, if we are to arrive at a deeper understanding of the interiorizing dynamics unleashed by spiritual disciplines proper to the Buddhist *upāya* ("saving means") and the Muslim faith. Buddhist "practitioners" arrive at their knowledge of consciousness through a rigorous spiritual training, a daily routine dominated by a variety of contemplative disciplines taking the mind out of its superficial, trivial, and habitual modes of thought, modes of cognition which but skim over the surface of existence; a routine which, instead, plunges the mind and soul into hitherto unsuspected depths of consciousness which are attuned to the true nature of Being. In terms of the Buddhist *upāya*, these deeper levels of consciousness are in harmony with the compassion pulsating at the heart of the Void; in Islamic terms, what is realized as *tawḥīd* ("unification") in the intellect radiates as *raḥma* ("loving compassion") from the heart.

When we speak about a daily routine of spiritual praxis, the modern Westerner needs to have it spelt out concretely: in his devotional life, the Dalai Lama is a "typical" Buddhist monk, and as such spends about seven hours in contemplative practice each day.[4] In passing, we might also note that this proportion of the day devoted to worship

3 https://www.bbc.co.uk/sounds/play/p003jht1 at 9 minutes. C. G. Jung seemed to be aware of this incommensurability between the traditional understanding of the soul and the subjective gropings of modern psychology. See Jung 1984, especially the chapter "Psychotherapists or the Clergy" (pp. 255–82). Jung is forced to confess: "every psychology—my own included—has the character of a subjective confession" (p. 136). "For the purposes of psychology, I think it is best to abandon the notion that we are today in anything like a position to make statements about the nature of the psyche that are 'true' or 'correct.'" The most he can aim at is to make a "true expression" of what is "subjectively noted" (p. 133).

4 https://www.dalailama.com/the-dalai-lama/biography-and-daily-life/a-routine-day#:~:text=After%20his%20morning%20shower%2C%20His,to%20use%20for%20his%20walk.

is remarkably close to the well-known practice (*sunna*) of the Prophet Muḥammad—he devoted eight hours of the daily cycle to worship in all its forms: formal prayer (*ṣalāt*), invocation (*dhikr*), recitation of the Koran, litanies, supplications, etc. (see Lings 1986: 210).

1. *Pāramitā* and *Makārim al-akhlāq*: Spiritual virtues

We begin our comparative observations with the following kinds of question in the background: In what ways can the various forms of prayer and meditation in the two traditions be seen as functionally or metaphysically equivalent despite their "theological" incompatibilities? Does the incommensurability between the Muslim focus on the Personal God qua Creator and the Buddhist denial of the necessity of positing a Creator perforce imply that their respective objects of worship and devotion are incompatible, and that their respective conceptions of virtue must therefore also be divergent? Is moral purification the fruit or the seed of spiritual contemplation? Given that Buddhism is founded on the realization of the Void—the emptiness of being—can Muslim prayers, addressed to the "being," *Allāh*, be authenticated from the Buddhist point of view? And conversely, given that Muslims believe that only prayers which are addressed to *Allāh* can be regarded as authentic worship, can Buddhist devotion (*pūjā*) to the various Buddhas and Bodhisattvas—together with their meditations and invocations—be regarded as valid forms of prayer? Such major themes cannot, of course, be exhaustively addressed within the compass of this chapter; it is, however, useful to have them as background "notes" in our effort to discern some harmonies and convergences between the contemplative disciplines of the two traditions, such as they are manifested through the two texts chosen for study here.

Turning first to the treatise on ethics, *Makārim al-akhlāq*, the title can be translated as "Most noble traits of character." It was composed by ʿAlī b. Ḥusayn (known as Zayn al-ʿĀbidīn, meaning "Adornment of the Worshippers"), who died in 713, and so was roughly contemporary with Śāntideva. Zayn al-ʿĀbidīn was the fourth in the line of Shia Imams, son of Imam Ḥusayn, grandson of Imam ʿAlī and Fāṭima, and thus, great-grandson of the Prophet. He is also regarded as one of the spiritual "poles" (*aqṭāb*, sing. *quṭb*) of the Sufi tradition, his name figuring in the spiritual lineage of virtually all the major mystical orders (*ṭuruq*, sing. *ṭarīqa*) of Sufism. He was the only survivor of the massacre of Karbala (680), being too sick to go to the battlefield in what was without doubt the most appalling atrocity to have taken place in nascent Islam—the slaughter of the Prophet's grandson, Imam Ḥusayn, together with seventy-two of his relatives and closest companions, who were killed by an army of several thousand for refusing to recognize and pledge the oath of allegiance (*bayʿa*) to Yazīd b. Muʿāwiya as the caliph of the Muslim empire (Chittick 1988: xv–xvii).[5]

Zayn al-ʿĀbidīn's response to this atrocity was very much in the spirit of Buddhist ethics: he refused to retaliate, to engage in bitter recrimination, or to sanction any

[5] We will be referring to the *Makārim al-akhlāq* text as found in this edition, and making minor modifications to Chittick's translation.

political activity aiming at the overthrow of the corrupt, illegitimate, and tyrannical regime of the Umayyads. Instead, he focused in an almost monastic fashion on the inner life, a life so dominated by prayer that, in addition to the epithet "Adornment of the Worshippers," he was referred to by the title of *al-Sajjād*, "The one [perpetually] prostrate in prayer." As noted by William Chittick in the Introduction to his translation of *al-Ṣaḥīfa al-Sajjādiyya* (the compilation of supplications and treatises of Zayn al-ʿĀbidīn, in which the latter's *Makārim al-Akhlāq* figures), "It is related that Imam Zayn al-ʿĀbidīn used to perform one thousand supererogatory cycles of *ṣalāt* every night, in conscious emulation of the custom of his grandfather, ʿAlī" (Chittick 1988: xxiii).

There are many striking parallels between the *Makārim al-Akhlāq* and Śāntideva's *Bodhicaryāvatāra.* To begin with, just as the latter text comprises a set of chapters devoted to each *pāramitā*—which can be translated as "supreme virtue," the sum thereof culminating in transcendent wisdom (*prajñā*)—likewise, the *Makārim al-akhlāq* consists of a series of supplications aimed at cultivating the virtues conducive to the spiritual realization implied in the saying of Zayn al-ʿĀbidīn's great grandfather, the Prophet: "I was only raised up for you [as a prophet] in order to perfect the noble traits of character (*makārim al-akhlāq*)."[6] Zayn al-ʿĀbidīn's treatise/supplication should in fact be read as a commentary on this prophetic utterance, which evokes the idea of the *prajñāpāramitā* as being the "Mother of all the Buddhas": just as the Prophet is implying in this *ḥadīth* that the entire purpose of his prophethood is to perfect the "noble traits of character," so the entire purpose of the *prajñāpāramitā* is to give birth to "sons of the Victors" (BCA 5:100), or, to quote Śāntideva's ostensible aim: "I would briefly like to describe according to the tradition how one resorts to the discipline of the Sons of the Buddhas" (BCA 1:1)—i.e., the discipline of the bodhisattvas.

It would therefore be instructive to study each of the *pāramitā*s of the *Bodhicaryāvatāra*, and find in the *Makārim al-akhlāq* echoes and intimations of the virtues described by Śāntideva. But neither time nor space allow us to do this kind of exercise. So, we will restrict ourselves to pointing out a few of the more remarkable resonances in respect of the theme of this chapter, by looking at the virtue of patience, and examining ways in which the implications and ramifications of this virtue transcend the bounds of conventional ethics, requiring us to delve into its spiritual roots and its metaphysical repercussions.

Śāntideva devotes Chapter 6 of *Bodhicaryāvatāra* to the perfection of this virtue, (*kṣāntipāramitā*); what he says in verse 2 is a useful starting point for comparison: "There is no evil equal to hate; there is no austerity equal to patience. That is why one should cultivate patience with effort in various ways." Schmidt-Leukel's comment here is important for taking us into a deeper understanding of the implications of *kṣānti*: "Śāntideva is not just interested in explaining *kṣānti*. His main concern is how to overcome hate or anger" (Schmidt-Leukel 2009: 258).

One discerns a clear resonance between this "main concern" of Śāntideva and the thrust of the message of the supplications in the *Makārim al-akhlāq*. In verse 8, Zayn al-ʿĀbidīn supplicates God: "Replace for me the animosity of the people of hatred with

[6] This *ḥadīth* is found in the collections of Aḥmad b. Ḥanbal, Bayhaqī, and Ḥākim al-Nīsābūrī; see, for discussion, Shah-Kazemi 2010: 73–8.

love *(maḥabba)*," doing so in a series of remarkable inversions which we will look at in a moment; all of these supplications will be seen as pathways by which the wronged soul can "overcome hate or anger," to use Schmidt-Leukel's apt words summing up Śāntideva's aim in cultivating *kṣānti*. It would be appropriate to emphasize at this point that, both in his life and his teachings, Zayn al-ʿĀbidīn was the epitome of non-violence: he robustly rejected any suggestion of exacting condign revenge upon the Umayyad regime for their slaughter at Karbala, instead urging his followers to pursue lives of impeccable virtue, piety, and devotion, following his example of renouncing this world, preparing for the Hereafter through rectification of character, seeking only the good pleasure of God. In the following sayings of Śāntideva, we see a clear parallel to Zayn al-ʿĀbidīn's unconditional renunciation of that egocentric worldliness which is the underlying cause of exteriorizing political activity:

> To pay homage to the Buddhas, today I shall become a servant for the world with all my heart. May crowds of people set their feet on my head or kill me! May the Protector of the World be satisfied with me!
>
> BCA 6:125–7

> All my lives and enjoyments, the merit that I will have acquired in the three times, I sacrifice without misgiving in order to realize the goals of all beings.
>
> BCA 3:10

> May they beat me without end, may they revile me, cover me with dust, may they play with my body, deride it, mock it. I have given them the body, so what do I care?
>
> BCA 3:12–13[7]

The following comment by Schmidt-Leukel on the meaning of *kṣānti* helps us to see that what is in question here is far from a passive acquiescence in the face of injustice; rather, *kṣānti* implies a potentially transformative spiritual power:

> The term *kṣānti*, often translated as 'patience,' has actually a number of connotations; it implies 'endurance,' 'toleration,' 'composure' and 'forbearance' . . . the last is of central importance in Śāntideva's understanding of *kṣānti* and even gets very close to the notion of 'forgiveness.'
>
> Schmidt-Leukel 2019: 258

The reference to 'forbearance" leads us to a key virtue in Islamic spirituality: *ḥilm*, which is one of the most "noble" of all the *makārim al-akhlāq*, a virtue for which the Prophet was particularly renowned. Again, the whole of the *Makārim al-akhlāq* can be read as an extended commentary on this all-encompassing quality of soul. *Ḥilm* cannot be translated by any single word into English, "forbearance" being its most common

[7] As Schmidt-Leukel (2019: 283) notes, "The Buddhist ideal of non-violence and non-retaliation has often been met with approval, respect and praise. Śāntideva combines this ideal with what appears to be a limitless endurance of any form of mistreatment."

translation. It is very closely related to the spiritual qualities inherent in *kṣānti*. Its subtlety and depth are evoked by the following family of virtues: patience, wisdom, composure, self-mastery—and all the immense strength of character implied in this quality—imperturbability, together with the qualities of kindness, mildness, and gentleness and the unfathomable power proper to the divine prototype of this virtue, one of God's names being *al-Ḥalīm*, ultimate source and possessor of *ḥilm*. The Prophet himself is described in the traditional sources as *aḥlam al-nās*: "the most forbearing of people"—the one with the greatest plenitude of *ḥilm*. He went so far as to say in his exhortation to emulate his own quality of *ḥilm*: "The *ḥalīm* is almost a prophet (*kāda'l-ḥalīm an yakūna nabiyyan*)."[8]

If *ḥilm* be the prophetic quality par excellence, this virtue must be at the very heart of the "noble traits of character" for the sake of which the Prophet was sent to mankind: "I was *only* raised up for you in order to perfect noble character-traits [emphasis added]," as noted above. Implicit in this saying—and in the treatise of Zayn al-ʿĀbidīn bearing this title—is the principle embedded in Śāntideva's avowal, cited above, that "there is no austerity equal to patience." If we understand by this word "austerity" not just the ascetic practices associated with the way of *tapas*, but the whole range of formal rites and rituals of a religious tradition, we see that Śāntideva may be alluding to the radical incommensurability between the interiorizing power of the virtue of patience (together with all of the spiritual qualities and interiorizing energies comprised within the family of virtues clustered around patience), on the one hand, and the merely outward, formal, or mechanical accomplishment of the rites and practices of a religious tradition, on the other. It is noteworthy in this connection that the Koran gives precedence to patience over prayer in the following verse: "O ye who believe, seek help in patience (*al-ṣabr*) and in prayer (*al-ṣalāt*)," and then adds: "God is truly with the patient," rather than saying that He is with those who pray (2:153).

These considerations lead to one of the esoteric, or shall we say "supra-confessional," implications of the synthesis between the two *ḥadīth*s, the sole purpose of the prophetic mission being the perfection of noble character, and the highlighting of the quasi-prophetic virtue of *ḥilm*. Taking the former *ḥadīth* at its word would lead us to the idea that everything else about the Prophet's mission—all the theological teachings, all the religious laws, all the rules and regulations of worship—are in some mysterious sense subordinated to the overriding imperative of perfecting one's character, of restoring or bringing to fruition the primordial nature (*al-fiṭra*) of the human soul, this innate human predisposition being identified in the Koran with "the eternally established religion (*al-dīn al-qayyim*)" (30:30).

One esoteric meaning that can be discerned here is the following: To the extent that the soul be adorned[9] by perfect virtue, all of the metaphysical mysteries by which the theological doctrines of the religion are governed, and all of the mystical realities at which the formal practices of prayer are aimed, will be spiritually magnetized and

8 Cited in the compilation of Muḥammadī Rayshahrī (2009: 311). Toshihiko Izutsu (2008: 236) claims, in one of his magisterial works on key Koranic terms, that it is not just the Prophet's character, but also the Koran "as a whole," which "is dominated by the very spirit of *ḥilm*."

9 We use the word "adorned" in line with the Arabic *ḥilya*, a key term in the vocabulary of Islamic spirituality and one which is used many times in *al-Ṣaḥīfa al-Sajjādiyya* as we shall see in a moment.

ultimately realized by the heart of the devotee. One might almost say, in accordance with the spiritual logic of the Prophet's *ḥadīth*, that all formal religious systems are subordinated to the existential imperative of perfecting the "noble character-traits" inseminated within primordial human nature. It is perhaps for this reason that, when asked which religion is most beloved to God, the Prophet refused to name any religion but replied with two words: *al-ḥanīfiyya al-samḥa*, which can be translated as "the primordial, generously tolerant quality of faith [epitomized by Abraham]" (al-Bukhārī 1976, vol. 1: 34).[10]

The passage from the *Makārim al-akhlāq* cited below (vv. 38–77) can be read as a commentary on the meaning of *ḥilm*, each of the vices of the "other" being confronted by its virtuous antidote. The remarkable similarity between this ethical inversion and Śāntideva's "reverse psychology" will be noted in a moment. But we should note first that, all such similarities notwithstanding, from the point of view of Zayn al-ʿĀbidīn—and, with him, the whole tradition of Islamic spirituality—nobility of character cannot be achieved without the grace of God, and the latter is not simply passively awaited, it is actively sought through spiritual praxis, including direct supplication to God: "Adorn me," cries out Zayn al-ʿĀbidīn, "with the adornment of the virtuous (*al-ṣāliḥīn*)" (MA:10): all of the virtues are so many beauties of soul, so many "adornments" bestowed by God upon His servants. The extent of the difference between this perspective, riveted as it is to the notion of the personal God as Creator and as the direct and indispensable source of one's virtue, on the one hand, and the perspective of Śāntideva, on the other, is evident;[11] the question of whether or not this difference is mitigated or transcended by mystical and metaphysical values will be addressed shortly.

2. Psychological inversion, ontological deconstruction

Returning to Śāntideva's discipline of inverting the self vis-à-vis the other: In the effort to establish an unconditional "equality" between oneself and the selves of all other beings—in other words, the ontological dismantling of the ego and its illusory sense of independence—let us bear in mind the startling spiritual statements and challenging psychological practices given by Śāntideva at Chapter 8 ("Meditative Concentration"[12]). These practices are aimed at producing in one's consciousness the sentiments of jealousy, rivalry, and pride (instrumentalizing these three vices in synecdochical fashion to represent vice as such, rooted in egocentric self-affirmation), that others may have toward oneself, in order to become as it were viscerally aware of the absurdity, the ugliness, and the noxiousness of these vices. This is akin to receiving a kind of

[10] The word *ḥanīfiyya* can be translated also as "original monotheism," the *ḥanīf* par excellence being the patriarch Abraham, who exemplifies primordial human nature, *al-fiṭra*, as noted earlier. As for the word *samḥa*, it connotes the notions of liberality, generosity, gentleness, easiness; it is thus closely related to *ḥilm*.

[11] See Schmidt-Leukel's very insightful commentary on Śāntideva's critique of belief in a Creator God (*Īśvara*) in Chapter 9 of the *Bodhicaryāvatāra* (*passim*).

[12] Or "Perfection of Absorption" in the translation of Ernst Steinkellner and Cynthia Peck-Kubaczek, used by Schmidt-Leukel in his commentary. The original Sanskrit here is *Dhyānapāramitā*.

"homeopathic" dose of the vice, which will produce an appropriate revulsion and thereby propel the meditator into a loving embrace of its antidote, that particular virtue of which the vice is an inversion or perversion. This contemplative antidote takes the form of a concrete presentiment, as opposed to a merely notional comprehension, of the virtue to which the vice is opposed. This would appear to be the initial ethical and psychological goal of the practice.

The power of the antidote can be seen, however, to go beyond these levels: According to a certain metaphysical logic, the antidote may be seen as catalyzing a process by which the pretensions of the ego are unveiled, and the root cause of every vice stands exposed—self-affirmation. Paradoxically, the ego is at the same time exposed as being devoid of ontological substance—despite its efforts at maintaining its identity as an authentic, existent entity. One hears an echo of the Koranic verse: "Nay, but the human being is rebellious; inasmuch as he deems himself self-sufficient" (96:6–7).

This process of uprooting the egotistic substratum of all the vices can be seen as a more subtle mystical goal of Śāntideva's discipline. Seeing through the existential emptiness of the ego can be discerned as the subjective counterpart to the metaphysical emptiness of the Void; in both cases—seeing through the microcosmic shadow to the metacosmic Light—what flows from the Void is, *mutatis mutandis*, impeccable wisdom, the chief repercussion of which is radiant compassion. Let us ponder the following passage from Chapter 8, "The Perfection of Absorption (*dhyānapāramitā*),"[13] which lends itself to comparison with a passage from *Makārim al-akhlāq*:

> 120. He who would like to save himself and others quickly should practice this highly mysterious exchanging of the other and oneself.
>
> 121. Since through exceeding love of a self, even a minor threat causes fear, who would not abhor this self, which is fraught with dangers like an enemy.
>
> . . .
>
> 129. All those who are suffering in the world are so out of longing for their own happiness. All those who are happy in the world are so out of longing for the happiness of others.
>
> 130. Why so many words? Just behold this gap between the fool who pursues his own goals and the wise one who acts for the goals of others!
>
> 131. It is certainly not possible to achieve buddhahood, how even happiness in the cycle of existences, if one does not exchange one's own happiness for the suffering of another?
>
> . . .
>
> 134. The troubles that the world offers, the many sufferings and dangers, all of this comes from grasping a self. So of what use is this grasping to me?
>
> 135. If one does not evade the self, one cannot escape suffering, just as one cannot escape being burnt if one does not evade fire.
>
> 136. To calm my own suffering and to calm the suffering of others, I therefore offer myself to others and adopt others as myself.
>
> . . .

[13] Translation by Ernst Steinkellner in Schmidt-Leukel 2019: 389–91.

140. Think of lowly and other beings as being yourself, and of yourself as being others, and then you may practice jealousy and pride without hesitation:

141. That person is honored, not me; I am not rich like he is; he (*ayam aham* M instead of *aham aham* V) is praised, I must be censured; I am unhappy, he is happy.

142. I do the work, while he stands around at ease; he, it is true, is important in the world, I am insignificant indeed and worthless.

. . .

148. If only my virtues would become obvious everywhere in the world, and if only no one would any longer hear about the virtues that are his!

149. Would that also my failures be hidden, the honor would be mine, not his! – Now I have easily become wealthy; I am revered, but he is not.

150. Finally, after a long time, we see delighted that he has been put down, a laughing stock to all the world, vilified here and there.

151. Since this wretch actually measures himself with me, does he really have so much erudition, wisdom, beauty, relatives and possessions?

152. When I hear such merits of my own being praised here and there, I savor a feast of joy, excited and with goose bumps.

153. Even if he had possessions, we would have to take them away by force and give him only enough to live on if he does our work.

154. And he must be deprived of happiness, laden with our distress forever. We have all been pained by him hundreds of times in the cycle of existences.

155. Innumerable eons have passed while you were seeking your own benefit. Through this great toil you have gained nothing but suffering.

156. So at my bidding apply yourself without hesitation to this [practice of exchanging the others and yourself]! You will see the advantages of this later, because the Buddha's words are true.

157. If you had done this work earlier, you would not be in this state, not to mention the bliss of perfection that is a Buddha's.

158. Just as you have formed, therefore, the notion of "I" with respect to someone else's drops of semen and blood, so cultivate this notion also with respect to others!

In the following passage from *Makārim al-akhlāq*, we see something akin to the "reverse psychology" of Śāntideva, inasmuch as Zayn al-ʿAbidīn pleads with God to grant him the virtuous antidote to the vicious attitudes of his enemies. It is a remarkable passage which is redolent with the Christian maxim "turn the other cheek" (Matthew 5:39), on the one hand, and on the other, evokes the immense spiritual power presupposed by the capacity to forgive those who are inflicting suffering ("forgive them, Father, for they know not what they do," Luke 23:34).

8. Replace for me the animosity of the people of hatred with love;
  the envy of the people of insolence with affection;
  the suspicion of the people of righteousness with trust;
  the enmity of those who are near with friendship,
  the disrespect of kinsfolk with devotion,

the abandonment of relatives
with help,
the false love of flatterers
with true love set right,
the rejection of fellows
with generous friendliness,
and the bitterness of the fear of wrongdoers
with the sweetness of security.

. . .
9. Point me straight to resist him who is dishonest toward me
with good counsel,
repay him who separates from me,
with gentle devotion,
reward him who deprives me,
with free giving,
recompense him who cuts me off,
with joining,
oppose him who slanders me,
with excellent mention,
give thanks for good, and shut my eyes to evil!
. . .

10. Adorn me with the adornment of the virtuous,
and clothe me in the ornaments of the godfearing, through
spreading justice,
restraining rage
quenching the flame of hate,
bringing together the people of separation,
correcting discord,
spreading about good behaviour,
covering faults,
mildness of temper,
lowering the wing,
beauty of conduct,
gravity of bearing,
agreeableness in comportment,
precedence in reaching excellence,
preferring bounteousness,
refraining from condemnation,
bestowing bounty on the undeserving,
speaking the truth, though it be painful,
making little of the good in my words and deeds,
though it be much,
and making much of the evil in my words and deeds, though it be little!

The resonance between the psychological and ethical aims—and even, at a stretch, the dialectical strategies—of our two authorities is self-evident. In both cases the aim is not just to displace a negative trait and replace it with a positive one; the spiritual strategies are at one in probing and uprooting the source of all vices—egocentricity. Hence the Imam's plea to God, at verse 3:

> Expand Thy provision toward me, but try me not with hubris
> Honor me, but afflict me not with pride
> Make me worship Thee, but corrupt not my worship with self-satisfaction (*ʿujb*).
> . . .
> Give me the highest moral traits, but preserve me from arrogance (*fakhr*).

The vices of arrogance, pride, and self-satisfaction all point to the false "god" which is "worshipped" instead of God: according to two verses of the Koran (25:43 and 45:23), this false god is "desire" (*hawā*). The convergence between the two traditions of Buddhism and Islam on this point is striking: the Koranic concept of *hawā* appears to play a role in the mystical traditions of Islam akin to, if not identical with, that of *tṛṣṇā*/*taṇhā* in Buddhism. In both traditions, egocentric desire is the chief obstacle in the spiritual life: in Buddhism it is the cause of all suffering, in Islam, it is the cause of covert *shirk*, the worship of false gods.[14] The worship of self-centered desire generates all vices, and even insinuates itself into the motivation of worship of God, thus "corrupting" this worship, in the words of Zayn al-ʿĀbidīn. One observes how this corruption of worship goes hand in hand with the violation or neglect of the ethical ideals of religion in a very short Koranic chapter, *Sūrat al-Māʿūn* ("Small Acts of Kindness"), a chapter whose swingeing critique of religious formalism and sanctimonious pretension would surely resonate forcefully with the worldview of Śāntideva:

> Have you seen him who gives the lie to religion?
> That is he who repels the orphan
> and does not urge the feeding of the needy.
> So woe to them who pray (*waylun li'l-muṣallīn*),
> those who are heedless of their prayers,
> those who wish to be seen [as pious],
> while withholding small acts of kindness.
>
> 107:1–7; translation by the present author

We return to the fundamental aim of both texts, to rid the human heart of the poisons of egocentricity, by means of the cultivation of authentic "altruistic" virtue—that is, ethical conduct untainted by any self-glorification or egoistic expropriation, being motivated by a sincere orientation toward "the other"; and, complementing this moral effort, by means of spiritual praxis, whatever be the "saving strategies" (*upāya*s) by which devotion to, or concentration upon, the absolute "Other" is achieved.

[14] See Shah-Kazemi, 2010: 87–92, for discussion.

3. The grace of contemplative praxis

We now need to address the extent to which the Islamic devotion to *Allāh* can be reconciled with the Buddhist denial of the existence of a Creator. That is, to what degree is there a functional equivalence, a mystical convergence, or a metaphysical identity between the respective object of worship/meditation in the two traditions? To help put this question into context, let us look at the very last verse of Chapter 8 of the *Bodhicaryāvatāra*, on "Meditative Concentration" (8:187):

> Thus, to banish all obscuring veils
> I'll bend my mind from the mistaken path;
> And constantly upon the perfect object
> I shall rest my mind in even meditation.[15]

Is this "perfect object" of contemplative concentration in any way identifiable with *Allāh*, the "object" which Zayn al-ʿĀbidīn worships, invokes, and concentrates upon? We have discussed this question at length in *Common Ground Between Islam and Buddhism* (Shah-Kazemi 2010: 29–78), so here we intend to address the theme from a different angle. First, let us take cognizance of the extent to which the two perspectives diverge on the plane of theology. This divergence is evident from the implications of the third verse of the *Makārim al-akhlāq*, where Zayn al-ʿĀbidīn pleads to God as follows:

> Relieve me from what would entangle me in worldly concerns;
> engage me in that for which you will hold me accountable tomorrow [i.e., at the moment of death];
> and free all my days in that for the sake of which you created me (MA 3).

Now it would be clear to those hearing this supplication that what Zayn al-ʿĀbidīn is alluding to in the statement "that for the sake of which you created me" (*fīmā khalaqtanī lahu*) is the following verse of the Koran: "I only created the spirits and mankind in order that they might worship Me (*illā li-yaʿbudūni*)" (51:56). The Creator created the creature solely for the sake of worshipping Him: on the surface, nothing could be further removed from the Buddhist perspective. However, if we recall the Prophet's avowal that it was exclusively for the sake of perfecting noble character that he was sent, the gap between the two perspectives narrows; or rather, the confessional plane on which this gap exists—and remains incommensurable—is surpassed by a metaphysical perspective.

Whereas according to 51:56 it appears that worship of God takes precedence over everything else—and that noble character is only a moral *conditio sine qua non* for this ontological imperative—we should remember that, as seen above, formal worship of

[15] This is from the translation by the Padmakara Translation Group (2008: 228). In the translation of Steinkellner (Schmidt-Leukel 2019: 404): "Therefore, to eliminate all obstruction, I shall draw the mind away from wrong paths and practice concentration constantly on the proper object."

God can be tainted by hypocrisy and ostentation, and that most insidious of poisons—referred to by Zayn al-ʿĀbidīn—self-satisfaction (*ʿujb*). By contrast, perfection of character can be seen, in the light of the prophetic utterance, as a magnet attracting the graces of God; graces which will generate knowledge of ultimate Reality, and salvation in the Hereafter—these two constituting the ultimate aims of the dogmas and doctrines of the faith, and the rules and regulations of worship.

If good character can thus be seen as attracting the grace of knowledge and salvation, concentration on the Real can also be seen as attracting the grace that perfects character. As Titus Burckhardt says, in his masterful summary of the mystical and ethical dynamics set in motion by the key Sufi practice of the invocation of the Name of God, "It is through its object, the revealed symbol, that concentration opens the way to the Grace which transforms the soul" (Burckhardt 1959: 108).

This leads us to consider what we could call the "grace of concentration." Whether we are speaking of personal prayer, formal worship, scriptural recitation, meditation, or invocation of an inspired formula or a revealed Name, the one thread that runs all the way through these modes of spiritual practice is concentration. And all types of concentration on "the one thing needful" (Luke 10:42) can be considered as so many modes of grace, if we understand this word in the sense suggested by Marco Pallis (2003: 71):

> In China, the Taoists have always spoken of the 'activity of Heaven'; for us to speak of the 'activity of enlightenment' is in no wise far-fetched. This is in fact the function of grace, namely, to condition man's homecoming to the centre from start to finish. It is the very attraction of the centre itself, revealed to us by various means, which provides the incentive to start on the Way and the energy to face and overcome its many and various obstacles.[16]

If grace be defined as the "attraction of the centre," and if this center in turn be defined as the immanence of the Absolute within the heart of human consciousness, then the following statement of Frithjof Schuon can be read as a definitive answer to the question of whether the supreme object of devotion in Buddhism and Islam is one and the same Reality:

> If it be admitted that 'the kingdom of Heaven is within you,' there is no logical cause for reproaching Buddhism with conceiving the Divine Principle in this respect alone. The 'Void' or 'Extinction' is God—the supraontological Real and Being seen 'inwardly'—within ourselves; not in our thought or in our ego, of course, but starting from that 'geometrical point' within us whereby we are mysteriously attached to the Infinite.
>
> Schuon 2018: 19

This observation helps us to discern the "transcendent Unity" of the absolute Object of the two traditions in terms of an "immanent Identity" within the relative subject: the

[16] See also Frithjof Schuon's insightful exposition of the meaning of "grace" in the Mahāyāna Buddhist context, in his essay "Dharmakara's Vow" in Schuon 2018: 123–33.

"geometrical point" constituting the essence and center of one's being and consciousness. And the realization of the immanent infinitude inwardly unfolding at the center can only come about as a result of grace, the merciful attraction exerted upon the periphery—the human subject—by the divine center, at once immanent and transcendent vis-à-vis the peripheral human subject.

Another point to be considered here is that in Islamic metaphysics the divine Essence (*al-dhāt*) cannot be worshipped. This is the startling insight of Ibn al-ʿArabī, who goes so far as to refer to the human being's worship of God as being "accidental" (*ʿaraḍī*): the servant praises God, he states, "with a praise worthy of God, *accident for accident* [emphasis added]" (Chittick 1989: 366). The dimension of divinity that is capable of being worshipped is "accidental" insofar as it is a self-disclosure (*tajallī*) of the Essence, and as such is ontologically subordinate thereto, consisting of the theophanic manifestation of one or more of the Names or Attributes of God.

At this point, let us cite a passage from the first sermon of the *Nahj al-balāgha* ("Path of Eloquence"), attributed to ʿAlī b. Abī Ṭalib, the first Imam of the Shiʿa, grandfather of Zayn al-ʿĀbidīn. This may help us see another important point of metaphysical convergence between the two traditions:

> The perfection of purification (*ikhlāṣ*) is to divest God of all attributes (*ṣifāt*) because of the testimony of every attribute that it is other than the object of attribution, and because of the testimony of every such object that it is other than the attribute. So whoever ascribes an attribute to God—glorified be He!—has conjoined Him [with something else] and whoever so conjoins Him has made Him twofold, and whoever makes Him twofold has fragmented Him, and whoever thus fragments Him is ignorant of Him.
>
> Shah-Kazemi 2006: 208

This negation of the *ṣifāt* is akin to the Buddhist concept of *anātman*: the negation of a "self" that can in any way be designated by means of *nāmarūpa*, name/form. In both cases, what is being denied or negated is not the metaphysical reality of the Absolute; rather, it is the incommensurability between the Absolute and all possible designations, conceptions, and attributes pertaining to the Absolute. This Absolute—the *dhāt* of *Allāh* or the *buddha-dhātu* ("nature of the awakened one")—cannot be realized by the individual, but only "through" the individual—that is, by virtue of the extinction of the individual and all modes of consciousness proportioned thereto, that "extinction" which is referred to as *fanāʾ* in the Islamic lexicon, and *nirvāṇa* in the Buddhist. These two terms refer to the selfsame ontological extinction of the ego, and this extinction is a grace, by definition—for the ego cannot extinguish itself. The worship offered to the Absolute through Its various modes of Self-disclosure—whether through the *ṣifāt* of *Allāh* or the various Buddhas and Bodhisattvas of Buddhism—culminates in this supreme gift of self designated as extinction or, bearing in mind the etymology of *nirvāṇa*, "being blown out." And this "de-spiration" of the ego results—according to both spiritual traditions—in a merciful radiance of blessings for the entire cosmos.

These principles are expressed with particular clarity through the esoteric exegesis of a Sufi in the school of Ibn al-ʿArabī, ʿAbd al-Razzāq al-Kāshānī (d. 1345). In his comment on the Koranic verse, "Truly, the righteous shall drink from a cup flavored with *Kāfūr*, a [celestial] spring wherefrom the slaves of God drink directly, making it gush forth abundantly" (76:5–6), Kāshānī writes that these "slaves" cause the flow of the spring to increase because "they are [themselves] the sources of this spring; there is no duality or otherness . . . were it otherwise, it would not be the fountain of *Kāfūr*, because of the darkness of the veil of egoity (*anā ʾiyya*) and duality" (Kāshānī 1283/1866: vol. 2: 360–1).

This metaphysical "slavehood" is realizable by the graces attracted by virtue and all forms of worship, and in particular, the remembrance of God (*Dhikr Allāh*), referred to by the Koran as the "greatest" form of prayer (29:45). The spiritual reality (*ḥaqīqa*) of this practice is, in the words of Imam ʿAlī, "that you forget your self in your remembrance (*tansā nafsaka fī dhikrika*)" (Shah-Kazemi 2006: 162). Herein lies the essence of "slavehood," complete loss of selfhood, attained through extinction, which, as noted above, is itself the effect of a grace, for the soul cannot extinguish itself; and this grace is galvanized or realized within the soul by means of the contemplative disciplines of remembrance, practiced within the framework of the moral disciplines aimed at purifying the soul, and eliminating defects of character.

According to the definition of grace provided by Pallis, above, we could say that the "activity of enlightenment" or the "activity of Heaven," which is "the very attraction of the centre itself," effaces the slaves who have dedicated themselves heart and soul to "the one thing needful," removing from them their separative egoity (*anā ʾiyya*). And it is for this reason that the blessings symbolized by the celestial fountain of *Kāfūr* flow through them: they have *themselves* paradoxically become *selfless* channels of divine grace, cascading down from Heaven to earth. In the words of Imam ʿAlī, "Down from me torrents do pour; up to me no bird can soar" (cited in Shah-Kazemi 2006: 185). We believe that Śāntideva would recognize here the cosmic function of the Bodhisattvas, "Sons of the Buddhas," through whom flow the blessings of the Pure Land, bringing about the enlightenment of all beings through their universal compassion:

> May a shower of lotus flowers fall, blended with fragrant water! It is seen as it puts out the hell-fires with a hiss. May the beings in hell be given the sight of the Bodhisattva Kamalapāṇi, wondering what it might be, and be unexpectedly gladdened by happiness!
>
> 10:12

> Come hither, come quickly, cast off your fear, brothers! We are restored to life! A youth with ribbons in the hair has appeared to us, ardently rendering us fearless; through his might all afflictions are gone, floods of joy have sprung, the spirit of awakening has arisen as well as compassion, the mother of deliverance for all beings.
>
> 10:13

> May the ghosts always be well fed and bathed, and may they be refreshed by rivers of milk flowing from the hands of the noble Bodhisattva Avalokiteśvara!
>
> 10:18

Despite the fact that much more could be said by way of substantiating this argument, we do not think we are going too far in claiming that the metaphysical essence and the spiritual fruit of contemplative praxis are one and the same as regards the *dīn* practiced by Zayn al-ʿĀbidīn and the *upāya* practiced by Śāntideva. Both spiritual traditions could almost be summed up by the old adage, "Practice makes perfect," so long as one adds these words: "Practice, *with faith and virtue*, makes perfect, *by the merciful grace of the Real*." Very relevant here is the "precious pith-instruction" given by Milarepa to his disciple, Gambopa. Milarepa lifts up his robe to reveal a body covered with sores and calluses, saying, "There is no profounder teaching than this. See what hardships I have undergone. The most profound teaching in Buddhism is '*to practice*.' It has simply been due to this persistent effort that I have earned the Merits and Accomplishment. You should also exert yourself perseveringly in meditation" (Milarepa 1989: vol. 2: 495). And both Śāntideva and Zayn al-ʿĀbidīn would most certainly agree with Bodhidharma's allusion to the mysterious reality veiled by all spiritual practice, when he stated that the enlightened ones are those who, while practicing the supreme virtues, "practice nothing at all" (Red Pine 1987: 7).

References

al-Bukhārī, Muḥammad b. Ismāʿīl (1976), *Ṣaḥīḥ al-Bukhārī: Arabic-English*, translated by Muhammad Muhsin Khan, Chicago: Kazi Publications.

Burckhardt, T. (1959), *An Introduction to Sufi Doctrine*, translated by D. M. Matheson, Lahore: Ashraf Press.

Chittick, W. C., trans. and ed. (1988), *The Psalms of Islam—al-Ṣaḥifat al-Kāmilat al-Sajjādiyya*, London: Muhammadi Trust.

Chittick, W. C. (1989), *The Sufi Path of Knowledge: Ibn al-ʿArabī and the Metaphysics of the Imagination*, Albany: SUNY Press.

Izutsu, T. (2008), *God and Man in the Qur'an: Semantics of the Qur'anic Weltanschauung* (Tokyo: Keio University Press, 1964), repr. Petaling Jaya: Islamic Book Trust.

Jung, C. G. (1984), *Modern Man in Search of a Soul*, translated by W. S. Dell and Cary F. Baynes, London: Ark.

Kāshānī, ʿAbd al-Razzāq. (1283/1866), (published under the title) *Tafsīr Muḥyi'd-Dīn Ibn al-ʿArabī*, Cairo: Būlāq.

Lings, M. (1986), *Muhammad: His Life Based on the Earliest Sources*, London: George Allen & Unwin with Islamic Texts Society.

Milarepa (1989), *The Hundred Thousand Songs of Milarepa*, translated by Garma C. C. Chang, Boston: Shambhala.

Padmakara Translation Group (2008), *The Way of the Boddhisattva*, Boulder, CO: Shambhala.

Pallis, M. (2003), *A Buddhist Spectrum*, Bloomington: World Wisdom.

Rayshahrī, M. (2009), *Mīzān al-ḥikma*, translated by N. Virjee et al., *The Scale of Wisdom: A Compendium of Shiʿa Hadith*, London: ICAS Press.

Red Pine, trans. (1987), *The Zen Teaching of Bodhidharma*, New York: North Point Press.

Schmidt-Leukel, P. (2019), *Buddha Mind – Christ Mind: A Christian Commentary on the Bodhicaryāvatāra*. With a new translation by E. Steinkellner and C. Peck-Kubaczek, Leuven: Peeters.

Schuon, F. (2018), *Treasures of Buddhism.* A New Translation with Selected Letters, edited by Harry Oldmeadow, Bloomington: World Wisdom.
Shah-Kazemi, R. (2006), *Justice and Remembrance: Introducing the Spirituality of Imam ʿAlī*, London & New York: I.B. Tauris.
Shah-Kazemi, R. (2010), *Common Ground Between Islam and Buddhism*, Louisville, KY: Fons Vitae.

Index

tajallī (self-disclosure) 233

www.ingramcontent.com/pod-product-compliance
Ingram Content Group UK Ltd.
Pitfield, Milton Keynes, MK11 3LW, UK
UKHW022140230126
467290UK00003B/26

9 781350 532335